T0177177

More Praise for
PARFIT

"Essential reading."
—JASON COWLEY, *The Times*

"An exemplary biography. It is thorough, revealing, and yet sympathetic."
—SIMON BLACKBURN, *Society*

"[A] companionable biography."
—*The New Yorker*

"[A] wonderful biography. . . . Offering more than a thinker's life and career,
Parfit is a crash course in the evolution of moral philosophy, and the best
account I have read of what 'doing philosophy' entails."
—HELLER McALPIN, *Wall Street Journal*

"*Parfit* is written engagingly, ably balancing philosophy and biography.
Readers outside the field will find Edmonds's descriptions of Parfit's
philosophical contributions fascinating and clear. . . . Parfit's philosophy
was philosophy at its best, and *Parfit* is an excellent introduction to that
philosophy and the life in which it grew to occupy such a central role."
—OLIVER TRALDI, *Washington Post*

"Lively."
—*The Economist*

"[A] gripping biography."
—JOE HUMPHREYS, *Irish Times*

"It is hard to imagine a more sympathetic, fair-minded, and appropriately skilled
biographer for Parfit than David Edmonds. . . . [An] excellent biography."
—FRANK B. FARRELL, *Commonweal*

"[A] fascinating biography."
—JANE O'GRADY, *Literary Review*

"Picture in your head: 'a philosopher.' Does he have a wild mane of white hair?
Does he ride an old-fashioned bike everywhere, speak in a British accent? Does
he have eccentric habits, like carrying a vodka bottle full of water? Does he spend

every second of his life trying to solve the most important problems of human existence, and is everyone who meets him in awe of his intellect? The person you imagined existed. His name was Derek Parfit, he was utterly fascinating and delightful and brilliant, and with this book David Edmonds has painted him a beautiful, thorough, and compelling portrait."
—MICHAEL SCHUR, creator of *The Good Place* and author of *How to Be Perfect: The Correct Answer to Every Moral Question*

"In his monumental biography of the moral philosopher Derek Parfit, David Edmonds renders the movements of a quicksilver mind, the allure of a charismatic personality, the drama of a cloistered life."
—SYLVIA NASAR, author of *A Beautiful Mind*

"Although Derek Parfit led a uniquely cloistered existence, immersed in his work, his life was not without drama, as David Edmonds's sympathetic but not uncritical biography shows. This is likely to be the definitive biography of this irresistibly intriguing, indefatigable, and finally elusive thinker: for many, the great moral philosopher of our time."
—JOYCE CAROL OATES

"To write an entertaining biography of the philosopher on whom, of all those I have encountered, the label 'genius' best fits, is quite a feat. David Edmonds does that in this beautifully written and thoroughly researched volume that also offers fascinating glimpses of academic philosophy and life in Oxford during the past sixty years."
—PETER SINGER, author of *Ethics in the Real World*

"Derek Parfit's electrifyingly original philosophy transformed thinking about who we are, what matters in life, and how we should care about the future. And the man was as original as his work. In this revelatory and fascinating biography, David Edmonds describes how the young Parfit's many passions contracted into a fervent, all-consuming search for moral truth."
—LARISSA MACFARQUHAR, author of *Strangers Drowning: Impossible Idealism, Drastic Choices, and the Urge to Help*

"Derek Parfit was perhaps the most important philosopher of his era. This scintillating and insightful portrait of him is one of the best intellectual biographies I have read."
—TYLER COWEN, author of *Stubborn Attachments: A Vision for a Society of Free, Prosperous, and Responsible Individuals*

Parfit

Parfit

A PHILOSOPHER AND HIS MISSION TO SAVE MORALITY

DAVID EDMONDS

PRINCETON UNIVERSITY PRESS

PRINCETON & OXFORD

Published by Princeton University Press
41 William Street, Princeton, New Jersey 08540
99 Banbury Road, Oxford OX2 6JX

press.princeton.edu

First paperback printing, 2024
Paper ISBN 978-0-691-22524-1
Cloth ISBN 978-0-691-22523-4
ISBN (e-book) 978-0-691-22525-8

British Library Cataloging-in-Publication Data is available

Editorial: Rob Tempio, Matt Rohal, and Chloe Coy
Production Editorial: Kathleen Cioffi
Text and Cover Design: Karl Spurzem
Production: Erin Suydam
Publicity: Maria Whelan and Carmen Jimenez

Cover photograph courtesy of Janet Radcliffe Richards

This book has been composed in Arno Pro

Printed in the United States of America

For Herbert Edmonds (1930–2022)

*He was a great Dad. He never read any of my books, but he made
damned sure everyone else he came into contact with did.*

CONTENTS

What Matters

'What do you do?' the American nurse asked the Englishman, Derek Parfit. It was the autumn of 2014 and the philosopher was hospitalized in New Jersey. He was in a terrible state—having nearly died when his lungs packed up after a bout of violent coughing. He looked exhausted and showing every one of his seventy-one years. He could barely speak. A succession of concerned visitors had been in to visit the white-haired patient, and the nurse was intrigued.

'I work', he replied, in a raspy voice, 'on what matters'.

. . .

On What Matters was the second and last of Parfit's books. The first was *Reasons and Persons*. So, only two books. But these two books are sufficient to have earned Parfit a reputation among political and moral philosophers as one of the greatest moral thinkers of the past century. It is not a unanimous judgement—he had trenchant critics—but it is widespread. Indeed, some go further, believing him to be the most important moral philosopher since his fellow British philosophers, John Stuart Mill (1806–73) and Henry Sidgwick (1838–1900).

That even one book appeared under his name came as a surprise to many who knew him. The word 'perfect' is thought to derive from the Middle English, *parfit* and Parfit, the ultimate perfectionist, was aptly named. His perfectionism would routinely cause him trouble—as when he repeatedly failed to meet publishing deadlines because the manuscript was not to his own satisfaction.

In the end, *On What Matters* was published in two volumes, weighing in at 1,440 pages (or 1,900 pages if you add the posthumously published Volume 3). *Reasons and Persons* is a mere featherweight, at 537 pages. Both Parfit's books have been described as enduring masterpieces. He also produced around fifty articles. He made seminal contributions on many topics, including equality, and 'personal identity': what, if anything, makes a person the same person through time. His ideas have very practical applications that affect us all; they change the way we think about punishment, about distribution of resources, about how we should plan for the future.

. . .

This book is in part a portrait of university life and academic philosophy in the second half of the twentieth century and the beginning of the twenty-first, as well as a depiction of the unique institution, All Souls, in which Parfit spent almost all his adult years. But it is essentially a book about one man.

For a chronicler of his life, Parfit poses a puzzle. I began this book with a clear conception of what sort of person Parfit was. I felt I understood his personality, what made him tick, and why he behaved the way he behaved. But the more people I spoke to about him, particularly people who had known him before he became a philosopher, the more I came to believe that my original view must be fundamentally wrong. That involved some agonizing and rewriting. Yet certain stories about Parfit kept nagging me; in the end I changed my mind for a second time. There is, of course, something ironic about a biographer attempting to grapple with the nature of a person who made the case that identity is not what matters.

For a biographer, he is both a nightmare and a dream. His life was, from one perspective, entirely uneventful. It was a cloistered existence—literally cloistered, from the cloisters of Eton to the cloisters of Balliol, Oxford, of Harvard, of All Souls, Oxford. It involved reading, discussing, and writing philosophy papers and books. That makes for unexciting copy. On the other hand, he was, at least in the second half of his life, a highly eccentric man—loveable but idiosyncratic. I was inundated with anecdotes.

Marshalling all this information has posed a few challenges. Broadly, the book follows a standard chronological narrative. But from about 1970, various patterns began to emerge in Parfit's life. There were, for example, the annual photographic trips to Venice and St Petersburg. There were the regular teaching gigs at Harvard, New York University, and Rutgers. There were his students. To return to these subjects repeatedly would be unsatisfactory. So I've chosen to present some of the latter part of Parfit's life thematically.

It also seemed to me that this structure meshed appropriately with his life. His early decades were rich with activities, and interests, and curiosity in multiple domains. The latter decades were dominated by a small number of fixations, which became increasingly compartmentalized. The first half of his life contains a lot of life, the second half a lot of philosophy. Beyond the details of his philosophy, one of my fascinations with Derek is that he represents an extreme example of how it is possible to prioritize certain values above all others—in his case, the urge to solve important philosophical questions.

He spent the last twenty-five years of his life anguished by philosophical disagreements he had with other philosophers. In particular, he grew increasingly upset that many serious philosophers believed that there was no objective basis for morality. He felt that he had to demonstrate that secular morality—morality without God—was objective, and that it had rational foundations. Just as there were facts about animals and flowers, stones and waterfalls, books and laptops, so there were facts about morality.

He genuinely believed that if he failed to show this, his existence would have been futile. And not just his existence. If morality was not objective, all our lives were meaningless. The need to refute this, the need to save morality, was a heavy emotional as well as an intellectual burden. How he came to bear this burden, and how it shaped him from being a precocious and outgoing history student into a monastically inclined philosopher obsessed with solving the toughest moral questions, is the subject of this book.

. . .

I must declare a personal connection to Derek Parfit. I did not know him well, but he was my dissertation co-supervisor in 1987, when I was studying for the Oxford BPhil degree. Since I am certain I would not have had the courage to ask him to supervise me, I assume the approach must have come from my other supervisor, Sabina Lovibond, my undergraduate teacher and a very different type of thinker. But Derek was an obvious choice. I had decided to focus my dissertation on some ethical issues to do with 'future people'—people not yet born—a sub-area of moral philosophy that Derek had done much to create. In the dissertation, I set myself the task of trying to solve the Asymmetry Problem—of which more later. I thought I'd cracked it. Derek disagreed.

Truth be told, I remember little of our meetings back then; there were probably only three or four. I recall my nervousness as I walked up the stone stairs of Staircase XI in the back quad in All Souls. For some reason, I recall the sofa I sat upon. I remember his red tie. And his long, wavy, already white-ish hair, though he was then only in his forties.

I had, of course, read *Reasons and Persons*, published just three years earlier, and it had had the same exhilarating impact on me as it had on so many others. No doubt it also increased my trepidation of the great man. I need not have worried. He read my work carefully, argued with me patiently. That I was a mere graduate student did not seem to matter to him.

When I started on this book, I reread my dissertation, which begins with a short acknowledgement:

> I would like to express my warmest thanks to my co-supervisors, Sabina Lovibond and Derek Parfit. Once I had become accustomed to their uncanny, almost psychic ability to disagree with each other on every fundamental point, I gained much from their fair and detailed criticisms, and was encouraged by their tremendous enthusiasm.

Derek's enthusiasm for philosophy never wavered.

Our paths did not cross again for many years, though I often heard his disembodied voice. Although I took a job with the BBC, I still had a philosophical itch that I felt compelled to scratch, and so I began a part-time PhD. This time my topic was the philosophy of discrimination, and my supervisor was Janet Radcliffe Richards, Derek's partner. I would visit Janet at her Tufnell Park home in north London; our meetings were invariably punctuated by a phone-call from Oxford, and I could just about make out Derek's distinctive baritone/tenor voice. 'I can't talk, I'm with David Edmonds,' Janet would say, though I doubt Derek remembered me.

That was in the 1990s. In 2010, and with a reference from Janet, I joined the Uehiro Centre for Practical Ethics, a branch of the Oxford University philosophy faculty. Janet had moved there in 2007. I am privileged to retain my association with the Centre as a Distinguished Research Fellow. In my first few years with Uehiro, I would visit weekly—and each time I went into my shared office I would glance at the four printed names on the door and receive a mini–dopamine kick. For, alongside my name and Janet's, was that of D. Parfit. He never actually showed up—preferring to work from home. But I occasionally boasted about this association of mine with a (never present) office-mate.

I should relate one other personal story—a truncated version of which appears in the Parfit obituary I wrote for *The Times*. In 2014, *Prospect* magazine ran a poll on the world's most important thinker. Their initial list included both Janet and Derek. Like most such lists, it was somewhat spurious, and Janet was perversely indignant that she had been included—blaming political correctness and affirmative action. In any case, I wrote to *Prospect* to ask whether they knew that two people in their poll were rather well acquainted. They did not, and a long-form article was commissioned—to which they gave the title, 'Reason and Romance: The World's Most Cerebral Marriage'.

As research for the article, I arranged to visit both Janet and Derek in Tufnell Park. Derek tolerated, but found tedious, my personal questions, but became more animated when we moved on to discussing philosophy. I had my laptop with me, and as he talked, I furiously typed notes.

Later, after completing a draft of the article, I sent it to Janet and Derek, because I wanted to ensure it contained no factual errors. It had taken me several days' grind, but I was satisfied, indeed proud, of it. Then I went for a long walk with my wife. At some stage, as we reached the top of a hill, I glanced at my email messages on my mobile. There was a note from Derek:

> Dear David,
>
> I hope you're well.
> I attach a message. I fear that you won't like it, and apologize for that.
>
> Best wishes, Derek

Distraught, I rushed home, and opened the attachment, in which there was a request that I desist from publishing the article, and a lengthy list of mistakes and misinterpretations. My heart pounding, I began to read through the list. As I did so, anxiety turned to puzzlement. For my first so-called 'mistake' was not in the article. Nor was my second. Or my third. Or, for that matter, my fourth or fifth. I wrote to him, explaining my bafflement.

Then, suddenly, I worked it out. I had not sent Derek my article, but the document of my notes and jottings from our Tufnell Park discussion. As I wrote in *The Times*, nobody—*nobody*—but Derek Parfit 'could have believed that this gobbledegook was intended for publication. If you told him that a set of rambling non sequiturs was to appear in a prestigious periodical, that was what he believed.'[1]

The story has a happy ending. He was pleased with the article. The only substantial change he requested was that I include some of the lavish praise for Janet's latest book, *The Ethics of Transplants: Why Careless Thought Costs Lives*, such as '"This is applied ethics at its very best"—Peter Singer'.

. . .

Notwithstanding *Prospect*'s designation of him as among the world's most important thinkers, Parfit was a philosopher's philosopher, not a public philosopher or a people's philosopher. There are some not particularly profound philosophers who have developed a high profile by taking a stand on matters of wide interest. There are a few significant thinkers who have also become well known through their public engagement. In the not-too-distant past, Bertrand Russell was an example—though very few people read the highly technical philosophy on which he built his early reputation. Parfit was fascinated by real problems beyond the seminar room, but he did not contribute to the conversation by giving media interviews, writing mainstream articles or op-eds, or briefing politicians or policy wonks. He did not campaign. He had no social media presence. He never sought fame. He remains, therefore, virtually unknown beyond philosophy.

I hope this book goes some way towards remedying this injustice. I hope it also shows that his response to the New Jersey nurse was true. He did indeed work on what matters.

ACKNOWLEDGEMENTS

Like Derek, I have perfectionist instincts, though not quite to his excessive degree. But stones I like to turn. Almost every time I spoke to someone about Derek, new ideas would emerge, or new suggestions would be made for another interview. Hunting down every fact and angle was time-consuming, and the burden was shared by my family. So my deepest thanks are to Liz, Saul, and Isaac. Before embarking on this project, I had co-written a children's book, *Undercover Robot*—and Saul and Isaac would have preferred that I write another one. They referred to this project as the BDB, 'the <u>boring</u> Derek book' and it's certainly true that this book has fewer flatulence jokes than the one aimed at their age group. But my main hope is that the reader finds their adjective inaccurate.

. . .

Derek tended not to discuss his background or his personal life, and even those who knew him best had surprising gaps in their knowledge. But without the crucial aid of certain people I could never have written this book. I should begin with the three most important.

I would not have proceeded at all with the book without Janet Radcliffe Richards's blessing. Being written about must evoke mixed emotions, but Janet was encouraging from the start of the process. Theodora Ooms, Derek's sister, was equally supportive, and essential in particular for reconstructing Derek's early years. Jeff McMahan, one of Derek's closest friends, was the third person I consulted from the outset and then continued to consult throughout the book's gestation. Janet, Theo, and Jeff all read the manuscript and made numerous improving points.

(Jeff is wasted as a renowned philosopher when he could have pursued a successful career as a copyeditor.)

Several philosophers read the entire book; special thanks are owed to Ingmar Persson, a close friend of Derek's, as well as to Saul Smilansky, who describes Parfit as 'the most original moral philosopher since Kant'. Thank you to my old friend Roger Crisp, who was instrumental, in the distant past, in persuading me to pursue philosophy graduate studies, and who, several decades on, saved me from several big errors. Four referees were approached by Princeton University Press to provide feedback on the book. They had the right to remain anonymous, but all chose to out themselves. Their comments were invaluable. Thanks to Ruth Chang, Tyler Cowen, Cheryl Misak, and Peter Singer.

I wanted the book to be accessible to civilians, a.k.a. non-philosophers. To check whether I had achieved this, I conscripted three more-or-less willing friends to read the manuscript. Two of them, the brutal comma tyrant Neville Shack and my Chicago chess buddy David Franklin, have been enlisted for previous books. David is solely responsible for note 17 in chapter 13. The recruitment of Danny Finkelstein made it a powerful trio. I am tremendously grateful to all three of them.

Each week during the Covid era, I went for a weekly lockdown-compliant walk around Hampstead Heath with Jonny Haskel. He tolerated much Derek-talk, and in so doing helped me think through some of my writing issues and dilemmas. Thanks too to octogenarian, proofreading supermum Hannah Edmonds, who had a tough time dealing with my father's illness during the latter stages of the writing of this book.

Many thanks to the following people who read sections of the book: John Ashdown, Quassim Cassam, Jessica Eccles, Bill Ewald, Adam Hodgkin, Michelle Hutchinson, Stephen Jessel, Guy Longworth, Peter Momtchiloff, Bill Nimmo Smith, Adam Ridley, Jen Rogers, Paul Snowdon (who sadly passed away in 2022), and Adam Zeman. I should single out too Robin Briggs, who read the Oxford and All Souls chapters and whose help I sought multiple times. He was Derek's tutorial partner at Oxford and then his colleague at All Souls. He answered all my many questions with grace and patience.

On my behalf, Sean McPartlin and Matthew van der Merwe tracked down the titles of all Derek's Oxford lectures and seminars. Johan Gustafsson is trying to piece together Derek's philosophical history—what he was working on and when—and provided many vital pieces of information.

As I mention in the Preface, I wrote a long article for *Prospect* magazine about Derek and Janet's relationship: 'Reason and Romance: The World's Most Cerebral Marriage'. Thank you to Jonathan Derbyshire for commissioning this back in 2014.

I have had to call on many administrators and archivists, and have plundered many archives, including those of All Souls College (Gaye Morgan), Balliol College (Bethany Hamblen), the Bodleian (Daniel Drury, Oliver House, Julie Anne Lambert, Alice Millea), the Church Mission Society, housed in Special Collections, University of Birmingham (Ivana Frian and Jenny Childs), Dragon School (Gay Sturt), Dulwich Prep (Ann Revell), Eton College (Georgina Robinson), Harvard University (Emily Ware), the Isaiah Berlin Literary Trust (Henry Hardy), the Liberty Fund (Carol Homel), New York University (Janet Bunde), the Oxford University Faculty of Philosophy (Pavlina Gatou), Oxford University Press (Martin Maw), Princeton University (Anna Faiola), the Rockefeller Archive Center, which houses the Harkness records (Bethany Antos), and Yale University (Eric Sonnenberg). Of these, Bethany Hamblen, Gay Sturt, Henry Hardy, Martin Maw, and Georgina Robinson merit special mention for their supererogatory dispositions. Thanks too to Miriam Cohen, for handing me some material from the personal archive of her father, G. A. Cohen.

This is my third book with Princeton University Press. Writers invariably grumble about their publishers, but PUP has been wonderfully professional throughout; more importantly, they've also been fun. I owe an enormous debt to Rob Tempio and Matt Rohal. PUP leapt on this book early, in part I suspect, because Matt was taught by Derek at Rutgers. They gave the manuscript an extremely close edit (these days one should not take that for granted in the publishing world). Rob sent me a note after reading the cat anecdote in the chapter on Derek's book *Reasons and Persons*, suggesting that it should have been titled *Reasons and Purrsons.* This is the sort of invaluable editorial intervention all writers crave. Thanks too to Matt McAdam, to whom Rob sent the book, and to those in the Princeton University Press team who worked on it: Kathleen Cioffi, Chloe Coy, Francis Eaves, Kate Farquhar-Thomson, Carmen Jimenez, and Maria Whelan.

I am grateful also to an institution, the Oxford Uehiro Centre for Practical Ethics. Julian Savulescu brought me into the Centre over a dozen years ago, and it has served as a great philosophical base ever since.

Thanks to my agents at David Higham, especially Veronique Baxter.

Finally, thank you to the literally hundreds of interviewees who helped with this book. Interactions occurred by Zoom, phone, and email, and occasionally in person. The emails I received and my interview notes, ended up being longer than *On What Matters*. I have tried to keep track of all those to whom I am indebted, but may (sorry!) have inadvertently left one or two out. In alphabetical order, I would like to acknowledge:

R. M. Adams, Timothy Adès, Jonathan Aitken, Gustaf Arrhenius, John Ashdown, Liz Ashford, Norma Aubertin-Potter, Simon Baron-Cohen, Raquel Barradas De Freitas, Simon Beard, Helen Beebee, Kathy Behrendt, Richard Bellamy, Michael Beloff, Selim Berker, Angela Blackburn, Simon Blackburn, Ned Block, Nick Bostrom, Andrew Boucher, Karin Boxer, Robin Briggs, John Broome, Krister Bykvist, Tim Campbell, Quassim Cassam, David Chalmers, Ruth Chang, Sophie-Grace Chappell, Anthony Cheetham (for Eton reminiscences), Bill Child, John Clarke, Mary Clemmey, Marshall Cohen, Miriam Cohen, John Cottingham, Tyler Cowen, Caroline Cracraft, Harriet Crisp and her father, Roger Crisp, Robert Curtis, Fara Dabhoiwala, John Davies, Ann Davis, Jonathan Dancy (who wrote a memoir of Derek for The British Academy), Judith De Witt, John Dunn, Jessica Eccles, Ben Eggleston, Gideon Elford, Humaira Erfan-Ahmed (a secretary at All Souls), William Ewald, Cécile Fabre, Kit Fine, Alan Fletcher, Stefan Forrester, Johann Frick, Stephen Fry, Sarah Garfinkel, James Garvey, Brian Gascoigne, Allan Gibbard, Peter Gillman, Jonathan Glover, Frances Grant, Johan Gustafsson, Steve Hales, Henry Hardy, David

Heyd, Cecilia Heyes, Joanna van Heyningen, Angie Hobbs, Adam Hodgkin, Stuart Holland, Brad Hooker, Peregrine Horden (for matters All Souls), poetry consultant Anna Horsbrugh-Porter, Tim Hunt, Tom Hurka, Edward Hussey, Michelle Hutchinson, Danial Isaacson, Dale Jamieson, Richard Jenkyns (who sent me his long and fascinating recollections of Derek at All Souls), the Jessel brothers, David and Stephen (David sent me a detailed summary of Derek's mentions in *The Draconian*), Shelly Kagan, Guy Kahane , Frances Kamm, Thomas Kelly, Anthony Kenny, Richard Keshen, Simon Kirchin, Charles Kolb, Christine Korsgaard, Douglas Kremm, Rahul Kumar, Nicola Lacey, Robin Lane Fox, Brian Leiter, John Leslie, Max Levinson, Paul Linton, Kasper Lippert-Rasmussen, Paul Lodge, Guy Longworth, William MacAskill, Alan Macfarlane, Julia Markovits, Jamie Mayerfeld, Iain McGilchrist, Jeff McMahan, Sean McPartlin, Matthew van der Merwe, Andreas Mogensen, Peter Momtchiloff, Alan Montefiore, Adrian Moore, Sophia Moreau, Ben Morison, Patricia Morison, Edward Mortimer (who sadly passed away in 2021), Liam Murphy, Jan Narveson, Jake Nebel, Bill Newton-Smith, Sven Nyholm, Joyce Carol Oates, Peter Ohlin, Martin O'Neill, Onora O'Neill, Bill Nimmo Smith, Alexander Ooms (Derek's nephew), Theodora Ooms, Toby Ord, Michael Otsuka, Paul Owens (co-poetry consultant—though he is better known for his majestic backhand, top-spin passing shot on the tennis court), Gavin Parfit (Derek's cousin), Michael Parfit (another cousin), Tom Parfit Grant (Derek's nephew), Richard Parry, Chris Patten, Catherine Paxton, Ingmar Persson, Hanna Pickard, Thomas Pogge, Michael Prestwich, Jonathan Pugh, Theron Pummer, Douglas Quine, Wlodek Rabinowicz, Stuart Rachels, Janet Radcliffe Richards, Peter Railton, Nick Rawlins, Judith Richards, Adam Ridley, Simon Rippon, Alvaro Rodríguez, Jen Rogers, Jacob Ross, Bill Ruddick, Alan Ryan, Anders Sandberg, Carol Sanger, Julian Savulescu, Tim Scanlon, Sam Scheffler, Paul Schofield, Paul Seabright, Amartya Sen, Kieran Setiya, Neville Shack, Thomas Sinclair, Peter Singer, Quentin Skinner, John Skorupski, Saul Smilansky, Barry Smith, Paul Snowdon, Sam Sokolsky-Tifft, Timothy Sommers, Richard Sorabji, Amia Srinivasan, Pablo Stafforini, Gareth Stedman Jones, Philip Stratton-Lake, Galen

Strawson, Sharon Street, Christer Sturmark, Jussi Suikkanen, Daniel Susskind, Richard Swinburne, Victor Tadros, John Tamosi, John Tasioulas, Charles Taylor, Larry Temkin, Patrick Tomlin, Peter Unger, Nick Vanston, David Velleman, John Vickers, Ben Vilhauer, William Waldegrave, Maurice Walsh, Nigel Warburton, Marina Warner, Ralph Wedgwood, David Wiggins, Dan Wikler, Dominic Wilkinson, Patricia Williams, Tim Williamson, Deirdre Wilson, Andy Wimbush, Susan Wolf, Bob Wolff, Allen Wood, Miriam Wood, Adrian Wooldridge, Aurelia Young, Ben Zander, Jessica Zander, and Adam Zeman.

Anyway, enough of the gratitude; I would like to start a trend of book acknowledgements ending on a note of petty ingratitude. During lockdown, research was hindered by constant interruptions in our wifi and internet connection. Multiple attempts to contact our broadband provider, Virgin Media, were thwarted by their system of dealing with faults and complaints—a system so labyrinthine and ingenious that it proved impossible to penetrate. Derek was remarkable in that he had no feelings of vengeance even towards those who had genuinely wronged him. I have tried to follow his admirable example, but with Virgin Media I have been unable to pull it off.

'Labyrinthine and ingenious' might serve as a description of Derek's philosophy, too. But I hope readers, after finishing this book, will see that philosophy to be both penetrable and important. Derek taught me when I was in my early twenties, and he helped inspire my lifetime's engagement with philosophy.

So, thank you Derek.

1

Made in China

All his life Derek Parfit had a missionary zeal. A zeal to solve the philosophical problems that matter and then persuade people that he was right.

Not only were both of Derek's parents missionaries; remarkably, all four of his grandparents were, too. He grew up in a household that had shed its faith but retained its missionary spirit. This spirit ran deep and centred on a fundamental urge: the urge to do good and help others.

. . .

One family theory is that the paternal side of Derek's ancestry, the Parfits, was descended from French immigrants—perhaps from the influx of Huguenot Protestants fleeing persecution in France in the seventeenth century, but more likely dating to the eleventh century and the Norman Conquest. References to Parfits, and variations of the name (Parfitt, Parfytt, Parfait), can be traced back hundreds of years.

The facts about Derek's family become more certain in the nineteenth century. Joseph Parfit was born in 1870, and raised in Cheshire Street, in Poplar, a deprived area of east London. Joseph's father had been a silk-weaver before becoming a postman, and they lived in a typical weaver's cottage. In 1894, however, after being ordained as a deacon and priest by the Church Mission Society, Joseph set sail for the Middle East, aiming to dedicate his life to preaching the gospel beyond British shores. He lived in various places—Bombay, Baghdad, Jerusalem,

Beirut—and wrote at least half a dozen books, with titles such as *The Wondrous Cities of Petra and Palmyra, Among the Druzes of Lebanon and Bashan*, and *The Romance of the Baghdad Railway*. He married his first wife in Baghdad in 1897, but within a year she was dead—passing away from influenza on a sweltering night. The Church Mission Society may have dispatched Norah Stephens to Baghdad with the intention that she become Joseph's second wife. They were married in 1902, and over the next decade Norah bore six children; Norman, the second eldest, arriving in 1904.

For a dozen years, the Parfit family lived in Lebanon, with Joseph serving as the canon at St George's Church in Beirut. That is where Norman spent much of his childhood. During the hot summers, the family would flee the city and retreat to a village in the hills, where Joseph taught English. Joseph and Norman had a problematic relationship, as Norman would with Derek. Norman wet his bed, and his father would beat him.

When they returned from the Middle East, following the outbreak of the Great War, the Parfits settled in Gloucester. Norman became a pacifist after so many of the senior boys at his school went off to fight in the trenches and never returned; he was also disgusted at being taught to stick bayonets into 'German' dummies.

He won a place to Brasenose College, Oxford, where he was a swimming champion and got a degree in physiology with a grade so terrible (fourth class) that it was considered something of an achievement. He then trained as a doctor at King's College Hospital, London. From 1931 to 1933 he worked in the Royal Free Hospital, in north London, which is where he met his future wife, Jessie.

Jessie Browne had a background that matched Norman's for exoticism. In 1896, just shy of the age of forty, her austere father, Dr Arthur Herbert Browne, abandoned a lucrative medical practice in Liverpool to become a missionary, first in Peshawar and then Amritsar, India. 'Whatever the temptations to stay at home,' he said, 'the needs, and the call abroad remain the same. I would prefer to stay at home, but duty calls me away.'[1] Dr Browne had a shock of white hair, uncannily like that of his philosophical grandson many decades later. He began one enlightened venture in which Christians and Muslims held open discussion. His medical support proved useful during the appalling famine at the turn of the century that devastated, in particular, the Bhils ethnic group. His services were again called upon after the 1905 earthquake in the Kangra Valley in Punjab, which killed around two hundred thousand people. The toughest part, he wrote in a letter home, was identifying and burying the remains.

As fate would have it, Arthur Browne suffered the same tragedy as Joseph Parfit: his first wife died before they could start a family. Like Joseph, he remarried (in 1909), this time to a nurse, Ellen. Jessie was born in 1910. Dr and Mrs Browne had their evangelical work cut out: they were supposed to carry the Christian message to a specific area in the Punjab covering around seven hundred villages and three hundred thousand people. But there were isolated communities of Christians who had arrived from elsewhere and who had settled in the Brownes' district. Ellen thought that 'unless discovered these would in all probability soon lapse back into Heathenism'.[2] Jessie had a low opinion of her mother and later wrote that 'her interest in the Indians was mainly as heathen patients with bodies to be cured and souls to be brought to the Lord'.[3] Although they were quite isolated, Jessie once received a letter addressed simply with her name and 'India'.

Arthur Browne died in August 1913 from a combination of septicaemia and diarrhoea. An obituary described his great heart, 'full of love [   ] but like all ardent lovers, he was capable of vehement indignation, and the way his nostrils would quiver at some tale of injustice or neglect of duty spoke of an element of the Sons of Thunder in his composition'.[4] Jessie was only three years old. She and Ellen returned to Britain, but when war broke out and Ellen went into army nursing, Jessie boarded with an uncle and aunt in Kettering, Northamptonshire.

Sent to various religious retreats in her holidays, Jessie became very devout herself. When, after the Great War, she moved back in with her mother, she told her that because the Second Coming was so imminent, she 'didn't see any point in working for exams'.[5] Nonetheless, she grew up to become a first-rate student and, like Norman, studied medicine (at the time, very rare for a woman)—first, from 1928, at the London

School of Medicine for Women and then at the Royal Free Hospital. Although she hardly knew her father, she was inspired by his career.

As part of her degree, she was sent to work for a spell in the casualty (emergency) unit—where Norman was in charge. He was in fact on the look-out for her, because a few months earlier Jessie had been on a religious camp on the Isle of Wight where she had met Norman's brother Eric, who reported back to Norman that she was 'a good egg'.[6]

Soon they were engaged, but because Norman was a few years older and had already completed his studies in London, he travelled alone to India to study tropical diseases and obtained a diploma from Calcutta University. He was back by 1934, the year in which Jessie won the London University Gold Medal for the top student—a previous winner was Alexander Fleming—gaining distinctions in surgery and pathology. All in all, she had picked up twelve prizes during her studies, the names of which were all recited at the annual prize-giving. The *Daily Mirror* even thought fit to print an article about twenty-three-year-old Jessie, managing to identify the real story: not one student's staggering academic accomplishments, but love. Headlined 'Romance of a Girl Doctor', the article opened with the applause of Jessie's fellow-students, 'ringing in her ears [. . .]. But as she walked back to her seat, a slim figure in cap and gown [. . .] her eyes sought only those of a tall, sun-bronzed young man seated among the audience. They smiled with mutual understanding.'[7]

A proud Dr Norman Parfit had a progressive attitude: 'our marriage will not be allowed to interfere with her career'.[8] Indeed, Jessie continued her studies, qualifying as a doctor in hygiene at the London School of Hygiene and Tropical Medicine, while Norman received a diploma in public health from the same institution.

At some stage Norman and Jessie joined the Oxford Group, an evangelical Christian movement founded in the 1920s by an American Lutheran priest, Frank Buchman, who had strong links with China. The movement believed that core human weaknesses, fear and selfishness, could only be overcome by surrendering one's life to God and by conveying His message to others. Although humans were not expected to attain the movement's four absolutes—absolute honesty, absolute purity, absolute unselfishness and absolute love—they were supposed to be guided by them. Part of the Group's practice involved individuals discussing their personal lives and decisions, owning up to their sins, and explaining the steps they were taking to alter their behaviour. (It is no coincidence that the founders of Alcoholics Anonymous had been members of the Oxford Group.)

Before Norman and Jessie married, they approached the Church Mission Society about working abroad as missionaries. The Society agreed (in late 1934) to send them to China, but recommended that they should not have children for the first two years away, so that they would have time to settle in and learn the language. This, of course, meant they would have to abstain from sex or practise birth control. They were not Catholic, but Ellen was so outraged by the demand and her daughter's agreement to it that she refused to attend their wedding.

This took place in North Oxford on 29 July 1935. On top of the wedding cake was the Oxford University motto, while the bottom tier had silver chains with maps of China—the country for which, a few months later, the newly married couple set forth. They arrived, via Canada and Japan, in late 1935, carrying in their luggage the top half of the cake (which was finally consumed on their first wedding anniversary). Their base was to be Chengdu, the capital of Sichuan in south-west central China, known in the West for its giant pandas. The couple's initial impressions were contained in a long letter in January 1936: 'We just feel that this is an amazing place [. . .] and we feel it is a very great privilege to be sent here by God.'[9]

Soon they would take up teaching positions at the West China Union University, run by Christian missionaries; the beautiful campus lay outside the medieval walls. But first they headed for a remote community in Mount Omei, a sacred Buddhist mountain, south-east of Chengdu, in part to immerse themselves in Sichuanese, a dialect of Mandarin. (Jessie picked up the language quickly, but Norman, much to his frustration, could not.)

Norman took the journey to the hills first, to prepare their bungalow, and Jessie followed with several others in mid-June 1936. The journey involved a terrifying episode on a boat trip to the area. The vessel was boarded by five or six bandits who ripped open boxes and bags, stole money, and took Jessie's watch, fountain pen, torches, mosquito net, and rings. Afterwards, Jessie was able to see the funny side. In an account dispatched back to the Church Mission Society, she described how one bandit had a revolver in one hand, a lady's compact powder case in the other, and some stolen ladies' underwear tucked into his belt. Somehow this story was passed down to Derek, but in mangled form. He would claim that although the pirates stole Jessie's money, they allowed her to keep either her wedding or her engagement ring. And, as we shall see, he used this as a case study to illustrate the difficulty of interpreting the maxims of the eighteenth-century German philosopher Immanuel Kant.

In 1937, Jessie and Norman began to teach in the public health department of West China Union University—on topics such as personal hygiene, nutrition, exercise, and how to ensure safe drinking water. They stuck to the no-children-for-two-years agreement, but in 1939 Theodora arrived, and on 11 December 1942 Derek Antony Parfit appeared in the world. 'I was born at the lowest point in human history,' he once said.[10]

He would always hate his given name, and envied his sister's classical one. Later in life, his Skype profile name was Theodoricus, because he playfully imagined he had a fictitious Roman ancestor called Theodoricus Perfectus.

Aged around nine months, Derek nearly died. He had become sick and was screaming incessantly. The local doctors were baffled, but Jessie correctly diagnosed intussusception, whereby the bowel folds around itself like a telescope, causing acute abdominal pain. She ordered the doctors to administer a water enema, which immediately resolved the problem.

. . .

By the time Theodora and Derek appeared in the world, war had already begun to impinge on life in Chengdu. In 1931, the Japanese had invaded and then set up a puppet state in Manchuria (north-east China), and in 1937, the year the Parfits moved to Chengdu, tensions between Japan and China erupted into a full-scale conflict. In the notorious massacres in Nanjing between December 1937 and January 1938, tens of thousands, possibly hundreds of thousands, of Chinese civilians lost their lives.

That was a thousand miles to the east of Chengdu, but as the fighting continued, refugees began pouring into the city. They brought with them many public health challenges, and Jessie and Norman were kept busy. The cost of living began to soar, contributing to worsening childhood malnourishment. In response, the Parfits were involved in the development of a milk powder made from soya beans. It was cheaper than dairy milk and the soya bean, it was said, was the cow of China. A manufacturing unit was set up on campus, and within the first eighteen months it had distributed forty thousand packets of powder.

Their other dominating public issue was student health. Dormitories were overflowing with students who had fled universities in other cities, including Nanjing. These were conditions in which tuberculosis flourished. In response, the Parfits helped organize a testing and quarantine system.

Chengdu remained beyond the reach of Japanese ground forces, but it was not invulnerable to attack from the air. Now and again, Japanese bombers would fly overhead. Jessie kept a careful count of the raids. Theodora remembers watching her looking up at the sky, wondering whether she was looking for God.

In fact, whilst both Theodora and Derek were absorbing Christian dogma as young children, their parents Jessie and Norman were becoming disillusioned with their faith. They played an active part in the missionary community—Norman became treasurer of the local mission and Jessie busied herself with the newsletter. But they didn't warm to their fellow missionaries, whom they regarded as racist. The American and Canadian missionaries were better resourced and quite grand, and most of them expected the local Chinese to enter houses only through the back door, the front door being reserved for higher-status guests. The Parfits came to believe that their religion had little to offer the ancient and sophisticated culture of China and certainly should not be imposed on the Chinese by outsiders; for a brief period, Norman became a Maoist, ingeniously interpreting this to be consistent with his pacifism. Then there were personal circumstances: they struggled financially and complained to the Church Mission Society that the rising cost of living made their salaries inadequate. Norman's unhappiness grew: he began to suffer bouts of serious depression.

. . .

In February 1944, after nine years in China, the decision was made by the Society to evacuate Norman and Jessie, despite the tide of the war against Japan having decisively begun to turn. The Parfits were long overdue home leave. However, January 1944 saw the start of the so-called Baby Blitz—a new Luftwaffe bombing offensive against Britain—and so, rather than return to Blighty immediately, Norman and Jessie sold all their material possessions and took a circuitous route back, heading first to the relative safety of the US, where Eric, Norman's brother, was living.

Jessie was now two months pregnant with an unplanned third child and she was sick throughout their long and gruelling journey. The trip began with a flight south to the city of Kunming on a Liberator bomber, for which Norman and Jessie had to practise parachute jumping, and during which Theodora and Derek sat on the floor under the gun turret by the cockpit. If the plane was attacked, the plan was for the pilots to strap the two children in their laps before parachuting out.

Then there was another flight, to Calcutta. From there it was a 1,200-mile train ride west to Bombay, where there were several thousand expats and refugees waiting around to be repatriated. The Parfits stayed for several days in a ramshackle hotel where one day Jessie 'found Derek lying in his cot absolutely covered with bed bugs'.[11] Eventually they were allocated a place on one of the two departing transport ships: non-American passengers were split alphabetically by name between a navy and an army ship, the 'P's being embarked on the latter.

They would spend nine weeks at sea, sailing first to Australia, where they dropped off a thousand Italian prisoners of war, and then across the Pacific through the Panama Canal, with Boston as the final destination. There were only two meals a day, and children were on the breakfast and supper shift, so Theodora and Derek went without food during the day.

Jessie and the few other mothers petitioned an army commander to allow them to give the children soup for lunch, which would otherwise be a supper course, and they offered to do all the serving and washing. The commander steadfastly refused: 'He said that women and children had no business to be travelling in wartime and he was going to do nothing to make it easier for them.'[12] Jessie resorted to smuggling items out of breakfast.

The strain on Jessie was almost too much for her to bear. She, Theodora, and Derek were in a cabin with nine others, while Norman was 'in bed most of the time on the men's side of the ship',[13] suffering from sea-sickness. There was a daily drill, when she and the children had to trail up to the top deck with their life-jackets. An exhausted Jessie washed Derek's nappies in cold sea-water. The children seemed to be blissfully unaware of their parents' mood. Theodora recalls loving the boat trip. Derek took his first tentative steps at the Panama Canal.

. . .

The Parfits wasted no time in Boston before continuing their trip to New York. They lived for two or three months in a flat on Claremont Avenue belonging to a Columbia University professor, and then moved into a cheap but 'dreary'[14] apartment in Washington Heights, in north-west Manhattan, a Jewish immigrant area 'where the shops always seemed to be shut for some Jewish holiday or other'.[15] Shortly afterwards, in October, Jessie booked into the cheapest hospital she could find to give birth to her third child, Joanna. Somehow, Jessie managed to combine looking after a newborn with studying behaviour problems among children, at Columbia. She took advantage of a diaper service, and 'a coloured girl'[16] came weekly to help clean. Norman couldn't earn money because his degree was not recognized in the US, but he visited various hospitals to upgrade his medical knowledge. He was on the steps of the Capitol in Washington, DC on 12 April 1945 when he heard the distressing news of President Franklin D. Roosevelt's death.

After the deprivations of China, the United States was a revelation, a land of 'plenty and luxury'[17], with crowded shops full of goods. The

Parfits were particularly captivated by the automats—fast-food vending machines. They couldn't believe that soap was only seven cents a tablet. Norman fell in love with the 'Chock-full-o-nuts' lunch counters that offered a nutted-cheese sandwich—cream cheese and nuts on raisin bread. They enjoyed several trips with Theodora and Derek to Central Park Zoo.

The aim was to get back to the UK, but a wartime passage across the Atlantic was impossible. Theodora and Derek were sent to the Horace Mann Nursery School. In one letter, Jessie described Derek as a curly-headed blond and a mischievous little rascal. He had been a very late talker, and Norman worried they might have to put him in a school for children with learning difficulties. But then he became chatty. His favourite word was 'No', and once when a trip to a park was suggested he delivered his longest utterance to date: 'No ball, no walk, no bus, no tram.'[18]

Baby Joanna's arrival added an additional bureaucratic hurdle to the family's UK plans. Born on US soil, she was a US citizen, and there was paperwork to be completed before she was permitted to travel back on a British passport. But with the war over, the Parfits bought tickets on the ocean liner the *Queen Mary*. This gargantuan vessel had been converted into a troopship during the war and the Parfits were passengers on its first peacetime (so blackout-free) sailing. They docked in June 1945 at Greenock on the Scottish west coast and took an overnight train journey from Glasgow Central to London King's Cross.

The family was finally home. For a short period after that, Derek developed a stammer. His parents believed it was because he was so over-excited.

2

Prepping for Life

The immediate post-war years in Britain were austere, melancholy, indebted, and famished. The rationing that had been introduced in World War II—which applied to such staples as meat, bread, butter, and eggs—was actually tightened for a period after Victory in Europe Day, and not fully abandoned until 1954.

The Parfits had no money, and uncertain prospects. For the first few months back in the UK they lived in several places, camping out with relatives, including in a suburb of north London with Norman's wealthy brother Cyril. Then, despite having no background in psychiatry, Jessie successfully applied for a job in a newly established psychiatric institution, the Roffey Park Rehabilitation Centre, near Horsham in Surrey, which aimed to treat individuals suffering from stress and anxiety and return them, rejuvenated, to the workplace. The Parfits relocated to the countryside, south-west of London. The position came with two attractive benefits: a comfortably-sized flat, and a day nursery for employees' children, to which Derek was sent.

Norman, meanwhile, was studying on a refresher course, and in the spring of 1946, he got a job with the title of deputy medical director of the Central Council for Health Education. The Parfits moved into a cheap, bomb-damaged property, 116 Croxted Road, Dulwich, in south London. A railway track ran at the bottom of the garden, and each morning they watched the luxury Golden Arrow boat train rush past on its way to delivering passengers to the Dover ferries. Derek's elder sister remembers Derek becoming fascinated by a worm wriggling in the garden and

11

deciding to cut it in half, and then being heartbroken at his own callousness. It was the only act of wanton cruelty he ever committed.

Jessie started a part-time job at the London County Council, which necessitated hiring a nanny to look after the three children. When the nanny left, they employed a succession of foreign au-pairs, including Belgian Simone; blond and sweet Michelle, whose husband was a French soldier fighting in Vietnam; Denise, who couldn't even scramble an egg; a nondescript Norwegian; and finally, Tati, a high-class Parisian.

In London, the family became so financially stretched that they could only furnish their new house by buying budget furniture at auctions. But their straitened circumstances were also a result of their spending priorities. For the next fifteen years, Norman and Jessie would devote virtually every spare penny they had to their children's education. When Derek was five years old, he was sent to the local independent boys' school, Dulwich College Preparatory School (now Dulwich Prep London), a ten-minute walk away. The school has a record of his attendance, misspelling his name ('Derek Anthony G. Parfitt born 11/12/1942—1947 to 1949'), but no further details.

Norman's inability to find a job he wanted made him suicidal. But in 1949, after several years of applying for better-paid, higher-status medical officer of health positions, he was finally offered one in Berkshire, based in the town of Abingdon, near Oxford. It was a decent enough position, and one he kept for the rest of his career. His twin preoccupations—some called them obsessions—were breast cancer and fluoridation; he campaigned for measures to screen for cancer and energetically advocated for more fluoride in the water to strengthen children's teeth. Other health fixations included his opposition to white bread, which he regarded as more or less equivalent to poison.

The Parfits settled at 5 Northmoor Road in North Oxford, an area which was not then, as it is now, beyond the reach of all but the wealthy. Still, it was a nice, quiet, leafy residential road. Just a few houses down, J.R.R. Tolkien had written *The Hobbit* and most of *The Lord of the Rings*. Also on Northmoor Road, Erwin Schrödinger, the Nobel Prize-winning physicist, had written a paper about a mythical cat which, according to the logic of the new quantum mechanics, was simultaneously alive and dead.

At the age of seven, after ditching ambitions to become a steam-engine driver, Derek decided his future lay in becoming a monk. Distraught that his parents had abandoned Christianity, he would pray for them at night. But within a year or so, he too had ditched his faith. He found it impossible to believe that a Christian God, a good God, would punish people, and send them to hell, as doctrine stipulated. Of course, he might have chosen to alter his beliefs about God; perhaps there was a God, but He was not all good? Or perhaps He did not permit punishment and there was no hell? These were coherent positions compatible with his stance on punishment. Instead, he chose to eschew Christianity altogether—and was never tempted by religion again.

After moving to Oxford, Derek attended the local Greycotes Junior School for a year. He was then moved to the Dragon School. This was Oxford's most prestigious prep school, and just around the corner from home. Although the Dragon allowed in a few girls, Theodora was packed off to board at the progressive, co-ed private school Dartington Hall, in Devon, a four-hour drive away. Norman was not a hugger, but his eyes would well up whenever his children went away.

Visitors to the Northmoor Road home recall its chaotic atmosphere. From the condition in which the property was maintained, one might not have guessed that the two grown-ups who occupied it were specialists in hygiene. Norman and Jessie did not get along and home life was often tense—perhaps one reason why all his life Derek was averse to conflict. When the children's friends came around for lunch, Norman could put on a show of being talkative and friendly, even witty. But alone with the family he was brooding and full of repressed rage. His anger could be provoked by mundane day-to-day domestic frustrations, such as the kids crying or misbehaving, but also by events that were entirely beyond his control, like the latest idiotic—as he saw it—government announcement. Nor did he attempt to conceal his temper from his children's friends. A friend of Joanna's remembers being shouted at for putting the butter knife in the jam.[1] A classmate of Derek's remembers Norman beating Derek savagely in public—though Theodora says she was never beaten.

Other visitors recall Norman's various eccentricities, some of which would be inherited by his son. He was a hoarder; one room was piled high with magazines and newspapers, and there were racks of old un-used suits. He was also frugal. He tried to save petrol by coasting the car downhill. Once he came into possession of some ham confiscated by the health inspectors, who'd judged it unfit for human consumption. He shaved off the green mouldy edges, cut it down the middle, kept one half for the Parfits and offered the other to some friends, who less than politely declined it.

When Norman appeared for lunch—he was usually the last at the table—he would bring a milk bottle full of water. (Perhaps Derek was subconsciously influenced by this. He later developed a habit of carry-ing around a vodka bottle filled with water.) Then he would plug in a plate-warmer—which for some reason involved unscrewing the bulb from above the dining-room table. He would explain to bemused visi-tors that he liked his food hot, as though what was unusual was the preference itself, rather than his pronouncement of it.

His relationship with all his children was strained. The child with whom he found it easiest to coexist was Theodora. She was bright, good-natured, and compliant. The child he rowed with most was the youngest, Joanna. These days, a child such as Joanna might be diagnosed as having a learning disability. In any case, she struggled academically and, perhaps to hide this, was naughty at school, and constantly in trou-ble; her parents despaired of her school reports and black marks. She played, but also quarrelled, with Derek, and in the car a peacekeeper had to sit between them to prevent fights breaking out. While her elder siblings were both good-looking, even glamorous, she was, by all ac-counts, peculiar-looking: preternaturally tall, with huge feet, bulging blue eyes, and frizzy red hair. She was needy, anxious and, like her father, unhappy. Like her father as a child, she wet the bed.

Derek, as the only boy, was the child on whose behalf Norman was most pushy, of whom he was proudest, and onto whom he projected his deepest paternal ambitions. Derek, however, remained an enigma to him. The boy showed little interest in the subjects and activities that Norman thought he should be interested in. In particular, Norman tried, unsuccessfully, to nudge Derek towards the sciences. He also hoped to excite his son by the sports which he himself was passionate

about—tennis, particularly—but again he was met with stubborn resistance. (Norman was highly competitive: it was the winning that mattered, not the taking part.) Movies were the one interest father and
children shared—and there were frequent visits to the Scala cinema in
the Jericho district of Oxford, a brisk fifteen-minute walk from home.

Every year, the Parfits put on a firework show on Guy Fawkes day,
5 November. On one occasion, after a rocket misfired, Norman ushered
them all inside with a force and aggression that shocked those invited
to the display. He was probably feeling stressed, for November was always a tricky month. It was then that Norman had to compile an annual
report for work, a task which should in theory have been relatively easy
to accomplish—and which Derek thought his clever mother could have
completed in an hour—but which Norman found agonizing. He
couldn't restrain himself from making partisan comments on fluoridation, and this landed him in trouble: the council once tried to dismiss
him, but his right to express his opinion was eventually upheld. Later,
Derek would draw parallels between his father's strenuous exertions
with the written word and his own. At all events, after sending off the
report Norman would head to the Alps with the local skiing group—as
the official doctor, he went for free—returning on Christmas Eve.

Jessie Parfit, meanwhile, was a kinder, warmer presence than her husband. Norman may have felt himself her intellectual inferior. Derek
claimed that his father read only two books as an adult, 'Thackeray's
Henry Esmond, which he was given, and *Away with All Pests*, which described a successful Chinese campaign to destroy disease-carrying
flies'[2]. Jessie, by contrast, was a voracious reader of both fiction and non-
fiction. Her domain was the living room, where she worked and knitted
elaborate sweaters which were beautiful to behold but had arms that
were too long. At weekends she would take the children for walks and
teach them about botany and fossils. She played proficiently on their
Bechstein piano, introduced the children to her beloved Bach, and on
Saturdays took them to the gramophone library, where they were allowed to borrow records. On 30 July 1954, for example, Derek borrowed
Pietro Mascagni's opera *Cavalleria rusticana*, whilst his mother chose
Delius's *A Mass of Life*. Jessie also sparked her children's fascination with

architecture through their visits to, and her enthusiasm for, churches designed by the seventeenth–eighteeth century architect Nicholas Hawksmoor. She worried about making sure Derek was stimulated because his 'early academic eminence, and his profound thoughts even as a small child, were a constant challenge.'[3]

Jessie's career rapidly outshone her husband's. She worked on a couple of research jobs at the Institute of Social Medicine—including a study comparing the weight gain of boys and girls during the first year of their lives—while at the same time earning a degree in psychology and physiology at St Anne's College, Oxford (because she was interested in learning more about child psychiatry). In September 1954 she joined the central medical staff of the London County Council, London's main local authority, and she was soon promoted to principal medical officer in child psychiatry, where she had a wide range of responsibilities for about thirty thousand disturbed, deprived, and disabled children.

The Parfit family thus had two salaries—with Jessie's the larger—but much of the money continued to go on school fees. Later, many people would be aware of, and comment on, Derek's apparently posh background—and he certainly received an elite and privileged education. But that had required sacrifice. The Northmoor home was cheaply furnished, the family couldn't afford a washing machine, and for many years there was no central heating. Holidays were also modest affairs.

Jessie's new job meant she had to stay in London during the week and so, from the age of eleven, Derek became a weekly boarder at the Dragon School, only returning to Northmoor Road at weekends. The fact that his parents had only two days a week to tolerate each other probably saved their marriage.

. . .

Most former pupils recall the culture of the Dragon School as being happy and easy-going, but others say it was arrogant and 'monstrously competitive.'[4] There were several hundred pupils, of whom about half were boarders. Some of these boarders had parents overseas, in the armed services or the colonial service. There were lots of bright kids; it was the school to which many Oxford dons sent their offspring. The school magazine, *The Draconian*, circulated around senior common rooms in Oxford colleges, where academics would scour the league tables at the back which revealed how their colleagues' children were performing.

Although masters were called 'Sir', the pupils gave them each a nickname, such as Hum, Ticks, Box, Inky, Tubby, Fuzz, or Oof.[5] On the whole, the teachers didn't mind being addressed by their nicknames, or overhearing them (this was even true of Mr Barraclough, a.k.a Putty-Nose). Some of the academic staff had fought in World Wars I and II, and bore the scars; and one teacher had bullet wounds sustained as a young soldier during the Boer War.

Some teachers were very strict—including one who made pupils sit in a wastepaper basket when they made mistakes. But, on the whole, it was not a school in which rules were rigidly enforced. As for dress code, there was a school blazer, but otherwise children could essentially wear what they wished. Once, when there was a flood at Port Meadow—the nearby riverside meadow of common land—and the water froze, the headmaster declared a day's holiday, and the pupils trooped off to ice-skate. The school encouraged pupils to think for themselves—perhaps one reason why it has produced so many philosophers (including Anthony Price, Richard Sorabji, and Galen Strawson).

Derek was an earnest boy—neither wildly popular nor unpopular. He exhibited early academic aptitude, improving as he progressed through the years. The pupils were taught Latin from the start, and Greek a year later, for two hours a day. Classes were streamed by academic ability, and there were frequent tests.

Derek's best friend at school was a boy named Bill Nimmo Smith, who was growing up in difficult home circumstances. Jessie helped look after him, taking him and Derek on many outings, including to Hampton Court Palace and a tour of the Oxford gas works. Bill and Derek had 'a friendly academic rivalry'[6]. Proudly displayed on a big school honours board, which they passed every day, were the names of pupils who had won scholarships to the top private schools. At the age of nine, Bill and Derek formed a plan to apply for a scholarship to the country's most famous school, Eton.

For several years, the two boys were close enough to have a joint birthday party. Theirs was a typical boys' friendship. They spent time at each other's houses, they built a tree-house, and developed a game of one-a-side bicycle polo, in which they would race around on their bikes, hitting a ball with a stick. There were other games, too: tiddlywinks, snakes and ladders, the strategy board game Halma, and some games invented by Derek. Bill later recalled, 'I wouldn't say that the rules were loaded in his favour, but authorship certainly gave him an advantage in spotting infringements.'[7]

At school, Derek played a full part in extracurricular activities. He neither shone nor embarrassed himself at sports. In his first year, there was a 'Baby School' football match against the junior school pupils, involving four balls, fifteen players on each side, and a sloping pitch. Derek played 'an excellent defensive game' whilst at the same time 'feeding the forwards'[8]. He excelled at arts-and-crafts and painting, and he was a keen chess player, winning the knockout chess tournament.

Decades later, a lengthy profile of Parfit in *The New Yorker* would claim that he couldn't play a musical instrument. In fact, he was a reasonably accomplished piano (and later cornet) player. At school he performed many piano solos in school concerts, including pieces by Chopin and Bach, and, in 1954, Mozart's 'The Turkish March' (*Rondo alla turca*): 'Parfit started well but later was carried away by the music.'[9]

He wrote several pieces for *The Draconian*. One was about a school trip to the Tower of London, where he marvelled at the crown jewels: 'my only recollection is a plain gold dish; for as I walked into the room the dazzle from this dish was so great that I could not see anything clearly for the next ten minutes.'[10] Poetry became a passion, and he was encouraged to develop his promising talent by an English teacher, Mr Brown (nickname Bruno). Derek no longer wanted to become a monk; now he had aspirations to become a poet.

Then there was drama and singing. Every autumn, the school put on a production of a Gilbert and Sullivan opera, and every summer there was a Shakespeare play. In November 1953, Derek was one of General

Stanley's daughters in *The Pirates of Penzance*. In subsequent productions he was in the chorus of nobles in *The Mikado*, Demetrius in *A Midsummer Night's Dream* (where he 'brought a virile force to his performance'[11]), and played Sir Toby Belch in *Twelfth Night*, complete with padded stomach, opposite his classmate Tim Hunt, who was Sir Toby's niece, Olivia. There were two complimentary reviews of the play in *The Draconian*. The first reviewer wrote in praise that Derek's 'acting ability made it from first to last impossible to think of him as much less than 50 years old'. The second recorded that Derek had raised 'gales of laughter'.[12]

. . .

For the summer holidays of 1952, 1953, and 1954, the school gave the boys diaries, and those who wished to could fill them in. Derek was happy to oblige. Only the last two of Derek's have survived (for the 1952 diary he received a 'First-Class' mark), but they offer a remarkable snapshot of young Derek, aged ten to eleven, in 1953 and 1954. The 1953 diary is 'DEDICATED To The READER' and an early entry—on 23 July—reads,

> I had heard before lunch that my grandfather,[13] who is 83, had died. I felt queer for a little while because he was the only grandfather I had ever had, but mummy told me that he had been unconscious for a week and that it was better for him just to die peacefully. That cheered me up considerably.[14]

He was sufficiently fortified to feel able on the same day to take the bus to a friend's house, where they played sports and an 'exciting' naval-war board game called 'Dover Patrol'. He was then to take the bus back, but, 'Unfortunately at Gloster green [sic][15] I absentmindedly spent all my money on an Ice cream! So I walked home!'[16]

Two days later, Derek read a simplified version of Plato's *Symposium*. And then it was off to France, where he would be dropped off to stay with a French family whose son, Jean de la Sablière, had stayed with them the previous year. Derek was pleased, because it would give him

the chance to improve his French. On arriving in France, he took in the
view from the train: 'There were two main things that I noticed were
different from England, otherwise we might have been in Surrey. First,
9 out of 10 men wore blue dungarees, and blue jackets; second, there
were no hedges, only fences.'[17]

When he moved in with his French hosts, he began writing sections
of the diary in French. But what is most notable about the diary is the
precociousness of both his interests—art, architecture, opera—and his
writing style. There are striking metaphors, vivid descriptions, and an
adult's vocabulary. One day, the family went on a long drive, and Derek
stared out of the window taking in:

> the majestic blue alps, rising and falling, in all their splendour, on the
> horizon [. . .]. After having enjoyed this view for about a quarter of
> an hour our car suddenly dashed down a ravine and under a hill; like
> a beetle quickly scurrying under a stone at the sight of a bird; and we
> saw the ALPS NO MORE!!![18]

He described the sun filtering through the leaves, cascading brooks, and
a spring, 'gently tossing its merry liquid life into the air'[19]. Readers who
can recall themselves at the age of ten will realize that the imagery and
linguistic maturity are not typical.

Notable, given the exclusion of gustatory pleasures from his future
life, is Derek's relish for French cuisine. There is a mouth-watering description of one meal, beginning with watery melon and five black,
slightly bitter, olives, 'a lovely prelude' to what came next, 'a delicate
lettuce' of oil, vinegar, watercress, pepper-plants and many other spices
and specialities.[20]

The second surviving diary, from when Derek was eleven, ran from
late July to September 1954. There are sweet descriptions of his family,
a wet holiday in Wales, table-tennis tournaments with his sisters and
mother, many book reviews (already a fast reader, he consumed a book
a day), descriptions of his oil paintings, including one 'composed of
three ripe apples, one overripe banana, one orange, a brown jug with
yellow spots, and a smaller glazed vase',[21] and an account of a trip to the
Morris Motors car factory:

Arriving at the Works, we waited in a big furnished room with outsize coloured photographs of landscapes on the walls, until a man entered and ushered us out where we were met by our guide. He led us through endless workrooms which all looked practically the same, with great steel girders and elaborate machinery, and rows upon rows of the metal ghosts of cars.[22]

There are few hints of any tensions at home, though he noted that on his Mummy's (*sic*) wedding anniversary on 29 July, there were no celebrations. There are also hints of Derek's lifelong aversion to mornings:

One thing I can never understand is how in all modern adventure stories written for children, the young boy hero always awakes at the crack of dawn and, the moment he opens his eyes, leaps out of bed, with as much vigour as a fresh springbok, and immediately rushes over to the window, flings wide the shutters, letting in a cold draught of damp morning air, as if he was half suffocated. This I have never, or ever will do.[23]

This is both funny and sharply observant. On 7 August 1954 Derek went to a production of Joseph Kesselring's black comedy *Arsenic and Old Lace*, at the Oxford playhouse. 'The plot of the play is fantastic yet morbidly humorous with two charming, and seemingly harmless old ladies, who have a habit of quietly poisoning lonely old gentlemen under the mistaken impression that they are "Setting the poor dears at peace!"'[24] A typical eleven-year-old might chronicle a wet day with the words, 'It rained.' This is Derek: 'Having been perfect for two days, the weather decided that it was being too lenient with us, and so this morning I was woken by an ominous drip-drop outside the window.'[25]

. . .

Derek's last year at the Dragon School was 1955–56. By this stage, the pupils were writing Greek verse—and for Derek this had become effortless: 'He could compose iambic pentameters like nobody's business.'[26] At the beginning of 1956 he won a school essay prize by writing about Sir Walter Raleigh. He also wrote an astonishing piece—called 'A Dream'—which appeared in the school magazine. It bears reproducing in full for its precocity. The narrator enters an enchanted and exotic garden, but turns against it and attacks its plants and buildings:

A large faded yellow manuscript floated towards me. It was slightly curved, as if it had once been rolled up. On it was written in a beautiful Elizabethan hand an intricate story of curves and finery. The sun smiled pleasantly on it, and reflecting that contentedness, it drifted towards me, strange but stately, until the words were as large as a row of oranges. The orange rays of the sun shone on it, and then through it, and the words faded away.

Beyond it I saw a peaceful glade with a ruined tower rising at the back. The tower was ruined, but it was never more peacefully happy than it was now. At one side a large purple wistaria climbed and twined over the warm stones, and on the other a red rose tree lazily spread itself over towards the centre. Below this was set a stone larger than those which surrounded it, on which was inscribed a strange, yet strangely lovely, cluster of delicate inscriptions. I looked closer, but it all floated past me, and I was in a paved courtyard. There was a row of pillars on either side of me, which supported a soft-orange tiled roof, which sloped upwards, and out of my sight. A graceful fountain arched up into the blue sky, then shattered and cascaded mistily downwards into a shallow clear pool.

The stones below me were warm, and the white pillars cast elegant shadows in perspective over their friendly grey surface. A few yards in front of me the terrace stopped, and some wide steps led down into a garden. A wave of warm cypress trees swayed gently in the sun. Through these I saw a row of pillars in crescent shape, with the wings curving towards me, over which draped an ivy, in contrasting shades of white, grey, and green. In the centre of this rose an arch, through which I saw a wooded hill with a white temple nestling close to the walls of a sundrenched village.

But now a strange feeling came over me, I scorned all this. I ran forwards, impatient, I leapt down the steps, brushed against the cypress trees, tore down the ivy, and kicked at the base of the archway.

I shouted, as loud as I could, 'You're all ugly and I hate you, and I'm going to see something much better than you!'

And the echo rang and whispered down the valley to the distant sea, and the breeze blew into a wind. The cypress trees shook, the fountain tottered crazily, and the ivy was ripped from the trembling pillars. The wind howled into a gale, the sky grew dark, the cypress trees were torn from the ground and rolled madly over the paving stones, the fountain hurled its sodden mist against the soft-orange tiles, spluttered, and died, and the pillars crushed into the dying lilies in the trampled grass below the first. The valley darkened and a thundercloud hung above. The last tree sank down, defeated, and all was black. And then I felt a change, everything was harsh, and uneasy . . .

I was staring at the blank ceiling of my room. A great rush of longing sadness came over me. I realised now the beauty of the things I had seen and scorned, and I wept bitterly because I knew they were lost for ever.[27]

It is a touch overblown and strains too hard for effect, but there is so much impressive writing here: the allegorical imagery—secret gardens, overgrown ruins—the Roman or Gothic settings, the use of various literary techniques (such as personification), the orange leitmotif, the sudden and startling moment of drama. Perhaps there are Kantian/Platonic and Christian themes present too: a world of transcendental beauty beyond human grasp, the temptation to sin, bringing regret and unhappiness. And all this is executed adroitly, with texture and pace, to recreate the phenomenology of dreaming. Derek had just turned thirteen.

The poetic and often light and carefree writing style of the boy would eventually be replaced by the rigid and narrow prose of the adult Parfit. This had much to do with the specific demands of philosophy. But there was more going on than that.

· · ·

Always hovering around the top of the class, Derek was now unchallenged. All the schools he attended were highly competitive. He would later explain to his *New Yorker* profiler that the competitiveness was enjoyable, since he was nearly always first 'except in mathematics'.[28] This was a false memory. He *was* top in maths. In fact, in the final term exams, he was top in the top class in every subject that was graded: classics, English, French, and maths. His friend Bill did well, too. Tim Hunt came bottom in classics and in French. He did, however, show some promise in biology, for which he later won a Nobel Prize (which led future BBC Paris correspondent Stephen Jessel, who had played Sebastian to Hunt's Olivia in *Twelfth Night*, to quip that he had once been married to a Nobel Prize winner). Derek would continue to insist throughout his life that he was hopeless at maths. In the United States, when he ate out with friends and it was time to pay the voluntary-obligatory 15 per cent tip, he would claim the calculation was beyond him, and leave it to someone else. This was patent nonsense. Possibly his arithmophobia arose because maths came less naturally to him than did other subjects. In any case, somehow he managed to convince himself that he was far worse at it than he actually was.

He collected an almost embarrassing array of prizes in his final year: the chess prize, the essay prize, the Latin prose prize, an art prize, the school prize for French, the reading prize, the English literature prize, and the overall Gold Medal prize. Mrs Parfit was asked to give an address to the school, presumably linked to Derek's success. She offered some jokey tips to pupils for filling out their school diaries—only Parfit and one or two others would have spotted the irony. It was essential, Jessie said, 'to have a very nagging and hard-hearted mother' and 'nice to have a kind and encouraging father, who will take you to interesting places that you can write about and give you something to stick in your diary'.[29]

Four years after they had conceived their ambitious plan, Bill and Derek took the Eton exams—the only two boys in the school to do so. They were accompanied to the school by an elderly teacher, Mr Jaques—Jacko—and the three of them all stayed at a bed and breakfast in the nearby town of Slough. The exams took place over several days. Derek was nervous about them, and nervous about his nerves: each day he weighed himself on the B&B scales, fearing that the stress was causing him to lose weight. It was the accepted role of any self-respecting B&B host in the 1950s to ensure that you left the lodgings heavier than when you had arrived, so inevitably she got cross: 'What, am I not feeding you enough?'[30]

Derek needn't have worried. Eton awarded him the top scholarship.

3

Eton Titan

'I was quite ready to see him become prime minister [. . .] but not a reclusive Oxford philosopher.'[1] Such was the future as imagined by Edward Mortimer for his closest Eton friend. Derek Parfit for prime minister? In any other school, such a prediction would seem preposterous, the fanciful dream of a naive and ill-informed child. But Eton College was not any other school.

When Derek began at Eton in the autumn of 1956, the British prime minister was Anthony Eden, an old Etonian. After the Suez crisis, which forced Eden's resignation, Harold Macmillan moved into Number 10, Downing Street. He too was an old Etonian. In 1963, Macmillan would be succeeded by Alec Douglas-Home, another old Etonian, whose son was one of Derek's Eton contemporaries. Douglas-Home's main rival for the premiership was Quintin Hogg, Lord Hailsham, another old Etonian. No other school in Britain is more connected in the public's eye with class privilege, nor has such historic and ongoing—and, frankly, outrageous—connections to power.

So, the idea that Derek might one day be prime minister was not so risible after all. Especially given his school record.

. . .

Eton was founded in 1440 by King Henry VI, who endowed the school with the money to finance the education of the poor. Those who do well enough in the entrance exam to receive a foundation scholarship are known as King's Scholars—and they are capped in number at seventy. Over the centuries, the school expanded to include those who paid their own fees, so that by the time Derek went to Eton there were over a thousand pupils. The non-King's Scholars, the vast majority, are called Oppidans (or 'townies', the Latin *oppidum* meaning 'town'). Derek was not only a King's Scholar, but the top King's Scholar of the fourteen in his year. His cohort was exceptional. In second place was Edward Mortimer; third was his best friend from the Dragon School, Bill Nimmo Smith.

The caste system dividing the King's Scholars from the Oppidans was, and is to this day, reinforced by ritual, dress-code, and material benefits. King's Scholars live in college and eat in College Hall, while the Oppidans live in various boarding houses in the town of Eton. Whenever Derek's name was mentioned in a school capacity—for example, in exam results—it was followed, as with every King's Scholar, by the initials KS. While all Etonians wear a uniform of tailcoats and white ties tucked into collars, for classes and chapel the King's Scholars also don a black gown. That's where they get their derogatory nickname 'Tugs', from the Latin *togati*, 'wearers of gowns'. As one former King's Scholar remarks, 'Hearty sorts of Oppidans who don't know Latin tend to take the word tug as an invitation to do so.'[2]

In the 1950s, an astonishingly high proportion of Oppidans—60 per cent—were the sons of old Etonians, most of whom were themselves the sons of old Etonians; they 'inherited the school like an old watch'.[3] These boys were drawn to a large degree from the British aristocracy and upper classes. The relationship between King's Scholar and Oppidan was one of reciprocal snobbery. The King's Scholars regarded the Oppidans as their intellectual inferiors. Nowadays, entry into Eton is highly academically competitive, but in the 1950s it was not. At least a quarter of the pupils, according to a contemporary of Derek's, 'were really thick'.[4] These dunderheads, it was felt, were intellectually equipped only for a career in the army, or stockbroking, or for a life as a backbench Tory MP. Meanwhile the Oppidans sneered at the King's Scholars for being eggheads and of lower breeding. Worse, some were even foreign. And worse still, in their eyes, it was rumoured that among them were one or two Jews.

. . .

Upon arrival in the Michaelmas (autumn) term of 1956, the first order of business for Derek was a ceremony in the splendid college library, where the King's Scholars knelt down and were inducted into Eton with a Latin ceremony. The headmaster at the time, Robert Birley, had centrist political views—but in the eyes of some Etonians that made him a revolutionary, and he acquired the 'cruel and ignorant'[5] nickname 'Red Robert'.

Initially, Derek was accommodated in what is called Long Chamber—a long room partitioned by curtains into cubicles, each with its own desk, little washbasin, bed, and ottoman in which clothes could be stored. The bed was made daily by servants—known as 'boys' maids'—and then with a hinge it could be lifted up to the wall to allow for more space.

The pace at the beginning was relentless. A butler, Mr Holmes, a robust ex-soldier, would turn on the lights at 6.50 a.m. and greet the thirteen-year-olds with a hearty 'Good morning, Sir'. The first class, before breakfast, was at 7.30 a.m. There was a compulsory chapel service at 9.50 a.m., at which King's Scholars sat together, wearing a surplice on certain saints' days. For the whole of Derek's first year, the chapel was being refurbished—so there was a walk down the high street to the parish church.

There was a strong sense of camaraderie among King's Scholars, with whom Derek spent much of his time. They took their meals together, and, because academic subjects were streamed according to ability, tended to be placed together in the top class. Most of his closest friends were King's Scholars. As well as Mortimer and Nimmo Smith, these included Anthony Cheetham and Francis Cripps. The group illustrates how easy it can be to exaggerate the social gulf between King's Scholars and Oppidans: Cripps was the grandson of Sir Stafford Cripps, a former Chancellor of the Exchequer, and Mortimer's father, as a senior bishop, became a member of the House of Lords. Derek was never a social snob, but he was, at least at Eton, an intellectual one—in his first year there he coined the word 'tritic', defined as 'the kind of person one would wish to be associated with'.[6] Edward and Francis were the right kind of people.

Eton was renowned then, and is now, for granting pupils freedom to develop their own ideas and interests. Unlike many elite private schools, pupils were afforded a degree of privacy. After 'graduating' from the Long Chamber, the boys had their own bedrooms. These were allocated according to academic rank. The top King's Scholar would have the pick of rooms—a system from which Derek would benefit.

. . .

Eton has its own vernacular. Teachers are 'beaks'. One young beak, David Cornwell, who taught languages during Derek's first two Eton years, would later become a writer under the nom de plume John Le Carré. (In the 1970s, a BBC crew hunting for locations in North Oxford discovered Northmoor Road, and shot a scene for the film adaption of Le Carré's book *Tinker Tailor Soldier Spy* in Derek's family home.) The cohort of pupils in college in each year is known as an 'election'. 'Terms' are 'halves', a particularly odd word, since there are three halves a year. At the end of each half there are exams, called 'trials'.

Derek was what one of his contemporaries called 'a high-class Rolls Royce academic machine'.[7] The exam results were read out by the headmaster and set the ranking for the next half. Apart from one half (summer 1958), in which he was pipped into second place, Derek was ranked top every time. It would annoy his friends that he would fret about these exams, since they regarded the outcome as inevitable. 'He was so much ahead of everyone else', recalled his friend, Anthony Cheetham, 'that we took his first place for granted. It was obvious to the rest of us that this was the natural order of things.'[8]

During vacation there were visits to friends. Aged fourteen, Derek holidayed with the Mortimers in north Wales, where he was caught trying to cheat at the card game racing demon. When he returned home, Mortimer's parents were upset that no thank-you letter was forthcoming, until one day a bulky envelope arrived containing an epic poem in which Derek described the holiday in verse. He also visited the Cheethams, and was present when Anthony Cheetham was learning to drive. '[Derek] was known to have originality of thought on just about everything. He was absolutely certain that if you wanted to turn the car to the right you turned the wheel on the left.' Derek lost a wager, and almost a car, testing his idiosyncratic hypothesis.

At school he excelled in extracurricular activities. Those who knew him only as a narrowly and feverishly focused adult would be startled by the range of his interests. There was music: Derek had graduated from the piano and now played the cornet/trumpet, participating in orchestra competitions between the houses. He performed in Ravel's *Bolero* and, in 1958, he received the biggest cheer of the evening when, defying tradition, he removed his tailcoat to play a version of Beethoven's eighth symphony in his shirtsleeves. He developed an obsession with Charlie Parker and became an evangelist, too, for Thelonious Monk. For a few years, he was part of a bebop group. Andrew Glyn (who became a well-known left-wing economist) was on clarinet, Nicholas Lowther (a viscount) was on trombone, and Brian Gascoigne played the keyboards. They were unmelodic as an ensemble, and not much better individually, except for Gascoigne, who later made a career as a musician, working on scores for films such as *Harry Potter and the Goblet of Fire*.

In the sixth form,[9] Derek became the editor of *The Eton Chronicle*. The paper covered school news, prizes, sports results, and shows, but there were also poems and reviews. On the whole, the boys were left to print what they wished, although Robert Birley discouraged any mention of Tap, a semi-clandestine bar off the high street, where senior boys were allowed to consume up to two pints of cider or beer. The headmaster was terrified that news of the licentious Tap would seep out to the wider world and lead to bad publicity. The only other time the *Chronicle* was censored was when Anthony Cheetham proposed they carry out and publish a survey on how many pupils' home addresses contained the word Hall, Manor, Estate, or Castle. Too socially divisive, the head judged.

Derek was known for his love of linguistic games and puzzles: he might, for example, take a poem and divide up the words or stanzas in a new way. Six decades later, a fellow pupil could still recall examples of his word play—such as a line he was doodling at his desk: 'have some fundamental knowhow about American canticle melody', which he

transposed into 'have some fun, dame, 'n' talk. Now how about a meri
can-can—ticle me, lady'.[10]

Besides music and journalism, there was the chess club, the literary
society, and drama. Derek's portrayal of Antony in the school staging of
Antony and Cleopatra received a solid review in the *Chronicle*: 'Parfit's
voice had a delicious scorn.'[11] He was also a 'virtuoso and gaping Cali-
ban'[12] in *The Tempest*. Each election would put on a cabaret at the end
of the year, and people looked forward to Derek's year, because he wrote
it and it was the funniest.

Eton had a philosophy club, to which various philosophers were invited, and Derek would go along—he may even have given talks himself. But the club was not particularly active, and Derek was much more
heavily involved in the debating society. When the topic was social or
political he spoke out on behalf of progressive causes. Usually debates
had clever-clever motions, to enable the self-possessed Eton boys to
show off their verbal gymnastics and urbane wit. Derek was clearly a
fluent speaker and cemented his reputation for being witty and
entertaining.

In September 1959, he gave an 'outstanding speech'[13] in favour of the
motion, 'The vote should be extended to those of eighteen and above.'
He suggested it might be a good idea to have some votes in which only
women took part, and others restricted to under-eights.

A more serious debate took place on 25 October: 'This House disap-
proves of punishment.' The topic is notable because of Derek's position—
one he was to hold consistently, throughout his life—that the world
could never be made a better place by suffering—even the suffering of
the guilty. 'Mr Parfit in one of the best speeches from the table that one
can remember confidently propounded a view that as chance, heredity
and environment are alone responsible for our actions, punishment is
surely invalid.'[14] This was a position philosophers label 'determinism'—
that all actions and events are determined by previously existing causes.
Parfit believed that if all our actions are caused—as he believed they
were—then we cannot have free will, as commonly understood. We are
no more free than the person forced to act because they have been un-
knowingly administered a hallucinatory drug that makes them highly

susceptible to suggestion. It's just that the causes forcing us to act are less obvious. The person who has been given the drug does not 'deserve' to be punished for their actions, and nor do we.

There was a more teasing motion in early May 1960: 'This House believes Columbus went too far.' For some reason Derek talked about Vladimir Nabokov's recently published *Lolita*, and 'twisted the English language to extremes of perversity.'[15] In July, he delivered a 'lengthy but brilliant oration, full of puns, epigrams, subtleties' on the motion, 'This House would fiddle while Eton burns.' It was not one of his virtuoso performances, and 'his funniest remarks went unheralded.'[16]

In October 1960 there was another solemn debate: 'This House believes a career in the armed forces is unworthy of the modern Etonian.' It was well attended, but the report on Derek's performance was unusually critical. Derek quoted Robespierre and 'some of the sillier and more mystic passages of Rousseau'. Although he spoke with great passion, the reporter-cum-critic delivered a damning verdict: his 'style had some of the emptiness of his material.'[17]

Such disparagement did not impede Derek from becoming president of the debating society. And after he took office there was a notable change in the tone of the motions, from the vague and facetious to the straightforward and grave. He delivered 'a fine performance'[18] on Sunday, 20 November 1960, supporting the motion that the House 'would abolish capital punishment completely'. It was a topical issue that had been debated in Parliament. Once again, Derek adopted an anti-punishment stance:

> In dramatic and eloquent tones, he described bitterly the degrading inhumanity of official murder, vehemently ridiculed all the usual retentionist arguments, and spoke movingly of the frail sanctity of human life. He yearned, with Thackeray, 'to cause this disgraceful sin to pass from among us, and to cleanse our land of blood.'[19]

The motion was carried by sixty-one votes to fifty.

Then, in February 1961, there was a rare excursion outside Eton, when a crack team of school debaters took on the Maidenhead Debating Society, a few miles away. Edward Mortimer, speaking in favour of the motion that 'the Public Schools should be abolished',[20] gesticulated wildly whilst advocating 'the destruction of the walls of class distinction'. Then 'Mr Parfit' took the floor. He 'was back on his usual revolutionary form with a scalding denunciation of the disastrous social split between public schools and other schools. "Putting a boy down for Eton at birth is like stamping a coronet on the baby's bottom", he asserted.'[21] His scorching speech was not enough to avoid defeat in the vote. But in March, as witness to his debating prowess, Derek and his debating partner Jonathan Aitken reached the finals of the English Public Schools Debating Competition.

. . .

In the English educational system, after O-Levels[22]—public exams taken at the age of around sixteen—pupils who remain at school then focus on just three or four subjects for A-Level qualifications. Derek took nine O-Levels in December 1958, including elementary and advanced maths. Thereafter the school ranking was fixed—with Derek as number one. There was an emphasis in Eton, as at the Dragon School, on Latin and Greek, and when he had the chance to choose subjects, Derek opted for modern history, 'not primarily because I wanted to do history, but because I wanted not to specialize in Latin and Greek'.[23] At Eton, 'modern history' meant anything after the Roman departure from Britain in 410 CE. He also studied for A-Levels in ancient history and English literature.

In his first year of Upper School, Derek won the Rosebery Prize, the top school history prize, despite being in competition with those who were one year above him. At around the same time, he also won a national literary competition sponsored by the *Daily Mirror* newspaper. Between 1959 and 1960, four pieces of his schoolwork were judged so exceptional that—in a practice known as 'sent ups'—they were shown to the headmaster. Three of the four topics were on eighteenth- and nineteenth-century French history and the fourth was a question about Italy: 'What forces governed the fact that Rome did not become part of the Kingdom of Italy during the 1860s?'

In late 1960, Derek entered for, and won, a Trevelyan Prize, for an essay entitled 'Wanton Beauty'. There was a word limit but, in a pattern that would become familiar, Derek thought he should be exempted from the rules, and that a charming and fulsome apology, combined with an (often casuistical) explanation, would suffice for any flouting to be forgiven. 'If my verbosity causes any trouble I can only apologise.' Although he had gone beyond the statutory length, it wasn't really breaking the rules, he claimed, because, 'much of what follows is in quotation'.[24]

The extended essay offered a fascinating disquisition on the nature of language; not the philosophical question of how language manages to refer to the world—a knotty topic that never much engaged him—but more about the phenomenology of language: how sounds and rhythms were experienced by the brain. What interested him in particular were 'the arbitrary qualities in the very nature of the sounds themselves [. . .] consisting, as they did, of a complex pattern of vowels and consonants—fricatives, plosives, labials and the rest'.[25] The essay reveals how highly attuned he was to the multiple subtleties of language, and explains too why poetry, at this stage in his life, so engrossed him. 'It is in poetry', he wrote, 'that we move from speech to song, that the very sounds we listen to play directly on our senses, and are no longer mere unacknowledged messengers of sense.'[26]

There was also a short section on how words look. Decades later, he would drive publishers crazy with his obsessive attention to the visual side of book production—and the seeds of this obsession are evident here, in his discussion of the brain's sensitivity to how letters and words appear on the page.

. . .

Typically, the teacher at Eton with the most influence on pupils was the housemaster—in Derek's case, for the first year, Stephen McWatters, and thereafter Raef Payne, both classicists and old Etonians. But it was a historian, Raymond Parry, who was to play a bigger role in his life. Parry, known as 'the Welsh Wizard', was a voluble and excitable man with a strong Welsh accent. He had won a cricket blue at Oxford,[27] was an expert on the English Civil War, and also taught a popular class on US history, about slavery and the secession of the southern American states. He was also something of an evangelist for his subject. It was obvious that Derek would apply for a place at Oxford or Cambridge, but when he broached the idea that he might study philosophy, politics, and economics—Oxford's famous 'PPE' degree—Parry replied, 'Nonsense boy, you'll do history.'[28] What made Derek easy to dissuade was the mathematical component of economics—he feared, rightly, that it would involve equations and symbols.

Oxford is a university that operates through a system of some three dozen independent colleges; the next issue was which one to apply to. For Parry that question, too, was easily resolved. He himself had been an undergraduate at Balliol and had maintained links with his history tutor, Christopher Hill, who was still teaching there. (It was these sorts of informal ties, of course, that gave already privileged pupils from private schools an edge and undoubtedly helped perpetuate the British class system.) On 2 February 1960, Parry wrote to Balliol in support of Derek's scholarship application: 'He won the top Eton scholarship from the Dragon School and, since then, he has remained consistently top of his election.' He went on, 'I can say, unhesitatingly, that Mr Parfit is the best historian I have come across in my fourteen years' teaching experience.' Having also detailed Derek's many extracurricular accomplishments, Parry wrote, 'Perhaps the most impressive thing about him is that, despite his considerable talent, he has remained a modest and charming person.'[29] A month later, Derek went back to Oxford for the scholarship entrance exam, held at Keble College. He did not have long to wait for the results. On 22 March 1960, news arrived that he had been awarded the Brackenbury, Balliol's top history scholarship.

. . .

A small fraction of children in the UK were (and are) educated at private schools, and a smaller fraction still were boarders, living away from home. Many boarders were lonely. Some were ill treated. Derek Parfit was never much of a one for introspection; a cache of letters sent from

Eton to his younger sister, Joanna, have survived, but these give few clues as to his mood and contain little information about what he'd been up to. But they are affectionate and jokey, and so unlike the tone of Derek's future self. On 11 October 1959 he addresses his 'dreamingest, darlingest sweetest gentlest sister', closing the letter with, 'Buckets of oodling LOVE, brother'.[30]

He wrote to Joanna on special occasions—on her birthday and to wish her good luck in her piano exam—but also sent ad hoc letters. He advised her not to over-work: 'Don't spend more than 12 hours a day working, dear; be like me, only spend 11.'[31] On 14 February 1960 he mailed an amusing Valentine's card in which he imagines a surreal telephone conversation between Joanna and an admirer, in which Joanna ends up asking, '[A]re you barmy? Only semi. Semi barmy, semi-nuts, semi-crackers, semi some chocolate for Christmas! Oh shut up.'[32]

His letters are on notepaper adorned with his Eton address (New Buildings, Eton College, Windsor, Berks). The sheets had been produced by Joanna on her own printing block. On 12 October 1960—the day the Soviet leader Nikita Khrushchev fashioned an enduring Cold War image by angrily thumping the rostrum at the United Nations after a Filipino delegate condemned the Soviet suppression of human rights in Eastern Europe[33]—Derek had a capitalist proposal to put: 'If you want to make quite a lot of money without much effort, I have thought of the way you could do it.' Many people had seen and admired his writing paper, and he offered to sell it for her 'at pretty high prices'.[34]

· · ·

Derek was by no means the only exceptionally clever student to have passed through Eton. Nonetheless, his accomplishments made him a legendary figure among the pupils. He was still being written about in the school magazine several years after he left. One might have expected his scholarly prowess to trigger resentment and jealousy. But he was never flashy, never condescending, never haughty, so he was disliked by few. If anything, he was seen as rather sophisticated, even cool. He told people he worshipped three gods and had come up with a catchy phrase for this Holy Trinity. He called them 'the Bird, the Bard, and Bardot': Charlie Parker, Shakespeare, and Brigitte.

The most prestigious society in the school—at least as far as the pupils were concerned—was the Eton Society, known as 'Pop'. Future members of Pop were elected by current members, and it was widely assumed that the name stood for 'popular'. In fact, it probably derives from *popina*, a Latin word for 'kitchen', 'eatery', or 'tuck shop'—where Pop originally used to meet. Membership was much sought after, because it brought privileges, such as the right to wear a brightly coloured waistcoat. It was a prefect society, so the Pop dandies would strut around Eton admonishing smaller boys for not having their shirts tucked in.

Pop was restricted to about twenty boys, and it is a sign of Derek's popularity that he was elected a member, especially after he had lambasted the club in the July 1960 debate on the motion that 'this House would fiddle while Eton burns'. His election also revealed a thirst for social status as well as a worldly understanding of human motivation: at the school concert the night before the election, he bought a box of marrons glacés and handed them round to his fellow ushers, mostly members of Pop.[35] On 9 February 1961 he wrote to his sister Joanna that he was having 'terrible trouble every morning as I lie in bed thinking of which of my waistcoats to put on.'[36]

'I can easily imagine', Derek wrote in his late sixties, 'how, with worse luck and cruel teachers or other boys, many other children have hated being at a boarding school. It is not a coincidence that the two most famous dystopian novels, *Brave New World* and *1984*, were both written by Old Etonians.'[37] Derek's own schooling, however, had been happy. He was already thoroughly institutionalized; and in institutions such as Eton, he thrived. His final school report catalogued the prizes and scholarships he had won in five years—sixteen in all. The Eton archivist had 'never seen so many prizes listed!'[38]

Had Derek stayed on at Eton until the end of the 1960–61 school year, he would automatically, as the top scholar, have become captain of the school. But, with his place already secured at Balliol, he felt there was little point hanging around, especially as he had just received a most unusual offer—an internship at an illustrious American magazine.

4

History Boy

'I received an invitation, out of the blue, from the editor William Shawn', wrote Parfit, half a century later.[1] Not many schoolboys get an unsolicited summons from a legendary editor to work on what was arguably the most prestigious magazine in the United States. I have been unable to find out how this dream offer from *The New Yorker* came about. The obvious route would be via Derek's well-connected New York-based sister, Theodora, but she says definitely not. Whatever the case, it was not an invitation anybody would turn down.

Exactly half a century later, the same magazine published a lengthy profile of Parfit, written by Larissa MacFarquhar:

> In the early summer of 1961, Parfit, aged eighteen, travelled to New York. He was nearly turned down for a visa—the immigration officer saw that he was born in China and told him the Chinese quota was already full. He protested that he was British; the officer consulted with a colleague and informed him that he would get a visa since he was the sort of Chinese person they liked. He went to work at *The New Yorker*, as a researcher for The Talk of the Town. He stayed in a splendid high-ceilinged apartment on the Upper West Side with his sister Theo and several of her friends from Oxford—mostly returning Rhodes scholars. He brimmed with enthusiasms and self-confidence and issued pronouncements on all sorts of subjects, which amused some of the Rhodes scholars and irritated others.[2]

'Talk of the Town' is and was one of *The New Yorker*'s feature columns. Parfit was set to work researching emerging African nations, especially Ghana. This was the decade of African decolonization—in 1960 Prime Minister Harold Macmillan had delivered his 'wind of change is blowing through this continent' speech. Ghana (formerly the Gold Coast) was near the front of the decolonizing pack—it had gained independence in 1957 and its American-educated leader Kwame Nkrumah was an advocate of pan-Africanism and a figure of endless fascination in the West.

The Cold War was at its frostiest. In April 1961, the CIA funded the catastrophic Bay of Pigs landing operation in Cuba, carried out by Cuban exiles opposed to Fidel Castro. In mid-August, a massive barbed-wire barrier was erected in the middle of Berlin, followed by the bricks and concrete and watchtowers that made up the Berlin Wall. Meanwhile, another international story was also of interest to the magazine. Whilst Parfit was in New York, the philosopher Hannah Arendt was in Jerusalem for *The New Yorker*, covering the war crimes trial of a leading Nazi, Adolf Eichmann. Her reports would be published in a series of explosive articles before being turned into a book, *Eichmann in Jerusalem: A Report on the Banality of Evil*; its analysis of Eichmann and the bureaucracy of genocide remains divisive.

Parfit was given E. B. White's office to work in. White, one of *The New Yorker*'s veteran writers who in his spare time wrote a series of successful children's books, was out of town. Closer to Parfit's age was another *New Yorker* staffer, Indian-born Ved Mehta. Mehta had not long before been a history student at Balliol College, Oxford, Parfit's own chosen educational combination. Parfit would later tell the story of how Mehta had saved his life, or at least saved him from serious injury, by pulling him back when he was about to walk in front of a car on East 43rd Street. Mehta was blind.

Parfit loved New York. He was entranced by the skyscrapers and the glimpses of sky and river. He was able to indulge his passion for jazz and saw several live performances by Miles Davis and Thelonious Monk. He also discovered the music of Billie Holliday, who had died in 1959. The shy *New Yorker* editor, William Shawn (about whom Mehta wrote a book), shared his musical tastes. He met Shawn on this first day at the

New Yorker offices, and that evening, when he went to a jazz club, he bumped into Shawn again. Both were sitting in the teetotal section; Shawn didn't drink alcohol, and Parfit was too young to order it.

. . .

After three months of noise and bustle in high-rise New York, and with his internship over, Parfit returned to the more sedate low-rise city in which he had been raised, and the sort of institution in which he felt most comfortable. Founded in the thirteenth century, Balliol is one of Oxford's oldest colleges. It has produced scores of notable alumni: famous politicians, archbishops, judges, diplomats, poets, novelists, and scholars.

For Parfit, there were new cloisters to navigate, and new rules and customs with which to become familiar. He committed one minor faux pas at the end of the first term, when he naively assumed that the practice of being presented to the college head for an academic progress report, known in Balliol parlance as 'Master's Handshaking', involved a handshake. Thrusting his arm out to Sir David Lindsay Keir is reported to have caused the Master of Balliol a degree of consternation.

Oxford terms are short—eight weeks—but intense. Undergraduates of that generation had two tutorials a week, and were expected to produce one essay, to be discussed with tutors and usually with one other tutorial partner. For a British history undergraduate, there was no better place to be than Balliol. When Parfit was there, the college had four history tutors. John Prest, of whom Parfit had a low opinion, was a kind but uninspiring expert on Victorian Britain and, according to the former Balliol student (and future cabinet minister, Hong Kong governor, and Oxford University chancellor) Chris Patten, a 'courtly man with apple cheeks and beautiful manners'.[3] The other three were significant figures. Maurice Keen was a brilliant specialist in the Middle Ages, who spent four decades in Balliol; a claim to popular fame was an appearance as the history tutor in Frederick Forsyth's novel *The Negotiator*.[4] Keen had a Socratic method of teaching, asking probing questions which revealed to the student difficulties or contradictions in their own arguments.

Patten remembers that he 'smoked filthy little cheroots and as he wandered about his room listening to undergraduate essays would occasionally stop to dip a finger in a pot of Oxford thick-cut marmalade which he would suck ruminatively in between puffing away'.[5] He was a diffident man, and later told Robin Briggs, Parfit's bright tutorial partner for medieval history, that he was intellectually intimidated by the Briggs–Parfit double-act.

Keen liked a drink, and in tutorials would sometimes be nursing a hangover, but his alcoholic consumption was pathetically amateurish compared to the quantities consumed by his great friend, Richard Cobb, who arrived at Balliol in 1962. Cobb was one of the world's leading authorities on the French Revolution and, in the early part of his career, wrote entirely in French. His interest was in 'history from below'—the poor not the rich, prostitutes rather than *les ducs*. A charismatic and inspiring teacher, who had a way of making the French Revolution feel vivid and present, he was also a coruscating writer whose initial reputation was built on his sparkling, and often damning, reviews of French history books. Oxford lectures would begin with his placing a pint of beer on the podium.

In person he could be as combative as he was on the page, and he would relish hurling insults at figures of authority. Once, after a dinner with friends at a restaurant, he returned to Balliol inebriated and swayed around the cars parked on Broad Street by the Master's Lodge shouting 'Fuck the Master!' When drunk, he was also known to stand at an open Balliol window and in fluent French carry off a perfect impersonation of the French president Charles de Gaulle.

Parfit had tutorials with Cobb on eighteenth-century English history and then again when he chose the French Revolution as his special subject. Of the four Balliol historians, Cobb undoubtedly had the most intellectual impact on Parfit, but the fourth Balliol historian would turn out to be more important for his career. Christopher Hill was a Marxist historian, who provided a new framework for understanding seventeenth-century English history, including the Civil War and the turbulent and revolutionary rule of Oliver Cromwell. The Hills and the Parfits had been family friends for years: North Oxford, where both

families lived was, and is, a small, socially interconnected area. The fact
that Hill had been a member of the Communist Party until the 1950s
proved no impediment to his Oxford career. He was everyone's favourite Marxist and a kind man, though 'he took a great deal of trouble to
avoid being caught in being kind'.[6] Soon after Parfit graduated, Hill was
elected Master of Balliol. Parfit would call upon him to support his
switch from history to philosophy.

Later, Parfit reported that he had always been less interested in history than philosophy. Indeed, in the second term of his first academic
year, he contemplated a switch to 'PPE': philosophy, politics, and economics. The economics component still deterred him; he was anxious
that the mathematics involved was beyond him. In order to test himself,
he began to read an economics textbook.[7] The first part of it—which
was about how there was a diminishing marginal utility from peas (the
more you ate, the less pleasure they gave you)—made perfect sense.

> Since I understood that claim, I told my friends at dinner in Hall that
> I was going to change to PPE. But after Hall I read a few more pages.
> I came across a symbol that I didn't understand, which was a line
> with a dot above and a dot underneath. I went to ask someone with
> rooms nearby what this symbol meant. When he told me that it was
> a dividing sign, I felt so humiliated that I stayed in History.[8]

Again, it is difficult to know how to interpret this story. Parfit wore his
mathematical illiteracy with pride, but it is hard to believe that the boy
who had come first in maths at school would not have recognized a divi-
sion sign. Be that as it may, however, everyone who studies PPE has to
learn some basic formal logic, and Parfit was pleased to have stuck with
history, because he would have hated that part of the degree and, 'as a
result, [. . .] might have been driven away from philosophy'.[9]

. . .

Academically, Parfit continued to flourish. According to one of his undergraduate contemporaries, Richard Cobb was in awe of his student:
'he thought he was a genius'.[10] Parfit impressed his tutorial partner, Robin

Briggs, with his powers of analysis and his skill at marshalling the relevant facts and arguments. He was the sort of historian who likes straightforward questions and solid answers; he would set out an intriguing problem and then seek a solution to it. At the end of the first-year exams he was awarded the H.W.C. Davis Prize for Oxford University's best performing history candidate.

As at Eton, Parfit pursued a smorgasbord of wider interests beyond the academic. Firstly, there was student politics. The Oxford Union, the 'establishment' debating society, was a playground and dress rehearsal for ambitious students who wished to enter party politics. Speakers were expected to wear black tie, and the elitist atmosphere was off-putting for many students from state-school backgrounds. Parfit joined the Union but did not become active in it. However, he was more heavily involved in the University's Labour Club, for which he organized a series of lectures, including some by brilliant academics; these included the philosopher and historian of ideas Isaiah Berlin (possibly on imagination in politics), the social researcher Richard Titmuss (on the welfare state), the Irish-born biologist J. D. Bernal (on the relevance to biology of the Marxist dialectic), and Stuart Hampshire (on psychoanalysis, freedom, and politics).[11]

Politically, he seems to have hedged his bets, however: he also became vice-registrar and then secretary of the Canning Club. The Club was named after an early nineteenth-century British Tory prime minister, George Canning, and it promoted and discussed Tory principles. It seems to have been, in the 1960s at least, a highly elite society. One of the senior members was the Warden (equivalent to Master) of All Souls, John Sparrow; another was the distinguished historian Hugh Trevor-Roper. The infrequent meetings would revolve around a speaker usually addressing a topic in political history—the Spanish Civil War, imperialism, fascism in Britain pre-World War II, Lord Canning himself—and would take place in student rooms. Parfit hosted one meeting at which, drawing on his *New Yorker* research, he spoke about Ghana.[12] He raced through a thousand years of Ghanaian history before arriving at independence and the feted figure of Kwame Nkrumah, whose quasi-deification, Parfit suggested, should not be taken too seriously. Parfit advocated a degree of forbearance for some of Nkrumah's repressive measures, which might be justified by 'the exceptional needs of an emergent country'.[13] As for the fear in the West that Ghana would be sucked into the Soviet orbit, this was misplaced, he said: Ghana remained overwhelmingly integrated with Western economies, and Nkrumah had no desire to become dependent on Moscow.

Each year, the Canning Club held a lavish annual dinner. Although the guest list for the 1961 dinner has been lost, it seems almost certain that Parfit was present. He didn't miss any Canning Club events and was about to be chosen as vice-registrar. The event occurred on 11 December 1961, so it is highly likely that Parfit spent his nineteenth birthday in the company of the British prime minister, Harold Macmillan. The dinner took place at the upmarket Dorchester Hotel in London, and the minutes show that the prime minister, who a year earlier had also become chancellor of Oxford University, 'took the chair as President of the evening'.[14] A toast to the Queen was proposed by John Sparrow, and there were toasts too from Lord Clitheroe (representing the House of Lords) and John Boyd Carpenter, the minister of pensions and national insurance (representing the House of Commons). Sparrow made a short speech about how the balance of power had gradually shifted from the House of Lords towards the House of Commons. (The prime minister thought that Sparrow got the history wrong and somehow found the time three days later to write a letter putting him right.)

What followed was a cut above a more typical student night out involving fish 'n' chips or a greasy kebab: after *Le Consommé au Fumet de Tortue* (clear turtle soup), the main course was *Le Filet de Sole au Champagne et Fleurons* (fillet of sole with champagne and pastry ornaments), followed by *Le Soufflé au Gruyère*, each course accompanied by an expensive wine (the sole was washed down with a glass of 1952 Château Mouton-Rothschild Pauillac).

The Canning Club was a discussion, not a debating society. Parfit did little public speaking at Oxford. However, there was at least one memorable occasion when he was reunited with his Eton debating partner Jonathan Aitken. A debate was arranged in the West London prison Wormwood Scrubs, on whether private schools were worse than prison.[15] (It is a curious fact that Aitken would himself end up with the personal experience to provide testimony for both sides of this motion: after resigning as a Conservative cabinet minister in 1995, he sued a newspaper for libel over allegations that he had been involved in shadowy dealings with some powerful Saudis. He lost the case and later pleaded guilty to perjury and attempting to pervert the course of justice, resulting in a prison sentence of eighteen months, of which he served seven.)

At the boisterous Wormwood Scrubs event, Parfit demonstrated 'the qualities of a high-class comedian' in arguing the demerits of private schools,[16] but he and Aitken were nonetheless heavily defeated. On the prisoners' team the star was the Cambridge-educated convicted spy George Blake, who had worked as a double agent for the Soviets. Exposed in 1961, Blake had been sentenced to forty-two years in prison. During the debate he claimed that if his punitive sentence was not cut, he'd cut it himself. That puzzled the university side—what could he possibly mean? Not so long afterwards, in 1966, the world would find out: with the aid of a rope ladder (and accomplices on the outside), Blake scaled the prison walls, eventually making it to Russia, where he lived out the rest of his long life.

Blake had handed the Soviets details of British spies, some of whom were executed. He believed that the glorious end—a communist society—justified the treacherous means. It was the sort of reasoning that in the future Parfit would write a great deal about. For the time being, however, his pen was engaged upon less weighty topics.

5

Oxford Words

As at Eton, Parfit dabbled in journalism. He edited and wrote jokes for a satirical magazine, *Mesopotamia*, produced in Balliol, and also tried to recruit people to sell it—as the historian and feminist Sheila Rowbotham discovered when she opened her (St Hilda's) college door to him. Finding Parfit 'aesthetic-looking', she took an instant dislike to him because his hair flopped over his brow in what she regarded as a 'peculiarly upper-middle-class way. [. . .] In two bounds he was on the other side of my room and was seated cross-legged on top of the wardrobe, looking down on me like the caterpillar in Lewis Carroll.'[1] Although Parfit was not from a privileged family background, his Etonian education guaranteed that 'posh' was how he was perceived.

Mesopotamia was not the main outlet for Parfit's scribblings. There were two university-wide student publications, *Cherwell* (the name of the Thames tributary at Oxford) and *Isis* (the name for the Thames within Oxford's boundaries). Parfit plumped for *Isis*, which was, then, a weekly magazine. It boasts of being the longest-running independent student magazine in the UK and has launched the careers of many journalists and writers; its contributors have included Evelyn Waugh and Sylvia Plath.

When Parfit first arrived at Oxford, *Isis* gained national notoriety for running articles critiquing and lampooning university lectures—as far as the university authorities were concerned, that was taking liberties with freedom of speech, and the magazine was temporarily banned. Parfit began writing for it within a month of arriving, however. He reviewed a cabaret, and in an unusual column reported on an Oxford Union debate on the motion that 'in the opinion of this House the machinery of mass publicity should be demolished'. It is odd in that he himself participated in the debate, and in the article served as both judge and defendant. As his own judge, he turned out to be less than lenient: 'the case against [was] impressively put by Robert Skidelsky, and flippantly by Derek Parfit'.[2]

He tried out a mixture of writing styles. There was a poem in his second term, a music review in the summer term, and more coverage of Union debates, including one about whether God existed. His existence was denied by Bertrand Russell's son, Conrad, and by the philosopher Antony Flew. One interruption so annoyed Flew that according to Parfit he went 'into tight-lipped fury. All Hell was let loose with hell as its object. A God of eternal damnation was not infinitely good but unspeakably bad. "You are worshipping a torturer!" he screamed.'[3]

On another occasion, Parfit gave a favourable account of a speech by the Conservative MP Enoch Powell, who 'had poor acceleration but great momentum in top gear'.[4] This was six years before Powell's infamous, racist 'rivers of blood' speech, which led to his sacking from his role as a frontbench party spokesman by the Conservative opposition leader, Edward Heath. Powell may have had few virtues, but he was rarely dull. Parfit found the following week's debate, by contrast, 'as grey as the order papers'.[5]

In June 1962, Parfit had a poem published in *The New Yorker*. This would have been an outstanding accomplishment even for a nineteen-year-old, but in fact it had been written two or three years earlier, when he was sixteen or seventeen, and had been reproduced in his Trevelyan Prize-winning essay at Eton. He later confessed to finding it 'embarrassingly overblown'.[6] That is an overly harsh judgement. The first verse is clumsy and contrived, but the imagery is inventive, and there are some poignant lines. It reveals a capacity for genuine empathy and is unrecognizably different from his later philosophical style. The poem was titled 'Photograph of a Comtesse' and its theme was that of ageing: a young girl whose photo 'time caught' is compared to the 'shrivelled, scorched, sun-wracked, fever-spiked' old lady. It was inspired by his revisiting an old French chateau where he had stayed, aged ten, on his French exchange trip. The occupants had all moved out of the chateau, apart from the housekeeper and an old lady, with whom he was alone for a few minutes. Although Parfit never himself drew a parallel between this poem and his subsequent philosophical work, it is hard not to see one. Are the young girl and the shrivelled, sick old lady one and the same person?

Her eyes blow wide some nectared anodyne.
Child brows replay the paleness of her chin.
Full, moon-blown bows surmount dark crystalline;
Dark, sweeping jets of hair, umber, wash by,
Flaking the skyline pallor of her skin.

The stern expression merely signifies
Mock-tragic gaiety in a girl her age.
Pale arms of porcelain touch. A necklace lies
Lightening her dress, whose whale-blown hoops of sky
Fade on exposure through the whitened page.

Time caught—a dying smile, caught, revived,
Fresh-watered in the lens, and duly shed–
Hangs shaded, where, behind noon shutters knived
By splintered light (whose fig-seed blaze outside
Bleaches the yawning stones), she lies in bed.

Shrivelled, how scorched, how sun-wracked, fever-spiked!
How winter frost has shorn this withered husk!
How many ravelled years have liked, disliked
This old, worn woman, many streams of light
Have lit this trembling mind, and how much dusk?

Nodding at some sweet thought, she half retrieves
The far, flushed sunrise, but the eyes which laugh
Are blind, the smile which wreathes those same lips leaves
A wasted rose. As darkness falls, she sleeps
Alone, with a little girl in a photograph.

The rhyme form is ABAAB; that much is obvious. But the methodical cast of Parfit's mind is revealed in the poem's carefully constructed sound-play. We know this because he set it out in two pages in his Trevelyan Prize essay. For example,

> Inside each structure, there is a relationship of rising and falling sounds between the interlocking rhymes, for B is in four out of five cases a relaxed complement to A—thus "ine" goes with "in", "ived" with "ed" [. . .]. Moreover, just as the effect of the repeated third and fourth rhymes in each stanza is to give the last line a sense of peace and relief, so a repeated use of the crying vowel I (as in line) throughout the first four stanzas gives the whole of the fifth stanza with its E rhymes, a feeling of calm and the abatement of passion.[7]

In the fourth stanza, he proceeds to explain that the harsh consonants and unexpected sense are intended to come as a shock, as it became clear in the unfolding narrative that the bed's occupant was an 'old, worn woman'.

. . .

Poetry was only one form of linguistic expression. There was also a short story, 'Like Pebbles' about a young man's holiday infatuation with a young woman.[8] (It would probably not be published today; it finished with the man entering the woman's hotel room at night, uninvited, to steal a kiss.) But Parfit's least successful literary form in *Isis* was satire. In the first term of his second year, there was a clunky parody of pro-apartheid publicity—a column funded by 'Suid Afrika Haus', which argued that the 'natives' were grateful for apartheid and that '[t]his is proved by the absence of riots'.[9] A second, equally unfunny spoof was written by Parfit in the guise of Conservative Central Office.

Thankfully, he abandoned attempts at lampooning political opponents and moved on to a style of journalism that came more naturally—forensic and opinionated pieces that reveal a cosmopolitan outlook and a curiosity about international affairs. Most controversially, he wrote about the dangers posed by the Christian Right in the United States, in an article entitled 'The Warfare State'. It was controversial not only because of its dark prophecy, but also because it bore a suspicious resemblance to material in a series of pieces in *The Nation* by Fred J. Cook. It was only after Parfit was accused of plagiarism that the magazine belatedly (the following term) acknowledged his principal sources. It has been impossible to establish whether the allegation against Parfit was justified: he claimed that he sent his sources with the original article, but that the *Isis* editor had chosen not to publish them. As for the content, he tried to pacify a furious American who objected to its 'woolly, irrational analysis'[10] by claiming, in a published response, that he had 'great hopes for America. I was merely setting down some of my fears.'[11]

Parfit also revealed antennae sensitive to injustices closer to home, in particular the appalling housing conditions of Pakistani immigrants living in Oxford. A column in the middle term of his second year was an impassioned plea for action to be taken to alleviate global poverty, and for more aid and technical assistance to be sent to parts of the world in dire need of it: '[If] we were to turn our backs on the East and South, if we were to leave the greater part of mankind lying in the gutter, it would be more than wicked. It would be mad. This is the most important subject in the world.'[12]

The theme was picked up again when, in the Trinity (summer) term of 1963, he became *Isis*'s editor. This was a position for which one had to put oneself forward, but for which one was chosen by the rest of the magazine's student editorial and production 'staff'. Among Parfit's *Isis* supporters and collaborators were Stephen Fry,[13] and his own close friend Edward Mortimer. Fry was studying physics, which he neither liked nor understood. He had secured his place at Trinity College after the dons interviewing him established that he was the grandson of the legendary cricketer C. B. Fry. He had no sporting ability, but inveigled them into believing that he would be an asset to the college cricket side. However, he was a talented photographer and graphic designer, and some of his covers for the Parfit editions of *Isis* are so professional that they could easily have graced a commercial publication.

And although their treatment didn't amount to investigative reporting—that would be too much to ask of a student magazine—the issues

Parfit spotlighted were ones that engaged with pressing contemporary concerns. A boxed paragraph on 1 May 1963 set out his ambitions for the period in which he would be at the helm. It fascinates
now, because his 'two kinds of suffering' would be ones he returned to
five decades on:

> No moralising this term. Just one starting-point: the aim of all actions
> should be to reduce suffering. Two kinds of suffering stand out
> above all others: the hypothetical suffering of a nuclear furnace
> (fuel: one third of the world, 1000 million bodies), and the actual
> suffering, now, of the other two-thirds. Two proposals, for the two
> kinds of suffering, appear on pages 10 and 11. People at least seem
> aware of the first problem, the potential death of our third. The sec-
> ond problem, the growing misery of the other two-thirds, will be the
> term's main theme.[14]

One might assume that by the 'actual suffering' of two thirds of the
world's population Parfit must have meant poverty. In fact, his own writing that term does not confine itself to economic hardship. There was
an anti–Vietnam War polemic (worth noting because this was well
before anti-war protests really took off in the United States); there was
an article highlighting the re-emergence of ex-Nazis into positions of
power in Germany; and there was what in retrospect seems like a preposterous and naive article about the likelihood of the Soviet Union
catching up economically with the US. In 1961, Yuri Gagarin had completed an orbit of the Earth and the Soviets looked like they were
winning the 'space race'; Parfit was hardly unique in believing that
Communism was proving an efficient system for achieving technical
breakthroughs and managing the economy, and hardly alone in failing
to foresee how a centralized economy was incapable of responding adequately to rapidly changing consumer demands. But he did at least
draw an interesting distinction: 'To ask which system—the Soviet or
the American—is better for achieving affluence, is quite distinct from
asking which system will be better once affluence is achieved.[15]

. . .

Besides journalism, there was another extracurricular interest that merits attention: women. Eton had been an all-boys establishment, and Parfit had had little opportunity to mingle with members of the opposite sex. Balliol was all-male too, but there were a few all-female colleges, including Somerville, five minutes' walk from Balliol down St Giles, and St Hilda's at the end of the high street on the edge of town. The male–female student ratio was about seven to one, which was not quite as evolution has designed it, so competition among the young heterosexual men was especially fierce. But the caricature of male students as being preoccupied less with studies and more with drinking, playing cards, and chasing girls hardly fitted Parfit.

Still, young women did now enter his life, though with a disastrous beginning. In early spring 1962 he fell for a twenty-five-year-old at St Hilda's, Diana. In a letter several years later to his younger sister Joanna, he revealed that she was the first girl he'd ever really been in love with and that she had broken it off after barely six weeks. 'I felt more miserable than I'd ever been [. . .]. I felt completely numbed and worthless.'[16] The worst aspect of it was the manner of the rejection: when he had confessed the depth of his attachment, 'she treated it simply as a great joke—to think that there might be any reason for _her_ to love _me_. So apart from my disappointment I felt completely humiliated—as if this was proof that I was unloveable.'[17]

His sense of dejection was brief. Notwithstanding this false start, Parfit was rarely short of attention from women. He had social status, intelligence, effortless public-school charm, and good looks—six feet tall, with fair hair and blue eyes. Unlike many young male Oxford undergraduates, he was not boorish. Plus, it turned out, he was a romantic. Soon after his first rejection, he met the woman with whom he would have an on-off relationship for several years. Mary Clemmey, studying for an undergraduate degree in physics, was a popular, sporty party-goer from Liverpool, attractive but fragile. 'He wrote the most beautiful love letters and cards. One of them had a photograph of a river, and he composed some accompanying poetry.'[18] There was an occasion when Mary went on a bus journey and had a scheduled stopover in Birmingham, an hour from Oxford; Parfit travelled to Birmingham to chat with her for the twenty-minute gap.

'The Pill' was not yet available as a contraceptive, and so the physical side of the relationship was constrained. There was a lot of what Mary Clemmey calls 'sweaty fumbling.'[19] She would later get her life together and have a successful career in publishing, but Oxford was not a happy period for her. For most of the Michaelmas term of 1962 (October–December), she was hospitalized in the Warneford, suffering a breakdown. Parfit visited her every day and helped to draft a note to the principal of Somerville for her to be permitted to return to her studies.

For a period, she was not allowed out of hospital. One day she asked Parfit to post a competition piece she had entered in the *Daily Herald* about what items should be taken to a desert island; it was designed to promote a Disney adventure film, *In Search of the Castaways*. The entry required payment by a postal order, but Parfit could not work out the system, and simply stuck the coins with sellotape onto the envelope. Somehow, the entry made it through, and it won. That Easter, having been released from hospital, Clemmey enjoyed a three-week round-the-world trip, all expenses paid.

Before and after her Warneford confinement, Mary and Derek communicated often, via the internal Oxford University postal system, which ran three deliveries a day. He kept some of her letters, many of which are exquisitely decorated with stunning little line drawings, Picasso-esque in form. In his personal papers, too, are what appear to be drafts of some of his own letters to her. Parfit spent his twentieth birthday, in December 1962, on a university skiing trip in the Austrian Alps, and holiday snaps of some of his privileged, well-connected friends appeared in the high-society magazine *Tatler*. But he told Mary that he was unable to get into the holiday spirit, and was mystified that '800 people should organise themselves into a massive expedition, split up into quasi-military training groups, grit their 800 chins and proceed to do nothing, for two weeks, but whoosh down hills and <u>curse</u> if they're not whooshing quite as fast as they meant to whoosh.'[20]

The (largely undated) letters give a clear sense of Parfit's infatuation with Clemmey:

I'm not at all drunk. I just want to be with you. Incredibly much. I can't even use words for it. I can just feel it, in my fingers, my ribs, my throat, hands, my knees, my chest. [. . .]

When you have to be away, at the other side of the world, then I don't feel alone at all, because if we just think of each other we are happy and real together. But when I know I could be with you, when you are just 800 yards away, then it hurts.[21]

At one stage he contrasts love for family—what he calls random love—with love one chooses: 'The first kind of love has an accidental base, but is real; the second, with all the powers of design and reason behind it, is reality at its highest peak.'[22] Meanwhile, the psychological turmoil that Mary is in is clear in many of her letters:

Derek, I am like a cork bobbing between elation and despair and always full of dreams. Theories unasked of people and thoughts hammer inside until I feel I am pregnant with dragons' teeth. Yesterday I was very happy. Today it is like a dry pain.

And,

My Dear Derek, Sorry to be so miserable last night but my imagination ran riot too deeply and too consciously. I think you may be right in saying that I am looking for something that cannot exist. And I think I may be right in saying that you are not ready to understand. My pain is real and lasts always; I am a fool not to wake up.[23]

One note simply reads, 'Dear Derek. I am sorry that I came to see you. I am sorry that I was impossible. I am very sorry.'[24]

In February 1964, he presented her with a seven-stone moonstone cluster ring and five-stone coral ring, as well as what she described as 'oceans and oceans' of roses.[25] She thanked him cryptically: 'Oh Derek, if only I were good and kind, but I am not, I am full of passions which are master of everything—so Hume would be pleased but I am not.' In another letter that year, he wrote to her, in gold ink, 'It is a strange new feeling that has come in the last few days now I <u>know</u>, that whatever happens, I will always love you, with a certain love that nothing could ever destroy (even another love) and that I will always look at the world partly through your eyes, and never feel anything for anybody, darling, except partly through you. For <u>you are part</u> of <u>me</u>.[26]

. . .

It was when returning from seeing Mary Clemmey in Somerville College one evening that Parfit suffered a close brush with death. In the 1960s, Balliol locked the gate at the porters' lodge at ten o'clock. Freshmen newly arrived in college were warned by the dean that they would be severely punished if they attempted to gain access to the ground floor after hours. But with a nod and a wink, the message was conveyed that climbing in through the first floor or above would be acceptable—since this at least posed a decent challenge.

There were several ways to get in, and all were hazardous, but Parfit's preferred route was via a drainpipe on the Magdalen Street side of the college. On Saturday, 18 May 1963 he left Somerville at around midnight. After successfully shimmying up the pipe, he had to shuffle along a ledge, and could then gain access by leaping to a window. But on this particular occasion, the breaking-in went calamitously wrong. He slipped and caught an arm on a set of metal spikes, causing a twelve-inch gash exposing arteries and nerves, and coming 'within a fraction of an inch of causing his death by loss of blood'.[27] A taxi driver he asked to take him to hospital refused: 'Wot—& muck up my cab!'[28] Instead, just in time, an ambulance was called.

This accident left Parfit with a permanent scar on his left arm. He was in no state to pen that week's *Isis* editorial, so the task fell to graphic designer Stephen Fry. In his debut article, Fry explained the fate that had befallen the magazine's leader. A delegation had gone to visit Parfit in the Cronshaw Ward at the Radcliffe Hospital and had passed on some of words of wisdom: 'If you go out, for God's sake don't eat late: because they won't give you an anaesthetic till 1.30 a.m. And they'll pump your stomach.'[29] What the patient was most upset by was the college's conflicting messages: 'I mean, they put the spikes there (a) to stop you climbing in, and (b) so you can use them as a foothold.'[30]

The group of friends offered to supply Parfit with some reading material: what would he like? The bed-bound editor requested a newly published book entitled *The Ethical Foundations of Marxism*, and for light reading a copy of the Sunday paper *The Observer*. After that a sign went up in college advising 'Gentlemen [. . .] not to use the climbing-in route until handles have been fitted'.[31]

. . .

It is often said of the Austrian-born philosopher Ludwig Wittgenstein that he published only one book in his lifetime, the *Tractatus Logico-Philosophicus* (1921). In fact, in the mid-1920s he also compiled a dictionary for children. Parfit is usually credited with writing only two books. This is true, but he also co-edited, and partially wrote, a third, *Eton Microcosm*, published when he was a student. It was, according to his friend and co-editor Anthony Cheetham, 'playful and a bit daft'.[32] Both young men were former editors of *The Eton Chronicle*, and they conceived the idea of compiling a collection of the best *Chronicle* articles into a magazine. Cheetham later met an editor who proposed turning it into a hardcover book. Assembled in 1963, it's an odd and patchy miscellany, divided into various aspects of Etonian life: 'discipline', 'recreation', 'crisis', 'public opinion'. There are extracts from famous old Etonians, such as Aldous Huxley, and articles on everything from love at Eton to the school's sport, the Wall Game.

Parfit never hid his Etonian background, nor did he campaign to reform a system in which a small elite received a privileged private-school education. The book presents an affectionate portrait of Eton, though the authors acknowledge that 'to those who hate the place, the average Etonian is seen as a cross between a conceited puppy and a brainless antelope'.[33] Parfit's personal contributions to the volume were a long, dark poem about fishing ('Delight and horror that the line you wound / Was tearing a pointed hook through flesh'),[34] and an article in defence of eccentricity, in which there are no capital letters:

attention, attention, this is your only remaining reporter with urgent news. a revolution has just taken place, yes, here on the front page of the eton college chronicle, led by a band of minuscule fanatics, vast masses of small letters have risen in revolt and seized the editorial headquarters. at one blow they have taken over the reins of government. flushed with heady victory, they are now proclaiming their manifesto[.][35]

Mimicking the style of Marx and Engels's *Communist Manifesto*, Parfit's manifesto calls for the overthrow of the capital letter and all existing typocracy: 'what has this smirking letter done to deserve its privileged finery? what shining merit raises it above its humbler fellows?'[36] Given the hundreds of subsequent anecdotes about Parfit, the manifesto's passage in praise of eccentricity is worth citing:

> why shouldn't i eat toothpaste? it's a free world, why shouldn't i chew my toenails? i happen to have trodden in some honey. why shouldn't i prance across central park with delicate sideways leaps? i know what your answer will be: 'it isn't done'. but it's no earthly use just saying it isn't done. if there's a reason why it isn't done, give the reason—if there's no reason, don't attempt to stop me doing it. all other things being equal, the mere fact that something 'isn't done' is in itself an excellent reason for doing it.[37]

Persecuted eccentrics received their own rewards, the article proclaimed. Those who stood on their heads had a fresh vision of the world around them. The person who 'strolls into chapel in pink shorts and turquoise bedsocks [. . .] will have the delicious sensation [. . .] of strolling into chapel in pink shorts and turquoise bedsocks'.[38]

Although they were not exactly able to retire on the royalties, Cheetham says they 'loved doing it. And some of it was rather good'.[39]

. . .

Parfit spent the summer of 1963 in Paris after being awarded a Cecil Spring Rice Travel Scholarship. Most of his days involved research in the national library, the Bibliothèque nationale de France, reading up about the subject he intended to specialize in in his final year—the

French Revolution—and he sought out city sites linked to it, such as the Café Procope (used by Maximilien Robespierre as a meeting place). But he also did the usual touristy things, like visiting Versailles and going to the theatre. He was appalled by the French translation of Shakespeare's *The Merchant of Venice*; hearing it was 'traumatic'.[40] It was the centenary of the death of the painter Eugène Delacroix, and Parfit went to three different Delacroix exhibitions. In part to perfect his French, he read the daily newspapers *Le Figaro* and *Le Monde*. His French was sufficiently fluent that at a dinner party he was able to engage in a lengthy discussion comparing the French and British national health systems. Upon his return, on Monday, 14 October 1963, he wrote to Sir David Keir, the Master of Balliol, to express his gratitude—this courtesy was expected, and a student who wrote an insufficiently long or effusive letter would be frowned upon. 'You have given me', Parfit wrote, 'the most enjoyable and useful summer I have had.' He had become so immersed in the language and culture that, '[i]n sum, by the time I came back to England at the end of September I felt as much French as English'.[41]

Then he was into his third and final undergraduate year. At the beginning of the first term, there was an optional exam for history students for the Gibbs Prize. The process of marking history papers obviously involves a greater degree of subjectivity than that of maths papers—it is therefore all the more remarkable that Parfit won again. What his tutors and examiners never found out was that he was not above inventing quotations in his exams. His motivation was simply to get the best possible marks—he mentioned to one friend that he had invented quotations from Otto von Bismarck. He loathed Bismarck more than just about any other historical figure, believing this nineteenth-century German statesman to be at the root of much of the evil unleashed in the following century.

The Finals exams would take place the following summer, but Parfit's thoughts now turned to life beyond his degree. He hoped to continue his studies, but fancied a change of scene. In November 1963 he filled in an application for a Harkness Fellowship, administered by the Commonwealth Fund, which would fund two years at a university in the US. What were his career plans, the form asked. 'I want to write on political and social problems, and perhaps later to enter government or politics.'[42]

His study proposal for the fellowship was woolly. The general aim, he wrote, was 'to see the future, and how it works'. He was interested in new developments in society, such as abundance, automation, and increasing leisure. These trends were more advanced in the US than elsewhere, and 'I want to ask whether traditional social and political theory can contain these developments: whether the new society can be democratically controlled by the old methods, whether traditional social and moral codes (eg attitudes to work) still fit the new facts.'[43]

What interested him specifically was whether a study of psychology and motivation could be applied to political and social theory. How do attitudes to work, wealth, success, and security affect social theory? 'Can a deeper study of motives—aggression, frustration, insecurity— explain the irrational events in recent history? At its simplest: how far do political and social systems give people what they really want?'[44]

Intriguingly, under the 'Activities' heading, he wrote little, made no mention of the University Labour Club, but put down that he was secretary of the Canning Club. Perhaps he felt that an American scholarship was more likely to be awarded to someone with centrist or right-wing political leanings.

His thin study plan gave every appearance of having been produced in haste and with little reflection. But then came the references. Parfit listed three: his old teacher, R. H. Parry, and two of his history tutors, Hill and Cobb. Their commendations made the award of the fellowship a certainty. 'If what follows sounds like extravagant praise I must point out that Mr Parfit is the most brilliant young man whom l have ever tutored,'[45] wrote Parry. Extravagant praise duly followed. Cobb wrote a short covering letter describing Parfit as 'an absolutely first-rate man, brilliant, charming and yet disarmingly modest'.[46] In the more detailed reference, he stated that his student was 'quite exceptionally gifted'. He was without doubt the best historian of his year in 'Balliol and probably in the University. [. . .] I have never felt so certain about any of my other pupils obtaining a First in the Honour School of Modern History'. He had many skills as a historian, not least that he 'has an extremely brilliant prose style, his essays and articles are little masterpieces'.[47]. Hill, meanwhile, wrote that Parfit 'is in many ways the ablest pupil I have ever had'.[48] He assured the Harkness committee that Parfit had a strong social conscience and that he was interested in applying high-quality academic research to making the world a better place in which to live.

The deal with the Harkness Fellowships was that Fellows had to agree to leave the US, for at least two years, once their fellowship was over. The form asked what applicants planned to return to post-fellowship; 'hopefully to an Oxford Research Fellowship. Not yet fixed,' wrote Parfit. The form also asked whether he was seeking funding elsewhere. Parfit wrote that he had applied for money from the grant-giving body the English-Speaking Union.

In fact, he had put in for funding from both Brandeis and Columbia universities, and this would cause him considerable anguish. Before their replies arrived, he approached various institutions to serve as his Harkness base—Harvard, the New School for Social Research, and NYU (New York University). And, it turned out, they all wanted him, as did Columbia and Brandeis. Columbia offered him five years of financial support for a Faculty Fellowship in sociology. Brandeis offered him a Wien International Fellowship. Parfit had been attracted to Brandeis because the German-born philosopher Herbert Marcuse taught there. Marcuse was a neo-Marxist associated with the Frankfurt School of philosophy, who in 1968 would be a source of intellectual inspiration for the student revolts. (European students marched under the banner of the 'three Ms': Marx, Mao, and Marcuse.)

What to do with this glut of offers? A friendly Commonwealth Fund official, John B. Fox Jr, wrote to Parfit in May to commiserate on his plight. He could see that Parfit was 'suffering from *embarras de richesses*'.[49] Inevitably, he would have to let some institutions down; he replied to Fox that the *embarras de richesses* 'has become a nightmare [...]. I feel like the cad in some Victorian melodrama being simultaneously sued for breach of promise by 3 wronged damsels, pursuing 2 others the while.'[50]

He had got himself into this mess and the Commonwealth Fund was inclined to let him find his own way out of it. 'It sounds to me as if you had discovered the formula for instant admission,' wrote John B. Fox on

15 May 1964. 'You should be able to sell it to your academically less fortunate colleagues at quite a high price. I will leave it to you to unravel the present situation.'[51]

Eventually, having studied the various courses available, Parfit concluded that he would like non-degree status at two universities—NYU and the New School, which offered courses in social psychology. Columbia did not make his withdrawal easy. After he told them that he was forsaking them, they wrote a wounded letter: 'We have with considerable disappointment noted that you will not be studying at Columbia next year. In order to attempt an evaluation of our position, may we ask you to drop us a note explaining the motives governing your decision as we should not like to lose students of your caliber in the future.'[52] Sugaring the pill, he apologized again, but wondered if he could enrol in a course entitled 'Utilitarianism, or John Stuart Mill', given by Professor Robert D. Cumming.

. . .

Oxford University degree classification rests solely on the performance in exams taken in the summer of the final year—putting what can be intolerable strain on students. Parfit, along with most other undergraduates, stepped up his work rate in his third year, though there was still time for some other activities, including social events. He was at a drinks party on 22 November 1963, hosted by Maurice Keen, when news came through that President John F. Kennedy had been assassinated in Dallas, Texas. He was 'distraught' at this,[53] much as his father had been at Roosevelt's death two decades earlier.

His immediate post-undergraduate future was settled in late March 1964. The Harkness Fellowships were highly competitive and sought after, but Parfit was used to success. In the letter of congratulation from the Harkness Foundation he was informed that a tentative booking had been made for him on the *Queen Elizabeth* ocean liner, to set sail on 3 September.

Before then, there were Finals (degree exams) to take. In any other year, it would have been a certainty that Parfit would achieve a First. But in 1964 the chief history examiner was Charles Stuart, 'a rather acidulated character',[54] who was a former student of, and would no doubt have been heavily influenced by, the snobbish, arrogant Hugh Trevor-Roper, who was himself on the board that year. Trevor-Roper believed that they should 'give no one a First who was not as good as himself (which meant, in his view, as good as Gibbon)'.[55] Yet, in a haughty *Sunday Times* article in which he compared students to horses parading in a paddock, he professed to care little about grades (though he clearly cared a lot): 'Some of my best research students and most admired colleagues got seconds and went on thinking. Some of the most brilliant firsts were so satisfied that they stopped.'[56]

The gruelling week began on Thursday, 4 June, and, including the Saturday, ran through to Wednesday, 10 June. The general paper was on the Monday. It wasn't a compulsory paper, but if you didn't sit it, you excluded yourself from the possibility of gaining a First. In 1961, candidates had to tackle three questions from a list that included:

> Would you agree that the destruction of the European Jews is the most important event of the first half of the twentieth century?;
> Is there any direct correlation between great art and a high state of civilisation?; and
> 'Freedom is never given. It is taken.' Discuss this dictum by Subhas Chandra Bose.

On the afternoon of 9 June and the morning of 10 June, Parfit sat the special papers on the French Revolution. Tuesday's papers were all compulsory and to be written in French. On the final, Wednesday, paper, he was given a choice of questions to answer, including one about the fall of Robespierre and a typically Oxford smart-aleck 'meta'-question on the Count of Mirabeau, a leader in the early stages of the French Revolution: 'Is Mirabeau's political significance exaggerated by the place given to him in this special subject?'

Day one of the exams provided a moment of high drama. Parfit was sitting in the North Room of the examination building and was about forty minutes into the paper when he suddenly went white in the face, rose from his chair, and staggered to the invigilator—a man called John Cooper, an ex-Fellow of All Souls, described by Robin Briggs as 'a large shambling figure with broad jowls and a pointed head [who] when agitated [. . .] had a mannerism of banging a large meaty hand on the back of his head'. This he began to do as Derek spoke to him. 'Then he turned and got up to ring the bell behind him and summon help. At that moment Derek fell down like a sack crumpling and hit the dais with a noise like doom; given the large hollow space underneath, it functioned like a drum.'[57]

On his zig-zag, stumbling route to Cooper, Parfit had careered like a drunk into other desks. His tutor Richard Cobb was summoned, as he described in a letter many years later:

> [Parfit] was having a fit, lay on the floor groaning and making dreadful vomiting noises after tipping over his table, the ink went all over a Somerville pupil of mine, also a P (Miss Pinder) and there was much distress in the M to Z room. [. . .] I took Parfit by the arm and walked him round and round the quad outside. His parents, both doctors, had given him two lots of drugs that had contrary effects.[58]

Briggs recalls that it took four large men to carry Parfit out and that he had appeared unconscious. When the paper was finished and Briggs left the room, he spotted Parfit sitting at a table in the lobby, having been allowed to resume the exam.

There was no further excitement during the week, and Parfit must have felt confident that, overall, he had put in a strong performance— for as soon as the last exam was taken he began to think about applying for a Prize Fellowship at All Souls. The Prize Fellowship lasted seven years and came with a decent salary plus room and board. The application process was usually exceptionally competitive, and without a First, there was no realistic prospect of a candidate being successful.

However, the All Souls exams were in early October—and he was due to be in New York from September. So a new idea began to germinate in his mind. Perhaps he could postpone the Harkness Fellowship a few months; instead of starting in the US in the autumn of 1964, he could begin in January 1965. He contacted NYU and the New School, who had no objections, and in a lengthy letter to the Commonwealth Fund on 29 June he set out three reasons to delay.

The first was that up until then he had been studying history; thus, 'My next year will have to be very largely spent in covering the basic groundwork in my three new disciplines—psychology, sociology, and moral philosophy.' Parfit appealed to the Fund's self-interest. He argued that he would benefit most from the courses in the US if he could do several months' intensive reading in advance. 'But this basic reading could as well be done in England as in America. I am very aware of the great responsibility I have been given as a Commonwealth Fellow [. . . and] I am convinced that it would be wasting the Fund's money for the time it took me to do this basic reading.'[59]

The second reason was that 'nearly all the courses in which I am most interested are not being given until next year'. The third, 'personal' reason was that it would enable him to take the All Souls fellowship examination in October. He thought his best chance of success was to apply in history, and not after he had changed to a new specialist subject.

As usual, Parfit got his way, the Commonwealth Fund agreeing to his proposal. The Finals results were announced in August; the examiners dished out a huge number of Third Class degrees, but only eleven Firsts, out of 299. Parfit got one, as did his tutorial partner, Robin Briggs. He sent a thrilled note to Mary Clemmey, bordering it with gold paint and adding a sprig of honeysuckle. He was now helping to prepare friends who had been called for a viva (oral exam) because the examiners were not sure which of two grades to award them. He was relieved not to have to go the US immediately, but would have to work flat-out for the next two months in preparation for the All Souls exam. He'd been perusing some old All Souls papers and 'found them very exciting'.[60]

He duly sat for the exams from 1 to 3 October—Thursday to Saturday—1964, along with only a dozen other candidates. Success depended entirely upon how he did in these three intensive days.[61] There were two papers on a chosen specialism (history for Parfit). Then there were general papers, which included questions of the type that undergraduate applicants to Oxford would face in their own general paper: '"It is easier for a camel to go through the eye of a needle than for a rich man to enter the kingdom of God." Do you agree?'; 'What is art?'; 'Is science compatible with religion?'; 'Do we owe duties to the dead?'; 'What are universities for?'; and so on. Robin Briggs remembers that the paper that year included something like 'Poetry set to music is poetry destroyed. Discuss.'

The most notorious part of the process was another three-hour exam in which candidates turned over a blank page, to be confronted by a single word, 'like a tiny incendiary device',[62] on which they had to compose an essay and display their erudition. A probably mythical story is that this was of such fascination to the outside world that even non-candidates would congregate outside the college to discover which word had been chosen.[63] Over the years, chosen words have been 'harmony', 'chaos', 'mercy', 'charity', and 'corruption'. When Parfit flipped over the page in 1964, he was confronted with 'innocence'.

Then, on the Saturday, came the final and most intimidating part of the process, involving a translation and viva. Candidates were given a minute to choose a passage from the Greek, Latin, French, and German ones on offer. They were then ushered into the gloomy common room and told to read and translate the passage in front of around fifty gown-swathed Fellows, who stared back at them in the half-light. (One failed candidate, a couple of decades later, described them as being 'draped around the room like vampire bats'.[64]) This was followed by some desultory questions from the Fellows about, for example, what research the candidate would pursue if they were successful. Aspects of the procedure were silly: for example, candidates could not be quizzed about their papers, because the Fellows had not yet had a chance to read them.

A vote among the Fellows took place about four weeks later, on or close to All Souls Day. Not coming top in an academic competition was a rare experience for Parfit. It must, therefore, have come as a shock to be rejected, and perhaps especially galling that the only Prize Fellowship that year was awarded to his tutorial partner, Robin Briggs.

Clearly, All Souls felt that there was not a second candidate worthy of a fellowship. Nonetheless, Parfit might have taken comfort from a letter from the Warden of All Souls, John Sparrow, who told him that the decision had been very close, and who encouraged him to try again. This he would do. But he could now take up his delayed fellowship to the United States—during which he would fall in love with a new discipline, to which he was to devote the rest of his life.

6

An American Dream

On 13 January 1965, Derek Parfit boarded the ageing *Queen Elizabeth* ocean liner at Southampton for the six-day Atlantic crossing to New York. For the next two years, he would be a Harkness Fellow.

The Harkness Fellowships had been established by Edward Harkness, son of Stephen. Stephen Harkness had begun his working life as an apprentice harness-maker and then made a vast fortune as a founding investor in what became Standard Oil. The fellowship programme was originally set up for Britons only, and to reciprocate the Rhodes Scholarships. In the 1960s, fellowships were principally awarded to bright and high-achieving students in their early twenties, who had recently completed an undergraduate degree. A few Fellows were a little older—Parfit's cohort, for example, included the novelist David Lodge, who was in his late twenties and already married with children.[1] Most Fellows were attached to a university, and the fellowship paid tuition and board.

To know the United States was to love it. At least that was the Harkness hope and aim. And, on the whole, it worked. The BBC broadcaster Alistair Cooke became fascinated by the United States during his fellowship in the early 1930s, and devoted most of his life to reporting and explaining America to a British audience. Parfit's love affair with the United States, which had begun with his *New Yorker* internship, deepened during his fellowship. He became more familiar with New York than with London.

. . .

Including Parfit, there were fifteen British Harkness Fellows that year. They were scattered in different universities across the country and their academic interests varied from chemistry to banking, anthropology to law, city planning to creative writing. Parfit was initially based in New York, and he chose as his first accommodation the chaotic, seedy, twelve-storey redbrick Chelsea Hotel on West 23rd Street, which maintained a louche charm and was a favourite haunt of numerous artists and writers. The Chelsea offered apartments that were ideal for a long-term stay. Arthur Miller moved there in 1961, following his divorce from Marilyn Monroe, and stayed on for six years. In the Chelsea, Miller wrote, there were 'no vacuum cleaners, no rules and shame',[2] and it was possible to 'get high in the elevators on the residue of marijuana smoke'.[3] At around the time Parfit was in residence, Miller would have breakfast with Arthur C. Clarke, who was developing *2001: A Space Odyssey* with Stanley Kubrick. Clarke was on the top floor and subsisting on tea, crackers, and liver pâté. No doubt their conversation turned at some point to the death of Winston Churchill, who passed away five days after Parfit moved in.

From 7 February until the end of May, Parfit rented an apartment on 144 East 22nd Street, before moving into Apartment 1E, 245 West 104th Street, on the intersection with Broadway. He was affiliated to both the New School and New York University. The fellowship afforded him the luxury of auditing courses without the obligation to take exams. We know what courses he planned to attend, but not how many he actually attended. His plans included classes on 'Democracy, Freedom and Responsibility', 'Social Psychology', 'Culture and Personality', and 'Psychoanalysis and Society'. At NYU, he had wanted to sit in on classes with Dennis Hume Wrong, a sociologist inspired by C. W. Mills. Wrong had recently written a much-cited article rejecting the notion that human behaviour was dictated by internalized social norms. (A better theory, he argued, was that it was governed by sexual urges and human nature.) But despite Parfit specifically citing Wrong in his application form, there is no evidence that he attended his class.

Parfit's hope was that his two years in the US, 'would give me the time to decide whether to do graduate work, and whether to try to change my subject from history to philosophy'.[4] Close to his Manhattan apartment was New York's oldest university, Columbia—and he did go to classes there. One was led by Sidney Morgenbesser who, in an admittedly uncompetitive field, is regarded as among the wittiest of philosophers— though the numerous Morgenbesser quips and anecdotes travel less well beyond the discipline. Asked for his view of pragmatism (which sees words and thoughts as tools to solve problems rather than to represent reality), Morgenbesser replied, 'It's all very well in theory but it doesn't work in practice.' During one conference at Columbia, the Oxford linguistic philosopher J. L. Austin pointed out that while in English you can have a double negative to express a positive, as in 'he is not unattractive', there is no example in English of a double positive expressing a negative. Morgenbesser interrupted, 'Yeah, yeah.' Then there's the story of his ordering dessert in a restaurant: the waitress said there was either apple pie or blueberry pie. He ordered the apple pie. She returned shortly to say that cherry pie was also an option, to which Morgenbesser responded, 'In that case I'll have the blueberry pie.' That's a classy joke, if you're an expert on decision theory. Morgenbesser covered a wide range of subjects; his switchblade-sharp intelligence and his way of interrogating students—Socratic with a Yiddish accent, to paraphrase one description—was daunting for students, and for Parfit, new to the discipline, it must have been eye-opening.

Of the various topics into which Parfit had planned to deep-dive, including sociology and psychology, it was philosophy that hooked him. He soon began to contemplate taking up the subject, post-fellowship, in Oxford. Oxford was known for its analytic philosophy, stressing the examination of concepts. In the 1950s, and partially inspired by the Viennese-born but Cambridge-based Ludwig Wittgenstein (who died in 1951), Oxford had become the centre of so-called ordinary language philosophy, according to which traditional philosophical problems could be dissolved if philosophers paid close attention to how words were actually used in an everyday sense—as opposed to how philosophers deployed them. Parfit told *The New Yorker* in 2011 that in America, 'I went to a talk [. . .] by a "continental" philosopher, which was on some important subject such as suicide, or the meaning of life, but which

I found very obscure. I also went to a talk by an analytical philosopher, on some very trivial subject, which was very clear. I remember wondering whether it was more likely that the continental philosophers would change, by discussing their important subjects in a clearer and better argued way, or that the analytical philosophers would change, by applying their clarity and logic to important subjects. I decided that the second seemed more likely, and I think I was right.'[5] Who was the obscure 'continental' philosopher? It's impossible to be certain, but it is likely to have been Robert Cumming, whose lectures Parfit had expressed an interest in attending, and who had studied at the Sorbonne in Paris. His interests included the existentialism of Jean-Paul Sartre.

The details are again sketchy, but we do know that at some stage Parfit paid a visit to the British philosopher Stuart Hampshire, who was at Princeton. Hampshire became a major influence on Parfit's switch to philosophy, not least because he too had started out as a historian.

. . .

The summer of 1965 was spent on the road. One of the aims of the Harkness programme has always been to encourage Fellows to immerse themselves in the United States through travel. When I was myself a Harkness Fellow, all Fellows received an air-pass, enabling them to fly wherever they wanted within the continental US over a sixty-day period: a vast number of mini-packets of pretzels and peanuts was consumed. But in the Parfit era, money was given for Fellows to purchase a car, and they were expected to spend the summer months traversing as much of the US as they could. Not everyone thought this was a worthwhile exercise, and one Fellow in Parfit's year gamed the system by writing a series of postcards from his US home and getting friends to post these from different cities.

Parfit, however, took the requirement seriously, learned to drive at his sister's house in New Haven at weekends, and then plotted a detailed and circuitous route from New York. He asked Mary Clemmey whether she would like to join him, and she eagerly agreed. He picked her up at JFK airport (only renamed, from Idlewild, eighteen months earlier, following Kennedy's assassination). From New York they went to Boston, Buffalo, Niagara Falls, Chicago, and across the Midwest. Parfit had planned sites to visit and things to do everywhere they went: in Buffalo, for example, they saw some Frank Lloyd Wright buildings. While driving between cities, they listened to local radio stations. Somewhere in the Midwest, they came across an outdoor dancefloor with young people dancing the twist to the recently released 'Dancing in the Street' by Martha and the Vandellas. Then they reached Snake River in Idaho and Crater Lake in the Sierra Nevada mountains. There, Parfit almost lost the car after getting out to appreciate the spectacular view whilst forgetting to put on the handbrake. Fortunately, the vehicle rolled slowly into the mountainside rather than over the cliff.

Eventually they arrived at San Francisco. They had planned to stay with friends of Parfit's sister, but had to move out after one night when one of their hosts received a cancer diagnosis. From Berkeley they drove to Stanford, where they picked up Anne Chisholm, a university friend of Mary's, and Anne's friend David Wiggins, who was at Stanford teaching a summer course. Wiggins would become an eminent philosopher; he was then in his early thirties and the philosophy tutor at New College, Oxford. He had been attracted to a summer posting at Stanford because he was fascinated by the then little-known work of Donald Davidson, who was developing an influential if byzantine theory about how language acquired meaning, which connected psychological states— such as intentions and beliefs—with a theory about when sentences would be true or false.

The quartet drove down the Pacific Coast Highway to Los Angeles, reaching there shortly after the Watts riots, which had erupted after a young African-American man was struck in the face by a police baton after being pulled over for reckless driving. Parfit had been reading up on the story and educated his fellow travellers with a detailed summary. Then they had a picnic on the beach with some people Anne knew, John Gregory Dunne and an aspiring writer called Joan Didion.

Next stop was Las Vegas, via Death Valley. As their car had no air-conditioning, they drove across Death Valley in the evening, making it to Vegas around midnight. The only accommodation available was one

room with two double beds—and in those chaste times the men decided to occupy one mattress and the women another. The discovery
that one of the beds had a quarter slot that, if fed, gently shook the frame
for a minute and a half kept them up and entertained for half the night.

After what Wiggins described as a disgusting Vegas buffet breakfast,
it was on to the Grand Canyon, which, because they were short of time,
they decided to see on an air tour. On the runway ahead of their small
plane they saw another plane that had clearly crash-landed and heard
their pilot shout to air traffic control, 'For God's sake get that thing out
of sight!'[6]

Back on land, they set off on a 1,200-mile journey to Nuevo Laredo
in Texas, through Arizona and New Mexico. Parfit drove all the way and
progress was measured, because he and Wiggins were discussing philosophy, and whenever debate became intense, Parfit would slow to a virtual
crawl. Parfit was never interested in linguistic philosophy, and it seems
unlikely that it was the writings of Donald Davidson that engrossed them:
far more likely is that Parfit received his first in-depth exposure to issues
of identity. In the autumn of 1964 (the Oxford Michaelmas term), Wiggins had given a series of lectures under the title 'The Absoluteness of
Identity'. He was interested in the question of what a substance is, or, as
he put it later, 'how the objects we speak of and think about—and must
ourselves interact with—are articulated or isolated or found or drawn or
formed or carved out in the world'.[7]

This was tied up with issues of identity. If a block of marble is a
substance, is it still the same substance when it is fashioned into a
sculpture? It is an ancient conundrum. Writing around 500 BCE, the
pre-Socratic philosopher Heraclitus is credited with claiming that it is
impossible to step in the same river twice. He also discussed the ship
of the legendary hero Theseus: Theseus's ship docked repeatedly in
port, and because its wood was rotting, its planks were slowly replaced
one by one. Eventually, not a single plank remained of the original ship,
raising the question of whether it was still the same ship. The puzzle
becomes even more headache inducing if one imagines the rotten
planks all being preserved and put back together. Now is *this* the original ship?

Humans are not inanimate objects like blocks of marble or ships, but a related puzzle applies: was Derek Parfit the same person at the end of the road trip as at the beginning? Was he the same person on the road trip as when he was a baby? If so, what made him the same person?

Parfit and Wiggins were the oddest of philosophical couples; over the next half century they would develop their thoughts across a range of issues but would share little intellectual common ground and would never become friends. Still, Parfit might consider himself fortunate that by chance the person sitting in the passenger seat was not only a brilliant philosopher but, at this stage, considerably more learned and immersed in the discipline than he was himself. And, with his interest in identity matters, Wiggins appears to have influenced significantly Parfit's future philosophical direction.

At Nuevo Laredo, Parfit parked the car and the four travellers boarded a deluxe train to Mexico City. In the few days they were there, they visited the National Museum of Anthropology and took a bus to the Teotihuacan pyramids. They watched the locals play a handball game, Basque pelota, which must have reminded Parfit of its ball-game cousin Eton Fives. Then the group separated, with Wiggins and Chisholm travelling to Yucatan and Parfit and Clemmey returning by train to pick up the car. Their long, final leg took them back to New York via Louisiana, Mississippi, and Alabama.

In Alabama they had an encounter with the brutal racism then pervasive across the American South. It was a pivotal period for US race relations. The civil rights revolution was built on twin legislative pillars: the Civil Rights Act of 1964 and the Voting Rights Act. The Civil Rights Act, among other measures, banned restaurants from discriminating against people because of their race or colour. The Voting Rights Act had just been signed by President Lyndon Johnson on 6 August 1965; it outlawed literacy tests and other bogus means by which African-Americans were disenfranchised. Johnson called it as huge as any victory won on any battlefield, but that's not how it was seen by most white voters in Alabama. Jim Crow practices persisted in many areas of life. On one hot and humid evening, Parfit and Clemmey went to eat at a small family-run burger joint. There was no air conditioning, just a revolving, throbbing ceiling fan. A white teenage girl, 'sweating profusely', handed them the menus. 'We were utterly flummoxed that it showed the burgers as costing $50.65 and a Coke as $50.15. When we queried this, she said in a Southern drawl, "Pay no mind to those prices, they're just for the coloured folk."'[8]

Parfit's Eton and Oxford friend Edward Mortimer was in New York when he and Clemmey reached Manhattan. The three of them went to a grungy jazz club on the Lower East Side called Slugs in the Far East. The jazz was invigorating, but they emerged a few hours later to discover that they had a flat tyre. None of them knew what to do, least of all Parfit. A passer-by, who may also have come from the jazz club, gave them a hand. He looked remarkably like John Coltrane, whom Parfit revered, and when they asked him whether he was, he said 'Yes'—but, says Clemmey, 'I don't think he was!'[9] Mortimer said something like, 'Then you must know Thelonious Monk?', to which he replied, 'Monk? Sure. He's out walking the dog right now.'[10]

In September 1965 another Harkness Fellow, Ben Zander, and his fiancée Patricia moved in to share Parfit's West 104th Street apartment. Ben was a talented cellist and conductor, and was in the US to study music. Patricia was a star pianist. Parfit saw little of them—usually only in the evenings—because he had already become semi-nocturnal. Zander particularly remembers his voice: 'There are only two people whose voices I can hear clearly when I picture them—Benjamin Britten, with whom I studied as a child—and Parfit. His voice was breathless, high-energy, with tremendous enthusiasm.'[11]

Patricia and Ben married in 1966 and divorced, amicably, in the mid-1970s. At some early stage, Parfit and Patricia began a relationship. There is evidence that it began during her engagement, which, had it become known, would have caused shock even within the liberal circles in which they moved. Patricia became a professor at Harvard and then at the New England Conservatory, one of the most prestigious music colleges in the world. She had been raised in a working-class family in Dorset; her father had become a gardener on the estate of the flamboyant and decadent socialite Stephen Tennant (who is thought to have inspired the character Sebastian Flyte in Evelyn Waugh's *Brideshead Revisited*). She had learned to play the piano, in fact, by sneaking into his stately home. Before she later developed a nerve injury, she accompanied one of the world's leading cellists, Yo-Yo Ma, on an international tour and made two recordings with him. Budding musicians would travel far and wide to be taught by her, and many famous composers would confide in her about their work in progress.

She had grown up in a house without a single book, and as a young woman she was insecure about what she regarded as deficiencies in her literary and cultural education. Eventually, she built up an impressive library at her duplex near Harvard Square, which included many works of philosophy. Parfit would recommend books. Most of their early conversations, however, were about music. In the mid-1960s Parfit was in a Bach phase. 'He was fantastically attuned to Bach,' remembered Ben Zander. 'It was as if it was written for him.'[12] He told the Zanders that there ought to be a loop in the universe that you could check into at any time and in which Bach's music was always being played.

. . .

The car conversations with Wiggins must have reinforced Parfit's growing interest in philosophy. In the autumn of 1965, he attended a class on ethical theory led by Robert Paul (Bob) Wolff at Columbia University. This was a topic in which Parfit had a keen interest. 'Derek showed up as a traveling student and asked whether he could sit in on my lectures on ethical theory. Naturally I said "yes". At the end of the semester, he asked whether he could submit a paper even though he was not taking the course for credit. Well, I thought, I am going to get a batch of 20 papers, what's one more? So I said yes.'[13]

That proved naive. Parfit soon showed up with an essay forty-eight single-spaced pages long. It turned out to be a defence of act-utilitarianism, the theory that in any situation we should always act to produce the best possible consequences (versions of which have been promoted by Jeremy Bentham, John Stuart Mill, and Henry Sidgwick). 'Needless to say, it was worth the time I took to read and comment on it.'[14] After that semester Wolff never saw Parfit again, 'but it will come as no surprise to learn that he stuck in my mind'.[15]

By January 1966, Parfit had decided definitely to apply for a BPhil, a two-year philosophy degree, and he wrote to the head of Oxford's philosophy faculty, Gilbert Ryle. Ryle was best known for his book *The Concept of Mind*, in which he argued that dualism—the idea that the body and mind are separate substances—was philosophically incoherent. Dualism was originally associated with the sixteenth-century French philosopher René Descartes; Ryle ridiculed it, coining the phrase 'the ghost in the machine'. Ryle sent Parfit an encouraging reply, but wondered whether he might consider taking three rather than two years to complete the BPhil—since he had no formal training in the subject. He also said he should send in two pieces of philosophical writing.

On 10 January Parfit wrote to one of the Balliol philosophy tutors, Alan Montefiore. He reminded Montefiore that he had seen him in 1962 when he was wondering whether to switch to philosophy, politics, and economics, but 'at that time, I quailed through fear of economics'. Before leaving for the US, he had been offered a place to study for a BPhil in politics. However, 'it has become obvious that my interests centre far more in philosophy'.[16] His two essays for Ryle would be on empirical value theory and moral emotions. He already had a draft of the first, but wondered if Montefiore would be willing to read the second before he submitted it.

He then approached three people to request references for his BPhil application: Stuart Hampshire, Bob Wolff, and Christopher Hill, his former history tutor, who had been elevated to the position of Master of Balliol. 'Give my jelly mind a year's freedom and I'm bound to wobble onto a new subject,' he wrote to Hill. He was worried that his degree in history would appear as 'woolly-mindedness to a philosophy board (they don't appreciate the subtler rigours of our subject)'. He nudged Hill with a suggested form of words: he was hopeful that 'my gentle argumentativeness (which you can hardly fail to have suffered from) might give you honest grounds for writing "he appears fitted for a course in philosophy". ("Fitted" in the sense "Damned".)'[17]

Over the next few weeks, all the references came in. Wolff said the paper Parfit had written for him, 'would have done well as part of a doctoral dissertation [...]. His skill in argument and command of the literature is remarkable for one who has had little or no formal training in philosophy.'[18] Hampshire was 'satisfied that he is very intelligent'. Parfit had read and understood a surprising amount of the twentieth-century literature, but 'he plainly still has a lot of reading to do, particularly in logic'.[19] Hill, who knew him best, was the most effusive: 'Mr Parfit is, in many ways, the ablest pupil I have ever had.' He went on to list the string of academic prizes that Parfit had won at Eton and Oxford. 'At every stage he has aimed for the highest honours, and has never failed to win them.'[20]

There was a section on the form for applicants to explain how they expected to finance their studies. Parfit expressed the hope that he would be awarded a State Scholarship. But, he wrote, he was not dependent on such a scholarship. The next box asked for details of how he would support himself in the absence of a grant or scholarship; his answer was, 'Parents?'[21]

On 18 March 1966, Gilbert Ryle informed Alan Montefiore that Parfit had been accepted on the course. He suggested reminding Parfit that it might be in his interest to take three years for the degree rather than the customary two. Montefiore passed this on and Parfit replied on 31 March 1966 to thank him for shepherding the application through. The letter is headed 'ELECTION DAY'—the Labour prime minister Harold Wilson had called a snap election, and this was the day he was re-elected in a landslide victory.

As was his wont, Parfit thought the rules as they applied to him might be permitted a degree of elasticity. He sought permission—granted—to delay the start of his BPhil until January 1967, so that he could spend the 1966 Fall semester at Harvard. On 2 May Bob Wolff wrote to the Commonwealth Fund to reassure them that in selecting Parfit for a Harkness Fellowship they had chosen wisely. 'Parfit has attended several of my courses and I have seen over 100 pages of his written work. Mr. Parfit is one of the three or four best students I have ever taught in my eight years at Harvard, Chicago, and Columbia. He is doing magnificent work and I only wish I could persuade him to stay on here. You could not have spent your money better.'[22]

The summer of 1966 was spent in Britain—apart from a trip to France for an Oxford friend's wedding. Parfit was back in the US by 26 August, in time to hear the welcome news that he had been awarded a Major State Studentship that would pay all his BPhil fees and a maintenance grant of £375, payable in three annual instalments.

. . .

During his semester at Harvard, Parfit met the professor who would blow the dusty lid off political philosophy with *A Theory of Justice*, a huge book that reinvigorated philosophical interest in questions of justice and equality, especially as these values pertained to liberal democracies. Since World War II, there had been some notable works of political philosophy—such as Karl Popper's *The Open Society and its Enemies* (1945) and Hannah Arendt's *The Origins of Totalitarianism* (1951). But the discipline had been hampered by the lingering impact of the Vienna Circle—a group of scientifically literate philosophers and mathematicians, who would gather in the Austrian capital in the 1920s and 1930s and who held that normative statements such as 'Murder is wrong' or 'Democracy is good' were meaningless, because they could not be empirically tested. Later, the ordinary-language philosophers dampened enthusiasm for political theory further by insisting that the task of the theorist was merely to analyse the way political terms—such as 'ownership', 'rights', 'power', 'democracy'—were used.

John Rawls, the author of *A Theory of Justice*, changed all that. He tackled substantial issues, and not through the narrow prism of linguistic analysis. He maintained that the principles of justice—and the just allocation of resources—could be derived from what he called the 'original position'. Rawls asked how we would distribute resources in society if we were behind a 'veil of ignorance' that screened us from any knowledge of our place in society, our class position, our race or sex, our interests or talents, or of whether we were good at maths or sport or art, or indeed whether we had any skills at all. Under these conditions,

Rawls claimed, we would adopt various rules of justice; most importantly, we would permit some inequality, but only to the extent that it was to the benefit of the least well-off group in society. It is likely, for example, that financial and other incentives to reward the ambitious and the capable are good for even the poorest in society. Although Rawls has suffered the fate of 99.99 per cent of philosophers in that, beyond academia, he is virtually unknown, it is hard to exaggerate his influence, which has been felt by vast numbers of people around the world. Whenever bureaucrats interrogate a potential policy and ask how it will affect the least advantaged, they are raising a Rawlsian query.

A *Theory of Justice* appeared in 1971, but it was the culmination of many years of thought, and Parfit was exposed to some of its ideas in late 1966. Parfit's personal introduction to Rawls was arranged by Dennis Thompson; he and Parfit had known each other at Oxford and Thompson was now a graduate in the Harvard department of government. Rawls immediately recognized that Parfit 'had a formidable philosophical intelligence and a very perceptive and penetrating mind'[23], and Parfit was clearly captivated by Rawls. He showed him his act-utilitarianism paper, and, in a letter dated Halloween, he wrote that the two of them had had 'particularly good talks'.[24]

In the past, Parfit had usually succeeded in bending institutional rules to his advantage. Rules, he seemed to believe, were for other people. On Thanksgiving, 24 November 1966, he tried his luck once more. The Harkness Fellowship had been awarded on condition that all Fellows leave the US for at least two years at the end of their fellowship. But Parfit had another idea. 'To my excitement', he wrote to the Commonwealth Fund, 'I have found that the moral philosopher here, Professor Rawls, is doing work extremely close to what I want to do. Partly for this reason, he and another professor with whom I have been working suggested to me a month ago that I should apply to Harvard for a grant to come back here in September and do a PhD.'[25]

Professor Rawls's approach to moral philosophy, he explained, differed markedly from that adopted in the UK. Rawls had a wider conception of the subject and brought in empirical assumptions. Parfit wrote that he wanted to write a thesis on empirical assumptions in morality, territory on which Oxford philosophers believed they had no business to tread:

> Professor Rawls knows (and likes) several philosophers at Oxford, but it is he who has warned me that what I want to do will not fit in at all well into the present Oxford framework. More broadly, several of my other interests in philosophy are in areas with which Harvard in particular deals (e.g., the work which a Professor Putnam is doing on the significance of artificial brains, or on the new linguistics at MIT).[26]

Rawls's PhD proposal was appealing: 'It seems to me that it would be particularly exciting and fruitful to start a career doing philosophy in England in three years' time with this American background.'[27]

It is fascinating to speculate how political and moral philosophy in the second half of the twentieth century might have changed had Parfit's plan been approved. He might have been drawn into political theory which, apart from one influential article he would write on equality, he for the most part avoided. He may also have shaped the arguments in *A Theory of Justice*. This book spawned a veritable cottage industry of books and articles, but Parfit himself found it vague and unconvincing.

On this particular occasion, however, his charm and persuasiveness hit a bureaucratic brick wall. The Commonwealth Fund would not budge. Parfit was heading back to Oxford and the BPhil. He had at least decided definitively to shift disciplines. As his friend Edward Mortimer put it, 'The rest is . . . well, not history I suppose.'[28]

7

Soul Man

Parfit already had his eyes on a bigger prize, but for the time being, he had a place on the prestigious BPhil course and he was back at Balliol, although living in the family home, 5 Northmoor Road.

Before the war, the most important philosophical developments in the UK had taken place in Cambridge—academic home to G. E. Moore, Bertrand Russell, and Ludwig Wittgenstein. But post-war, the action had moved, decisively, to Oxford. The BPhil was (and is) a two-year postgraduate degree. Students were graded both on exams and on a dissertation. In other Oxford disciplines, the BPhil was rebranded as an MPhil, to reflect its master's status. But the Oxford philosophy faculty argued successfully that the BPhil was so well known in the philosophical world that they should stick with the original nomenclature. In the 1960s, the BPhil alone (without a doctorate) was considered a sufficient qualification for budding philosophers to apply for prestigious academic jobs.

At the time, Oxford moral philosophy was mainly focused on meta-ethics; that is to say, it examined the status of moral claims. If I say, 'Murder is wrong,' am I stating an objective fact? If so, how are such 'facts' to be understood? Over the previous decade, Oxford had established itself as *the* centre for ordinary language philosophy—in which traditional problems were thought to result from misunderstandings about how words are normally used. J. L. Austin was the leading exponent of linguistic philosophy, and his approach inevitably seeped into the study of ethics.

The rest of Parfit's BPhil cohort had begun their degree in October 1966. As with his Harkness Fellowship, he had stretched the rules and sought a postponement. He was there for the start of the second term (known at Oxford as Hilary term), on 15 January 1967. His tutors reflected the strength and depth of Oxford's philosophical squad. He was taught by Alfred Ayer, Peter Strawson, David Pears, and Alan Montefiore. In his first book, *Reasons and Persons*, he also thanked, among his first teachers, R. M. (Dick) Hare. Several of these men were colossal figures in philosophy.

Montefiore was from a prominent Jewish family; partly perhaps for this reason, his interests included the issue of how far one was in control of one's own identity. He was unusual in Oxford in that he was well acquainted with, and sympathetic towards, many continental philosophers, such as Maurice Merleau-Ponty. David Pears specialized in Wittgenstein. As an Oxford student, he had discovered Wittgenstein after jumping out of a window at the upmarket Randolph Hotel to escape a brawl: he snatched *Tractatus Logico-Philosophicus* from a friend as he was being carried to the ambulance and became bewitched by the book whilst recuperating in hospital.

Ayer and Strawson had wide-ranging philosophical pursuits and they, along with Hare, made important contributions to ethics. The flamboyant 'Freddie' Ayer was another old Etonian. He had a reputation—well justified—for being an incorrigible womanizer, earning disapproval from some of his peers (and envy from others). In the 1930s, he had imported into the Anglo-American world the (by the 1960s discredited) ideas of the Vienna Circle, mentioned earlier. The Circle pushed what was known as logical empiricism (sometimes called logical positivism), and its associated Verification Principle. This claimed that for propositions to have meaning they must either be true by definition ('All triangles have three sides') or checkable ('There are 417 bridges in Venice'). That had radical implications for ethics. Since moral claims, such as 'Murder is wrong', are neither true by definition nor testable, they were, according to the Circle, meaningless.[1] Ayer extended the ideas of logical empiricism and held that moral statements were simply expressions of emotion. His emotivism (sometimes called the 'boo/hoorah theory') translated the statement 'Murder is wrong' into 'Murder. Boo!'

For a period the Vienna Circle was all the rage in philosophical circles, but it turned out that aspects of its framework, including the Verification Principle, were riddled with difficulties. For a start, the Verification Principle seemed to flunk its own test—since it was neither true by definition nor testable empirically. Shortly after Parfit began the BPhil, a volume of *The Encyclopedia of Philosophy* was published in which logical positivism was declared 'dead, or as dead as a philosophical movement ever becomes'.[2]

More influential when Parfit was doing the BPhil were the writings of Hare, who became the White's Professor of Moral Philosophy in 1966. (The White's Chair was Oxford's oldest philosophy professorship.) Hare had returned to Oxford after surviving World War II as an exhausted, emaciated prisoner, forced by the Japanese to work on the 'death railway', connecting Burma and Thailand. Still, his experiences did not convince him that morality was objective, that there were some actions that were objectively right or wrong. Instead, his first two books, *The Language of Morals* and *Freedom and Reason*, heavily shaped by Austin's linguistic philosophy, established his reputation with an analysis of moral terms. What did terms such as 'ought', commit us to, as when we say, for example, 'I ought to tell the truth'? His answer was that they imply a command for everyone to tell the truth in similar circumstances. The command also holds for situations in which we are not the agent, but at the receiving end of the action. To discover what I ought to do, I must want the action not just from my own perspective, but must imagine myself in the shoes of each and every person affected by the action and be willing to accept it from their point of view as well.

The last of Parfit's tutors was Peter Strawson, who was best known for his paper 'Freedom and Resentment', which had been published when Parfit was an undergraduate. It argued that even if we thought that humans had no genuine free will and were part of a deterministic world, subject to the laws of causation like everything else in the universe, we would still be bound to have what Strawson called 'reactive attitudes' towards others. In other words, even if we believed that in some sense a person who had wronged us had had no choice—because they were responsible neither for their character nor for the situation in which they found themselves—we would still be bound to feel anger and resentment towards them.

All of these ideas influenced Parfit, though mostly in a negative way, in that he resisted them. In particular, he was puzzled by Strawson's position, because he, Parfit, did not have the strong reactive attitudes that Strawson insisted were natural. If somebody was mean to him, he could feel a degree of hurt, but not resentment or the desire for revenge.

Agree or disagree, he was finding philosophy exhilarating. He later recalled attending his first philosophical debate, at the Oxford Philosophical Society. Responding to a talk, a philosopher commented that all the arguments in the talk were invalid, based on false premises, and the conclusions, even if true, were trivial. 'I thought, "Wow"!'[3] Parfit disapproved of people who enjoyed boxing and wondered whether this attitude was compatible with the relish he took in these philosophical slugfests.[4]

. . .

For the time being, Parfit's aim was simply to absorb as much philosophy as he could. He must have come across the work of Henry Sidgwick when he was in the US—he later reported that he bought a secondhand copy of his 1874 Methods of Ethics[5]—but in Oxford his love deepened further for this 'great, drab book'.[6] Methods of Ethics, written when Sidgwick was only thirty-six, contained a central theme that came to obsess Parfit: the competing pulls of egoism (the claim that I ought to act in my self-interest) and consequentialism (the claim that I ought to act so as to produce the best consequences overall). For Parfit, Sidgwick provided the template for how philosophy should be done. Sidgwick was a truth-seeker, pure and ego-free enough to follow the logic of an argument and courageous enough to reach conclusions that challenged Victorian norms. Parfit believed that he too should pursue the truth, even when this was uncomfortable.

Both Parfit and Sidgwick came from families steeped in religion (Sidgwick's father was a reverend). Both were educated at upmarket

English institutions (Sidgwick was at Rugby and Cambridge). Parfit would develop a writing style similar to Sidgwick's—unpretentious and straightforward, with sentences that strove above all for clarity. *Methods of Ethics* has been described as 'a philosophical gold mine',[7] and Parfit would make a deep impression on students when he strode into the room, dropped *Methods* on the table with a loud thump and declaimed, 'This is the greatest work of moral philosophy ever written.'[8]

. . .

'My life here (as far as Luv goes) is very, very empty at the moment. Not unhappy or anything, just a blank (Perhaps I'm too selective, I don't know [. . .].(Or perhaps they all run a mile etc. etc., self-pity [. . .]).'[9] So wrote Parfit to his twenty-two-year-old sister, Joanna, on 27 June 1967, shortly before his All Souls exam. Joanna had temporarily moved to New Haven, Connecticut, to help Theo out with her young kids. Parfit was responding to a letter she had written, requesting some advice about her own love life. She was having a torrid time in New Haven with an intense and unstable boyfriend called Jon, a student at Ohio's Oberlin College. Did her relationship with Jon have a future? Jon was returning to Ohio and Parfit counselled that his feelings might change: 'I think women are just much better at being faithful over long distances because their love is more "spiritual" etc. etc.'[10] He told her that he himself would be cautious about becoming involved with somebody if he knew they were leaving Oxford.

But Joanna had also asked for advice about whether she should sleep with her boyfriend. Jon was pressuring her to do so; his psychiatrist, he claimed, had suggested that this would be beneficial for his mental health. Parfit cautioned against it.

I don't think you should sleep with Jon JUST because you think it might help him get over his emotional difficulties (as his psychiatrist suggests). My reason for this is not that I think it would be immoral; on the contrary, I think it would be a very moral and kind thing to do. But the trouble is that if this is your reason for it you may find it distasteful, and this would be a pity, as it would start you off on the wrong foot.

For a woman (here speaks the man of the world!!!) it takes some time to get acclimatised to sleeping with people; it's normally a great disappointment to begin with, and only later becomes more and more significant.[11]

There were also other potential consequences to think about, of course. The contraceptive pill was now available, but it was not until the Supreme Court ruling of *Roe v. Wade* in 1973 that the right of American women to have an abortion was guaranteed. Parfit never wrote about the ethics of abortion, but by 1967 his position was unequivocal. He told his sister that in the unlikely event that

one occasion has had any effect, tell Theo at once, and the whole thing can be over in less than a week. (It's only later on that it's more traumatic.) I, and Theo, have known so many people (I won't name names, but almost everyone) who've taken almost-invisible foetuses in their stride (the boring bit being the cost). I don't express myself very directly, do I? If you need this, and if you've talked to Theo, I'm sure she'd know where you could be fitted out. If you don't want to talk to her, I happen to remember that New Haven is where a very nice agnostic doctor started a clinic two years ago for birth control for unmarried women, and it would probably be in the phone book. [. . .] For my money, if I were a girl, I'd vastly prefer a pill.[12]

The letter then moved on to happier topics. The Beatles had released *Sgt. Pepper's Lonely Hearts Club Band* a month earlier. Joanna had asked her brother to buy her a copy, but he pointed out that this would be 'a bit stupid' because the record was exactly the same, track for track, in the US, except cheaper. He had heard the album already; particularly good, he reckoned, was the last track on side two ('A Day in the Life'). He didn't have much further news. Papa 'has his occasional bad moods but in between is pretty cheerful'. His own life, he reported, was uneventful. He finished the letter with the hope that Joanna's spirits would lift: 'Look after yourself, because I'd hate to think of my favourite kid sister upset.'[13]

Unsurprisingly, the relationship between Joanna and Jon did not flourish. The end seems to have been abrupt. Joanna must have written a despairing letter to her brother about how she felt unloved. That, he reassured her, was nonsense. Everybody who knew her at all well cared for her; the problem was that she didn't know many people in America. 'I'd bet that though I, for instance, know more people than you do, a smaller proportion of the people I know love me—I know several people who really <u>hate</u> me.'[14] Since few people, if any, seem to have actually hated the young Parfit, this may have been written simply to lift her spirits.

Part of Joanna's angst was worry that, intellectually, she was insufficiently stimulating. Parfit might have chosen to deny this. Instead, he told her that in his opinion being intellectually stimulating was overrated.

> Here's the truth, sister dear—since I came back from Harvard in January I've been searching and searching for the girl of my dreams, and failed to find her—because all the 5 or 6 girls I've tried going out with have been intellectually stimulating and nothing else. I was consoling a very bright and witty girl about a month ago who's been pretty miserable, and her main problem is that she just can't feel any strong emotions for anyone. The brain takes over and the heart withers away. (Why do you write so much better letters than me—because mine are self-conscious and indirect and yours are sincere and direct.) The only girl I've ever really felt I might have married (if she hadn't been engaged of course)—(This is a STRICT SECRET)—is the least 'intellectual' girl I've met —Patricia, Benjy's wife. She had a great inferiority complex and often complained to me that she couldn't discuss things the way Benjy could—but she was so much more sensitive and understanding than Benjy. (<u>Secret</u>). So for Albert Einstein's sake don't you start thinking that what men want in a woman is someone who can discuss the rival merits of different orchestra conductors! (one can read that in a paper.)[15]

. . .

In late August 1967, Parfit drove to northern Italy with Edward Mortimer and his then girlfriend and future wife, Elizabeth (Wiz). The itinerary took in Venice. In *Reasons and Persons*, Parfit claimed he was travelling that year in Spain with the philosopher Gareth Evans, but unless he had access to a teletransporter that would have been physically impossible. The trip with Evans must have taken place the following summer.

Parfit had already determined that upon returning to Oxford he would reapply for an All Souls Prize Fellowship. His previous attempt, in 1964, had been in history—the subject at which he'd excelled both at school and university, with the marks and extensive list of awards and scholarships to prove it. It is an indication of his self-confidence—some might call it chutzpah—that he now thought himself ready to put himself forward in philosophy, with virtually nothing to demonstrate either past performance or future potential.

Once again, he sat through the three-day exam process, beginning on a Thursday. In 1967, the single-word essay topic was 'space'. Of course, and as was the point, this allowed the candidate to pursue one or more of the multiple ways the term can be understood—but whether consciously or unconsciously, the exam-setters had surely been influenced by the intense and ongoing Cold War space race.

The next step was for All Souls to seek references. The dominating figure and head (Warden) of All Souls was John Sparrow, a barrister, a reactionary, a polemicist, and a man with a hot temper who 'would invent an argument against himself if no-one else obliged'. He liked the world as it was, and if he could have stopped it revolving, he would have. He loathed agitators among the 'bearded and unkempt student generation'.[16] His friend, the historian of ideas Isaiah Berlin, described his top three interests as '1. Himself. 2. Sex. 3. At a great remove from these, old books.'[17]

On 31 October 1967, Sparrow wrote to his opposite number at Balliol, Christopher Hill.[18] Hill immediately sought the views of Parfit's Balliol tutor, Alan Montefiore, who responded the next day, All Souls Day. Montefiore had discussed Parfit's case with his Balliol colleagues. The historians regarded Parfit as clever but frivolous, Montefiore wrote. 'Now he has come to philosophy, however, there is no doubt whatsoever about his entirely serious commitment to the subject. He is immensely hard-working and thorough, but what really strikes me about him is the intensity of philosophic imagination. I think he is capable of producing, one day, work of great originality and power[.]'[19]

Hill then wrote to Sparrow, not once, but twice. The first letter was sent in the knowledge that it would be seen by all those with voting rights at All Souls. It listed Parfit's many academic awards. 'He [Parfit] is in many ways the ablest pupil I have ever had,' Hill wrote.

> Three years ago, I had the feeling that, though outstandingly able, Derek Parfit had not really found himself. History was, like everything else he turned his hand to, just something he could do superlatively well. Since then, however, he has clearly and firmly decided that he is a philosopher [. . . . It] was always clear that he was going to go to the top in something.[20]

But Hill then wrote a second letter. The initial letter might have been read by Robin Briggs, still a Prize Fellow at All Souls after having been selected in 1964 ahead of Parfit, his Balliol tutorial partner. The second letter was for Sparrow's consumption only.

> We were delighted three years ago when you chose Robin Briggs in preference to Derek Parfit. Up to that time Derek had always been number one and Robin (just) number 2. We felt that All Souls saw through the superficially greater cleverness of Derek to the solider worth of Robin Briggs. I think, in fact, that your decision did Derek a great deal of good. It was his first real defeat in competition. But he has now purged himself of his silly cleverness, and is a serious person as well as about the ablest man of his age I know.[21]

To put it another way: success had come too easily to Parfit; for his own good, he had needed to be taken down a peg or two. But the charge that Parfit had been somehow frivolous in his studies, or more generally in life, seems an odd one, and wide of the mark. Frivolity was not a Parfitian vice.

Soon, Parfit received notice that he had been elected to a Prize Fellowship, the other available fellowship being awarded to John Clarke, a historian. Hill wrote to Parfit to congratulate him, and on 9 November 1967

Parfit replied: 'It was my con-man performance in the general papers that helped me I'm afraid—it will still be some time before I make the grade as a professional (rather than amateur) philosopher. (Not a move I wholly want to make anyway.)'[22] This is a cryptic remark. What was he hinting at? Perhaps he was not yet convinced that philosophy should be his vocation. Perhaps he thought that as an amateur he retained an outsider's perspective on philosophical problems—enabling him to see more clearly through complications. More likely, he meant it in a mundane sense: what didn't appeal to him about a professional philosopher's life were the accompanying commitments, most especially, teaching.

In any case, such drudgery was postponed for up to seven years. For he would now enter the rarefied atmosphere of All Souls, and so be in the privileged position of being able to focus purely on research and his declared subject, 'philosophy, in particular philosophy of mind and moral philosophy'.[23] He could not have known that All Souls would in fact become his home for the next forty-three years.

. . .

The high street is Oxford's busiest traffic street, the main artery in and out of the city. During the day it's clogged with buses, taxis and cars, all trying to avoid the weaving and sometimes seemingly kamikaze cyclists. But through the thick wooden doors of the porters' lodge, as one enters the 'College of the souls of all the faithful departed', commonly known as All Souls College, there is an almost eerie quiet. It's too quiet for some. One secretary in the college left within a week because she couldn't cope with the absence of noise. A college librarian jestingly claims that 'World War III could erupt outside the college and we wouldn't notice'.[24]

There are few other academic institutions in the world where researchers are free from teaching. One of them is the Institute for Advanced Study (IAS) at Princeton, founded in 1930. Abraham Flexner, the brains but not the money behind the IAS, envisaged a place which 'should be open to persons, competent and cultivated, who do not need and would abhor spoon feeding' and 'in which there would be an absence of distraction either by worldly concerns or by parental responsibility for an immature student body [. . .]. It would be small [. . .] but its propulsive power would be momentous.' And it would offer 'above all tranquillity'.[25] All Souls, established in the 1430s during the reign of its formal co-founder King Henry VI (and just a few years before that monarch's foundation of Eton College), had a five-hundred-year head start over the IAS. The original All Souls Fellows were expected to pray for the souls of those killed in the wars with France. But even then, they were principally there to study; and then, as now, the college was an undergraduate-free zone.

The current organization of the college can be traced to reforms in the late nineteenth century which introduced various categories of fellowship—including the Prize Fellowship. Nonetheless, All Souls is a college that for much of its existence has valued tradition over reform. The All Souls political philosopher Jerry Cohen once wrote a paper defending his objections to change. It begins as follows:

> 'Professor Cohen, how many Fellows of All Souls does it take to change a light bulb?'
> 'Change?!?'[26]

When Parfit became a Prize Fellow it was still an all-male college. There were many Fellows around who were determined to keep it that way and block any changes made in the name of 'progress' or 'moving with the times'. One such was the prolific historian A. L. Rowse, who was of the opinion—one he was happy to disseminate—that all other historians were second-rate. It was not an institution that was short of confidence. While Fellows regarded it as the academic pinnacle, visitors were struck by its degree of institutional self-importance.

Old Etonians and old Balliolians were vastly overrepresented. 'Diversity' was not on the agenda. Warden Sparrow reluctantly acquiesced when the college elected a Ghanaian, William Abraham, in 1959,[27] and was highly amused when one of the servants complained he couldn't make Abraham out against the mahogany furniture.[28] Sparrow encouraged Abraham to return to Ghana.

Of course, and as we shall see, there have been some important developments in the way the college is run, and fundamental changes in the fellowship demographic, but the pulse, the beat of the institution has remained largely unaffected. It caters for most of its Fellows' basic needs. There's breakfast, lunch (in the Buttery) and a formal dinner—at which the Warden says grace in Latin and gowns are mandatory. Order Marmite for breakfast and it will arrive in a jar with a silver screw top on a small silver tray. Each afternoon in what's called the Smoking Room there are freshly baked cakes and tea in china cups. The dinner table is festooned with an array of cutlery and glasses and the novice has to learn which utensil to pick up for which course. As for your room, there is no need to clean it: this is done by 'scouts', nowadays almost always women, but in the 1960s all men.

Parfit was allocated Room 4 on Staircase XI in the North Quad—designed in the early eighteenth century by Nicholas Hawksmoor, whose churches Parfit had traipsed around as a child. In fact, it was a suite of three rooms—a small bedroom, a small office, and a decent-sized lounge, with an electric heater that he put in the fireplace. It would be impossible to tire of the stunning view of the quad and, beyond, the domed Radcliffe Camera. Number 5, Northmoor Road was within walking distance, and Parfit frequently and dutifully visited there; but it was no longer home.

Some Fellows take a while to adjust to life in college. A few never fully reconcile themselves to it. Being served at meals, never having to clear up your plate, never being addressed by staff by your first name: that strikes some Fellows as awkward and alienating. Not Parfit. He was never rude to college staff; he was far too kind and solicitous for that. But he had spent his life being waited upon in ancient institutions. Some young Fellows, arriving at All Souls in their early to middle twenties, could feel intense social pressure: guests sitting next to them at dinner might include a cabinet minister or high-ranking civil servant, a diplomat or a judge. Parfit was impervious to such anxieties; he had an undeveloped sense of status, and was uninterested in and unimpressed by the lives and achievements of more worldly others.

It is impossible to exaggerate the impact of All Souls on Parfit. But how that impact operated is harder to assess. Did All Souls allow him to be the person he always was—to give expression to his authentic self? Or did it warp him, slowly transforming him into the monomaniac he became?

. . .

For the time being, Parfit continued with his BPhil studies—and continued to astound his tutors. David Pears wrote in a March 1968 report that 'for someone who began philosophy so recently, his work in the philosophy of mind this term is astonishingly good, and original'.[29] He would have received this degree in the summer, but, encouraged by John Sparrow—for whom formal qualifications were irrelevant slips of paper—he decided to switch from the BPhil to a doctorate, or, in Oxford vernacular, a DPhil. His supervisor was Alan Montefiore and Parfit's proposed thesis title was 'The Philosophical Concept of Personal Identity'. But he would never complete that, either. As a result, the sum of Parfit's higher-education qualifications for philosophy remained for ever an undergraduate degree—in history.

Parfit's lack of formal training in his discipline, though not unique, was rare. One consequence was that he had a narrower philosophical range than his peers. There were vast swathes of philosophy—such as logic, or the philosophy of science—in which he had no grounding. There were philosophers in the canon of whom he had scant knowledge, such as Leibniz and Wittgenstein. If you look in the *Reasons and Persons* index for the name of Aristotle, you will search in vain. Parfit, however, saw an upside to this, telling *The New Yorker*, 'Because I never took a degree in philosophy, I have only read those books and articles that I wanted to read. That has helped me to love the subject.'[30]

. . .

The summer road trip to Spain with Gareth Evans, mentioned earlier, probably took place in 1968. Evans was four years Parfit's junior. He had come first in his year in the PPE Finals and was then given a year's scholarship at the college known simply as Christ Church. It is unclear how Evans and Parfit met; it was probably through Strawson, who taught them both. In any case, intellectual stars have a habit of locating each other. Evans's own philosophical interests were in logic and the philosophy of language.

Evans would have a short life, the most dramatic moment of which occurred in the late 1970s when he was driving in Mexico City with a friend, the son of a prominent Mexican politician. An attempted kidnapping by four men left his friend, Hugo Margáin, dead and Evans, mistaken for the bodyguard, shot in the knee.[31] Not long after he was diagnosed with lung cancer; he was in so much pain that during his last tutorials he lay on the floor. His book *The Varieties of Reference* was published posthumously. It addressed the issue of how names (in, for example, 'The Morning Star was clearly visible today') or pronouns ('He went to the bookshop') refer to, or 'denote', their objects. The subject had preoccupied the German logician Gottlob Frege as well as Bertrand Russell. Take the names of people. Russell had argued that a name— 'Derek Parfit', for example,—served as a description (equivalent in this case to, say, 'the author of *Reasons and Persons*'). But under criticism from an American logician, Saul Kripke, this view came to be discredited. If I used the name 'Derek Parfit', it would still pick out Parfit, even if it turned out that Parfit hadn't written a word of *Reasons and Persons*, but instead had paid another philosopher to write it. *The Varieties of Reference* aimed to partially rehabilitate Frege and Russell.

Such questions in the philosophy of language were not ones that much engaged Parfit, and it is not known what the pair discussed on their long car journey. By all accounts, Evans was astoundingly sharp and deep. After his death, Parfit would write, 'I hoped to become a philosopher and as we drove through France I put to him my fledgling ideas. His merciless criticisms made me despair. Before we reached Spain, hope returned. I saw that he was almost as critical of his own ideas.'[32]

Language and morality heavily overlapped in Oxford. As outlined above, 1960s moral philosophy centred around the meaning and status of ethical propositions. This was an abstruse topic. Neither metaethics nor linguistic philosophy concerned itself with practical moral questions, such as abortion or capital punishment, both of which were live controversies in the 1960s. Abortion was legalized in Britain in 1967 and capital punishment was finally abolished two years later. Social, cultural, and political worlds were in flux. In 1968, the Vietnam War escalated with the Tet Offensive, the Soviets invaded Czechoslovakia, Martin Luther King and Robert Kennedy were assassinated, two African-American athletes gave the Black Power salute at the Mexico Olympics. There were student-led protests in Paris, at the London School of Economics, and elsewhere. The Oxford protests were more muted, although All Souls received some heat. A Wadham College undergraduate, Mike Rosen,[33] wrote a lacerating article about John Sparrow and All Souls privilege in the *Cherwell* student newspaper: if you asked someone 'to invent an object that was too incredible for the mind to cope with at one sitting, then he would be hard put to produce a concept more hairy-fantastical than All Souls'[34]. And three other members of the Oxford Revolutionary Socialist Students wrote directly to Sparrow, to inform him that 'the rationale, structure and working of your institution [. . .] contradicts everything for which revolutionary socialists stand'.[35]

But most of the 1960s ferment passed Oxford philosophers by. A few of them addressed practical moral issues and involved themselves in practical affairs. Elizabeth Anscombe, for example, had fought a campaign in 1956 to prevent Harry Truman being awarded an Oxford honorary degree, because he had ordered the use of atomic bombs in Japan. Michael Dummett campaigned tirelessly for immigrants and ethnic minorities. Isaiah Berlin, like Dummett a Fellow of All Souls, had delivered an influential lecture in 1958 entitled *Two Concepts of Liberty*, about the nature of political freedom. It drew a distinction between negative liberty—the absence of coercion or interference—and positive liberty, which consists in the freedom to be self-governing, to have mastery over one's thoughts, values, and passions.

But applied ethics was not on the Oxford syllabus. Parfit, along with the young philosophers Jonathan Glover and Jim Griffin (who taught at New College and Keble College respectively) conceived the idea of holding a class on real moral issues such as punishment, civil disobedience, abortion, euthanasia, charity, and poverty. Glover proposed that they call it 'Life, Happiness, and Morality'. Parfit suggested a catchier title, 'Death, Misery, and Morality'.

It took place in 1970, on Tuesday afternoons in the summer term— Trinity term, in Oxford-speak—and proved an immediate success. It was attended by many distinguished philosophers, such as the legal philosopher H.L.A. Hart and the White's Professor R. M. Hare, as well as by postgraduates who would later make their mark, including a young Australian, Peter Singer.

The Trinity-term trio would reunite several times over the next few years, though the class title and venue varied: 'The Quality of Life', in 1973; 'Rights, Interests, and Possible People' in 1974; 'Utilitarianism' in 1975; 'Problems of Ethics' in 1976. The format was that either Griffin, Glover, or Parfit would give a talk, to which one of the others would reply, having been sent the paper in advance. Questions and points would then be put from the audience. While each of the trio of young philosophers was impressive, Derek was 'the star',[36] one philosopher comparing him to the Wimbledon champion Rod Laver and describing 'his Laver-like ability, wherever the ball came from, to return it at speed'.[37] The impression he made on Singer lasted a lifetime: 'Of all the philosophers I have known since I began to study the subject more than fifty years ago, Parfit was the closest to a genius. Getting into a philosophical argument with him was like playing chess with a grandmaster: he had already thought of every response I could make to his arguments, considered several possible replies, and knew the objections to each reply as well as the best counters to those objections.'[38] The seminars managed to generate a sense of excitement rare in the philosophical world. 'We all felt that we were sitting in a philosophical laboratory, which unlike a science lab, was taking place in Derek's mind!'[39]

Parfit's distinctive mode of communication was on display for all to hear. His voice had a baritone range and his delivery was monotonic, but every fifteen words or so he would abruptly *emphasize* a word, as though suddenly roused from sleep. It was in this seminar that many of the ideas for which he would become famous were first aired in inchoate form. This is not the chapter for an exegesis of Parfit's now famous arguments about future people, but Jonathan Glover was among the first to hear them. One afternoon it was going to be Parfit's turn to lead the discussion, and he promised to show Glover the paper, but kept delaying and delaying. He was unhappy with it, and so wanted to continue to tinker—never being satisfied was a trait buried deep within his psychological make-up. Eventually, the day arrived for the seminar, and still there was no paper. 'With absurd over-confidence, I said, "That's OK, Derek, I will listen and reply off the cuff." Little did I know.' It turned out that Parfit had been agonizing over population paradoxes—having to do with the balance between quality of life and population size. He covered a blackboard with diagrams. When at the end Glover tried to offer some objections, Parfit had some ready responses, 'at least four or five moves down the line. I felt like a novice chess player who had blundered into a game with a grandmaster.'[40]

In fact, during the seminar series Glover introduced several fascinating ideas of his own. One involved the issue of how an individual act is to be assessed when the badness of this act in and of itself is negligible, and it is only when everyone acts in the same way that there is a significant harm. This puzzle occurs frequently in the world beyond the seminar room. Many people believe that they needn't bother to curb their individual carbon emissions, because their contribution to global warming is close to zero.

In response to this type of argument, Glover devised an ingenious thought experiment. Imagine there is a village with a hundred unarmed inhabitants. As they eat their lunch—a plate of a hundred baked beans— a hundred hungry armed bandits arrive and they each take a plate. Each bandit has harmed a villager in a significant way. But some of the bandits start having moral qualms. The following week they raid the village again. This time, however, they steal in a clever, if slightly slower, way. Bandit 1 takes only one bean from Villager 1, another bean from Villager 2, a third bean from Villager 3, and so on. He causes negligible harm to each villager, since one bean makes no discernible difference to the villager's lunch. Bandit 2 does the same, taking one bean from each villager's plate. And so do Bandits 3 to 100.[41] The result is that each bandit ends up with a hearty lunch of a hundred beans, and each villager ends up with an empty plate.

Are we to say that during the second raid each bandit did no wrong? That, argued Glover, would clearly be an absurd conclusion. Parfit agreed. We will see this puzzle re-emerge in Parfit's first book, with the case of 'the harmless torturers'.

. . .

When would that first book appear? Although Oxford University Press later developed a dominant position in the philosophy publishing market, in the 1960s and 1970s Cambridge University Press was the leading publisher in the field. But at a social event in December 1968, Parfit met a senior OUP academic editor, Dan Davin, who expressed an interest in his research. A month later, in January 1969, Parfit wrote to say that if his DPhil on personal identity was 'passable',[42] he would be delighted to adapt it into an OUP book. But that, he wrote, would not be for a couple of years. Over the next dozen years, OUP editors would learn to be sceptical of Parfit's timetable and declared publishing ambitions.

. . .

Parfit's first major setback had been in 1964, with his failure to be awarded the All Souls Prize Fellowship. The second came in 1970. A year earlier, the Balliol logician Arthur Prior had died in his mid-fifties, creating a vacancy for a Tutorial Fellow in philosophy. Parfit applied, as did several others, including another young British philosopher, Kit Fine, and a Canadian, Bill Newton-Smith.

The job was to teach undergraduates taking PPE. There were six people on the interview panel—two who taught classics, Jasper Griffin and Oswyn Murray, two who taught politics, Steven Lukes and Bill Weinstein, and two who taught philosophy, Alan Montefiore and Anthony Kenny. In theory, the appointment was for seven years. In practice, it was a job for life. Parfit was obviously eager to get it, but after the interview something odd happened. For some reason, he came to believe that Kit Fine had been offered the position. How this occurred is unclear, but, now worried about his future and in an agitated state, he sought out Newton-Smith to report this baseless news. Later, Newton-Smith paid a visit to Kit Fine to congratulate him, taking a bottle of champagne. Fine had heard nothing, so was baffled. The following day, Newton-Smith received a call informing him that he had been selected for the position.

According to Anthony Kenny, the decision was not taken purely on grounds of philosophical ability:

> Derek brought wonderful testimonials from the history tutors who had taught him as an undergraduate and he had won a great array of prizes. It was possible (and indeed it turned out) that he was more talented as a philosopher than Bill. But in the end we decided to elect Bill, partly because his field in philosophy was close to Arthur's, and partly because we felt Derek was likely to be more interested in his own research than in the hands-on job of teaching philosophy to undergraduates.[43]

That was an astute judgement. Not only would Parfit have been called upon to teach tutorials for at least twelve hours a week, but he would also have been expected to teach topics in which he had no interest and even less expertise. The first year of PPE required undergraduates to study John Stuart Mill's *Utilitarianism*, David Hume's *An Enquiry Concerning Human Understanding*, and some basic logic, through a book called *Beginning Logic* (by John Lemmon). Parfit had no training in logic and would have been incapable of teaching the latter text. What's more, Balliol had recently accepted two students to study philosophy with physics, and it was seeking ideally a tutor who could take them on. Newton-Smith had a background in a related area, mathematics and philosophy.

These were all sound reasons for not employing Parfit. And there was another one. He still didn't have a dissertation to his name, let alone a publication. That was about to change.

8

The Teletransporter

'I think that no young philosopher has got as far as I did on the basis of a single article.'[1] The article that Parfit was referring to was published in *The Philosophical Review* in 1971. It made his reputation. Parfit said that on the basis of this twenty-four-page paper, many people invited him to give talks: 'My introducers often said, "the author of such articles as 'Personal Identity . . .' and then realized that they hadn't read anything else by me.'[2]

The core philosophical issue about personal identity is straightforward. A baby, who was called Derek Antony Parfit, was born in 1942. Somebody with the same name wrote a book called *Reasons and Persons*. Derek Parfit died in 2017. But was the Derek Parfit born in 1942 the same individual as the person who wrote *Reasons and Persons*, and the same individual as the Derek Parfit who died in 2017? What, if anything, made them the same? To put the question a slightly different way, when did the Derek Parfit born in 1942 cease to exist?

The question does not baffle non-philosophers, and many of our ordinary actions and values are rooted in a commonsense understanding of identity. A person may feel shame and guilt for a bad act committed many years ago and such an emotion only makes sense if they think they are the same person as the one responsible for the act. The obligation of Person A to Person B to fulfil a promise that in three months' time they will return a £100 loan is comprehensible only if the person who repays the loan is Person A. Similarly, I put money into a personal pension pot because I implicitly assume that the ultimate beneficiary, the retired person, will be me! Non-philosophers have no trouble thinking of themselves as thus being the same individual over time. They see themselves as being the same individual as some newborn child in the past. If pressed to justify their view, they will likely do so on the grounds that they have the same body.

It initially seems a compelling response, but it cannot be quite as simple as that. For what does it mean to have the same body? When did my body begin to exist? Did I exist as a single-celled zygote or did my body begin to exist at some later point? How should I respond to the biologist who tells me that the body writing this sentence is composed of almost entirely different cells from the body to which my mother gave birth fifty-eight years ago? And, if I am my body, to the extent that my body will continue to exist as a corpse, it seems that I will survive death.

. . .

'Beam me up, Scotty.'

It would take someone unusually detached from popular culture not to have heard this phrase. But Parfit never watched *Star Trek* and rarely read science fiction. People familiar with his work might find that hard to believe; for his writings on personal identity are peppered with thought experiments that might have been lifted from the TV series, which originally aired in 1966. In particular, Parfit has a transporter, not dissimilar to the one that can dematerialize Captain Kirk and other members of the USS starship *Enterprise*, and have them rematerialize in another location.[3]

Parfit was by no means the first to use thought experiments to test our beliefs about personal identity. The seventeenth-century English philosopher John Locke imagined the souls of a prince and a cobbler being swapped, so that all the memories of the prince were in the body of the cobbler and vice versa. We want to say, wrote Locke, that the person once in the body of the prince is now in the body of the cobbler. Surely what matters for identity, he argued, is memory.

Such thought experiments were developed in the twentieth century by the American philosopher Sydney Shoemaker, and by David Wiggins, who had been in the passenger seat on Parfit's American road trip. Shoemaker imagined a technique that made it possible to remove a person's brain and place it in another skull. Wiggins imagined a variation whereby, instead of a brain being transplanted whole, the left and the right hemispheres of the brain were separated and transplanted into different bodies.[4]

So Parfit was following in a rich tradition when his first philosophy article appeared. Much of the material would later reappear in modified form in Section III of *Reasons and Persons*, and it is this version that I present here. It's worth reproducing the first page, to illustrate Parfit's style, and to show how, at its best, his writing managed to combine depth, clarity, and elegance.

I enter the Teletransporter. I have been to Mars before, but only by the old method, a space-ship journey taking several weeks. This machine will send me at the speed of light. I merely have to press the green button. Like others, I am nervous. Will it work? I remind myself what I have been told to expect. When I press the button, I shall lose consciousness, and then wake up at what seems a moment later. In fact I shall have been unconscious for about an hour. The Scanner here on Earth will destroy my brain and body, while recording the exact states of all of my cells. It will then transmit this information by radio. Travelling at the speed of light, the message will take three minutes to reach the Replicator on Mars. This will then create, out of new matter, a brain and body exactly like mine. It will be in this body that I shall wake up.

Though I believe that this is what will happen, I still hesitate. But then I remember seeing my wife grin when, at breakfast today, I revealed my nervousness. As she reminded me, she has been often teletransported, and there is nothing wrong with *her*. I press the button. As predicted, I lose and seem at once to regain consciousness, but in a different cubicle. Examining my new body, I find no change at all. Even the cut on my upper lip, from this morning's shave, is still there.

Several years pass, during which I am often Teletransported.[5] I am now back in the cubicle, ready for another trip to Mars. But this time, when I press the green button, I do not lose consciousness. There is a whirring sound, then silence. I leave the cubicle, and say to the attendant: 'It's not working. What did I do wrong?'

'It's working,' he replies, handing me a printed card. This reads: 'The New Scanner records your blueprint without destroying your brain and body. We hope that you will welcome the opportunities which this technical advance offers.'

The attendant tells me that I am one of the first people to use the New Scanner. He adds that, if I stay for an hour, I can use the Intercom to see and talk to myself on Mars.

'Wait a minute,' I reply, 'If I'm here I can't *also* be on Mars.'

Someone politely coughs, a white-coated man who asks to speak to me in private. We go to his office, where he tells me to sit down, and pauses. Then he says: 'I'm afraid that we're having problems with the New Scanner. It records your blueprint just as accurately, as you will see when you talk to yourself on Mars. But it seems to be damaging the cardiac systems which it scans. Judging from the results so far, though you will be quite healthy on Mars, here on Earth you must expect cardiac failure within the next few days.'[6]

Noteworthy here is Parfit's use of narrative. His philosophical style is famously (or notoriously) succinct. He uses the minimum number of words to express his thoughts with the maximum degree of intelligibility. Economy and clarity are two key virtues in his writing. Yet here we have a polite cough, a dramatic pause. The pause contributes nothing to the substance—it is inserted for theatrical impact and to stress the enormity of the moment. It suggests, at the very least, that Parfit placed some value on readability—a quality distinct from clarity.

Over the course of some 150 pages, Parfit's fanciful thought experiments were used to make the following claims. First, there is nothing over and above my body and its brain and an interrelated series of mental and physical events that makes me *me*. It would be misleading to say, 'I am David Edmonds and I (David Edmonds) have this brain and this body, these overlapping memories, etc.,' because this implies that I am a separately existing entity. Rather, I am constituted by my body, brain, and psychology over time. Parfit calls this 'reductionism'. René Descartes was quite wrong to posit something like a soul.

This point is related to a second one. Sometimes there is no true answer to the question of whether a particular person continues to exist. If there was a separately existing entity to my body and brain, etc., then, so long as that entity was maintained, I would continue to exist. There is no such entity; as a result, we can know all the facts and still not have a definitive answer as to whether a person has continued to exist. Whether that person still exists may be *indeterminate*. What is more, and third, identity is not what really matters. This was the claim to which Parfit was most committed. What should matter to me is whether some future person will be psychologically connected with me. And this is not a question of all or nothing. This is a matter of the degree of my psychological connection to the future person.

To see that personal identity is not what matters, consider an example Parfit adapts from David Wiggins. Imagine I am one of three identical triplets. My body is fatally injured, as are the cerebral hemispheres of my two identical brothers. The two hemispheres of my brain, each of which is capable of supporting my psychology, are separated and each hemisphere is transplanted to a body. 'My brain is divided and each half is successfully transplanted into the body of one of my brothers. Each of the resulting people believes that he is me, seems to remember living my life, has my character, and is in every other way psychologically continuous with me. And he has a body that is very like mine.'[7]

You might object that, since this could never happen, it is not a question worthy of consideration. But in the treatment of epilepsy some patients have had the connection between their two brain hemispheres cut, and have then been discovered to have two separate streams of consciousness. There was one patient with a split brain who was religious in one hemisphere and an atheist in the other.[8] It was these sorts of experiments that triggered the philosophical discussion of split brains. And although we are a long way away from the triplet operation being viable, Parfit argued that this was merely a technical constraint, and did nothing to diminish its value as a thought experiment to test our intuitions.

So what are your intuitions? How do you respond to the triplet case? If a person has two brothers, and one of his brain hemispheres was transferred into each of the bodies of these two brothers, would he have ceased to exist? Or would he continue to exist? Many people will feel that he continues to exist. But if so, would he be one brother or the other, or both? The answer cannot be that he survived only in one brother; that sounds too arbitrary. Why one brother rather than the other? But, logically, he cannot be identical to both, since then they would have to be identical with each other. And they cannot be identical to each other, because if they both carried on living they would soon have different experiences and memories. In any case, it's implausible to suppose that the original person survives as one person in two bodies and two minds.

Parfit's claim is that in this case, neither brother with the transplanted brain can be identical to the first brother. But that, he argues, is not the important issue. What matters is that the first brother's psychological continuity would have branched. In fact, it would be maintained in two bodies—a sort of bonus, like 'two for the price of one'.[9]

. . .

A person ceases to exist, argued Parfit, when there is nobody in the future who is psychologically continuous with their present self, or when psychological continuity branches, as in the case of the three brothers. But in the latter case, what really matters, namely psychological continuity, is preserved.

Not everyone is convinced by his arguments, but even critics concede that no serious and extended philosophical discussion on personal identity can ignore them. Still, some readers might put the 'So what?' question. Since psychological continuity cannot branch in real life, why should we care?

Well, first one should acknowledge how radically Parfit's position departs from common sense. He is encouraging us to ditch an intuition that is deeply held, if not by philosophers, then by almost every non-philosopher—that in each of us is a separately existing entity, distinct from our brain and body and experiences; that in each of us there is some underlying thing that makes us *us*, some deep fact about us that is all or nothing.

If we embrace the radical Parfitian position, there will be implications for how we think about ourselves and perhaps too in how we behave. One implication might be a weakened relationship between us now and our future selves. The future me will be 'me' because we are sufficiently connected psychologically, not because of some unique fact that I and the future me have in common. Our identity over time consists in such things as having memories of our past and desires for our future, but such psychological connectedness is a matter of degree. Tomorrow, next week, next year, hopefully in a decade, there will be a person who will use the name David Edmonds, and who will have some of the memories and desires and inclinations that I have today. Then, at death, the person with my name will cease to exist. But there will be other people—other beings who themselves are bundles of thoughts, memories, and desires—who will remember me. They may even be influenced by me. Parfit's work makes the boundaries between me today and me tomorrow, as well as the boundary between me and others, seem more fluid.

This, in turn, may have radical repercussions for how I act, or how I ought rationally to act. On the one hand, since there is no fixed line between me and others, perhaps I should care about others more, and do more to help them. On the other hand, perhaps I should be less committed to looking after the interests of my future self, for example in saving now to spend later. Why should I not splurge more of my money to have fun today, and to hell with this forthcoming, attenuated version of myself?

Then again, perhaps I should be discouraged or prohibited from harming my future self. Many citizens in liberal democracies take a view similar to that of John Stuart Mill as to what individuals should be allowed to do. Mill's famous harm principle states that adult humans should be free to do as they wish so long as they do not harm others.[10] But if our future selves are more tenuously linked to our present selves than is traditionally thought, should we regard *them* as 'others', or at least as *more like* others? On Parfit's view, this is a matter of degree. Our future selves become increasingly like other people as they become less psychologically connected to us over time.

The list of issues affected by Parfit's arguments is endless. Take 'advance directives', in which we set out in a legal document how we want to be treated if we are not in a position to make a decision ourselves. Suppose an individual develops dementia but there exists an advance directive. Is the earlier self that signed the directive sufficiently close to the later demented self in ways that matter to have authority over this later self?

There are consequences of Parfitian personal identity for blame, responsibility, and moral desert. Imagine a person commits a crime, but this goes undetected for many years. And imagine over those years that person's character has evolved. Or suppose the person forgets about the crime altogether. In other words, suppose there's a very thin psychological connectedness between the person who committed the crime and the future person. A Parfitian account seems to imply that a person is less responsible for this past action in so far as they are less psychologically related to the person who committed the crime.

For Parfit, however, the most important impact of his findings was on how he viewed death, expressed in one of his most widely quoted passages:

> When I believed that my existence was such a further fact, I seemed imprisoned in myself. My life seemed like a glass tunnel, through which I was moving faster every year, and at the end of which there was darkness. When I changed my view, the walls of my glass tunnel disappeared. I now live in the open air. There is still a difference between my life and the lives of other people. But the difference is less. Other people are closer. I am less concerned about the rest of my own life, and more concerned about the lives of others.[11]

Buddhists will feel an instinctive sympathy with Parfitian reflections on personal identity, for they are taught that we have more in common with other people and less in common with our future selves than we typically believe. Parfit was aware of the similarities between his writings and Buddhism and discussed them in a short appendix to *Reasons and*

Persons, pointing out that the Buddhist term for an individual is *santana*, or 'stream'.[12] Later, he was delighted to discover that Buddhist monks had been heard chanting passages from the book.

The story is this. A Harvard philosopher, Dan Wikler, was trekking through northern India with a scholar of Tibetan religion and mentioned the affinity between Buddhists' and Parfit's views of the self. Wikler knew Parfit slightly and later had him sign a copy of *Reasons and Persons*, which he sent to his trekking partner. On a future trek, Wikler and his friend visited a monastery. The friend explained that he had shared *Reasons and Persons* with the abbot at this monastery, and the abbot had included some passages of the book for the monks to study and chant and for cross-examination. For a philosophy book, that's an unusual impact.

. . .

'It is impossible to read off a person's personality from their ideas. Discuss.' One could imagine such a question in an All Souls general paper. And there are cases where there seems indeed to be no connection. The special theory of relativity provides no clue to Einstein's genial personality. Parfitian philosophy, however, *is* bound up with aspects of his character.

To start with, his conclusions on personal identity downplayed the role of the body, which was of a piece with the atypical relationship he had with his own body. His body was a vessel in which the brain resided. It was necessary to keep the vessel afloat and in good working order, for if it ran aground or floundered, the brain would suffer or die. Paying tribute to Parfit at an award ceremony, a friend used another analogy: 'Derek really does seem to live wholly in his mind [. . .]. He treats his body like a mildly inconvenient golf cart he has to drive around in order to get his mind from Oxford to Boston to New York to New Brunswick. [. . .] And he sees others as pure minds similar to his.'[13]

Regular workouts on an exercise bike were a means to keep the brain, the most vital of organs, functioning through the healthy functioning of the other organs. But it was pointless to 'treat' or 'pamper' the body.

Many people love lying in the sun, luxuriating in the feel of rays on their back. This, to Parfit, was a waste of time. Many people will spend hours preparing a delicious meal, to be consumed with a glass of wine. The evidence suggests that as a younger man, Parfit relished his food. As he aged, such quotidian physical gratifications were increasingly discarded.

There are certain norms with regard to the body. Either Parfit did not recognize these norms, or, if he did acknowledge them, they exerted no tug on him, no sense of compulsion that he adhere to them. Take 'personal space', the area surrounding our body which is felt to be ours—like the area of sea encircling an island state which falls within the state's jurisdiction. To breach this personal space seems rude or threatening. The degree of personal space varies from culture to culture, but all cultures have it. Parfit had almost no sense of it, however, and as early as his student days, this made people uneasy. He would sit or stand rather too close to his first philosophy supervisor. 'I would shuffle along and try and gain another six inches of space.'[14] When students visited him in his rooms, he would place himself very near them on the sofa. It might take them some time to realize that this was entirely innocent.

Nor did he absorb the social message that display of the body was immodest. He would sit on his exercise bike either naked or in his underpants, regardless of whether there were others in the house. And if he felt uncomfortably hot, he would simply strip off items of clothing (why would one not?). One sweltering day in Venice, he 'removed his jacket and his shirt and, with a bare torso, walked around the city'.[15] In All Souls, he would dash upstairs to the bath entirely naked, startling the girlfriends of the male Fellows on his staircase.

· · ·

Between 1968 and 1972, Parfit's own romantic life became increasingly byzantine. This was in part because he found it embarrassing to extricate himself from unwanted entanglements. He once spent about a week at Robin Briggs's house hiding from a woman.

In addition to these transitory affairs, he remained emotionally involved in his two serious relationships with Mary Clemmey and Patricia Zander. In 1968, Mary Clemmey was corresponding with him regularly from her new base in New York. On 3 February 1968 Parfit wrote, 'Your letter was wonderful to get. I am so certain in my feelings about you that even though you're now away in New York, thinking about you is like switching on a clear and warm light. I love you very much. (I didn't realise how much until you had to go).'[16] Her letters began 'My darling Derek' and 'My dearest Derek'. Mostly introspective in nature, they nonetheless offer snatches of news from a wider world: the feminist demonstrations in Atlantic City on 7 September against the Miss America pageant, broadcast live on TV, and in October the massive, chilling political rally for the pro-segregationist American Independent Party candidate George Wallace at Madison Square Garden. Clemmey correctly predicted that victory in the November presidential elections would go to 'Dirty Dick Nick'.[17]

On 25 July 1969 Parfit arrived in the US to spend a few weeks visiting his elder sister in New Haven. On the visa application form he was asked to describe his complexion (fair, ruddy, etc.). He wrote, 'pink'.[18] He had planned to go to New York to see Mary during his trip, but then received a phone call from her. A visit would no longer be welcome. She now had another partner, with whom she was going on holiday to Greece. After Parfit put the phone down he composed a twelve-page letter, which it seems he never sent.[19] 'Dear Mary,' (it began):

Thank you very much for ringing me and saying what you did so tactfully. It was obviously the right thing for you to have done [. . .]. I don't feel any kind of jealousy—my feeling for you is not possessive at all, and I like to think you may be happy. And I'm not at all unhappy myself (no self-pity). So please don't feel that by ringing me you did anything to hurt me.[20]

He was currently single, he wrote, but in recent years he had 'got fairly entangled with four different girls', though none of these 'involvements' was like his relationship with her. None had 'left any permanent mark on me at all. (Surprisingly, I can hardly even remember how I felt). But you have made a completely permanent mark; I can't even imagine losing my fondness and tenderness for you. This is why my thoughts keep returning to you. But it's a quiet tenderness, and it's been there so long that it doesn't mind keeping quiet even longer.' He wanted her life to go well, and if the relationship with her new partner lasted, so much the better. But if it did not? Well, he, Parfit, had no intention of getting married for many years, and it gave him 'delight to think it's a smallish possibility (even if about one in a hundred) that I might, when I've begun to have grey hairs, start wooing you again.'[21]

Although Mary had to be struck off his US itinerary, he could still visit Patricia Zander in Cambridge, Massachusetts. The nature of their relationship at this stage is unclear, but at the very least it was an intense friendship. Parfit saved a heap of letters from Patricia during this period, all undated. There are, naturally, many musical references and music-related opinions. When it came to chamber music, Zander held that 'the piano is the skeleton on which everything else hangs—because it is responsible for the harmony—without harmony there is no structure',[22] and she complained that 'writing about music is even harder than writing philosophy because there is virtually <u>no</u> language to describe sound.'[23]

It may have been after his 1969 trip that she wrote to Parfit, 'Seeing you was quite wonderful—I have found it necessary to reconsider a number of things as a result, and it is mostly rather exhilarating. It still slightly amazes me that you have been and are an important part of my life, and yet there is no pain involved.'[24] In another letter she writes, 'I seem to miss you more and more.'[25]

Her letters chart the demise of her marriage to Ben, as they grew apart and began to live separate lives. A letter in what was probably 1970 saw her situate her unhappiness in a wider pattern of gender relations. The year 1970 was memorable for feminism, with the publication of both Kate Millett's book *Sexual Politics* and Germaine Greer's *The Female Eunuch*. Patricia was brought to the 'amazing realization' that

I am a woman, and that it is extremely unsatisfactory to be a woman! I don't know what I've been doing during these years—I feel like Rip van Winkle [. . .]. I had thought that so many of my attitudes, professional fears, inability to communicate with large numbers of people, were all my own fault, or the result of an unsatisfactory transplant from a working-class background to a "new life", etc. etc. some of which remains true, and that the way my life was set up was so much better than so many women I could think of, that there was no point in moaning about it [. . . . P]sychiatrists must be having a hard time now trying to persuade all these increasingly frantic women to stay with their suburban dreams and part-time pretend jobs.[26]

While her letters are full of her feelings, she writes at one point that she had little idea about how he was doing, partly, she presumed, because he was not 'a great gnasher of teeth'.[27]

. . .

Things would soon become more complicated still. On 3 July 1970 Parfit wrote to his sister Joanna. She was, as usual, having personal problems. The letter to which Parfit was responding no longer exists, but it appears that she was on the pill, had concerns that it had not worked, and had undergone a pregnancy test, which turned out negative. 'Poor you. It must be a nightmare,' wrote Parfit. 'I think I can imagine it though I can't quite appreciate the mixed feelings that one would have if one were a woman.'[28] If she wanted extra peace of mind, he advised her, she could avoid her fertile period. As for him, he was supposed to be writing an article for a philosophy conference 'on LOVE of all embarrassing subjects [. . .]. What do I know about it I ask, except from my own rather peculiar case.'[29] No record of this tantalizing lecture exists.

Two weeks earlier, on 18 June, the Conservative Party had unexpectedly won a general election; the now ex-prime minister, the Labour leader Harold Wilson, had left 10 Downing Street and Edward Heath had moved in. Parfit was upset, but took some comfort from discovering that a majority of the Fellows in college preferred Wilson to Heath.

About a year after his personal identity paper appeared, Parfit began dating a young American-born Oxford undergraduate, Judith De Witt.

Having previously met Parfit at a social event, she paid a visit to his rooms at All Souls to ask for some jazz record recommendations for her then boyfriend; like Mary Clemmey, she was at the all-female Somerville College. Meanwhile, however, Patricia Zander was due to visit the UK. Judith was understandably not keen on Parfit seeing Patricia, and he must have passed on the message. The relationship between Parfit and Judith provoked ambivalent emotions in Patricia, who was under the illusion that her ties to Parfit were more exclusive than they actually were. 'Letting someone else into this totally unexpected and wonderful friendship from which I feel I have derived so much strength,' she wrote to him, 'is not a question of coping with jealousy, rivalry—because I want all possible nice and good things to happen to you—but it seems to involve making a kind of adjustment.'[30]

Parfit and De Witt were together, on and off, for several years. 'He was a lovely boyfriend. I was a pain.' They holidayed together in St Petersburg, Paris, and Venice. They went to the cinema and the opera. He bought her a moonstone necklace and a pretty white dress. 'He was romantic and sentimental.' They discussed getting married, and whether to have children, but 'these issues were unresolved'.[31] Whilst she was still living in Oxford, in the northern suburb of Summertown, they socialized a lot. All Souls Fellows were allowed to purchase bottles from the extensive All Souls cellar at the price they had been purchased for, so Parfit would provide fine wines, selected by Judith, at negligible cost. Among those invited to the house was W.V.O. Quine. Quine had carved out a distinctive empiricist philosophy—empiricism being the view that all knowledge is based on experience. He was known to collect interesting facts and kept notebooks of anything that caught his imagination. Parfit may have been made somewhat nervous by the looming arrival of the eminent American, for he and Judith devoted more time to gathering facts that might amuse his guest than Judith spent preparing the meal.

After a year and a half of their relationship, De Witt moved to London, where she was employed as a social worker. It's a sign of how serious the couple were that they bought a house together: 46 Elfort Road, Drayton Park (within kicking distance of the Arsenal football stadium). But they never actually cohabited. Room 4 on Staircase XI in All Souls remained Parfit's principal home.

Few Fellows in All Souls knew of De Witt's existence. 'There were rumours of a girlfriend, though no one seemed quite sure, and there wasn't even much speculation about the matter,' according to a college friend. 'There was a kind of purity about [Parfit] that inhibited gossip.'[32] Judith De Witt, like Mary Clemmey, is insistent on one point: Parfit was not especially odd. Perhaps his only odd habit, she says, was that when he found a jacket that he liked, he would buy two more. 'I thought at the time that that was eccentric. Now it makes perfect sense. People who achieve things don't waste time.'[33]

If he wasn't unconventional then, something—or several things— must have happened later.

. . .

At the age of thirty, Parfit's standing within the philosophical community was already secure. Great philosophical figures sought his advice and feedback. R. M. Hare asked for help with a long review of Rawls's *A Theory of Justice*, because he was 'fearful of having misrepresented him; I have tried very hard not to, but he is just so damned slippery.'[34] Parfit suggested multiple changes, including the recommendation that Hare tone down his hostile language.

Parfit's Prize Fellowship was coming to an end in 1974. He understood how privileged he had been. Academia and grumbling are old friends, with three primary forms of grievance: low pay, heavy teaching, boring paperwork. For seven years, Parfit had been provided with an income that met all his needs, he had no teaching obligations, and the college and university authorities essentially left him alone. There were very few such positions in the UK. Who would want to give this up? Certainly not Parfit. But his fellowship had produced thin publication pickings, at least in terms of quantity. The originality of the personal identity paper had led it to be hailed as a masterpiece by philosophers. There were, however, far more lawyers and historians than philosophers at All Souls, and they were less forgiving of his poor productivity.

At the time, it was possible to move seamlessly from a Prize Fellowship to a seven-year Junior Research Fellowship, with the approval of the governing body (made up of the Warden and All Souls Fellows), and without having to face external competition. But Parfit assumed he would have an internal rival—his Prize Fellowship-twin, historian John Clarke. In theory, both could have been elected to a Junior Research Fellowship, though there was no precedent for that.

There are differing accounts of what happened next. It was certainly believed by a number of Fellows that Parfit had been pushy, campaigning for himself with unseemly vigour. This was not the All Souls way. It was important that he secure a position without teaching, he argued to anybody who would listen, so that he could concentrate on his philosophical work. John Clarke recalls being asked by Parfit whether he intended to job-hunt elsewhere, and giving a noncommittal reply. The gossip among other Fellows was that Parfit had done his best to dissuade Dr Clarke from applying. There were even accusations flying around that he had denigrated his opponent, though this seems implausible, and if true, would have been wildly out of character.

Parfit's application for the fellowship was delivered in October 1973. It required setting out a study plan. He hoped, he wrote, to produce three books, one on personal identity, the second on rationality, giving an account of what reasons individuals have for action, and a third book covering the same ground as the second but from the point of view of society rather than the individual.

The process required references, and Parfit sought out some of the leading philosophers of the second half of the twentieth century, who duly obliged. They included Peter Strawson, R. M. Hare, A. J. Ayer, and John Rawls. This was the equivalent of a pianist receiving testimonials from Daniel Barenboim and Alfred Brendel, or a footballer from the likes of Diego Maradona and Johann Cruyff.

Strawson wrote that Parfit was 'one of the two or three outstanding philosophers of his generation in this country; and of that small number he is the most remarkable for the originality of his thinking, the thoroughness with which he works out his thoughts and the clarity with which he presents them.'[35] David Pears concurred: 'He is one of the two or three philosophers of his decade who should be given the opportunity to continue their research without the interruption of a heavy load of teaching.'[36] There were generous references too from Ayer and Thomas Nagel. Hare worried that, were All Souls not to award Parfit the fellowship, he might seek work abroad and be lost to Oxford forever. 'The seminars that he has been doing with Glover and Griffin on various applications of moral philosophy, and in which he has been perhaps the leading spirit, are the most exciting thing that has happened in moral philosophy in recent years [. . .]. Considering that he came into philosophy without having read for a first degree in it, I think it would not be going too far to say that he has a genius for the subject.'[37] Finally, there came a reference from John Rawls, whom Parfit had first met in his Harkness years: 'He seems to me extremely gifted. I believe there is no one among the younger philosophers, say those under forty, who is likely to make a greater contribution to ethics.'[38] There is a tendency in academic references towards the hyperbolic; nevertheless, it would have been nigh impossible to ignore such endorsements. It is notable that they came from thinkers from all subcategories within the discipline. Rawls was a political philosopher, Hare a moral philosopher, Pears a leading expert on Wittgenstein.

In any case, Parfit need not have worried about competition. Although John Clarke was keen to graduate to a Junior Research Fellowship, John Sparrow made it clear to him that this was not going to happen. Instead, Clarke was granted another two years at All Souls, but on the condition that he make use of the time to seek employment elsewhere. The previous decade had seen a huge expansion in the British university system, and the assumption was that he would not find it difficult to secure a job.

Few would have foreseen that the Warden would become a Parfit promoter. He and Parfit had no obvious affinities. But Sparrow was a talent spotter; he must have recognized that Parfit was an exceptional intellect, and he had a vision of All Souls as a college whose unique environment existed for the benefit of great men (yes, in his view, *men*). Not that Sparrow was interested in research; Isaiah Berlin reported that

Sparrow 'couldn't care less about the intellectual quality of the college, not in the least. He liked clever people [. . .] who amused him or could be good company for him and so on.'[39] The gossip was also that Sparrow had a sexual interest in Parfit. He was particularly taken by, and repeatedly complimented him on, his long, flowing hair.

Having Sparrow as an ally was helpful, especially because, without being aware of it, Parfit had begun to develop college enemies. The main cause of the hostility was that he took a nonchalant approach to norms and rules. One of his trifling transgressions concerned trifle. After the trifle, Eton mess, or apple crumble, a second dessert (consisting of fruit, cheese and booze) was served in a separate room (the common room) from that in which the starter and main course were served (the splendid hall). Staying for dessert was the 'proper' thing to do, yet Parfit started to skip it the last course to save time. It was hardly a revolutionary act—Academics of the world unite, you have nothing to lose but your camembert—but it encouraged others to follow suit, and some of the older Fellows tut-tutted. The tut-tutting intensified when Parfit abandoned his dessert boycott in the run-up to his fellowship renewal, so that he could seek out Sparrow for a chat; to other Fellows, this seemed cynical and inauthentic.

Another unwritten college meal convention was (and still is) that when you take your place at the lunch scrum or at the dinner table, you avoid prolonged shoptalk (about your research topic), you do not monopolize conversation, and you converse with the person on your left and on your right and with the person sitting across the table. Just as the general papers at All Souls were designed to allow potential Fellows to display their breadth and intelligence, so you were expected to hold your own at mealtimes, displaying curiosity, knowledge, intellect, sharpness, and wit. All Souls valued the well-rounded over narrow specialists.

This was not Parfit's way. He wanted to talk about philosophy. When he brought a guest to dinner, it was always someone related to work. And he would converse with them exclusively. Usually, he had no guest, and then he would nab one of the few philosophers and say, somewhat conspiratorially, 'Let's sit together.' To outsiders this might seem another insignificant foible. But All Souls academics carry out their research, for the most part, in isolation, and mealtimes function as social glue.

Parfit had by now established a nocturnal schedule. The bursar, Charles Wenden, was appreciative, since 'he acts as an unpaid night-watchman'.[40] It caused amusement among the college porters, who learned that if they telephoned him before lunch it would serve as a wake-up call. So as not to disturb him, the cleaners left clean sheets outside his room. Parfit's body clock ran several hours behind other people's—more Greenwich Village than Greenwich Mean Time—and he had begun to suffer from chronic insomnia. He told a student that his circadian rhythms did not follow the twenty-four-hour rotation of the Earth's orbit around the sun. One solution was to read novels that were neither so terrible that he couldn't read them at all, nor so interesting that he wanted to carry on reading: Trollope fitted this Goldilocks mean. But the strategy was only partially effective. A doctor prescribed Amitriptyline, an anti-depressant. Parfit thought it sensible (it is not) to wash this down with a tall glass of neat vodka, and so began a routine that would persist for the rest of his life, as he fought each night to pull the shutters on consciousness.

He now began to emerge from his suite of rooms for meals, seminars, and little else. His ever-deepening single-mindedness constituted a new facet to his character. Larry Temkin, later one of his closest friends, traces this development to a dawning awakening:

I believe that when Derek was younger, he regarded his relationship with academic subjects as a kind of game. A very enjoyable one that he was really good at. He enjoyed the combative side, of 'beating a foe' on the field of intellectual debate. When he was doing history [...] it made sense for Derek to 'play the game' he was so good at, while retaining the characteristics of a normal, very smart, young person enjoying themselves and the company of others, as well as a host of stimulating pursuits. But, when he realized that he could be massively successful at philosophy, and then, more particularly, that

he could make important and lasting contributions to moral philosophy, he was now dealing with issues that really mattered.[41]

Parfit was changing. He was becoming more of a loner and more
reclusive. The change was gradual, bit by bit, like that of Theseus's ship.
But in some ways he would end up almost unrecognizable from the
Parfit of his more open, carefree youth. He would become, some might
say, a different person.

9

A Transatlantic Affair

'I have long regarded myself as part-American,'[1] Parfit once wrote. To many Americans he seemed quintessentially English. He spoke the Queen's English and had a distinctly British sense of humour. He enjoyed Monty Python and the Jeeves and Wooster books of P. G. Wodehouse. But as evidence for his US attachment, Parfit cited the fact that when faced with a variety of newspapers in a college common room, the first ones he picked up, even when he was in the UK, were *The New York Times* and the *International Herald Tribune*.

Certain features of Parfit's life were cyclical. Two such patterns stand out and warrant discussion separately from the linear narrative. One was his annual photography pilgrimage to Leningrad and Venice (see chapter 13). The other was his regular sojourn at American universities. During the course of his life, he took more than forty teaching trips to the US. He had spells at Temple University (Philadelphia), the University of Colorado (Boulder), Rice University (Houston, Texas) and Princeton University (Princeton, New Jersey). But the three universities with which he had the closest and longest relationships were New York (NYU), Harvard, and, much later, Rutgers. His motivation was partly financial—until the millennium he needed money to pay for his photography habit. But more important was the opportunity these trips afforded to test out his ideas and to collaborate with, and learn from, other philosophers, especially Tim Scanlon and Thomas Nagel.

Parfit came to regard Scanlon and Nagel as two of his closest friends. Scanlon was a genial Hoosier (a native of Indiana), whose grandfather had been a working-class Irish immigrant and whose father had been a successful litigator. He had gone to Princeton as an undergraduate, and his original plan had been to specialize in mathematics before returning to Indiana to work in his father's legal practice. That was before he became hooked on philosophy.

He met Parfit for the first time in October 1972 in North Carolina, at a weekend Chapel Hill colloquium in philosophy. This was one of the numerous invitations Parfit received following his acclaimed first paper. Scanlon and Rawls addressed the colloquium on the Friday evening, and Parfit spoke about personal identity on the Saturday afternoon (21 October). At the close of the weekend, Scanlon and Parfit found themselves sitting in a group together in the coffee lounge of the airport waiting to fly out, 'and to our amazement, Derek began squiggling on napkins. He was sketching out his Repugnant Conclusion argument.'[2]

Scanlon spent his academic career first at Princeton, and then, from 1984, at Harvard. He began to specialize in moral and political philosophy in the 1970s, and his masterpiece, *What We Owe to Each Other*, appeared in 1998, a year after his first joint seminar with Parfit. It grappled with the two principal questions that animated him: how do we judge the moral worth of an action; and why should we be moral? His prose has been compared to a Le Corbusier edifice, 'without ornamentation and constructed with [its] purpose always in mind'.[3]

The book contains a widely cited thought experiment. 'Suppose that Jones has suffered an accident in the transmitter room of a television station. Electrical equipment has fallen on his arm, and we cannot rescue him without turning off the transmitter for fifteen minutes. A World Cup match is in progress, watched by many people, and it will not be over for an hour. Jones's injury will not get any worse if we wait, but his hand has been mashed and he is receiving extremely painful electrical shocks. Should we rescue him now or wait until the match is over?'[4] Scanlon's intuition, widely shared, is that we should not wait. Many philosophers have had a go at trying to explain this intuition. What it shows, according to Scanlon, is that we must reject at least crude forms of utilitarianism. We cannot just aggregate harms and benefits. It is wrong to allow someone to be severely harmed to save a large number of people from a minor harm. There is no collective perspective to judge these matters: we should ask, instead, whether any of the millions watching could—as individuals—reasonably object to the match being stopped. And, in Scanlon's view, they could not.

In his review of the long-awaited *What We Owe to Each Other*, Thomas Nagel described its publication as 'a philosophical event'.[5] A positive review from Nagel was not unexpected. He and Scanlon were close and had charted similar philosophical trajectories. Like Scanlon, Nagel had followed his undergraduate degree with a Fulbright Scholarship in Oxford, where, like Scanlon, he had studied philosophy. Like Scanlon, he received his PhD from Harvard. Like Scanlon, he taught at Princeton; he moved to NYU in 1980. Belgrade born, New York raised, he was another philosophical heavyweight, and an elegant writer. He had the rare skill of being able to reflect deeply on a topic, sometimes over a period of many years, and then synthesize complex thoughts on it into lucid, pithy prose.

If Nagel rated a philosopher, he could be a supportive ally, and Nagel rated Parfit. Parfit reciprocated; Nagel's *The View from Nowhere* (1986) was his favourite work of contemporary ethics. It is indeed a remarkable book.[6] Nagel lighted upon a unique human characteristic: our ability to make a detached assessment of our lives and actions. We can, as it were, look down upon ourselves, judge ourselves, assess ourselves, as though from outside our skins. We have a view from nowhere.

The fact that we have an inner and an outer perspective, a subjective and objective view, is at the root of many philosophical puzzles and psychological tensions, suggests Nagel. From an outer perspective, we may be struck by the thought that we are infinitesimally tiny dots in a vast universe. Or that we, like everyone else, are going to die. Our struggle to promote a cause, or pass an exam, or finish writing a biography, which a few minutes ago seemed so vitally important, can abruptly evaporate. The sense of the absurd emerges from this bird's-eye view.

Or take ethics. Is it acceptable to harm someone for a greater good? From the objective standpoint we might conclude that what matters is the greater good, what is best overall. But the subjective view resists this. We think it wrong to torture someone even to save a life, and we don't want to betray a friend to maximize the happiness of others.

Or take an issue philosophers feel compelled to contemplate—free will. Do we have free will? We certainly feel free in most ordinary situations: we feel free to choose between dishes on a menu, to order pizza or pasta at a restaurant. On the other hand, when we take the objective standpoint and consider that the world is subject to causal laws, scepticism about free will creeps in. Presumably the choice to select the pizza rather than the pasta is governed by prior conditions, including prior beliefs and desires (perhaps I find pizza tastier than pasta, for example). In what sense, then, is the choice really free? Free will comes to seem like legerdemain, an illusion.

Consider another puzzle: how to account for and categorize the weird phenomenon of consciousness. On the one hand, from the outer perspective, we want to explain it in scientific terms, in the language of neurons and synapses. But our subjective experience resists a reduction to science; a description in purely physical or material terms misses something. Nagel illustrates this in his most famous article, 'What Is It Like to Be a Bat?', published in 1974. You can give a complete scientific description of how bats operate—how they navigate, using sound like sonar, for example. But that doesn't tell us how it *feels* to be a bat.

. . .

Parfit's first US teaching gig was a three-week spell in 1971 as a visiting lecturer at Harvard. There, he was reacquainted with John Rawls, under whom he had studied during his Harkness Fellowship. It was the year that *A Theory of Justice*—now required reading for every student of political theory—was published. Parfit always acknowledged that Rawls had done political theory an enormous service by making the subject feel newly relevant and urgent. But, as he aged, he grew more critical of Rawls and frustrated by the dominance of *A Theory of Justice* within the discipline; there was a period when almost every work of political theory appeared to be a response to Rawls. As one critic, Robert Nozick, put it, 'Political philosophers must now either work within Rawls's theory, or explain why not.'[7] The book did not merit this monopoly of attention, Parfit complained. Still, in 1971 he enjoyed talking to Rawls, and, as we have seen, Rawls was sufficiently impressed by the young Englishman to act, later, as one of his referees.

Rawls credited Parfit with shaking him out of a certain complacency. The American was a leading opponent of utilitarianism, the core of his critique being that it failed to give weight to the axiomatic fact that human beings are separate. Utilitarianism provides an impersonal measure of how to act, adding and subtracting pros and cons, benefits and harms, happiness and misery. Rawls's insistence on our separateness was accompanied by his stricture that, for example, we cannot—as utilitarians say we can—always be morally permitted to harm one person for the greater benefit of one or more others. Our distinctiveness prohibited the sort of crude moral reasoning that would necessarily allow for an act that hurt Jane so long as it produced a bigger gain for John. Until reading Parfit, Rawls had barely considered the issue of personal identity, believing it to be a subset of his discipline cocooned from ethics and political theory. Now he was forced to reconsider. For if Parfit was right, the claim about separateness of persons rested on a metaphysical error.

. . .

The following year, 1972, Parfit had his first spell teaching at NYU, organized by the American philosopher Bill Ruddick. They had been introduced through a mutual friend at All Souls, and Parfit mentioned that he would be interested in teaching in New York, having already lived in Manhattan twice—once during his internship at *The New Yorker* and again during his Harkness Fellowship. Ruddick questioned him about his philosophical interests and promised to do what he could. He was as good as his word. In the autumn of 1972, Parfit was accompanied to the US by his girlfriend, Judith De Witt, who had leave of absence from Somerville College. She was a tourist whilst he worked at NYU during the day; in the evenings, they took advantage of New York's cultural riches, including the opera.

NYU now hosts one of the world's leading philosophy departments. That was not so in the early 1970s. Then, like the city itself, it was at a very low ebb. It had nearly gone bankrupt, and there had been a drastic reduction in the number of academic staff. Parfit was hardly famous at this stage, even in philosophical circles, but he had a growing reputation, and his association with NYU was helpful to the university as it sought to rebuild.

On future trips, Parfit travelled to the US alone. Sometimes he would stay in university accommodation, but more often over the years he would stay with a member of the faculty, such as Bill Ruddick. Because of his unusual hours, he tended to see very little of his host. Those who put him up once were not always inclined to do so again—it could risk the wrath of their partners, who complained that Parfit talked incessantly and only about philosophy. Patricia Zander, however, did host him several times, as did the philosopher Frances Kamm.

The dedication of one of Kamm's books is to 'the love of morality'.[8] The daughter of concentration camp survivors, she had powerful reasons to share Parfit's earnestness about ethics. Her philosophical life was devoted to unearthing and formulating moral principles with the aid of brilliantly imaginative, if often bizarre, thought experiments. Many of these were extensions of the famous trolley problem, which runs as follows.[9] Imagine a runaway train is about to kill five people who have the misfortune to be tied to a track. You could press a switch that would divert the train down a spur, thus saving the five lives. Unfortunately, one person is tied to the spur, and if you redirect the train this person will die. What should you do?

Now imagine an alternative case. Once again there is a runaway train heading towards five people. This time, you are standing on a bridge overlooking the track, next to a heavily built stranger. The only way to save the five people is to push the man over the bridge: the fall would kill him, but his bulky body would be enough to halt the train. Should you push him?

Most people believe that in the first scenario you should save the five lives, even at the cost of killing one. By contrast, most people believe that you should not push the man over the bridge. So why the difference? After all, in both cases you could kill one to save five. The search for an answer has been a long-running philosophical crime mystery, and

Frances Kamm has served as Agatha Christie, author of multiple trolley-type dilemmas. Drawing on ever more intricate hypothetical cases, she has elicited moral distinctions so subtle and nuanced that they had never occurred to anybody before. 'I feel that I've been admitted to a whole world of distinctions that haven't been seen by others, or at least not by me. And I'm taken by it as I would be by a beautiful picture.'[10]

Parfit was very taken with one particular thought experiment, about whether 'nearness' mattered to moral obligation. Many of us will have a stronger emotional response to news of a terrible episode in a neighbouring street than one in a distant country. But do we have a stronger moral obligation to help those near to us than to help people further away? Kamm argued that there was something to the intuition that we *do* have a stronger obligation to those who are near, but she first wanted to clarify what we mean by near. Only Kamm could have concocted the array of scenarios she uses to achieve this, including one Parfit thought ingenious. 'Suppose I stand in one part of India, but I have *very* long arms that reach all the way to the other end of India, allowing me to reach a child drowning in a pond at a distance. Is this case treated as one where the child is near or far?'[11]

Parfit's philosophy was less reliant on thought experiments than Kamm's, but there were certainly similarities in their styles. In their characters, too: 'She is the person who is most like me,'[12] Parfit said. He once discovered that the plughole was blocked in her kitchen sink; she hadn't noticed because she had never used it.

. . .

In the United States, Parfit was generally left to lecture on whatever he wanted—which invariably meant the topics on which he was working. He gave his courses general titles: 'Metaphysics', 'Ethics: Selected Topics', 'Advanced Ethics'. He stubbornly resisted taking on any administrative tasks, to the irritation of some colleagues. On the other hand, he had no objection to another widely disliked academic chore—marking. In the mid-1990s, he made a most surprising suggestion to Thomas Kelly, his teaching assistant at Harvard, whose job it was to read and grade undergraduate papers. Why didn't Kelly send every paper to him, and he would mark them; in other words, do all of Kelly's work. 'When he first explained this new plan to me, I literally didn't understand what was being proposed.'[13] But it made sense, explained Parfit without a hint of arrogance, because he could accomplish the task more quickly than Kelly. Quickness didn't mean superficiality, however. 'In order to really appreciate just how generous Derek was when it came to giving people feedback on their work, you'd have to take into account all of the initially indifferent undergraduates who turned in some half-assed five-page double-spaced paper that they probably fired off the night before it was due—only to receive back two days later (often to their astonishment!) three single-spaced pages of incredibly incisive comments from one of the greatest living philosophers.'[14]

The duration of Parfit's US visits varied, but they were either for a whole or half semester; he liked to bunch two classes in a week, so that he could minimize his stay. Often, he taught joint classes. At Harvard, he taught half a dozen packed classes with Tim Scanlon. The two of them argued a lot, with civilized passion, and 'both were quite capable of getting carried away'.[15] Each week, the two of them would move on to the same Thai restaurant after their class and continue their discussion.

Many of Parfit's deepest philosophical relationships were forged with former students. In the Fall terms of 1977 and 1979, Parfit had visiting appointments at Princeton, where a smart young Wisconsinite, Larry Temkin, was a graduate. Temkin, like Nagel and Kamm, was Jewish, and it was family discussions about the Holocaust when he was growing up that nudged him into philosophy—along with the possibly somewhat naive assumption that implanting reason and logic into debates about ethics and politics might prevent any such horror from recurring.

Parfit and Temkin would become close, but in 1977 the teacher inadvertently nearly stymied the career of the student. Temkin was preparing for his oral exam, a 'comprehensive' exam, which would partially be about utilitarianism and which he was required to pass to move to the

dissertation stage. 'What should I read?' he wanted to know. 'Sidgwick's *The Methods of Ethics*', Parfit replied. Temkin had to travel to
New York to get hold of a copy, and when he'd read this huge tome,
he went back to Parfit. 'What should I read next'? 'He replied, "Reread
Sidgwick."' Temkin reread it and approached Parfit again; 'Is there
anything I should read on utilitarianism besides Sidgwick?'. Parfit advised him to reread Sidgwick a third time, rather than devote energy
to inferior writings. Eventually it came to the oral exam. Temkin was
questioned about various standard books and papers in the field, but
not having read them was unable to comment. One examiner was
exasperated: "*Larry*, this is supposed to be a *comprehensive* exam—
what *have* you read?!!!" At which point another of the examiners,
Derek Parfit, 'raised his finger and emphatically interjected, "He has read
Sidgwick!!!"'[16]

Some years later, when Temkin was teaching at Rice University,
in Texas, he arranged for his erstwhile teacher to visit. And when Temkin transferred to Rutgers, in New Jersey, Parfit became a regular visitor
there, too. Rutgers had built up a very strong faculty, including two
other former students of Parfit's, Jeff McMahan and Ruth Chang (of
whom more later). When he was visiting Rutgers, he would stay in the
basement of McMahan's house, which McMahan labelled 'The Parfit
Suite'. For seven weeks, badger-like, he would remain underground, eating austere, cold meals, and only emerging into daylight for his classes
and then a very late night chat with his host.

The association with Rutgers, which began in 2007, was important
for crude financial reasons. Parfit's attitude to money was not entirely
disinterested. From his US host organizations he would enquire about
pay and allowances, but he eschewed tough haggling. However, as part
of their rivalry with nearby NYU, Rutgers tried to snatch Parfit by making an offer he couldn't refuse—half the time commitment for double
the pay. The plan was only partially successful. Parfit agreed to teach at
Rutgers, but drew up a schedule that allowed him to continue at Harvard and NYU, and which involved teaching half a semester in each
place every two years. And, armed with the Rutgers financial package,
he 'suggested' that Harvard and NYU agree to similar terms. It meant

his US salary rose to around $160,000 per annum. Suddenly, teaching in the United States became lucrative.

But in the early 1970s, financial windfalls lay in the future. For the time being, Parfit would need to safeguard his position at All Souls. Unbeknownst to him, several of his colleagues were beginning to question whether he merited his position in their elite college.

10

The Parfit Scandal

Young academics are usually desperate to publish as much and as quickly as possible, for there is no more effective route to career advancement. This was not the Parfit way. True to the ancient meaning of his surname, he was reluctant to commit anything to print unless he thought it incapable of improvement. Everything he wrote went through dozens and dozens of drafts—and this was pre–word processor. Richard Jenkyns, a classicist at All Souls, says Parfit told him that 'most of this [. . .] was a search for perfection of expression.'[1]

Signs of his chronic publishing constipation were evident as early as 1974. Oxford University Press had been in talks with him about a book on personal identity since late 1968. This would develop arguments and themes from his first article. On 1 July 1974, Parfit wrote to the OUP philosophy editor, Nicholas Wilson—who had asked for news of the identity book—but deflected the enquiry with details of the three books he had promised All Souls. 'I may decide in, say, three years' time, to push ahead with one of the three books; but I'm not even sure which that would be.'[2]

Parfit was safely ensconced in All Souls for another seven years, so the immediate pressure to publish had eased. He agreed to help the philosophy department out by taking on one or two minor burdens, including in at least one year the marking of the moral philosophy paper in PPE. He kept a tally of the philosophers name-checked by the undergraduates. Immanuel Kant received the gold medal, David Hume the bronze. Silver went to the White's Professor, R. M. Hare.

There was an ironic consequence of his 1974 promotion. In part due to what some perceived as his unseemly behaviour, the college decided that internal promotion from the Prize Fellowship with no open competition was incompatible with modern equal-opportunity practice, and a working party was established to devise a new scheme. Both Parfit and Robin Briggs were on this committee, though Briggs felt more discomfort at hauling up the ladder on which they had both climbed than did his former tutorial partner. A new system, open to outsiders, took effect in the late 1970s.

There was further internal college business to attend to, including the election of a new Warden. John Sparrow retired in 1977 and Parfit— along with Isaiah Berlin and some younger Fellows—approached a potential candidate to succeed him. Bernard Williams was Parfit's senior by thirteen years and the living philosopher he most admired. Respect ran in both directions: Williams was hugely impressed by Parfit's work on identity.

Like Parfit, Williams had had a glittering start to his academic life, the top First in Oxford and a Prize Fellowship at All Souls. But in personality the two men could hardly have been more different. Williams was a social creature, charming, charismatic, and dazzling in conversation, more cerebrally agile than Parfit. After listening to an academic lecture he might say, 'I have five objections to your thesis,'[3] and would then reel them off one by one. Observers suspected that he had plucked the number 'five' at random and was making it up as he went along. It was a way of challenging himself while peacocking his brilliance to others.

There were two reasons to become a philosopher, Williams once said. The first was to discover truth, the second to have fun (which, for Parfit, was a bizarre motivation). He had a highly evolved sense of the absurd, wore a wry expression, and enjoyed puncturing pomposity with lacerating witticisms. An inane question from an audience member would be met with a less generous rejoinder from Williams than from Parfit.

Nor did the two men share much intellectual common ground. Parfit's rooms might increasingly resemble a rubbish tip, but he wanted to tidy up moral philosophy and sought definitive answers. Williams's office was neat and ordered, but he thought moral philosophy was intrinsically messy, and that the search for ultimate truths was futile. Parfit was a builder, Williams a demolisher. Parfit's philosophy was ahistorical—philosophical truths were immutable—while Williams's approach was both socially and historically rooted.

Aged just thirty-eight, Williams had become the Knightbridge Professor of Philosophy at Cambridge. But he lived an active life beyond the ivory tower, participating in the practical world of politics and ethics. His first wife, Shirley, was a prominent Labour Party politician, who in 1981, after Labour had lurched leftwards, became one of the founders of the breakaway Social Democratic Party. Williams himself served on several government commissions and committees, including on drug abuse, on gambling, and, most famously (in 1979) on pornography. 'I did all the major vices,'[4] he joked.

And as regards philosophy, he made many seminal contributions. In ethics, for example, he generated an enormous secondary literature when he introduced the phrase 'moral luck', of which a classic illustration runs as follows. Suppose two people drink heavily at a party and then choose to drive home at night. Driver One encounters no traffic and reaches home safely. Driver Two rounds a bend, where a pedestrian is crossing the road. The alcohol has slowed his reactions, and he runs the pedestrian over. Most people would agree that Driver Two should be far more severely punished than Driver One. Yet, in a sense, both drivers are equally culpable. They both drank and drove. It was mere luck that Driver One harmed nobody.

Williams spotted that much of our moral life has this feature and that this was a profound philosophical problem. Many factors that affect the judgements people make about us are beyond our control. A different type of example is the person who devotes their life to philosophy whilst neglecting friends and family and all the other ingredients of a normal human life. That may eventually prove to be a justifiable decision (or more justifiable at least) if the person produces a significant body of work; but that is impossible to guarantee in advance.[5]

More closely related to Parfit's work were Williams's writings on utilitarianism. He shared none of Parfit's consequentialist instincts. He did not believe that we should always aim at bringing about the best consequences. He emphasized fundamental aspects of our moral lives, such as what he called 'integrity'—consistently pursuing our own projects—that could not be adequately accommodated within a utilitarian framework. His objections were set out in a slim 1973 book—now a staple on undergraduate philosophy reading lists—*Utilitarianism: For and Against*, in which an Australian-based philosopher, J.J.C. Smart, advanced the 'For' side whilst Williams put the case for the opposition.

His case is built on two hypothetical scenarios. First there is George, an unemployed chemist who is offered a job developing biological and chemical weapons. George is adamantly opposed to such weapons, but knows if he doesn't take the position, somebody else will, and will pursue the work with far more zeal. Plus, George needs the money.

Then there is Jim. Jim is on a botanical expedition in South America when he comes upon a terrible scene. Twenty indigenous villagers have been tied up, and a heavy man in a sweat-stained khaki shirt, who turns out to be the captain in charge, explains that all twenty are about to be executed for protesting against the government. However, since Jim is an honoured visitor from another land, the captain offers him the choice of killing one of the locals himself, after which the others will be set free. If Jim doesn't take up the offer, the captain's men will execute all twenty.

The consequentialist has an easy response to both cases. George should take the job, and Jim should shoot one of the villagers. From a utilitarian perspective, this would ensure the best result. But, argued Williams, this is to miss a key facet of these scenarios. For George to work in the biological warfare industry would run counter to everything he believes. We each have personal projects and special obligations to people, and these cannot, or should not, be ignored or downplayed. Of George, Williams wrote, 'It is absurd to demand of such a man, when the sums come in from the utility network [. . .] that he should just step aside from his own project and decision and acknowledge the decision which utilitarian calculation requires. It is to alienate him in a real sense from his actions and the source of his action in his own convictions.'[6]

Equally with Jim. Perhaps, on balance, Jim should kill the villager. But, thought Williams, that is surely not quite as obvious a conclusion as the utilitarian would have us believe. True, if Jim does not kill one man, twenty will die. But this doesn't make Jim *responsible* for their deaths—at least in the way that the captain, who orders their killing, would be responsible. If Jim pulls the trigger that kills one villager, he *is* responsible for this man's death, in a much more direct way than if he refuses to take up the captain's offer and the man dies anyway. That, at least, was the influential argument put by Williams, and a challenge to which consequentialists such as Parfit felt they had to respond.

. . .

Williams was no doubt flattered that Parfit et al. urged him to apply for the wardenship at All Souls, and he allowed himself to be persuaded. He stood on a reform and modernizing platform—the contrast with the old-fashioned Sparrow needed no spelling out. Parfit campaigned vociferously for his friend, and, based on what Fellows had told him, reported back to Williams that 'he was home and dry'.[7] His chief rival was Patrick Neill, a besuited lawyer, decent, dependable, albeit, according to Isaiah Berlin, 'not exactly first rate'.[8]

The convoluted electoral system, devised by philosopher Michael Dummett, involved a single transferable vote method, but also the option of 'No Election'—this is the chance to express a preference to rerun the race with fresh candidates. It turned out that polls of All Souls Fellows were no more trustworthy than national ones. At the final shoot-out, many Williams supporters ranked Neill second, while Neillites conspired among themselves to enter 'No Election' as their favoured alternative.

Isaiah Berlin reported that Williams was 'crushed'[9] by the defeat, but according to his second wife, Patricia, it came as 'a considerable relief. He had not realized before quite what an inward-looking and conservative institution All Souls had remained.'[10] Berlin's diagnosis was that some Fellows thought Williams too young and, what's more, that 'he was a philosopher [and] wore a duffel coat'.[11] Parfit informed one friend that when the results of the last round's voting were announced in college, 'there were gasps of astonishment'.[12]

Neill may have been the traditionalist's candidate, but as so often, the electorate failed to appreciate who they were electing. The pressing issue on Neill's agenda was women. Should All Souls' overturn a 1926 statute which stated no woman should become a member of the college? The vote on whether to admit women was taken at roughly the same time in many Oxford colleges, but the internal debate was unusually divisive in All Souls. A change of statute required a two-thirds majority and, although they were still a minority, the college had more than its fair share of dyed-in-the-wool misogynists. For a few Fellows, an influx of women threatened to sully their institutional Eden. In the end, however, they were swept aside: no dam could hold back the tide of social revolution, even one constructed in dinosaur-era All Souls limestone. The reformers, supported by Neill, won convincingly.

In this mini–culture war, Parfit was one of the leaders of the pro-reform faction, baffled by the worldview of opponents who seemed to think that the smell of perfume might inhibit the enjoyment of college port, or who resorted to petty logistical objections, such as inadequate toilet provision. At the college debate in 1979, he was somewhat more persuaded by an elegant speech in which a Fellow drew an analogy with Victorian architecture: we go to enormous lengths to preserve Victorian architecture, even when we don't necessarily find it beautiful; and we do so because we think it valuable to preserve something distinctive. The same argument applied to all-male colleges, the Fellow pronounced.[13]

The vote was only the beginning. For it was one thing to allow that there was an abstract woman in the Platonic realm who met the required standard, and quite another to believe that a living and breathing female could do so. The first real test came in January 1981 when, under the rules that Parfit had helped to formulate, there was an open competition for a 'Thesis Fellowship', a two-year postdoctoral appointment. Would All Souls once again reveal that it was 'a hotbed of cold feet'?[14] The two leading candidates were both female, but several All Souls Fellows insisted that neither was up to scratch. A decision required a simple majority. Parfit was an unhelpful campaigner for the female cause— 'counter-persuasive',[15] according to one Fellow—alienating his colleagues by pointing out their irrationality. After the first ballot, there was no clear result. A second round ensued, then a third and a fourth. 'We didn't have black and white smoke, like the papal conclave, but the vote held that sense of excitement,'[16] recalled Paul Seabright. Eventually, American-born philosopher Susan Hurley, Parfit's preferred candidate, was elected. She became the first female Fellow in October 1981.

Hurley grew to love All Souls, but the most obnoxious of the chauvinists set out to make her and her immediate successors feel unwelcome. Upon seeing a female Fellow come down for dinner, the geneticist E. B. Ford stood up, declaimed, 'There is a woman present', and promptly fled the room. When he bumped into another of the early XX-chromosome Fellows, the geneticist swung his umbrella at her and screeched 'Out of my way, henbird!'[17] Opinion differs over whether the reactionary ultras reflected more deep-seated institutional and cultural problems in the college. One frequent visitor says the venomous atmosphere went beyond a few toxic individuals and that All Souls 'cultivated hostility'.[18]

After his wardenship ended, John Sparrow just about managed to reconcile himself to modernization and the exotic new intake. Even so, over the next few years, he became a tragic figure, descending into an embarrassing state of drunkenness. He remained attached to Parfit, however. When he came to dinner and Parfit was present, he would bellow, 'What's the most beautiful thing in this room?', before answering the question himself: 'Parfit's *chevelure!*'

. . .

In the first two years of his 1974–81 fellowship, Parfit worked on issues linked to a subject hitherto largely ignored by philosophers. Other things being equal, it is wrong to cause pain to a neighbour or even to a person on the other side of the world. That is uncontentious. But what about future people? On the face of it, it seems obvious that certain actions taken today, such as the depletion of resources, might be wrong because of their impact on subsequent generations. But is 'harm' to people who are not yet born comparable to harm that I might inflict on people currently alive?

Clearly it was, Parfit thought. But he also thought that there were more taxing questions about future people. These arise from two effects we can have on the future. First, we can affect the identities of those who will be born (for example, prospective parents might put off having a family, and if they do so, the child born later will not be the same child as the child that would have been born had they not delayed). Second, we can affect the numbers of people born—the size of the future population.

In so far as philosophers had previously reflected on future generations—and those who had included Parfit's hero, Sidgwick—their arguments had been largely dismissed for being philosophically arid, even facile. This began to change in 1967, when Jan Narveson published a provocative paper entitled 'Utilitarianism and New Generations'. Utilitarianism, wrote Narveson, appears to demand that we produce as many people as possible, so long as their happiness outweighs their misery. And he regarded this as a crazy implication.

The following year saw the publication of a doom-laden book, *The Population Bomb*. Echoing the fears of the English economist Thomas Malthus, 170 years earlier, the authors, Paul and Anne Ehrlich,[19] predicted that there would shortly be worldwide famine because food supplies could not keep up with the rapidly rising population. Hundreds of millions of people would soon die. Steps were urgently required to control population size, and the book made multiple suggestions, including incentives for men to agree to be sterilized.

So population concerns were in the political air, though it was Narveson who really provoked Parfit into reflecting philosophically about future people. As early as 1971, Parfit had written to John Rawls, 'The more I think about population policy, the more puzzling I find the subject.'[20] One question was how to evaluate population size. Would it be better to have a smaller population in which each person enjoyed a high quality of life, or a larger population with a lower quality of life? With a series of bar-charts, Parfit illustrated a fiendish conundrum that, to his exasperation, he couldn't crack.

Nobody else could crack it either. Many tried, for Parfit had begun to circulate his unpublished writings to the global philosophical community. Nevertheless, he made sufficient progress on the philosophy of future people to consider bringing out a book. In the end, he became disillusioned with the idea, feeling he had to come up with solutions, not just problems. So instead, he switched to another topic: rationality and our reasons for action. This culminated in a lengthy essay, 'Against Prudence', which in 1977 was awarded the triennial T. H. Green Prize, and addressed the notion that the ultimate reason for me to act in a certain way is self-interest: in other words, that I should care most about what is best for me. Parfit argued, however, that if people act selfishly, the results will be worse for everyone—that self-interest is in fact self-defeating.

Meanwhile, OUP was pressing him for his long-promised manuscript on personal identity; but as usual, his plans were in flux. On 13 May 1977, he invited Nicholas Wilson and his successor as OUP's philosophy editor, Adam Hodgkin, for lunch at All Souls. His new proposal, he told them, was to turn his prize-winning essay into a book. They expressed enthusiasm (they had no real choice, other than severing their relationship with him), and Parfit set to work. Within months he had generated enough fresh material for what he thought might make another book. Some of these new thoughts were delivered in the annual philosophy lecture at the British Academy, under the title 'Prudence, Morality, and the Prisoner's Dilemma'.[21]

On 9 August 1978, Hodgkin pleaded with Parfit to send the 'Against Prudence' manuscript within two years and not, as Parfit was now threatening, in three or four: 'We have no wish to rush you into premature publication but interest in your work is clearly building and we should encourage you to think about early publication.'[22] The White's Professor of Moral Philosophy also urged OUP to pile on the pressure. On 28 October, Hare contacted Hodgkin. 'I hope you will give Derek Parfit every encouragement. I think he is the best moral philosopher of his generation that I know, and it is without question that a book by him would be worth publishing. However, he does have a tendency to go on and on writing, so anything you could do to get a reasonably short book out of him quickly would be highly appreciated by the public.'[23]

Finally, in November that year, a contract was agreed for *Against Prudence*. The contract stipulated that the book would be delivered by 30 April 1981. Parfit would receive the princely advance of £900, a third on contract, a third on delivery, a third on publication. The book would be succinct, at around sixty thousand words.

. . .

The fact that neither this, nor any of the other books Parfit had proposed up to this time, ever appeared in print would land him in trouble. But during the course of his 1974–81 Fellowship he did publish shorter pieces—in fact, he wrote chapters in three edited collections, and produced four journal articles. One of the chapters was on personal identity. Of the other published works, three were about the ethics of future people and two had to do with puzzles about morality. Those arguments were all to re-emerge in his first book, *Reasons and Persons*.

The final article, however, merits brief discussion here. It was published in the summer of 1978 and was a patient demolition of an influential paper, 'Should the Numbers Count?', by John Taurek. This paper had caused a philosophical buzz. Taurek imagined a life-saving drug and that six people would certainly die if they were not treated with it. One of the six requires all of the drug to survive; the other five only require one-fifth of it. Taurek claimed that since every life is of equal weight, we should be morally indifferent as between using the drug in one way (to save five people) or the other (to save a single person). The numbers do not matter. In defence of his argument, he argued that suffering was not additive: we should not do sums in moral reasoning by combining the suffering of different people. 'The discomfort of each of a large number of individuals experiencing a minor headache does not add up to anyone's experiencing a migraine.'[24]

If Taurek was right, there were dramatic implications for how we distribute resources, including health resources. We should be indifferent as between funding Drug A that could save five thousand lives and Drug B that could save one thousand. But this conclusion jarred against Parfit's deepest moral instincts. He believed Taurek had gone badly wrong and that he needed to preempt the damage the article would do if it became more influential. He slowly and painstakingly took Taurek's arguments apart. He argued, for example, that just as it made sense to say that fifty minor headaches could be worse for one person than a single migraine, it made equal sense to say that fifty headaches each felt by a different person might be worse—involve more total suffering—than a migraine. Suffering *was* additive. And he pointed out some absurdities of Taurek's position; it seems to commit us to the ludicrous notion that we should be no more obliged to save one person's life than another person's toe. He concluded, 'Why do we save the larger number? Because we do give equal weight to saving each. Each counts for one. That is why more count for more.'[25]

Was that true of publications, too? An average of one (relatively short) publication a year was hardly prolific, bearing in mind Parfit had none of the teaching and bureaucratic commitments of most university employees. On the other hand, the quality of his output had established him as a major figure in the discipline. What's more, there were other All Souls academics with far less distinguished publishing records.

. . .

On 10 August 1980, Parfit's brilliant friend Gareth Evans, with whom he'd once driven to Spain, died of cancer. He was just thirty-four. Parfit had not been aware of the speed of Evans's illness, and his death jolted him. He wrote to a friend five days later, 'We are all in a state of shock here. I wish Gareth had let us know before. I would have wanted to write to him. I feel now full of a resolve to make more of the rest of my life. I shall try at least to cling to this resolve, in his memory.'[26]

What did making more of his life mean? In October, Parfit had a revealing exchange with R. M. Hare about the latter's forthcoming book *Moral Thinking*, in which it was argued that there were two levels of moral thinking: the intuitive, which relied on simple rules, and the critical, when we have to reflect more deeply on how to judge or behave, such as when our intuitions conflict. Parfit sent many pages of suggested improvements, accompanied by the unwelcome recommendation that Hare delay publication. It was more important for posterity that Hare get it absolutely right, argued Parfit. No, replied Hare, perfection was not necessary. 'I don't hope to write an ethics-book to end ethics-books.'[27] What mattered was that the book set off a discussion: 'I am afraid', Hare wrote, 'that we disagree fundamentally about the art of writing books.'[28]

The following year—the year of Susan Hurley's arrival at All Souls—was also the year that Parfit's Research Fellowship was due to end. He had been at the college for fourteen years altogether. In late March 1981 he received a letter from the Warden, Patrick Neill, reminding him that his Fellowship ran out in November. Parfit had lost track of time. He replied on 26 March; he was 'ashamed to confess' that he had assumed it would expire the following year. That meant he would be late applying for a Senior Research Fellowship, which he now intended to do, and which could be considered by the college at its June meeting. This might appear to put undue pressure on the college, he wrote, for Fellows might be concerned that if they turned him down, he would be out of work. But they needn't fret. In the Michaelmas (autumn) term of 1981, he would be in Princeton, and between the second (Hilary) and third (Trinity) terms, he would be teaching in Boulder, Colorado. He could support himself with these teaching posts and, in any case, he could probably find a permanent teaching post in the United States.[29]

Should we read this letter at face value? Probably. But written by someone with more guile than Parfit, it would be natural to interpret it as a boast and a passive-aggressive assertion of the author's credentials—a not-so-subtle message that he was in considerable demand elsewhere, so All Souls should feel jolly lucky to have him.

The letter contained a confession. Before the award of his second seven-year Fellowship, Parfit had said that it would enable him to produce three books. 'That hope was over-ambitious. But I am depressed and humbled at having to report that I have not yet published any of my projected books.' He went on to summarize what he had achieved to date and what he hoped to accomplish in the future. He would finish off the three books he had begun. Also, he was working on a new edition, for OUP, of Sidgwick's *The Methods of Ethics*, 'a neglected classic'.[30] Although he did not go into details, the reason this project was so important to him was that the edition that was currently in print included revisions that Sidgwick had made in the margin as he was dying. Parfit felt many of the changes made the text worse.

Academics in his first discipline, history, had an advantage over philosophers, Parfit lamented. When philosophers were stuck, they could only await inspiration. Stuck historians, by contrast, could always read or transcribe another source. In defence of his record, he highlighted some mitigating circumstances. He had only switched to philosophy in 1966; 'I was therefore simply learning until about 1970.'[31] He had supposed that he would be able to make the case for a further Fellowship on the basis of unpublished work. 'It has now been suggested to me that I should not have assumed this, since the College may take the view that little weight should be given to unpublished work. I can only reply that the College has not in the past taken this view, and that, if it does so now, it is not clear that I ought to have predicted this decision.'[32]

. . .

The Senior Research Fellowship was, effectively, a tenured position, a research post for life, a rare and precious jewel within the British university system. The discussions about whether Parfit should be offered it turned nasty.

One of those leading the campaign against him was Rodney Needham. Needham was a veteran of World War II, who became a prolific social anthropologist. Before an acrimonious falling out with Claude Lévi-Strauss, he helped to import Lévi-Strauss's structuralist ideas into the UK. The structuralists maintained that there were consistent patterns across different societies, which reflected universal aspects of human nature. Myths and rituals had surface differences, but deep parallels. An All Souls loyalist, Needham was a passionate defender of college rituals— when he died in 2006, one of his obituaries reported that he had 'revelled in both [Oxford's] great traditions and its petty ceremonies.'[33]

But Parfit's principal adversary was a sociologist of religion, Bryan Wilson, who had become an All Souls Fellow just a few years prior to himself, and who made his name with the first sociological study of religious sects in the UK. He, too, according to a colleague, had 'an unhealthily intense and possessive love of the college.'[34] Wilson took an early dislike to Parfit and had gone so far as to warn younger Fellows about him. In a vaguely threatening manner, one new All Souls Fellow, who spent many mealtimes in animated philosophy conversations with

Parfit, was taken aside and told that if he wanted to be on the right side of the influential forces in college he should not be seen to ally himself with somebody who was so friendless there. The contention that Parfit had no supporters was untrue. But he was certainly developing a reputation for eccentricity. He was courteous to everyone but was increasingly finding small talk a challenge. If he had to converse with a non-philosopher, his two opening gambits were, 'What are you working on?', or, 'What title are you thinking of for your book?' Meanwhile, non-philosophers feared expressing any interest in Parfit's work, because invariably an invitation to read and comment on a hundred-page manuscript would follow. There were many Fellows whose names he couldn't remember, and when he had a guest he would explain, *sotto voce,* that he couldn't introduce them to other people at the table for that very reason.

Each year in August, the All Souls kitchens close, to give staff time off. This obliges the Fellows to eat elsewhere. In the 1970s, University College, across the road, agreed to take in the hungry refugees. Every day Parfit would sit with Gareth Evans, at a separate table from other Fellows, such as Richard Jenkyns, who watched 'the two of them debating furiously with their mouths full. One or two [Fellows] disapproved— they should be making small talk to other people—but I thought it was magnificent to see such intellectual excitement, and the sense that no hour should be lost to the pursuit of truth.'[35]

Parfit's obsession with his subject was deepening. This ex-historian had a zealotry common among converts. When non-philosophers were elected as Prize Fellows, Parfit would suggest they abandon their discipline and take up philosophy. It was within their rights to switch subjects, he explained. Adrian Wooldridge, a future star columnist at *The Economist,* was one of the historians on the receiving end of this advice. He arrived in All Souls in 1980. 'I was trying to work out how to structure my PhD, and he said, "It's pointless. Philosophy is much more important." This wasn't particularly helpful.'[36]

Meanwhile, those who visited his room found it slowly disappearing under stacks of books and paper. A palaeontologist or dendrochronologist could have dated a manuscript by how high in the pile it was located. 'If you looked in the room', says his friend Bill Ewald, 'you would think the occupant was mentally ill.' The outer room, bad enough in itself, was still more presentable than his little study or his bedroom. Nobody was permitted in his bedroom, 'but I peeked in, and there were vodka bottles everywhere, food lying around half eaten. It was a health hazard.'[37] The rooms were also brimming with papers, pens, pencils, coins, and dental floss. The college cleaners were barred from entering.

Parfit's door remained closed until late morning. And each night, as other Fellows retired to bed, he would start playing Wagner—usually *The Ring Cycle, Tristan and Isolde*, or *Parsifal*—and the music would float across the North Quad for several hours. Parfit had once enjoyed live opera, but now claimed he could not see the point in going to a concert. He recommended that other Fellows do as he had done—buy the most expensive stereo equipment available, after which the finest musicians were at your disposal at the time of your convenience.

. . .

Despite his show of insouciance about promotion, Parfit was nervous. He needed two-thirds support among the Fellows, but he was not so unworldly as to remain unaware of hostile feelings towards him. He embarked on a 'charm' campaign. This carried a risk of backfiring, since he was not adept at messaging. He told colleagues that teaching would be a distraction that would impede progress, irritating Fellows who, behind his back, groused that he did actually teach—in America, for which he received an income on top of his Oxford salary. He did not explicitly state that his work was more vital than that of other scholars, but he could not successfully disguise that he believed this to be the case. On 7 April 1981, his friend Thomas Nagel wrote to him with avuncular advice: 'You have sometimes been inclined to argue that this sort of near-total freedom was a necessity for you, that without it your research would dry up. That is an argument that is more likely to put people off than persuade them.'[38] What was more, Nagel added, it probably wasn't true; more teaching might prove a catalyst to productivity.

In support of his application, Parfit produced another A-list suite of referees: Ronald Dworkin, Jonathan Glover, R. M. Hare, John Mackie, Thomas Nagel, Tim Scanlon, and Bernard Williams. Dworkin and Mackie are the only two of these characters we have yet to meet. The Australian-born Mackie was a philosopher of broad interests, though in the years to come it was in particular his scepticism as to whether morality could be objective that most exercised Parfit. As for Dworkin, or Ronnie as he was known to friends, he held (from 1969) the Oxford Chair of Jurisprudence and was fast developing a reputation as the most original philosopher of law in the English-speaking world. An American, educated at both Harvard and (as a Rhodes Scholar) Oxford, he initially made his reputation by his trenchant attacks on the then-dominant legal positivism. This was the notion, to put it crudely, that law was merely a convention or construct, independent of morality. Dworkin insisted that humans had moral rights and that these rights existed in law, whether or not they were codified. Linked to his anti-positivism was his rejection of 'originalism'—the idea that in the US judges should settle legal disputes by asking, 'How did the framers of the Constitution intend the law to be interpreted?'; or, as later original-ists would put it, 'What did the words of the Constitution mean when they were written?' He expressed his views forcefully, in lengthy, stylish essays in *The New York Review of Books*.

Several of Parfit's referees made excuses for his poor publishing rec-ord. 'He is not as other men are,'[39] explained Hare, meaning that Parfit held on to his manuscripts because his standards were higher than other people's. Rawls cautioned that he should not be rushed; the sort of book Parfit will eventually produce 'should be allowed to mature and not be expected too soon.'[40] What would probably happen, predicted Dworkin, is that he would publish a great deal in one burst as the various strands of his project come together. 'This is a fairly typical pattern among good philosophers,'[41] wrote Dworkin, citing Rawls as an example. But the real problem, wrote Jonathan Glover, was Parfit's perfectionism, which 'verges on being neurotic.'[42]

It was not just his perfectionism, though. More than one referee men-tioned that Parfit expended a colossal amount of energy commenting on the work of other philosophers, and that this was bound to affect his progress on his own projects. Regardless, All Souls was urged to acknowledge the value of this to the profession as a whole. 'He is sought after as a critic', wrote Dworkin 'because his criticism is so good—detailed, sympathetic and intelligent.'[43]

There was unanimity about Parfit's smartness and originality. However, both Dworkin and Nagel expressed reservations about his unpublished work on future people that had been circulating for years. Nagel thought there was simply no answer to one of the central problems Parfit was addressing—how to compare the value of existence of two groups of people and 'the attempt of an inexhaustible philosopher to find one will generate more heat than light.'[44] Glover, however, wished that Parfit's work on future people would appear in a journal or book: 'There is something absurd about a whole field where everyone takes as a starting point an unpublished piece of work.'[45]

All the referees endorsed Parfit's application. 'If he does not deserve a Senior Research Fellowship, I cannot imagine who does,'[46] wrote Glover. Only Nagel's endorsement had a tepid qualification: 'He will not become a philosopher of truly broad scope and power like Dummett or Strawson. But within his chosen area he is extremely good: clearly no one of his generation is better. I confess that I do not know the standards for a Senior Research Fellowship at All Souls, but my sense is that Parfit is a plausible candidate.'[47]

Towards the end of April, Parfit finalized his arrangements to be in Princeton in the Fall semester. Tim Scanlon had found him accommodation. He was to be paid $11,000 in remuneration, and $8,500 for travel, board, and lodging. Parfit had not negotiated hard, and this represented something of a bargain for Princeton, one of the world's richest educational institutions.

As for All Souls, Parfit's anxiety levels must have fallen dramatically when he discovered that the Academic Purposes Committee—which assessed the academic record of the applicant and the outline of their proposed research—had unanimously recommended his election. His future was now assured—or so Parfit supposed. On 11 May he wrote to Adam Hodgkin, at OUP: 'I'm happy to report [...] that our College

Committee has met and recommended that I be elected at our College Meeting in June.'[48] Hodgkin wrote back to congratulate him: 'This is news which is as welcome as it was expected.'[49]

Not so fast. The All Souls meeting was held on 13 June 1981. Parfit was, of course, not allowed to be present. He assumed that Fellows would simply take their lead from the Academic Purposes Committee. But it turned out several of them carried not a rubber stamp, so much as a sharpened knife. Although details of college meetings are supposed to be secret, it is possible to reconstruct what occurred. One of Parfit's champions, Isaiah Berlin, was unable to attend the vote, but had originally promised to send a note of support to be read out by the Warden. An unfortunate consequence of Parfit's backing by the Academic Purposes Committee was that Berlin too thought the election was a mere formality and that his own assistance was superfluous.

Parfit had many other powerful allies, including the Canadian philosopher Charles Taylor (who was the Chichele Professor of Social and Political Theory) and the Conservative MP and All Souls Fellow William Waldegrave; and, especially, the Bengali-born philosopher/economist Amartya Sen (the Drummond Professor of Political Economy). Parfit had helped persuade Sen to move to Oxford from the London School of Economics. 'It's the best place for philosophy,' he insisted, 'and you should define yourself as a philosopher rather than an economist.'[50] Sen's formative experiences had been as a boy in pre-independence Bengal, seeing emaciated bodies during the 1943 famine in which up to three million people died, then witnessing vicious Muslim–Hindu clashes. In the mid-1940s, an unemployed Muslim labourer staggered into his family compound, having been looking for work in a predominantly Hindu area, and subsequently died; he'd been set upon by a Hindu mob, who knifed him in the back. As he became weaker, he explained to the young Sen that his children had no food at home. 'For that, he lost his life.'[51]

These early encounters shaped his future interests, straddling philosophy and economics. He would eventually win a Nobel Prize for a body of work that included breakthroughs in social choice theory— the study of how collective decisions should be made from a set of individual choices, and how to derive a measure of social wellbeing from different individuals' wellbeing. (There is a story, so apt it must be apocryphal, of a waitress, not realizing whom she was serving, asking Sen and his fellow diners, who were hesitating over their meal selection, 'Don't you people know how to make a decision?').

At the Parfit vote, Sen was outraged that 'some silly idiots thought that it should all depend on how many books you'd written.'[52] 'The great men defended him,' Waldegrave remembered, whilst 'the less distinguished middle-aged scholars who were very proud of their own mediocre publishing lists were the ones who criticised him.'[53] At all events, Parfit's opponents contended that he had a legitimate case to answer. His publishing record did not justify elevation; a Senior Research Fellowship at All Souls was one of the most prestigious positions in British academia, and it was not unreasonable to require published evidence of excellence. At some stage, probably recognizing that they lacked the votes to scupper his application altogether, Parfit's detractors proposed an amendment. This would deny him the Senior Fellowship but grant him an extension of his existing Junior Fellowship for another three years, with an ultimatum that by the end of this period he must have brought out a book. That faced Parfit's supporters with a tricky dilemma. If they opposed the amendment, there was a risk that they would fall short of the two-thirds majority required for his promotion. And that would leave Parfit out of college, out of work, and out of luck.

The amendment received overwhelming backing.

. . .

For Parfit, the outcome was, to put it mildly, 'rather a shock.'[54] A number of people wrote to him to commiserate. Parfit developed a theory about how he had alienated a minority of Fellows. 'I know that I've a small band of enemies, whom I've made because of the moral indignation with which I attacked their view about the admission of Women Fellows, the way I started the great Walk Out before Dessert when we dine in Common Room (five years ago nearly everyone felt constrained to stay; but I decided to get up and go each day, and like the Pied Piper carried most people with me. So Bryan Wilson thinks I've changed the College from a College to a Faculty Club or even Family Hotel).'[55]

One of his correspondents, the philosopher of law Marshall Cohen, excoriated the All Souls Fellows for being 'stupid or treacherous'.[56] But an emollient Parfit imagined how the decision might seem reasonable from the perspective of other Fellows. They may have thought that '[i]f we give him a three-year renewal, while he finds a job elsewhere, he will have had 17 years. That is more than anyone, however good, should be given. We would spend our resources both more equitably, and in a way that would promote research more, if we gave a larger number of shorter Fellowships to more people.'[57] In fact, Parfit believed such an approach would make perfect sense. However, since no such scheme had been adopted, he decided that he would do what he'd effectively been ordered to do—publish and reapply in 1984.

Moreover, because he was sympathetic to those who were risk-averse and had backed the amendment, he claimed not to 'nurture any resentment'.[58] Isaiah Berlin was mortified by the result—particularly because he had failed to produce his promised supportive note. Parfit tried to assuage his guilt, but Berlin was still ruminating about it several months later when, in a letter to Bernard Williams, he referred to 'the so unjustly persecuted Parfitt [sic]'.[59] Later, in conversations with his biographer, Berlin recounted the whole episode, calling it, 'the famous Parfit scandal'.[60]

. . .

Did Parfit really not nurture resentment? The question justifies a short digression on an intriguing aspect of Parfit's psychological make-up. Most of us have what philosophers call retributive instincts. That is, if a person, let's call him Bryan, commits a bad act, then we believe that it's right that Bryan faces sanction or is punished in some way, even if this only involves a mild ticking off. Typically, the idea that Bryan 'deserves' punishment is conditional upon his having committed the bad act freely. If he had to do it under duress, perhaps because somebody was holding a gun to his temple, it seems inappropriate to blame or punish him for it. But such cases notwithstanding, there are times when punishment, proportional to the crime or bad act, seems right and proper.

Yet Parfit found it obscene to suppose that we could have a moral reason to cause a person to suffer for no good effect. Philosophers routinely grapple with issues at an intellectual level without feeling any emotional attachment to either side of an argument. This was not the case with Parfit's loathing of retribution. 'He was very emphatic about this,' says the philosopher Nick Bostrom. 'The passion, the intensity is what surprised me.'[61] When his close friend Shelly Kagan wrote a book on moral desert, Parfit would not consider its inclusion in a series he was editing, on the grounds that he did not believe in moral desert. Another young student asked Parfit to read an article he had written on the implications for moral desert of brain fission—of the type Parfit had discussed in his writings on personal identity. If a person committed a bad act, and then their stream of consciousness was split in two, what were the implications for how punishment should be meted out? A fascinating question; but Parfit refused even to look at the article because, in his view, punishment purely for retribution was always unwarranted. A discussion about desert outside Jeff McMahan's New Jersey house, with some stellar philosophers, ended with Parfit saying, 'I would die happy if I could convince the five of you not to believe in desert.'[62]

This attitude to pain and punishment can be traced back to his childhood. Recall that Parfit said he abandoned his religious faith aged eight, when he discovered that the Christian God punished sinners. He found it impossible to suppose that a good God would send people to hell.

Even when people behaved badly towards him, he appears genuinely to have had no retributive urges. He could not summon up blame or resentment. Jonathan Glover recalled one episode when he and Parfit were discussing what to do about dangers produced by scientific developments or breakthroughs. Parfit came up with the idea of an organization of scientists who could warn about the risks. They wrote a paper together, along with a lawyer, who submitted it to the journal *Nature*. Glover was infuriated to discover that his and Parfit's names had been removed from its authorship. But Parfit took it calmly. What was important, he said, was that the article was published.

The most extreme—indeed shocking—example of Parfit's instincts on desert concerns a film about Adolf Hitler. Just as Parfit believed that the world could in no way be better if someone was unhappy, or made to suffer, so he also believed the converse—that every bit of happiness should be welcomed. All other things being equal, it was better that a person be happy—even a person who had committed bad acts—than that they be unhappy. He once saw footage of Hitler performing a little jig, celebrating the French surrender to Germany in June 1940. (In fact, though Parfit didn't know this, the film had been doctored, and was an early example of 'fake news'.) What was Parfit's reaction to Hitler's jig? 'At least something good came out of the German victory.'[63]

Parfit was sufficiently self-aware to recognize that such a response was atypical. He sometimes endeavoured to self-ignite the full range of reactive attitudes experienced by ordinary people. In 1991, during Operation Desert Storm, the US-led air attack on Iraq following the Iraqi invasion of Kuwait, Parfit tried to build up feelings of hostility for the Iraqi leader Saddam Hussein—feelings that were being given full expression by the media and by others around him. He read all the horrific details about the gassing of thousands of Iraqi Kurds in 1988. But, try as he might, he could not summon up any hatred.

One student recalled a meal with Parfit in Harvard at a Chinese restaurant. 'He was making a point that I'd hear him make many times—how no one deserves to suffer. He spoke about this with such depth of emotion that it shook me. I remember looking at the tears in his eyes as I sat eating my Chinese food and thinking that nothing I worked on had ever moved me to tears.'[64]

As an All Souls colleague pointed out, there was a 'chilling' counterpart to Parfit's claim about punishment. For if nobody deserved punishment for bad acts, nobody deserved praise for good ones. Equally, it followed that 'one cannot properly feel gratitude to anyone for anything. One can go through the outward expressions of gratitude; one can say one's thank-yous, but one cannot mean them.'[65]

. . .

Parfit had been told that the Warden was upset by the outcome of the college meeting. On 22 June 1981, he and Neill met and had a long and awkward conversation. The Warden had an unwelcome suggestion. Parfit should drop all his other activities for the next three years and work flat out to produce a substantial book. Neill acknowledged that this would involve big sacrifices, but making these sacrifices would strengthen Parfit's position in three years' time; it would be hard then, he argued, for the college to deny him the right to reapply.

Taking the advice would mean letting Princeton down, just three months before Parfit was due to teach there. But, given what was at stake, he felt that he had no choice, and wrote to Princeton to inform them. His decision must have caused considerable inconvenience, forcing the philosophy faculty to scramble to put in place alternative arrangements. Nevertheless, Tim Scanlon sent him a remarkably supportive note. Parfit's decision was clearly best in the light of the All Souls's 'foolish decision'; when his book eventually emerged, it would be 'splendid'. Scanlon would 'fight like mad' for Parfit to visit in 1984–85 instead.[66]

However, Parfit's prospects were uncertain. All Souls had been home since 1967, but he now contemplated being rebuffed in 1984. He had been slapped down once; it was conceivable that he would be slapped down again. 'Perhaps I must then leave Air Strip One for good.'[67]

Hurt and upset though Parfit was, the All Souls snub in 1981 was the best thing that ever happened to him.

11

Work, Work, Work, and Janet

Parfit was not obliged to produce all three of the books he had outlined
in his Fellowship application; the demand was 'merely' that he produce
at least one. His approach was to corral his many disparate ideas into a
single manuscript. This would include his material about rationality,
personal identity, and future people. He would call it *Reasons and Persons*.
There were many sceptics who believed that no book of any title
would ever appear. For several years, he had been promising a book, and
had always found reasons to defer publication. Nothing could be published
unless it were perfect, and perfection was always just beyond the
horizon. But now he had no time to wait.

He contacted OUP. The sixty thousand word *Against Prudence* would
be ditched, he explained, and folded into a far longer tome. Adam
Hodgkin agreed and promised to keep the price of the book down.

There were three All Souls Stated General Meetings (SGMs) a year,
one a term. Parfit's first opportunity to reapply for the Senior Research
Fellowship would be March 1984, so the book needed to appear, or be
about to appear, a month or two earlier. Normally, a publisher requires
a year to shepherd a manuscript from delivery through the process of
editing, copyediting, proofreading, typesetting, cover design, and printing.
Working backwards, Parfit calculated that he only had about twenty
months to turn the book in.

In the history of philosophy, there have been some heroic efforts to
hit deadlines. The philosopher Karl Popper nearly killed himself producing
The Open Society and Its Enemies during World War II—he called

it his 'war effort'. Parfit's book—like Popper's—would occupy almost every waking hour of almost every day.

It was the most stressful period of his career and accelerated a grow-ing retreat from the non-philosophical world. Of course, there were humdrum non-philosophical activities essential for health and survival. But Parfit would accommodate these by minimizing the time and effort expended on them, or by running them in parallel with philosophy. He began to develop some distinctive habits. In tooth-brushing, for exam-ple: teeth had to be cleaned, but that was no reason for philosophy to stop. Parfit was an enthusiastic and comprehensive tooth-brusher; no incisor, canine, or molar was neglected. Tooth-brushing took up more of his time than eating. He would buy toothbrushes in bulk with a brush attrition rate of roughly three per week. And during one tooth-brushing session he could read fifty pages.

Likewise, staying fit. The exercise bike was philosophy-compliant; it was perfectly possible to combine cycling and reading. Sometimes he would brush his teeth while cycling. Clothes, food, and drink were more problematic, but Parfit devoted as little time to them as possible. He wore the same outfit every day—grey suit, white shirt, red tie—so that there was no time-wasting and energy-sapping decision to be made each morning. He drank coffee, but boiling a kettle became an unnecessary luxury; so he would throw a dollop of instant coffee into a mug, and fill it with hot water from the tap. Sometimes, cold water would do. The caffeine was what mattered. He would run to appointments. Food was a pitstop; he would rush down to the Buttery to fuel up and be quickly back in his rooms. He once finished off what was left of the communal fruit salad, helping himself to a large portion and explaining to the per-son next in line that it was reasonable and rational that he, Parfit, should have it all, because it was his first meal of the day. 'Would I have gone into the jungle with Derek?', asks Richard Jenkyns. 'No, I would not. He would have found a morally and logically compelling reason why the jaguar should eat me rather than him. The loss to philosophy if he were the one consumed would be unthinkable.'[1]

Parfit told Hare (in the latter's capacity as chairman of the Philosophy Panel) that, with time being so precious, he could not supervise anybody until his 'substantial' book was produced. It had to be substantial, he explained, 'because length is regarded by many Fellows here as of considerable importance.'[2] When he informed Hare that he also had to bank a few more hours by forgoing a weekly discussion group, the White's Professor replied, 'I am not sure that you are right, from the point of view of your future, to turn yourself into a recluse.'[3]

Although he cancelled his Princeton teaching trip in 1981, Parfit fulfilled his obligation to travel to Boulder for six weeks over spring 1982. The Falkland Islands (or Malvinas) were invaded by Argentine forces in April 1982, and Margaret Thatcher's decision to send a task force to recapture them transformed her popularity in the polls. Parfit's host, Dale Jamieson, recalled Parfit's vigorous support for the British war effort. 'I was shocked by how nationalist he was!'[4] This is incongruous: Parfit did not reveal any strong patriotic impulses at any other time, and he was certainly anti-imperialist. He was, however, thoroughly culturally British—and perhaps this had a subconscious influence. There were, of course, solid arguments for objecting to Argentine aggression and not wanting the Falkland Island inhabitants to come under the rule of a brutal military junta.

Debate with other philosophers was not entirely a proscribed activity, since it was useful to stimulate his own ideas and, once back in Oxford, Parfit did attend a few seminars and discussion groups. There were lots to choose from, including one in All Souls on moral, political, and legal philosophy. Small invitation-only discussion groups had always flourished in Oxford; the philosophy faculty is so large and unwieldy that like-minded philosophers have tended to form breakaway circles, sometimes centred around a particular subdiscipline, such as aesthetics, the philosophy of mind, or the philosophy of mathematics.

For many years, the most elite of these gatherings was the so-called Tuesday Group, originally set up by Freddie Ayer in 1960. It met, as one might expect from specialists in conceptual precision, on Tuesdays, from 5 to 7 p.m. to be exact, and the format was a paper, then a break, followed by discussion. Members took turns to host, which could be expensive. Half-time drinks were expected—decent wine, vermouth, and whisky. The older members drank gin and tonics.

It was arguably one of the strongest discussion groups in the history of Western philosophy. When Parfit joined (in either 1968 or 1969), and for many years after, it was dominated by the illuminati Ayer, Michael Dummett, Philippa Foot, David Pears, Peter Strawson, and (at a later stage) Bernard Williams, all born before 1930. Ayer, Williams, Strawson, and Dummett were all knighted, and the latter two reminisced in one meeting about the investiture process, both of them struck by the shortness of the royal sword.

Slightly younger were Dworkin, who developed a habit of always asking the first question, and David Wiggins, who remained surprisingly quiet, until he would interject with a killer objection. Younger still, and in Parfit's age cohort, were John McDowell, Simon Blackburn, and Gareth Evans, all active members at varying times. If a star was in town—such as Thomas Nagel, Donald Davidson, the philosopher of mind Jerry Fodor, or the logician Saul Kripke—they too would be invited along. Kripke caused confusion by requesting a half-time cocktail, a Harvey Wallbanger, unfamiliar to that term's host, Paul Snowdon. The following week, when Snowdon had gone to the trouble to assemble the ingredients—vodka, orange juice, Galliano, and cherry for garnish—the logician ordered a dry sherry.

For most meetings, for many years, the room was full of smoke. The smoking only ceased when one member got cancer—and a smoking interval was introduced, during which the non-smokers who remained in the room were banned from talking philosophy. Ayer, Dummett, and Strawson were all heavy smokers. Dummett had a habit of running his fingers through his hair, and he smoked so much that it became tinged yellow.

Within Oxford, the Tuesday Group aimed to recruit the smartest philosophers, with existing members agreeing which new members to invite. Once you were in, you were in for life. (When Jerry Cohen became Chichele Professor of Social and Political Theory in 1985, Hurley, the secretary that term, mistakenly fired off an invitation to L. J. Cohen, of The Queen's College, instead. He became a loyal participant and went to his grave unaware that the honour had been bestowed on him on account of his name, not his talent.)

Younger members found the atmosphere intimidating. Foot spoke a lot and chuckled whenever she regarded an argument as incoherent; Dummett was a bully and lost his temper (Peter Strawson was the only person who could restrain him); Williams wore his disconcertingly sardonic smile. It took Galen Strawson (Peter's son), over a year to pluck up the courage to speak. Once, when he raised a point, Williams scolded him: 'That's such a *boring* objection.'[5] Parfit, in a matter-of-fact way, told Galen Strawson that others in the group had decided, in his absence, that he was not quite first-rate.

There were also clashes and tensions between various members. Dummett was so rude and disdainful about a talk delivered by Colin McGinn on what was called the syntactic theory of mind—the idea that our thoughts are empty symbols without content—that McGinn determined never to return. Williams and Stuart Hampshire had a heated exchange over whether and how one could justify entering a burning building to save an animal. Williams and Foot constantly goaded one another. The atmosphere, says one member, 'was often one of deep self-satisfaction'.[6] But others report that the older members, such as Foot, could be intellectually supportive. Hanna Pickard was one of a handful of women in the group, becoming a member when she was twenty-five years old. She joined in with the drinking, in part to still her nerves. 'I experienced the old guard's drinking together as reflecting an attitude towards doing philosophy that was very serious but also involved having a lot of fun. There was a joy in philosophical conversation that seemed to come very naturally to them and that has always stuck with me as part of what we should want from academic life.'[7]

In the end, the Tuesday Group ossified, with many of the youngest members, such as John Campbell, Bill Child, Quassim Cassam, Adrian Moore, and Tim Williamson, preferring separate gatherings with more intellectual spark and less booze. But Parfit, who was indifferent to hierarchical structures and status, remained a regular attendee throughout the 1980s and 90s. He had, from the beginning, struck Freddie Ayer as 'a very clever man',[8] but several members were hostile to his approach to moral philosophy as well as to his views on personal identity, and so he sometimes found himself under concerted attack.

The Tuesday Group was organized informally. But Parfit also participated in a formal series of seminars, primarily aimed at postgraduate philosophy students. This was his own brainchild, but he recruited two heavyweight co-panellists, both roughly a decade older than himself, Dworkin and Sen. Neither Dworkin, Parfit, nor Sen was trained in philosophy: Dworkin was a lawyer, Sen an economist.

The weekly Parfit-Dworkin-Sen seminars had begun at 5 p.m. on the first Wednesday of the 1979 Trinity (summer) term. The location was the rectangular wood-panelled Old Library at All Souls College, with its green baize-covered tables. Each week, the three men would take turns to open a discussion—but with some rough remarks, rather than a formal, read-out paper. They all had impressive argumentative energy, word quickly spread, and the seminars became postgraduates' favourite. They repeated the formula (moving to St Cross College) in the Hilary terms of 1980 and 1981, with the titles, respectively, of 'Preference, Welfare, and Responsibility' and 'Preference, Welfare, and Value.'

For Parfit, however, life was now mostly devoted to the gestating book. And as it grew in size, there developed the nagging thought that he was at real risk of missing his deadline. So, he came up with an ingenious, if unorthodox, idea. It dawned on him that if he dribbled in the manuscript, chapter by chapter, OUP could be carrying on with the production process—including copyediting—whilst he continued to work on the later chapters, buying him precious extra days and weeks. The book could still be revealed to the world in January 1984, as planned.

Meanwhile, he was sending off draft after draft to scores of philosophers in the UK and around the world, requesting feedback. In those pre-email days, that necessitated having to spend hours in the college office, photocopying piles of paper and then mailing them out. One of the secretaries, Humaira Erfan-Ahmed, helped him out. 'He was gentle and humble, not at all patronizing. There was no sense of a hierarchy as there often is with other Fellows. He photocopied a lot himself, but he would ask me too. We got through several forests.'[9] The process clogged up the office and irked other Fellows. One Fellow, noticing how many American tourists there were in Oxford that summer, commented wryly that they were probably dodging the draft.[10]

Comments began pouring back—the most extensive from Shelly Kagan, credited by Parfit in his acknowledgements as 'the person from whom I have learnt the most.'[11] Kagan had originally wanted to become a rabbi, a plan that was thwarted when the seminary rejected his application. Instead, he turned to philosophy, and met Parfit while a postgraduate at Princeton. The young (mid-twenties) philosopher had recently begun to teach at the University of Pittsburgh when Parfit sent him part of what would become *Reasons and Persons*. Kagan mailed back a few comments and, two weeks later, the phone rang. These had been much appreciated. Would he read the rest of the manuscript, Parfit wanted to know. 'I was flattered but I demurred. I said, "I don't have much time, because I'm hoping to turn my dissertation into a book." So he made me an offer I couldn't refuse. "If you give me comments on the rest of my manuscript, I'll give you comments on yours." Now, I knew a good offer when I heard one!'[12]

Kagan mailed off a hundred pages of single-spaced comments. Parfit felt obliged to respond to the points made by Kagan and many others, and worked manically on revising the text, keeping himself going with a cocktail of (legal) drugs. This went on day after day, seven days a week. John Broome spent a year as a Fellow of All Souls as the final deadline approached: 'This was crazy behaviour,' he recalls.[13] Broome was a trained economist who switched to philosophy, in large part under Parfit's influence. In those final few months of the book's maturation, Parfit would turn up at Broome's All Souls flat asking him to read a chapter, before delivering it to the publisher the next morning.

Truth be told, this process did not always improve the text. The early versions of *Reasons and Persons* were more streamlined than the published book. The forest was being lost among the trees, and trees would be unnecessarily sacrificed for the ever-expanding manuscript; Parfit was dealing with objections that were not fundamental and need not have detained him. The arguments in the early versions were those he had ruminated over for years. As the deadline approached, he was introducing ideas that he had reflected upon for barely thirty minutes. Understandably, this made him feel insecure, and he became dependent on a few close confidants to double-check every sentence. In fact, some key editorial decisions were taken by others, and a page and a half of Appendix H was written entirely by Broome; he is credited in a byline.

Parfit's personal papers contain evidence of the scramble to the finish line. The arrival of individual chapters was acknowledged by OUP. And the publisher maintained the pressure for more. In a representative note, on 16 August 1983 Parfit's OUP editor wrote, 'I return your printout of Chapter 11 read "by eye" for literals. We shall expect five more chapters by Monday 22nd at the latest.'[14]

Helping him with the bibliography and checking references were philosophy doctoral student Jeff McMahan and his then wife, Sally. McMahan's thesis was on population ethics, and although he was officially supervised by Bernard Williams, in practice he was learning far more from Parfit, who was reading and commenting on all his work. McMahan had arrived in the UK as an American Rhodes Scholar; Oxford was far from his roots in rural South Carolina. Like most boys where he was raised, he had been a keen hunter; his father owned several guns and was a Republican Party activist who wanted his son to become 'a young athlete who would go into the military. What he got instead was a weedy hippie.'[15] McMahan Senior was unimpressed when a teenage Jeff announced, after seeing a shot and wounded dove, that he was turning vegetarian.

Despite support from the McMahans, by the final week of his final deadline, Parfit was on the brink of a breakdown. He was up all night every night, before seeking some pill- and alcohol-induced rest. On the penultimate day, he rang two friends, Susan Hurley and Bill Ewald. He had finished a draft of the conclusion, but his brain could no longer process the text. 'The words are swimming on the page,' he said. 'I've got to sleep.'[16] He asked them to proofread the last chapter—and to ensure it reached OUP before the deadline.

The opening sentence of the short concluding chapter was arresting. 'When he was asked about his book, Sidgwick said that its first word was *Ethics*, and its last *failure*.'[17] The chapter Ewald and Hurley received from Parfit ended with a quotation from Nietzsche:

At last the horizon appears free to us again, even granted that it is not bright; at last our ships may venture out again, venture out to face any danger; all the daring of the lover of knowledge is permitted again; the sea, *our sea*, lies open again; perhaps there has never yet been such an 'open sea.'[18]

After both Hurley and Ewald had read the chapter, they held a consultation. Hurley thought it could be improved upon in many places. 'The sentences are too staccato, they're marching in fascist lock-step,'[19] she opined. Both Hurley and Ewald agreed that they could smooth out some sentence transitions. Then they reached the denouement. Above the Nietzsche quotation was a rather insipid paragraph, preceded by one that concluded as follows:

> Belief in God, or in many Gods, prevented the free development of moral reasoning. Disbelief in God, openly admitted by a majority, is a very recent event, not yet completed. Because this event is so recent, Non-Religious Ethics is at a very early stage. We cannot yet predict whether, as in Mathematics, we will all reach agreement. Since we cannot know how Ethics will develop, it is not irrational to have high hopes.[20]

Ewald had a neat idea. This seemed like the perfect end. Sidgwick's book had closed with the word 'failure', so why not complete Parfit's book with 'hope'? It was a clever contrast. Parfit was fast asleep and could not be roused—he had disappeared for twenty-four hours—so his two friends took a bold and unilateral decision. They ditched the dull paragraph that followed this one and moved the Nietzsche quotation to an epigraph at the front.

By the time Parfit emerged the following midday, Ewald had already walked to OUP with the floppy disk containing the last chapter. Ewald explained what he had done over the phone. There was a long—and nerve-racking—pause.

Then Parfit agreed that they had made an improvement.

. . .

In fact, the Nietzsche epigraph had itself been an afterthought. The quotation encapsulates poetically Parfit's enthusiasm for a fresh secular morality. Parfit once summed up the entire history of ethics in four neat steps:

1. Forbidden by God.
2. Forbidden by God, therefore wrong.
3. Wrong, therefore forbidden by God.
4. Wrong.

We were, he believed, in the fourth phase. *Reasons and Persons* would apply reason and logic to ethics without the distorting influence of God. Parfit would often repeat the point that secular ethics was a toddler taking its first stumbling steps. As a former school chess player, he liked to compare the study of ethics with the research on chess openings. He complained that far more attention had been devoted to a single opening move by black (c5 in response to e4; that is, the Sicilian Defence) than to the fundamental questions about morality. But now we had an exciting opportunity, he thought. Once we had unshackled ourselves from the chains of religion, we could reflect on moral issues anew, bringing logic and rationality to issues that had hitherto been resolved by superstition. Nietzsche's open sea image strikingly mirrors Parfit's ethical optimism.

Except that's not why it's there. Parfit had an independent motive for using the quotation, which was only tangentially to do with its philosophical meaning. He had set his heart on a particular cover photograph— one he himself shot in Venice. It shows a misty lagoon, a modern boat emerging from the right, and in the background the shadowed form of San Giorgio Maggiore—an old island monastery that had captured the imagination of Monet, too (who made a series of paintings from almost the very spot where Parfit took his photo). It's undoubtedly an exquisite photograph, but what does it have to do with reasons, or, for that matter, persons? Well, not much. The Nietzsche quotation about the open sea provided a rationale for the cover picture.

. . .

The chapter-by-chapter delivery was a Parfitian publishing innovation; novel too, at least for OUP, was the process by which the book was typeset. Parfit was an evangelist for, but no expert in, the emerging computer technology, and he wanted—and insistently requested—that the book be typeset straight from his word-processing files. That was no easy task in the early 1980s; it was fiddly and time-consuming, and in the end required hours and hours of overtime to be put in by Catherine Griffin (the wife of philosopher Jim Griffin), who was employed at the Oxford University Computing Service. The programme they had for converting text to type was rudimentary and, for example, did not allow for words at the ends of lines to be split with a hyphen.

The cover itself involved a lot of back-and-forth negotiations. Parfit discovered that while most books had a four-colour printing technique (using cyan, magenta, yellow, and black), some of the fanciest art books used six colours (with the addition of orange and green). Could they not print his cover with six colours? They managed to deflect this request and also conveniently overlooked his proposal that he go to the printers as the covers were emerging, to check they had it right.

But then came a new and disastrous headache for OUP, having to do with Nagel's Brain. 'Nagel's Brain' was the title of Appendix D, which was a response to some unpublished writings in which Thomas Nagel argued that he, Nagel, essentially consisted of his brain. Ironically, given Parfit's split-brain cases, 'Nagel's Brain' had been cut in two, with one half of this section being inadvertently omitted. Such mistakes were virtually inevitable, given Parfit's drip-feed manuscript delivery. The OUP solution was to plonk the second half of Appendix D after the index and to include an erratum slip in each copy of the book. So instead of flowing on from page 471, 'Nagel's Brain' would resume on page 538.

Parfit had an alternative solution, which occurred to him after a conversation with the Warden of All Souls. Patrick Neill had been approached by Isaiah Berlin who, without consulting Parfit, had suggested that Parfit's promotion be considered in June, not March, 1984. Perhaps Berlin wanted the book to be published in good time for All Souls Fellows to have a chance to read it. In any case, the Warden believed it to be a sensible proposal, and put it to Parfit, who agreed.

By late October 1983, three thousand copies of *Reasons and Persons* had been printed and were ready to be transported to bookshops. But

Parfit thought that, since the crucial All Souls meeting had been delayed by three months, OUP should take more time. How about they reprint the book, with 'Nagel's Brain' intact? It would require altering page numbers on the Contents page, and while they were at it, they might as well take the opportunity to rectify a few more mistakes he had spotted. . . . If they were worried about the cost, well he, Parfit, would gladly bear it himself. In a rare moment of self-awareness, Parfit wrote to Adam Hodgkin, 'I have caused you and Angela[21] so much trouble already that, despite your generous denials, you must be fed up, and wish you could simply now forget this blasted book.' But, because of the new, more generous timetable, they 'COULD forget this blasted book at least for a fortnight.'[22]

As usual, Parfit prevailed. They knew he could be infinitely patient in his stubbornness. Three thousand books were pulped. Nevertheless, many errors remained. First editions of the hardback version of *Reasons and Persons* are rare, but if you get your hands on a copy and examine it closely, you'll notice some publishing idiosyncrasies. For example, footnote 15 has something in common with Santa Claus: neither exists. And the same goes for footnotes 26, 45, 49, 50, 51, and 52 of Part I, footnotes 30, 60, 67, 96, and 104 of Part III, and footnotes 4, 12, 29, 43, 47, 48, and 52 of Part IV. Parfit had removed some of the footnotes at the last minute, and the system did not update automatically. Reviewers of the book, it had to be hoped, would either not notice, or not care.

. . .

In the two years before submitting *Reasons and Persons*, there were few departures from book writing. Yet there was still time for Parfit to start first one relationship, and then a second. Both were with philosophers. The first fizzled out within a year or so. The second persisted a lifetime.

Academically, Susan Hurley, the woman who broke into the monastic male world of All Souls, resisted any pigeonholing. She had trained in law as well as philosophy, and her first book was about how humans choose to act when they're pulled by conflicting values. But she later became better known in the field of philosophy of mind. She was inspired by Wittgenstein, but unlike the type of philosopher who thought conclusions could be reached a priori, without rising from the comfort of the armchair, she drew on empirical findings in cognitive neuroscience and kept abreast of research in the social sciences.

The view she propounded is now regarded as less outlandish than it seemed when she proposed it. She thought that it was arbitrary to insist that the skull was the perimeter of the mind. She rejected what has been called the 'sandwich model' of the mind, by which 'perception' acts as input into the mind, with 'action' being output from the mind to the world, and 'thought' being the filling in the middle. She was particularly interested in the discovery of 'mirror neurons'. If a monkey performs an action—for example, ripping a piece of paper—certain neurons will fire. These same neurons will be fired in the brain of another monkey who's merely watching this behaviour. This occurs directly, without any complex perception–thought–action sequence. Humans, argued Hurley, had to be understood as embodied creatures existing in a physical and social world. Parfit was not a philosopher of mind, but this was an outlook with which he would have felt instinctive sympathy.

Hurley had a striking impact on All Souls and its culture. Paul Seabright was at the meeting that elected her. 'There is no delicate way to put this: [. . .] Susan was a visual as well as an intellectual phenomenon, an issue about which a bunch of largely boarding-school educated men even as late as the 1980s found it difficult to take an uncomplicated view.'[23] She was not only beautiful, but had a unique style of dress. She had a penchant for vivid, vibrant colours—gold and orange, turquoise and cyan. The word 'exotic' comes up frequently at mention of her name. She died in her fifties, of cancer, by which time she was happily married and with two children. At her memorial she was described as appearing 'to others like a bird of paradise blown by some freak of the weather to live among the sparrows of an English garden.'[24]

Her relationship with Parfit was passionate, but short-lived. Its prospects were never promising. Parfit, of course, was far from being an uncomplicated long-term romantic prospect, while Hurley suffered, in her twenties and thirties, from bouts of depression. The issue of children came up; Parfit was not keen, and this was a cause of irreconcilable tension. In a happy moment, Hurley snapped a photograph of Parfit, handsome, smiling, with thick, flowing hair, wearing a casual shirt and holding his jacket nonchalantly over his right shoulder. It's the cover image of this book and the image that is often used to accompany articles about him. Many of those who knew him later can barely recognize the Parfit captured in it—he seems so carefree and relaxed.

. . .

In 1983, after one of the Parfit-Dworkin-Sen seminars, Parfit saw Amartya Sen talking to a tall and beautiful dark-haired woman. After she left, he went up to Sen: 'Who was that?' 'She's a philosopher,' Sen explained. Sen knew her through her striking ex-partner, a towering and fierce Canadian-born philosopher, Ted Honderich, with whom she had lived in London and from whom she had moved to Oxford to escape. Her name, Sen told Parfit, was Janet Radcliffe Richards. During the course of this short conversation, Sen gave Parfit her phone number; and 'the next thing I knew, they were a couple'.[25]

In fact, the 'courting' process had been protracted and decidedly strange and, although competition was something he tended to relish, it did not occur to Parfit that he might be in rivalry with other men. His first step, which she later described as a sort of audition for herself, was to purchase a copy of Radcliffe Richards's book *The Sceptical Feminist*.

This had been published just three years earlier and had caused a stir, in part because it irritated everyone. The chauvinists objected to its feminism, and the feminists objected to its scepticism. It was banned in at least one feminist bookshop. Radcliffe Richards claimed that many traditional feminist arguments were sloppy or illogical. At the same time, she exposed some of the risible arguments that men have often used to justify their positions of power and privilege.

She considers a rule such as 'Women should be barred from driving buses'. That might strike most people as ludicrous today, but the issue felt much more urgent in the 1970s: women could not drive buses for London Transport before 1974. What's wrong with this rule? It can't be merely that it implies different treatment for men and women. After all, in a labour market distinctions are inevitable. Alcoholics are not allowed to become pilots, but it would be foolish to conclude that alcoholics are thereby victims of discrimination. What is wrong, Radcliffe Richards argues, is that the rule cannot be justified, even in terms of the general standards set by those who propose the policy. Most of these people profess to believe in a meritocracy, and this moral standard is not consistent with the arbitrary disadvantaging of one group.

The point was inspired by John Stuart Mill. If Parfit's favourite philosopher was Sidgwick, Radcliffe Richards's go-to utilitarian was his predecessor, Mill. Often those proposing a rule such as the one prohibiting female bus drivers will insist that women aren't good enough drivers to be permitted behind the wheel. But as Mill wrote, 'what women by nature cannot do it is quite superfluous to forbid them from doing'.[26] In a genuine meritocracy, in other words, if all women were really hopeless at driving buses, neutral criteria would ensure that they wouldn't be employed—it would be unnecessary to have an additional rule categorically excluding them. Irritating many feminists, Radcliffe Richards argued that one could condemn a law keeping women out without needing to attack the conservative premise that women were mentally and physically inferior to men.

Like Mill, Radcliffe Richards argued that, since women's roles and passions have been so shaped by oppressive rules and expectations, we can have no real idea of what women are capable of doing, or whether men and women might on average have different dispositions or 'natures'. Indeed, far from ruling out the notion that there were group differences between men and women beyond the anatomical, Radcliffe Richards would later accept the evolutionary case for recognizing that these were inevitable. But the truth about 'natural differences' would only emerge when women had genuinely equal opportunities to pursue their freely chosen goals.

The book met with Parfit's approval: Radcliffe Richards had passed the main audition. Later he explained that he'd been impressed by her Houdini-esque ability to extricate herself, time after time, from traditional arguments put by standard feminism. In any case, after finishing the book, he wrote to her with what she describes as '[t]he most remarkable chat-up letter in history', written with some capitalised words and in such formal language that it was impossible to make out his intentions.[27] A day or two later he phoned to invite her to his All Souls philosophy seminar, to be followed by dinner.

At the seminar, he was extremely cool, but grew friendlier over dinner, during which, when she complained about having trouble sleeping, he tried to encourage her to adopt his pill regime. In his rooms after dinner, he suggested she rent an old desktop computer that he had bought from Ronnie Dworkin. She did take it, though the subject of payment was never raised again. (Later, he told her that the renting proposal was so that she didn't feel under any obligation.) He then switched off the lights to listen to music.

Over the next few months, the normal signals of a wooing campaign were entirely absent. There were neither flowers nor chocolates. He phoned a couple of times to tell her when there was a good concert on BBC Radio 3. He invited her to his rooms to listen to music. He would 'put his arm around me, but nothing happened'.[28] The only things he sent in her direction were the complete keyboard scores of Bach. Clearly something was going on, but what? Radcliffe Richards wondered whether he might propose before he even kissed her. Then, the Dworkin computer broke down. 'It was an indication of the strangeness of what was going on that when Derek suggested he come round at midnight to deal with the computer, I thought he meant it.'[29] He didn't.

In their early relationship, Janet was living in Oxford—in Glebe Street, in St Clements, about five minutes' cycle ride from All Souls—but teaching at the Open University. The OU was established in 1969, and remains the most durable legacy of the then Labour prime minister Harold Wilson. Its students study long-distance, many of them are mature students, and, compared to other universities, more students are working-class.[30] Its headquarters are in the new town of Milton Keynes, an hour's drive from Oxford, but the work for teachers largely involves writing courses; teaching staff are only obliged to travel there for meetings.

. . .

Janet's family would have been called at the time 'northern educated'. Her parents came from Liverpool, and her father was an Oxbridge scholar who became a Unitarian minister in Yorkshire. Her mother was a primary school teacher who, like Derek's mother Jessie, eventually specialized in children with special needs. Like Derek, therefore, she had a religious background, and like him too, she had abandoned her faith. She did so later than Derek, as a teenager, not a seven-year-old, because, as she puts it, 'Unitarians do not have hell to contend with.'[31]

There was never any question of fee-paying schools. Unlike with the Parfits, no amount of juggling could stretch the family income that far. They eventually moved to London, and Janet attended a girls' grammar school which, although good, never thought of encouraging its pupils to apply for Oxford or Cambridge. In any case, her father was keen that she attend Keele University, the first of the new UK universities established in the 1960s. It had what was regarded as a radically new approach—four-year degrees, with students living on campus, and all students taking courses in humanities, sciences, and social sciences. It was here that Janet discovered, and became passionate about, philosophy.

After Keele, Janet spent a year in Borneo, working for Voluntary Service Overseas. From there, she moved to Canada (Calgary), for a master's degree, before returning to the UK, and earning an Oxford BPhil. A first and too-early marriage to a clever and extremely nice young man, also from a Unitarian family, did not work out. The subsequent years in London with Ted Honderich were miserable. Honderich had an eclectic range of philosophical interests, including consciousness, free will, and the rationale for political violence. He also had a reputation as a womanizer and carried an aura of menace. He was known for hosting drunken soirees with guests drawn from the intellectual illuminati.

Parfit and Radcliffe Richards shared several interests and tastes, such as music and architecture. They talked, of course, about philosophy, but took a deliberate decision not to be too closely involved in each other's work. They had at least one deep psychological trait in common: perfectionism. Parfit's perfectionism impeded completion of his big task, his book, while Radcliffe Richards was typically trying to deliver on multiple tasks; he called her 'a promiscuous perfectionist'.

At the beginning of their relationship, Parfit would spend his days at All Souls and every night at Glebe Street. He was entering his forties and Janet was in her late thirties. The subjects of children and marriage did not arise—Janet believed there were already too many people in the world. Had they got married at that time, it seems unlikely that it would have had much impact on Parfit's essentially solitary existence. It might indeed have tested to the limit the standard philosophical example of an analytic statement: 'All bachelors are unmarried men.'

12

Moral Mathematics

Imagine going into a local restaurant to discover the menu offered an odd mixture of dishes that are not traditionally combined: pizza, sushi, burgers, curry, plus a hundred little tapas dishes. Reading *Reasons and Persons* is the philosophical equivalent of such a smorgasbord. If the book has an overarching theme, it is that we should be more impartial in our ethics—we should focus less on ourselves, our family, and our own friends, and more on the common good. But that's a loose common thread. The four chunky sections into which the book is divided are in most ways very distinct. It is, nonetheless, a deeply original and richly textured book. Provocative arguments, novel ideas, wild thought experiments leap out of every page.

'Like my cat, I often simply do what I want to do,'[1] begins the introduction. One can see why Parfit believed this to be a strong and arresting start. The book would examine what we have reasons to do, including ethical reasons. Humans differed from cats: we can reflect on our reasons for action. For example, I can decide that some actions are morally wrong, even if they might benefit me. Cats cannot do this (though one study suggests that if cats *were* people they would be psychopaths).[2]

So, a nice, slightly wacky, opening. The only drawback with it was that it was misleading. Parfit did not have a cat. At this stage in his life, a cat would have been as needless a distraction as a child. For a leading moral philosopher to begin a major work of moral philosophy with a half-lie was obviously short of ideal.

It took a visit to his sister Theodora, in Bethesda, Maryland, for the problem to be pointed out. He had presented her with a copy of the book. 'But Derek,' she said, after turning the cover, 'you do *not* own a cat!'[3] A solution lay in a deal struck with her son, who drew up a pseudo-contract regarding their aged black-and-white shorthaired cat, Diamond, so named because of the diamond shape of his fur from his nose to his brow:

> I, C. Alexander Ooms, do hereby declare that Derek A. Parfit is the new owner of Diamond, male, feline, born July 1972. This said feline exhibits some of the characteristics of personhood as you so felicitously acknowledge in the first line of your book, *Reasons and Persons*. A portrait of your cat, Diamond, is enclosed for you to display prominently in your abode thereby maintaining your moral credibility if anyone should inquire: 'I didn't know you owned a cat?!'[4]

In the contract, Tamara, Alex's elder sister, was appointed Diamond's guardian, thus releasing Parfit from any onerous duty of cat care. In exchange for acquiring a pet, he had to agree to visit the Ooms household on every future US trip, a codicil that he singularly failed to honour, technically putting him in breach of contract. Another condition was 'that you make no reference to "my" dog, parrot, or any other animals in future writing [. . .] as we would not be able to help you out of another moral lapse.'[5]

. . .

The first of the four sections in *Reasons and Persons*, and arguably the most challenging, is on what Parfit calls self-defeating theories. Suppose we were all selfish. Like Diamond the cat, we did what we wanted, when we wanted. This could involve a more sophisticated set of self-interested actions than Diamond was capable of. We did not just drink milk when we wanted. We broke promises when it was in our interest to do so. We broke the law when it was in our interest to do so. We betrayed friends when it was in our interest to do so. We sought only our pleasure and our own advantage.

The seventeenth-century English philosopher Thomas Hobbes was the first systematic exponent of self-interest theory; he suggested that the rational policy for each of us was to pursue our own interests. Parfit, like his hero Henry Sidgwick, was struck by the competing claims of egoistic theory, in which we only take *our* wellbeing into account, versus universal theories, such as consequentialism, that take *everyone* into account. He set out to demonstrate that some theories about how we should act—most especially egoism or self-interest (which he shorthands to 'S')—are self-defeating.

There are different ways a theory can be self-defeating. One of Parfit's examples has an autobiographical subtext. It concerns Kate, an imaginary young writer who cares so much about producing good books that she works all hours, even though she believes this will not make her happy; indeed, she eventually collapses with fatigue. If her strongest desire instead was that her life go as well as possible, she would not drive herself to this state of exhaustion. But then she would care less about her writing, and, ultimately, she would feel less fulfilled and find life less meaningful. Parfit must have constantly interrogated himself about how he could justify a life dedicated almost exclusively to philosophy.

Consequentialism, he argues in *Reasons and Persons*, is also indirectly self-defeating. Take utilitarianism, the version of consequentialism that states that one should act so as to produce the most happiness or wellbeing: if in all our decisions we tried to be as utilitarian as possible, the result would be disastrous, even judged by utilitarian standards. There is a child currently suffering in the world more than my child: utilitarianism seems to demand that I neglect my own child to help this more needy child. But a world in which we did not feel special obligations to our own children, and failed to prioritize their wellbeing over the wellbeing of others, would be a miserable, impoverished one. It would not be the best world, even judged on consequentialist criteria. Does that show that consequentialism should be abandoned? No. It merely indicates that consequentialism should endorse and encourage non-consequentialist dispositions—including the disposition to feel a special bond with one's offspring. These commonsense dispositions are justified on consequentialist terms. Consequentialism is therefore only *indirectly* self-defeating.

But there are also moral theories that Parfit calls *directly* self-defeating. A theory is directly self-defeating when we all *succeed* in achieving its aim, and yet doing so results in the aims of each of us being less well achieved than if none of us had successfully followed the theory. This sounds contradictory. Parfit explains what he means by borrowing from basic game theory.

When Parfit was working on *Reasons and Persons*, game theory—the modelling of human behaviour using simple games—was still only a few decades old, and game-theoretical tools were burgeoning in many of the social sciences, most especially in economics. All Souls at this time had a remarkable number of stellar economists—several of whom were also interested in philosophical matters. There was an elderly past Nobel Prize winner, John Hicks, as well as a future one, Amartya Sen. John Broome and Jon Elster were both visiting Fellows at the college. Paul Seabright and John Vickers were young and rising economic stars. So it is not surprising that Parfit absorbed some of the game theory buzz and integrated it into philosophy.

The classic game is the Prisoner's Dilemma, which goes like this. Two prisoners are accused of a crime. If Prisoner A confesses, and Prisoner B does not, Prisoner A will be released while prisoner B will receive twenty years' hard labour. If Prisoner B confesses, while Prisoner A remains silent, the reverse will be the case: B will be released and A will be handed down the lengthy sentence. If they both confess, they will each receive a sentence of ten years. But if neither confesses, the police and courts will have little evidence to go on, and they will only be locked away for five years.

Here's why the result is both peculiar and important: a quick comparison of options shows that whatever A does, the best thing for B to do is confess. Likewise, whatever B does, the best thing for A to do is confess. As a result, both A and B end up confessing, and receive a sentence of ten years each. But had they both remained mum, it would have been better for both. They would only have received five years.

The Prisoner's Dilemma is relevant to many real-life cases. It might be better for each of us to take the car rather than the bus, but if we all drove we would be worse off than if we all took the bus. The game is used by economists to explain why cartels like OPEC are so inherently unstable. If a group of oil producers can co-operate in restricting supply, they will each benefit from pushing the price of oil up. On the other hand, they each have a motive to sell (sneakily) more than their allotted quota. If they all follow this strategy, the price of oil will drop; they will all suffer.

Prisoner's Dilemma cases, Parfit claims, show that self-interest theory can be *directly* self-defeating. If we all successfully achieve what's best for us individually, the result is worse for us. One solution to many coordination problems might be to have a dictator forcing certain actions upon us. This is a Hobbesian solution. Hobbes believed that if we all acted in a state of nature, without society or a government, life would be 'solitary, poor, nasty, brutish, and short'.[6] What is needed is a powerful individual or assembly to enforce cooperative deals. But a less scary solution is for individuals to operate with a degree of basic decency and fairness. If fish stocks are limited, it might be better for each trawler to catch as much fish as possible, but it will be worse for each if everyone does so. If we all cared about the welfare of others, and, for example, did not take more than our share, then that would turn out better for us—as well as for others.

Parfit maintains that the inherent contradictions and inconsistencies of theories of self-interest are more fundamental than they are for other theories about how we should act. But the upshot of his panoply of examples is to nudge consequentialism, commonsense morality, and self-interest theories closer together. In other words, even if I am an egoist, for example, and believe that it is rational for me to pursue my self-interest, and for you to pursue your self-interest, I should still prefer that we all had dispositions to care about others, because that would be better for me than if none of us did.

. . .

The Prisoner's Dilemma is set up as a 'game' with just two people. Many of our moral dilemmas involve multiple people. Parfit offered some fiendish puzzles about what he called moral mathematics. His ambition was to generate a general theory about how we should act that would cover all cases.

One conclusion was that we should think about our acts, not in terms of what they alone achieve, but rather in terms of what they achieve given the acts of others. For example, suppose the lives of a hundred people are in danger. 'These people can be saved if I and three other people join in a rescue mission. If any of us fails to join, all of the hundred people will die. If I fail to join, I could go elsewhere and save, single-handedly, fifty other lives.'[7] Parfit thought it was obvious, in this case, that I should join the rescue mission, though my 'share' of the group contribution is only twenty-five lives, compared to the fifty lives I could save on my own. We should act, Parfit argued, in ways that would benefit people the most overall.

But there are other subtleties that a general principle of action has to cover. It has to fit cases of 'over-determination'. Suppose that 'X tricks me into drinking poison, of a kind that causes a painful death within a few minutes. Before this poison has any effect, Y kills me painlessly.'[8] Assume that Y did not know about X. Surely any acceptable principle has to judge Y to be morally culpable, even though, because of what X did, Y has not harmed me?

Then there are actions that have a minuscule or imperceptible impact. At a fairly trivial level, the All Souls sign 'Do not walk on the grass' may exist to stop damage to the quad lawn. But, if I am the only person to ignore this injunction, the lawn would remain, at least to the naked eye, pristine. Numerous decisions have a similar structure. I might believe that it is environmentally irrelevant whether or not I conserve energy in my household. Failure to turn off lights in my house will not accelerate global warming to any discernible degree.

Yet Parfit argues that such reasoning is flawed. Consider his 'harmless torturers', who resemble the baked-bean bandits we came across in chapter 7. Suppose a thousand torturers have a thousand victims. At the start of each day, each of the victims is already feeling mild pain. Each of the torturers turns a switch a thousand times on some instrument. Each turning of a switch affects some victim's pain in a way that is imperceptible. But, after each torturer has turned his switch a thousand times, he has inflicted severe pain on his single victim.[9]

Few would disagree that each torturer has acted wrongly, although no individual act of switch-turning made any perceptible difference. We might want to say that each torturer has acted wrongly because each torturer's acts, taken together, inflict severe pain on their victim. But now suppose that each of the thousand torturers presses a button, thereby turning the switch once on each of the thousand instruments. The victims suffer the same severe pain in the end. But none of the torturers makes any victim's pain perceptibly worse.[10]

If we continue to insist that there can be no imperceptible harms, then the 'harmless torturers' can have harmed nobody. This is plainly absurd. Parfit uses these cases to suggest that there *can* be imperceptible harms and benefits. You can do something wrong, even if the wrongness is not felt. It is wrong to pollute, even if one's contribution to overall pollution is negligible or imperceptible. This is a conclusion that clearly matters.

· · ·

Part II of *Reasons and Persons* is about our reasons for actions—an issue that Parfit puzzled over throughout his life. He drew a distinction between three approaches. 'P' was the theory that we only have reason to do what satisfies our current goals and desires. What I want *now* is what I have most reason to do. Then there's 'morality', the view that I have reason to do what will be best for everyone affected by my actions overall. And then there's 'S', which is the theory that I have reason to do what is best for me overall (not just what is best for me now, but what is best for my life considered as a whole). The argument is complex, but what Parfit shows is that S is caught in a pincer movement; it can defend itself against P, but only in a way that means it is defeated by morality.

Part II is also where Parfit discusses time. Should we care about yesterday as much as we care about tomorrow? Through some ingenious thought experiments, he suggests that our attitude to time is irrational. Imagine you are in hospital. Given the choice between a very painful operation and a less painful operation that has the same chance of success, obviously you will choose the less painful. But what if the operations are at different times?

> I am in some hospital, to have some kind of surgery. This kind of surgery is completely safe, and always successful. Since I know this, I have no fears about the effects. The surgery may be brief, or it may instead take a long time. Because I have to co-operate with the surgeon, I cannot have anaesthetics. I have had this surgery once before, and I can remember how painful it is. Under a new policy, because the operation is so painful, patients are now afterwards made to forget it. Some drug removes their memories of the last few hours.
>
> I have just woken up. I cannot remember going to sleep. I ask my nurse if it has been decided when my operation is to be, and how long it must take. She says that she knows the facts about both me and another patient, but that she cannot remember which facts apply to whom. She can tell me only that the following is true. I may be the patient who had his operation yesterday. In that case, my operation was the longest ever performed, lasting ten hours. I may instead be the patient who is to have a short operation later today. It is either true that I did suffer for ten hours, or true that I shall suffer for one hour.
>
> I ask the nurse to find out which is true. While she is away, it is clear to me which I prefer to be true. If I learn that the first is true, I shall be greatly relieved.[11]

Parfit questions whether the bias against future pain is justified. He imagines a character, Timeless. Timeless is as distressed at being reminded about a painful event in the past as when he learns about a painful event to come in the future. Timeless might seem very alien to us, but Parfit argues that we should become more like Timeless. We should be no more motivated by future pleasures and pains than by past ones. In fact, in some ways, being like Timeless would make sense of some of our intuitions. For example, Parfit imagines being in exile, having left behind his widowed mother. She is fatally sick, but news about her rarely arrives.

I am now told something new. My mother's illness has become very painful, in a way that drugs cannot relieve. For the next few months, before she dies, she faces a terrible ordeal. That she will soon die I already knew. But I am deeply distressed to learn of the suffering that she must endure. A day later I am told that I had been misinformed. The facts were right, but not the timing. My mother did have many months of suffering, but she is now dead.

If past pain mattered little, Parfit should feel relief. But this is not how most people would feel. Most people would be more like Timeless and be terribly distressed to discover that their mother died painfully, even if the pain is over. Although he did not try to demonstrate this in *Reasons and Persons*, Parfit was inclined to believe that the passage of time was an illusion, in that 'tense', in the sense of, for example, yesterday and tomorrow, was not a part of the fabric of the world. A pain was a pain, and it should not matter to us, from our perspective today, whether it has occurred in the past or will occur in the future.

· · ·

Section III of *Reasons and Persons* deals with personal identity, and its contents have already been sketched in the discussion in chapter 9 above of his celebrated 1971 paper. That brings us to Section IV—future people.

Future people are people who will exist but who are yet to be conceived. We have strong views about future people. Many of us worry about the impact of climate change on forthcoming generations. We worry about the depletion of resources. We worry about bio-diversity. Some of these worries are linked to concerns about overpopulation. But we also worry about the risks of bioterrorism or nuclear conflict, and the potential annihilation of tens of millions of people.

What should be the nature of our concern for future generations? What are our duties towards them? Is it relevant that these people are not yet born? So long as lives are happy—or at least better than nothing—should we try to create as many lives as possible? Before Parfit, the philosophical literature on population ethics was sparse, especially on the topic of our obligations to merely possible people. Parfit fashioned a sub-genre of moral philosophy and triggered a mini-industry of journal articles.

His basic starting point was this. Just as it makes no difference whether a life is harmed one mile from my home or a thousand miles away, it is as bad to harm a life in the future as a life now. If I leave broken glass in the undergrowth of a wood, and a child steps on it in a hundred years, what difference does it make if this child is not yet alive?

But there are far tougher puzzles. Here is one:

Imagine a 14-year-old girl. Let's call her Angela. She chooses to have a child. Because she is so young her child (let's call him Bill) has a bad start in life. It will still be a life worth living. But had Angela waited for several years, she would have had a different child, who would receive a better start in life.[12]

Most people believe that it would have been better if the girl had waited. But Parfit noticed an intriguing feature of this case. Angela's bad decision, to have the child, made nobody worse off. If she had delayed having a child, Bill would not have been better off, since Bill would not have been born. Another child would have been born in his place. How strange. Can an action be wrong if nobody is wronged by it?

Philosophy is an ancient discipline. Its problems are ancient. Most of the thorniest ones have been around for centuries, if not millennia. What can we know? Do we have free will? What makes me the same person over time? How should we understand consciousness, and what is the link between mind and matter? What is beauty? What is truth? Exceptional minds have addressed these problems; making progress has proved slow and strenuous. There are very few *novel* problems.

One of Parfit's most important achievements was to identify a new problem: the Non-Identity Problem. After he spotted it and applied his usual rigour to drawing out its implications, it became impossible to view crucial aspects of morality in the same way again. More than that, it seemed such an obvious conundrum that it was a wonder that nobody had ever noticed it before.

A fundamental assumption in moral philosophy had always been that, in the area of morality concerned with benefits and harms, an act can be wrong only if there is someone for whom it would be *worse*, or *on balance* bad. What Parfit showed is that there are a great many acts that seem wrong even though there is no one for whom they are worse— indeed, even though they are on balance good for everyone they affect. These are acts that cause bad effects in the lives of people who would never have existed had the acts not been done.

Immanuel Kant and Jeremy Bentham recorded the dramatic impact of reading David Hume. Kant wrote that Hume had woken him from his 'dogmatic slumbers'.[13] Bentham wrote that Hume had 'caused the scales to fall' from his eyes.[14] Reading Parfit on future generations had a similar impact on some philosophers. According to Jeff McMahan, Parfit's work on future generations came as a comparable revelation to many contemporary moral philosophers: 'It revealed that explanations we had complacently accepted of why many acts are wrong were in fact mistaken. It thus compelled us to seek alternative explanations, all of which seem to have implications that radically conflict with common sense moral beliefs. The effect has been revolutionary.'[15]

The relevance of the Non-Identity Problem is not restricted to hypothetical philosophical thought experiments. In fact, many of our actions and decisions run up against it. Each of us is the product of a union between a particular sperm and egg. Reader, you are extremely fortunate to be here. Had someone rung your parents' telephone at a crucial moment, or had your elder sibling cried out for milk at an inopportune time, or had there been a transport strike, such that Mum or Dad was late home, or had there been something better on TV that evening, you might not exist: possibly somebody else would be here instead.[16]

Now, imagine a choice between two environmental policies. Suppose that '[as] a community, we must choose whether to deplete or preserve certain kinds of resources. If we choose Depletion, the quality of life over the next two centuries would be slightly higher than it would have been if we had chosen Conservation. But it would later, for many centuries, be much lower.'[17] Parfit makes the point that our choice of policy will affect who is born, and that we can plausibly assume that after three centuries there would be no one living in the community who would have been born had we chosen the alternative policy. If we find this difficult to grasp, Parfit suggests we ask ourselves whether we would still be here if railways and cars had never been invented.

The Non-Identity Problem has other implications for many debates. Although Parfit applies it exclusively to the future, one can also see how it might discombobulate attitudes to the past. Adolf Hitler made the lives of scores of millions of people much worse—but not the life of this author. This author (a child of refugees) certainly owes his existence to Adolf Hitler. Given Hitler's disruptive impact on the world, the same is probably true for most readers. Should I regret this monster's ascent to power and the destruction he wrought? There are obvious implications for reparations of various kinds. As philosophers who support reparations are aware, descendants of slaves are not worse off because of slavery—in the sense that they exist only because of slavery.

But back to the future. Parfit argued that the issue of identity makes no difference. Take his clever medical example:[18]

There are two rare conditions, J and K, which cannot be detected without special tests. If a pregnant woman has condition J, this will cause the child she is carrying to have a certain handicap. A simple treatment would prevent this effect. If a woman has Condition K when she conceives a child, this will cause this child to have the same particular handicap. Condition K cannot be treated, but always disappears within two months. Suppose next that we have planned two medical programmes, but there are funds for only one; so one must be cancelled. In the first programme, millions of women would be tested during pregnancy. Those found to have Condition J would be treated. In the second programme, millions of women would be tested when they intend to try to become pregnant. Those found to have Condition K would be warned to postpone conception for at least two months, after which this incurable condition will have disappeared. Suppose finally that we can predict that these two programmes would achieve results in as many cases. If there is Pregnancy Testing, 1,000 children a year would be born normal rather than handicapped. If there is Preconception Testing, there would each year be born 1,000 normal children rather than 1,000 different handicapped children.

Parfit believed that we should be indifferent as between these two programmes. This and other examples led him to make the following claim. If in either of two outcomes, X and Y, the same number of people would live, we should choose the outcome in which the people have a higher quality of life. It makes no difference whether there are no *particular* people for whom the decision is bad.

. . .

One tricky issue Parfit attempted to resolve was originally raised by Jan Narveson. Suppose a woman knew that, if she had a child, this child would have a terrible and painful life for a few years, and then die. It seems wrong, says Narveson, to have this child—in part (if not mainly) because it is bad for the child. Does it follow from this that, other things being equal, we have a reason to create—to bring into existence—a child whose life is worthwhile? This seems counterintuitive. Of course, once children exist, we should want their lives to go as well as possible. And we think that parents can have a variety of reasons for having or not having children—but benefiting a child by bringing them into existence is not one of these, nor is populating the planet with one more happy life.

It's not easy to explain the Asymmetry Problem: the asymmetry between what Parfit called the Wretched Child and the Happy Child. And it draws us into the most intractable problem of all: what is the ideal population size? If the choice is between a future in which there is a happy life and a future in which there is an unhappy or a less happy life, we should choose the former. This is what Parfit calls a same-number problem. That's easy. But different-number comparisons are far trickier.

What is the optimum population for a country, or a planet? Should we aim at the greatest possible total quantity of happiness, or the highest

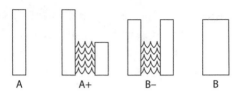

FIGURE 1. An illustration of Derek Parfit's
Mere Addition Paradox.

average level of happiness? Compare one scenario in which the world
has five billion people, each with a high quality of life, with another in
which there are twenty-five billion people, each with a much lower quality
of life. Most of us would opt for the former world. We instinctively think
that in this case average happiness is what matters; that is, quality rather
than quantity. However, Parfit's solution to the Non-Identity Problem
seems to imply that a world with more people is preferable to a world
with fewer people, so long as these people are happy. After all, if we have
a reason to cause a better-off person to exist rather than a less well-off
person, should I not have a reason to cause a well-off person to exist
rather than no person?

Parfit also produced an inventive but dense argument, known as the
Mere Addition Paradox, which rejects the average argument, and leads
us down an apparently inexorable path that bumps us into his 'Repugnant Conclusion'. Suppose there was a population A (see Fig. 1). The
height of A represents the quality of life each person has; the width
represents the size of the population. Let's assume that everyone in A
has a wellbeing or quality-of-life level of 100. Now imagine that there is
another group of people, represented by the second bar, A+, whose lives
are worthwhile, better than nothing, but not as good as the lives of all
those in A. Let's say they have a wellbeing or quality-of-life level of 50.
Still, A+ can't be a worse state of affairs than A, insists Parfit, for A+ is
just A with the addition of some worthwhile lives.

We could try to fall back on the average principle. Average happiness
in A+ is lower than in A. But the average principle is not viable. It would
lead us to conclude that a world in which there existed only one very
happy couple would be better than an alternative in which there were a

billion equally happy people, plus one satisfied but mildly grumpy person.

Suppose next that we compare A+ to B−, where everyone has a well-being level of 98 rather than 100. This looks much superior to A+, because the total wellbeing is greater, and it is more equal. Now consider B. B is simply the two B− groups merged into one single group.

Parfit seems to have shown that A is no better than A+, which is worse than B−. It follows that A must be worse than B. But with the same reasoning, we can go to C, D, E, and all the way down to Z, in which there are zillions of people whose lives are only just better than nothing. That, to Parfit, is a repugnant conclusion.

Parfit expresses his Repugnant Conclusion as follows: 'For any possible population of at least ten billion people, all with a very high quality of life, there must be some much larger imaginable population whose existence, if other things are equal, would be better even though its members have lives that are barely worth living.'[19] His label for this conclusion makes it clear that he regards it as unpalatable, but he and other philosophers have found the logic that got him there hard to refute.

As a historical footnote, it is interesting that an earlier philosopher had identified a related problem, also describing the conclusion as 're-pugnant'. In the first half of the twentieth century, the Cambridge don John McTaggart contrasted, not different numbers of lives, but two single lives. He imagined one life which, in terms of 'knowledge, virtue, love, pleasure, and intensity of consciousness, was unmixedly good', and another life 'which had very little consciousness, and had a very little excess of pleasure over pain, and which was incapable of virtue or love. The value in each hour of its existence, though very small, would be good and not bad. And there would be some finite period of time in which its value would be greater than that of the first life [. . .]. This conclusion would, I believe, be repugnant to certain moralists.'[20]

Had Parfit stumbled across this passage? He was extremely well-read in moral philosophy, and it is possible that he had. Perhaps his use of the term 'repugnant' was unconsciously influenced by McTaggart, though he nowhere credits him. Unlike Parfit, McTaggart swallowed the logic: we must be at fault, he believed, in assuming that the shorter, higher-quality life was to be preferred to the life that was much longer and much lower quality: 'I can see no reason for supposing that repugnance in this case would be right.'[21]

. . .

Parfit was immensely troubled by his Repugnant Conclusion. He tried desperately to find what he called 'Theory X'. Theory X was a theory that solved the Non-Identity Problem but avoided the Repugnant Conclusion. It was a theory that would somehow manage to reconcile all our conflicting intuitions about population ethics. Theory X surely had to exist, he thought. He searched for it for several decades. He was still searching for it when he died.

13

The Mind's Eye in Mist
and Snow

Parfit's close friend Larry Temkin tells a story that is as remarkable as it is baffling. Sometime in the mid-1990s, Temkin was visiting Oxford, and went to visit Parfit in his All Souls' rooms, when he saw one of the most stunning photographs he'd ever seen. It was a view from Parfit's room, through the All Souls wrought-iron gates to the Radcliffe Camera, the domed, eighteenth-century neo-classical building that graces so many postcards of the city. A light sprinkling of snow had settled on the gates and on the Radcliffe Camera.

After Temkin expressed his admiration for the photograph, Parfit explained how it had been produced. It was his favourite of the thousands of pictures he had taken from the same spot. However, not entirely satisfied with it, he had gone to London to employ the services of a photographic developer—a man so skilled, and so costly, that besides Parfit, he was used only by professional photographers. 'I want less yellow,' Parfit had requested. And a new version was produced.

Parfit, however, was still unhappy. The yellow was fine, but he now demanded less pink, and the developer again went through the painstaking retouching procedure—charging his usual fee. It was an improvement, Parfit thought, but it was not perfect. Eventually, after seven iterations, with Parfit travelling back and forth by train to London, the photograph emerged that was now on the wall in his study. 'Here, if you like it, take it,' said Parfit, offering it to his former student. Given the expenditure and effort that he had put into the photograph, this was an outlandishly generous offer, and one Temkin felt obliged to refuse.[1]

A year later, Parfit arrived at Rice University in Houston to teach a course, which Temkin had fixed up. He carried with him one small canvas bag, in which he stuffed everything he thought he needed for his three-week visit, and before even unpacking he told Temkin that he wanted to hand him a gift. He rummaged around in the bag, pulling out shirts and underpants and books, until he found what he was looking for—the photograph Temkin had so admired. It was completely ruined. He'd crumpled it up.

Horrified, Temkin later took it to the best art restorer in the city, who worked for Houston's Museum of Fine Arts. It took him six months to iron out the folds as best he could, and then Temkin paid another hefty sum to have it beautifully framed. Now it is prominently displayed in his home office. But, to this day, it still has one massive wrinkle across the bottom, and other tiny wrinkles are visible elsewhere. 'Who does this? Only Derek could do this.'[2]

How could Parfit be so careless with a photograph that had cost so much in both money and time, and which he had worked so hard to perfect?

. . .

Parfit's long-running obsession with photography began when he was young. His first camera was given to him around the age of fourteen as a gift from his father's elder brother, Cyril. When he lost it, Cyril bought a replacement. Cyril was a successful businessman and the richest member of the Parfit family. He wore impeccable double-breasted suits, and once took his nephew to his tailors on Savile Row to have a suit made. But the camera generated much more excitement. By the time he was a university student, Parfit was already taking many photographs, though not yet in any serious way.

As he sloughed off most of his interests, Parfit retained only philosophy and photography. For two decades, he was a duomaniac. One was his profession, the other his hobby. But a hobby is typically pursued for pleasure or relaxation, and Parfit's engagement with photography was too intense to be captured by these terms. He told a friend, 'If I had to choose between having children and my expensive hobby, photography, I would choose photography.'[3]

He loved, above all, photographing buildings. He had always loved architecture. He adored the skyscrapers in New York and Chicago: when his on-off girlfriend Mary Clemmey arrived for their US tour in 1965, the first thing he showed her was the brutalist, octagonal Pan Am Building on Park Avenue (detested by New Yorkers).[4] He admired some modernist architecture, such as the buildings of Ludwig Mies van der Rohe. But he believed that, in general, architecture over the past century had become uglier.

Oxford was one of three picturesque cities he photographed. The others were Venice and Leningrad (now St Petersburg). Oxford, Venice, and Leningrad were, he thought, the world's most exquisite cities. Venice was his first love; on an early trip he said to his Eton schoolfriend Edward Mortimer that 'once you've been to Venice you don't need to go anywhere else'.[5] He paid a single visit to Rome and Florence, but never bothered to return to them.

He went to Leningrad for the first time in the winter of 1974, accompanied by his then girlfriend, Judith De Witt. This was still more than a decade before glasnost and the easing of state control. They stayed in a hotel with inedible food and were starving until they found dumplings being sold on the street. They wandered around the city and went to the opera. There were tight restrictions on tourists, but several times they managed to evade the state Intourist guide to visit sites outside Leningrad.

The city made a deep impression on him, so much so that he returned almost every year until the millennium; he travelled annually to Venice too. In Oxford, he would rarely appear before lunch, but in Venice and Leningrad he would set his alarm for 4:30 a.m. He liked to photograph buildings in different lights, but he preferred the slanting golden rays of sunrise and sunset to the direct midday sun. (This matched an aversion to overhead artificial lighting.)

He would take shots of the same building countless times. 'I may be somewhat unusual in the fact that I never get tired or sated with what

I love most, so that I don't need or want variety.'[6] In Venice and Leningrad, there were only a few buildings he was interested in photographing. In the former, he photographed churches designed by the sixteenth-century architect Andrea Palladio, including San Giorgio Maggiore and Il Redentore, as well as the Grand Canal, and the Doge's Palace, one of Venice's most familiar landmarks. In Leningrad, favourite buildings included the Winter Palace and the General Staff Building.

He would go to Venice in October, and Leningrad in January or February when there was snow on the ground and the skies were an oppressive grey, which he preferred to blue. Rain, hail, sleet, or snow: he would sit for hours, until he clicked the shot he was aiming for. Mostly he used Nikon cameras and he carried a variety of lenses, including what is called a tilt-shift lens, which allowed him to photograph at a wide focal length whilst straightening the lines that appear to converge in the distance. When waiting for the ideal light, he would read a book. If the conditions weren't right, he would return to his lodgings without taking a single photo and start again the following day. On one occasion, when he had been taking photos all morning of the River Neva, a passing Russian picked up some snow and started smothering it over Parfit's face. Thinking he was being attacked, Parfit tried to push the man away—but it turned out he had seen signs of frostbite on Parfit's face. Parfit believed this stranger saved his nose. He nearly lost two or three toes. Back in Oxford, Edward Hussey, an All Souls Fellow and specialist in ancient philosophy, asked him (out of genuine medical curiosity) 'if I might inspect the said toes, which he was happy to let me do; it was a frightening sight'.[7]

The photographs of Leningrad and Venice have common elements—especially mist and water. Most of Parfit's favourite buildings had classical or gothic columns. He also liked arches and domes. What he found appealing was the fusion of building and nature, stone and sky. He poured water on the Tetrarchs, sculptures on the external facade of St Mark's Basilica in Venice, to make them glisten more.

His photos are reminiscent of early Turner paintings, though Turner's smoke and steam, billowing clouds and turbulent water, carry more menace. Parfit's images, by contrast, are serene and romantic and have a timeless quality. He had very strong views on colours. He disliked both pale blue and saturated blue. He liked the green of spring but not the green of summer. In fact, he disapproved of bright colours more generally (he once said that the gorgeous red and orange leaves in the New England fall were 'too violent'[8]), and he thought most buildings (and most faces) looked best in black and white. However, he did not think that was the case with many buildings in Venice and Leningrad. In Leningrad in particular, he liked to capture the white pillars against the painted stucco plaster.

Upon returning to Oxford, he would examine his photographs, and jettison the vast majority. Only a very few passed his exacting aesthetic standards. But, even so, this was not the end of the process. Well before Photoshop and Instagram filters, he would use techniques to enhance his images. Initially, he employed a man in southern Italy, but when this business closed, he discovered a specialist at the Gilchrist Studios in Clerkenwell, London, who was highly skilled if not, Parfit felt, quite up to the Italian's standard. Parfit was capable of spending thousands of pounds on a single print. Indeed, as already described, his teaching trips to the United States were in part driven by the need to earn money to pay for his prints and photography-travel. Receipts in his private papers reveal that the basic cost of one trip to Leningrad in the late 1980s was £1,700, and after he returned from Leningrad with his All Souls colleagues in 1982, the invoice for the first print enhancement was for £925.75. Given how prized he must have been as a customer, it's surprising to find the invoice made out to a 'Derek Parfitt of All Saints College'.

The photographic developer was set a variety of tasks. Small adjustments to colour were the easiest. More complicated were demands that he remove anything that obscured the building or cluttered the image. Telegraph poles, wires, scaffolding, drainpipes, traffic signs, and litter had to be erased. Once, he even had to remove an army truck that defaced the view of the Winter Palace. Cars had to go, and people, too. 'It seems to me', wrote Frances Kamm, 'that [Parfit's] highly impartialist view of ethics might seem to some as another way to get rid of people.'[9]

Parfit later embraced digitalization, which made it possible for him to alter photographs himself, though he rued his inability to smooth out the blue gradient in the sky from the pale blue near the horizon to the strong blue high up. He normally worked on his Photoshopping late at night. In the end, he kept just a few hundred of the tens of thousands of photographs he had taken. He thought of himself not as an inspirational photographer, but as a competent critic. He believed that if he took enough shots, he was capable of identifying the few great ones from among them. In total, he kept only ten portraits, including one of a couple kissing under a column and another of two Venetian nuns walking across a piazza.

What motivated his photographic manipulations? There are two possible interpretations. Either he was trying to improve on reality, or he thought that by ridding the image of eyesores he was laying bare the beauty of reality. This latter explanation is supported by one of his photographic rules: while he was willing to erase parts of an image, he would never add to an image—he would never Photoshop anything in, only out. He wrote in one email, 'I wouldn't want to destroy the sense that we are looking at the buildings themselves, not a representation of them. I don't invent anything, since every part of every image was taken from somewhere in the original image.'[10]

In that way, Parfit believed, his photography was different from the work of an artist. But his 'erase, don't add' rule was somewhat arbitrary. Raindrops were multiplied, tree branches were extended, clouds were shunted around, and in one case (breaching his usual rule), a moon was added from another print. Parfit would manipulate shapes and sizes of buildings and street furniture. The buildings he loved most had harmony and proportion, but if he felt the sense of harmony or proportion could be improved, he was not above extending a spire or altering the distance between domes.

. . .

I was told by several people close to Parfit that his trips to Venice and Leningrad were taken alone. But while this was true in later years, in the early years there were a few occasions when he was accompanied to Leningrad. Marshall Cohen, one of the founders of the journal *Philosophy and Public Affairs*, was a visiting Fellow at All Souls in 1976–77, and with his wife Margaret travelled to Leningrad with Parfit in March 1977, along with the All Souls classicist Richard Jenkyns. The following year, the Oxford philosopher Tony Quinton and his American wife, Marcelle, escorted Parfit, along with a young All Souls Fellow, Iain McGilchrist, who was Parfit's nearest neighbour in college (with rooms virtually opposite Parfit's on Staircase XI). Quinton and Parfit had common interests in utilitarianism and P. G. Wodehouse. McGilchrist and Parfit shared a room in Leningrad, and what McGilchrist principally remembers is Parfit's long nocturnal wind-down, involving pills, alcohol, and a warm bath.

Why Parfit desired companionship is a mystery. Simon Blackburn was invited along to Leningrad in 1981. Blackburn was also a keen photographer and took a single Leica camera and three small lenses. It soon dawned on him that his principal function was to be camera-caddy. Parfit had 'an armoury of cameras and lenses, which he didn't want to put in the aeroplane hold. So I carried on board his huge bag of films— at least 40 rolls.'[11]

The two philosophers had contrasting approaches to photography and so would part early in the morning. Blackburn shot in black and white, and whilst Parfit did not want his photographs marred by human beings, Blackburn, influenced by photographers such as Henri Cartier-Bresson, aimed to capture the chance dramas and spontaneity of street life. Parfit thought that modern photography erred in trying to resemble snapshots that a non-artist might have taken. They didn't argue about this and rubbed along well enough, but for Blackburn it was a 'cheerless' week.[12]

The following year, from 5 to 12 February 1982, Parfit led a group of mainly junior All Souls Fellows to Leningrad, including Peregrine Horden, Susan Hurley, Paul Seabright, John Vickers, Simon Walker, and Adrian Wooldridge. In what could have provided the material for a Tom Stoppard play, they flew to the USSR with two other groups, a party from the Tunbridge Wells Women's Institute, and a bunch of UK communists who all sported beards and were hoping to discover what sort of post-revolution utopian future awaited the British. Parfit stocked up on insomnia-curing vodka at the duty-free. In Leningrad, the rest of the All Souls Fellows followed a standard tourist itinerary—visiting the Hermitage and the Summer Palace of Peter the Great. Parfit disappeared each morning to take photos, wearing a heavy overcoat, but otherwise making few concessions to the Russian winter, 'to the evident amazement of the locals'.[13] One member of the All Souls party recalls seeing him one day on the frozen Neva, oblivious to an ice-breaker heading his way.[14]

They stayed at the Hotel Leningrad, a monstrous concrete block. Its chief virtue was that the view of the city looking out from the hotel windows was the only one not blighted by the Hotel Leningrad. It also had, as you might expect, a selection of fine vodkas. The days were short, and so a fair quantity of vodka was drunk. Parfit told the others exactly where and when you had to be on a particular Leningrad street corner to capture the right mix of light and shade. Susan Hurley was at that time deeply immersed in the philosophy of the later Wittgenstein. The group had one intense discussion about Wittgenstein's claim that a private language—a language that was comprehensible only to a single person—was incoherent. They wondered whether the KGB was listening in.

In fact, they may well have been under observation. The Fellows would eat at long tables alongside the women from Tunbridge Wells, the hirsute communists, a bunch of inebriated Finns, and a mystery Soviet woman who sidled up to them. She claimed to have studied at Oxford and adored the 'Blackies Bookshop' (sic).[15] The All Souls academics assumed she was in the pay of the secret service.

What the Soviet authorities made of Parfit is difficult to guess. When he first began to travel to Leningrad, Leonid Brezhnev was the general secretary of the Communist Party, the Cold War world was divided into two hostile blocs, and the Berlin Wall seemed indestructible and everlasting. Both sides dispatched spies to penetrate the institutions of their enemy and to gather information. Western tourists had to book their trips to the USSR through the state tourist agency, their itineraries were agreed upon in advance, and their movements were monitored. Yet here was a man who returned each year under a suspicious photography pretext—an intellectual based at All Souls, the heart of the British establishment. It would be delicious but not surprising to discover that the KGB had wasted valuable resources tracking this eccentric, harmless philosopher and that in the KGB archives Parfit has his own file. He was more than once stopped by men who asked him questions and made it patently clear whom they represented. Iain McGilchrist recalls Parfit being briefly taken in for questioning one day and emerging from the episode unscathed and unfazed. And Simon Blackburn believes their room on the earlier trip was bugged. When he and Parfit were unpacking their bags on their first evening in Leningrad, Blackburn remarked to Parfit that one of the lamps in their room didn't work. Planning to mention this to reception in the morning, they went down for dinner. By the time they returned, somebody had been into the room to sort the lamp out. They concluded that their complaint had been overheard.

The 1982 trip may have been the last time Parfit went to Leningrad with company. He had been due to travel there in February 1984 with the philosopher Bill Ewald, who had agreed to take one of his equipment bags to the airport. In the event, Parfit failed to show up at Gatwick Airport, having mislaid his passport. Ewald had already passed through customs and so was forced to go on to the USSR alone; the flight was delayed for an hour whilst they hunted for, and then removed, Parfit's camera bag from the hold.

Towards the end of the 1990s, Parfit's enthusiasm for photography began to wane. He felt he had completed his work in Venice. Meanwhile, the winters in what was by then St Petersburg became milder, and Parfit was frustrated that he travelled there several times when it didn't snow. Even when it did, he grumbled that the snow was now the wrong shade of white. On his last trip, in 2002, he had the time to reread all of Kant's *The Metaphysics of Morals* and *Groundwork of the Metaphysics of Morals*.

. . .

What can be said about Parfit's aesthetic sense, his appreciation of beauty? Oddly, his visual sensibility was at its most acute when mediated, usually through the lens. Once when he was staying in Colorado, he refused an offer to go hiking, but enjoyed a scenic drive near the Rockies—he wouldn't get out, preferring to see the view framed by the windows as though he were observing it through a camera. He watched wildlife documentaries on television, but had no interest in experiencing wildlife in nature.

Although he loved art, he told his friend Frances Kamm that going to exhibitions was no better for him than looking at reproductions of art-works in books (a view that paralleled his preference for musical recordings over concerts). His taste in paintings ranged from Jan van Eyck (c. 1390–1441) to Turner (1775–1851). As a critic, Kamm says, he would focus on some things 'that didn't seem worth noting, at least in evaluating the merit of a work, e.g., if people were or were not fully depicted'. But he also 'appreciated many things worth appreciating'.[16] When they went together to the New York Museum of Modern Art, Parfit immediately saw in one of the works of abstract expressionist Philip Guston (1913–80) a connection to the brushstrokes and water lily paintings of Claude Monet (1840–1926).

Were there links between the substance of Parfit's philosophy and his photography? If there were, they were quite tenuous. But both activities were the product of the same character, and there were certainly similarities in motivation. Parfit was a philosopher who wanted to impose reason and order on morality, to iron out wrinkles. That was true, too, of his approach to photography. Both his philosophy and his photography were practised with fanatical intensity. The perfectionist urge propelled both pursuits in a way that few others could match or comprehend.

. . .

The significance Parfit attributed to beauty and aesthetics is evinced by one of the lesser-known aspects of his life: his two-decade-long involvement with Oxford's streetlamps. This began in the 1970s, when Oxford was replacing its old streetlamps. The original black wrought-iron lamps were called Winsor lanterns.[17] They were parallelogram-shaped, narrow at the bottom, broader at the top, and capped by a cylindrical chimney vent. The principal problem was that they were gas lights, neither as safe nor as effective as electric lighting. But they were also poorly maintained, often in the wrong place, and many students, particularly female students, complained that they felt unsafe walking through Oxford after dark. As a consequence, these lamps were gradually being scrapped, and replaced by electric ones, described by one author as 'the last word in sheer ugliness'.[18] The old lamps were fixed to the walls; the modern ones, in a mishmash of styles, were often on stand-alone poles, soon disfigured by stickers advertising services or events or promoting causes.

To counter this anarchy, a working group was set up by the recently formed Oxford Civic Society, an independent organization aiming to preserve and enhance Oxford's beauty. The society wanted to persuade the city council to take aesthetic considerations into account. Parfit was a driving force in this group, and it was no fleeting involvement. He remained the group convener from 1973 into the 1990s.

The working group proposed that the city use a replica of the Winsor lantern. That was uncontentious; more complicated was how to fix it to Oxford's ancient walls. Parfit became particularly friendly with an eccentric American engineer, Robert Maccoun, whose home was a barge. Maccoun designed a bracket, which Parfit financed. The prototype was installed in a few places, including outside All Souls—and the replica brackets were soon rolled out in most of Oxford's smaller streets.

Then, from the late 1970s, it was the turn of the main streets to be upgraded—the final gas lamp was switched off in 1979. This involved new standing lamps as well as those attached to walls. Parfit came up with some drawings of a new design for the former, which were then worked up by a draughtsman, Richard Lewis. These, effectively, are the lamps that exist in the city centre today, with one alteration to Parfit's vision: the standing lamps, too, required a bracket at the top, and the city engineers demanded more metal there, to strengthen the fixing. One way of doing this was by metal crenellations. In a long letter to John Ashdown, the city's conservation officer, on 13 March 1993, just as he was flying off to teach in the US, Parfit pleaded for a rethink. He was 'becoming agitated' by the thought of the crenellated brackets, he said. 'I even had a nightmare about them last night!'.[19] In the end, the council determined that Parfit's upset—about a small modification that was not visible at street level—was outweighed by considerations of safety and durability.

Parfit had acquired such expertise in lamping that All Souls called upon him in 2001 when its splendid eighteenth-century Codrington Library was renovated. The rich benefactor Christopher Codrington had been a slave owner in the West Indies, an unfortunate fact which was more or less overlooked until his name was dropped from the library in 2020. But it was still the Codrington when Parfit was at All Souls, and the former librarian, Norma Aubertin-Potter, says that its lighting became Parfit's domain. He would balance precariously on a ladder to inspect the lights and recommend alterations. 'We just did what he said.'[20] When he showed visitors around the library, he would sometimes bring them in in darkness and then switch on the lights to reveal its architectural magnificence.

. . .

Parfit suspected that his fascination with photography was at least partially to do with a condition he had that has only recently acquired a label: aphantasia.[21] Venice makes an indelible impression on most tourists, and after they've left the city, they'll be able to conjure up images of it in their mind's eye. A small number of people are, like Parfit, incapable of doing this. It wasn't that he couldn't describe Venice—he could tell you where the Bridge of Sighs was, its shape and dimensions, its colour; but he couldn't 'see' the bridge. He could not do what most people can do—close his eyes and picture the beautiful Venetian locations as though he had a set of internal postcards. Nor could he imagine anyone's face.

Aphantasia is a condition estimated to affect around 2 per cent of the population. It was first diagnosed by the Victorian scientist Francis Galton (a cousin of Charles Darwin). He asked subjects to picture their breakfast table—Darwin himself said he could do so as distinctly as if there was a photograph in front of him. A few others could not. However, it was only in the mid-2000s that a British neurologist, Adam Zeman, revived interest in aphantasia (coining the term in 2015—*phantasia* is the Greek word for 'imagination'). Zeman was fascinated by a patient who lost the ability to picture images after a heart procedure.

(*Above left*) Welcome to the world: baby Derek, with his father Norman and sister Theodora, Chengdu, China, 1943. (*Above right*) Toddler Derek, with his mother Jessie and sister Theodora, New York, 1944. (*Below*) Derek with his sisters Theodora and Joanna, London (c. 1949).

DEMETRIUS SPEAKS TO THESEUS

(*Above*) Derek and his close friend Bill Nimmo Smith, Eton, 1956.
Courtesy of Bill Nimmo Smith. (*Below*) Derek in a Dragon School
production of *A Midsummer Night's Dream*, 1955.

Derek, sixth-former at Eton, flaunting his 'Pop' waistcoat.

(*Above*) Derek and Mary Clemmey, at the start of their 1965 US road trip. (*Below*) The Parfit family, c. 1975; from left: Derek, Norman, Theodora, Jessie, Joanna.

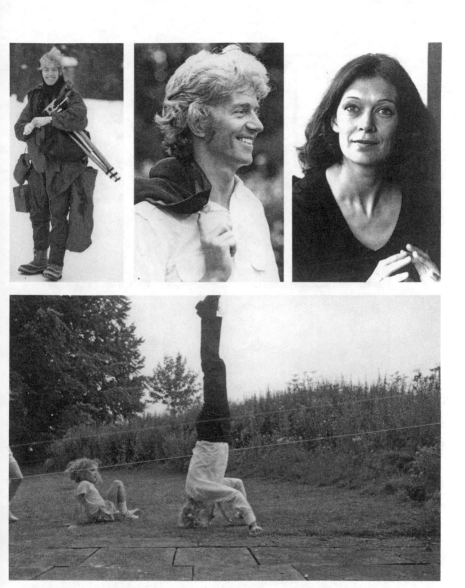

(*Above left*) Well-equipped Derek, taking photographs on an early trip to St Petersburg. (*Above centre*) Carefree Derek (c. 1982), photographed by Susan Hurley. Courtesy of Nicholas Rawlins. (*Above right*) Janet Radcliffe Richards, photographed by Peter Johns around the time of the publication of her book *The Sceptical Feminist* (1980). Copyright Guardian News & Media Ltd 2022. (*Below*) Upside-down Derek (c. 1989).

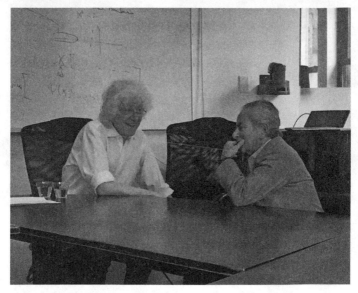

(*Above left*) Oxford, All Souls College: the view from the landing next to Derek's rooms, over Hawksmoor's North Quad. (*Above right*) Lighting up Oxford: a Derek-designed lamp. (*Below*) Derek in conversation with his friend Tom Nagel, 2015. Courtesy of David Chalmers.

(*Above*) Derek and Janet, 31 August 2010: post-wedding picnic. (*Below*) Derek and Janet's West Kennett House: 'like falling for a pretty face'.

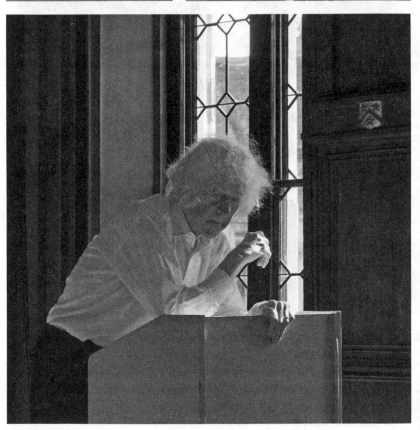

(*Above left*) 1,900 pages of *On What Matters*, Volumes 1, 2, and 3. (*Above right*) Kayaking in Maine, 2015. (*Below*) Lecturing in Oxford, 2014. Courtesy of Toby Ord.

The condition is still not well understood. It appears to run in families. People with aphantasia are more likely to experience difficulties in social interaction. Often, those with aphantasia have a weak autobiographical memory—that is to say, they're unusually poor at being able to conjure up details of their own past. Finally, there may be a connection between aphantasia and face recognition. The problem Parfit had with faces was probably not so severe that, had he ever sought a diagnosis, he would have been diagnosed with prosopagnosia (the neurological disorder characterized by the inability to recognize faces), but there are countless examples of him struggling to identify people he'd met before. He often failed to recognize his former students; after this happened to Jake Nebel, Parfit sent an apologetic email.[22] And one of his All Souls' colleagues, Amia Srinivasan, wrote that when he passed her he 'would smile in a way that didn't entirely convince me I was recognised'.[23]

14

Glory! Promotion!

Parfit had risked delaying the vote on his All Souls promotion. The strategy worked.

The reception for *Reasons and Persons* was everything that he could have hoped for, and more. 'Something close to a work of genius', proclaimed Alan Ryan in *The Sunday Times*.[1] In *The Times Higher Education Supplement*, John Gray declared it 'the most notable contribution to moral philosophy since Sidgwick's *Methods of Ethics*'.[2] Samuel Scheffler in *The Times Literary Supplement* also drew a comparison with *Methods of Ethics*, describing Parfit's book as extraordinary [. . .] brilliant [. . .] astonishingly rich in ideas'.[3] While taking issue with aspects of the book, Roger Scruton nonetheless considered it 'a work of great suggestiveness and power'.[4] In *The New York Review of Books*, Peter Strawson praised its 'scope, fertility, imaginative resource, and cogency of reasoning'.[5] Strawson's review was edited by *NYRB* supremo Robert Silvers who, after his death in 2017, was described as 'the greatest literary editor there has ever been',[6] but who inserted multiple errors into the text that Strawson had to insist be removed. Of all the reviews, Parfit was probably best pleased by the one in the *London Review of Books*; for it was written by the thinker he admired above all his contemporaries—Bernard Williams. Parfit had uncovered deep questions, Williams wrote. It was a 'very original' and 'imaginative' book, 'brilliantly clever', 'strange and excitingly intense'.[7]

Inevitably, there were detractors—for some, it was over-long and stodgy. David Wiggins did not condemn it publicly, but privately considered it 'weird', and likened the experience of reading it to 'being stabbed relentlessly by a tooth-pick'.[8] Only two negative reviews appeared in print, each, in its own way, bizarre. The first was by the philosopher Mary Warnock, who a few months earlier had been anointed Dame Mary.[9] (The Warnock report on human fertilization and embryology was about to be published; it would recommend that embryos under fourteen days could be used for research.) Her review appeared on 26 April 1984 in *The Listener*, and described the book as 'quite simply unreadable'. She took umbrage at the lengthy list of acknowledgements. 'The ordinary reader who was not consulted, may be forgiven for feeling that all these advisers came between him and the author. It is as if private conversation, conducted in the code-language of friends, has been interrupted, or simply overheard. The conversation may be clever, funny, or even, as I believe, of great importance. But before it can be understood, it must be translated.'[10]

Being incomprehensible was at least a lesser charge than that levelled by the political philosopher Shirley Letwin, however. In the lead review in *The Spectator*, she accused Parfit of destabilizing society, no less. Her lofty article, peppered with misinterpretations, warned that Parfit presented 'a profound attack on Western civilisation'. What particularly perturbed Letwin was the section on personal identity which, she fulminated, stripped bare Parfit's 'bland indifference to millennia of philosophical reflection on the identity, continuity, and existence of persons'.[11] Taking these views seriously, she warned, would undermine the Judaeo-Christian values by which our society is constructed.

Parfit was not inclined to respond to Warnock, but he felt the Letwin review was so misleading that it could not be ignored. On 21 May, he wrote a letter for publication.

Dear Sir,

Mrs Letwin writes (Books 19 May), 'for Parfit, altruism is always opposed to self-interest'. I wrote, 'On all plausible theories about self-interest . . . it may not be true that the altruistic choice will be worse for us' (p. 87). Mrs Letwin writes, 'Parfit . . . speaks of a person as a synonym for a

Cartesian Ego'. I wrote, 'we might have been such entities. But all of the evidence is against this view (266)'. Mrs Letwin writes, 'Parfit asserts that there is no more reason to believe in persons than in unicorns'. I wrote, unsurprisingly, 'persons exist' (p. 473). Mrs Letwin writes that my view 'dispenses with human personality'. I wrote, 'what matters is what makes us persons' (p. 446). Readers may decide for themselves whether what I actually wrote is 'a profound attack on Western civilisation'; but they will be disappointed if they hope to find in my book the claims that Mrs Letwin has imagined.

Parfit must have mentioned this letter to one or more people and received advice that it was not a good idea. He withdrew it before publication.

He was probably in no mood for conflict because, two days after he wrote his letter, his father Norman died at the breakfast table, of a heart attack. Derek had a troubled relationship with his angry and depressive father—but he dutifully paid regular visits home, and always wanted to please him. The timing of his death, just as the two of them should have been basking in review glory, must have exacerbated Parfit's grief. At least before he died, Norman had seen the prominent display of *Reasons and Persons* in the window of Oxford's Blackwell's bookshop.

· · ·

The world of philosophy is a small one, but within it *Reasons and Persons* caused a sensation. For once, the publishing cliché 'an instant classic' is not hyperbole. Philosophy books which are not aimed at a popular market do not sell well—very few reach five figures. It was hardly *Hollywood Wives* (that year's blockbuster, by Jackie Collins), but *Reasons and Persons* sold tens of thousands and became OUP's best-selling academic philosophy title of the past fifty years, and perhaps ever.

For certain scholars, *Reasons and Persons* was life-changing—they became transfixed by its problems and arguments, and devoted their careers to engaging with them. A generation of younger philosophers, such as Shelly Kagan, were profoundly influenced by it. 'It was eye-opening. It opened up new vistas.'[12] It had a similar impact on some non-professional readers. Many years after publication, one online book purchaser described it as the philosophical equivalent of a neutron bomb.[13]

Its impact was a product of its style as well as its substance. This is not to everyone's taste, but Parfit had an inimitable writing voice: a Parfitian paragraph is unmistakable. Mary Warnock's accusation of unreadability was unjust. Some philosophers are guilty of not caring about clarity or, far more disgracefully, are wilfully obscure. Not Parfit. His overarching ambition was lucidity and the exclusion of ambiguity. The trickiest points were the ones he worked hardest on explaining. The desire for clarity stimulated a staccato pace, in which distinctions were carefully stated and points were often repeated and reinforced. To take a few lines at random from *Reasons and Persons,*

> I distinguish between what I have most reason to do, and what, given my beliefs, it would be rational for me to do. If my wine has been poisoned, drinking this wine is not what I have most reason to do. But, if I have no reason to believe that it has been poisoned, I would not be acting irrationally if I drink this wine. My main question is what we have most reason to do.[14]

. . .

The early 1980s was a dark time for British philosophy. Margaret Thatcher's Conservative government had come to power in 1979, pledging to curtail public spending. The financial cuts that followed led to the closure of several philosophy departments; others were facing the chop. Parfit was optimistic that his book's reception cleared the route to an All Souls Senior Research Fellowship. However, after being stung in 1981, he was taking no chances. The British job market may have stagnated but, unbeknownst to the college, he was in discussions with various American universities about his future. News of his Oxford troubles had spread, and several departments saw an opportunity to swoop, and burnish their faculty team-sheet by adding his name. Negotiations with various universities ran in parallel.

In the short term, Rice University, in Houston, Texas, wanted him for a month in January 1984 and then another eight weeks from late March 1984. An initial offer of $12,000 was raised to $16,000 (to include travel, board, and lodging). Janet, meanwhile, had a one-semester appointment at UCLA. For Parfit, there was also a longer-term and more enticing proposal: a letter from Robert Nozick, on 12 May 1983, offered him a full-time job at Harvard.

Nozick was a brilliant philosopher in his own right, and the author of *Anarchy, State, and Utopia* (1974), which was seen as the most compelling of all the responses to his colleague John Rawls's *A Theory of Justice. Anarchy, State, and Utopia* remains the libertarian bible; it argued that the state should have the minimum possible functions—ensuring safety and enforcing contracts. Parfit read the entire draft manuscript and provided detailed comments. The book contains the famous Wilt Chamberlain argument;[15] for the twenty-first century, we can update this to the LeBron James argument. If a hundred million people around the world were willing to pay James $1 each week to watch him perform for the Los Angeles Lakers, and each fan engaged in this deal freely, then, according to Nozick, James would be entitled to his weekly $100 million, and even though he would be wildly rich (even more wildly rich than he currently is), it would be unjust—and an infringement on his liberty—to force him to surrender a portion of this money in tax.

Channelling his inner Chamberlain, Parfit enquired about the Harvard salary. 'This is not what would most affect my decision, but it would help a decision.'[16] He mentioned that he had also received an overture from NYU. This may have been a tactic designed to play one university off against another, but, if so, it was ineffective. The official Harvard offer from the dean's office was surprisingly modest—the starting salary would be $48,000; slightly more if Parfit chose to start in the Fall semester of 1984, rather than in 1983. Parfit expressed his gratitude but wondered whether his decision could be delayed until June 1984, by which time he would know whether he was being ousted from Oxford. He was again being tactical: if the All Souls Fellows were aware that he had a back-up plan, he felt that they would have fewer qualms about rejecting him for promotion.

Meanwhile, there were ongoing negotiations with NYU, most of which were conducted through his friend Thomas Nagel. Nagel had for some years been reassuring Parfit that if he was fed up with All Souls, he could fix him up with a permanent job at NYU, on the assumption that this would be a full-time appointment. When Parfit expressed a desire for a part-time role, NYU reluctantly agreed; they yielded, too, to his unusual scheduling demands. Parfit's idea was that every other year he teach the full Fall semester and a portion—March and April— of the Spring semester. He then proposed the same deal to Harvard. This was a year before his father's death, and to Nozick he explained that there were two reasons for this offbeat arrangement:

> While either of my parents is still alive, and living in Oxford, I am reluctant to increase the number of full semesters that I spend away from Oxford. I see my parents twice a week or more, and they are unhappy for me to go away for a full semester. My absence for six or eight weeks is better for them. The second advantage is that, by coming in March and April, I do not miss much of the Hilary and Trinity Terms in Oxford. This means that I lose none, or little, of my All Souls salary. When I miss a whole term in Oxford I lose a quarter of my annual salary.[17]

While these negotiations were underway, Parfit had to resubmit an application for All Souls promotion, containing his research programme for the next seven years. He decided that this would not include an investigation into central questions in metaethics—such as whether moral claims are 'objective'. He wanted to steer clear of metaethics, because he believed it would entangle him in areas in which he had insufficient expertise—the philosophy of language and 'objectivity' in non-moral areas. In addition, he thought that, since many moral philosophers already worked in metaethics, it made sense for him to specialize in something else. As he explained to John Rawls, the questions he did intend to address were sufficient to 'keep me busy for the rest of my life'.[18]

Indeed! Perhaps All Souls should have learned by now not to take Parfit's goals too seriously. But he laid out an ambitious list of tasks and topics which he planned to address were he to be promoted. First, he was going to produce the long-promised new edition of *The Methods of Ethics*. Then he would edit a new series of books on ethics, also for OUP. After that, he intended to re-examine some aspects of *Reasons and Persons*. He had discussed in the book what a person has most reason to do, but he needed 'to consider different kinds of irrationality, such as self-deception and weakness of the will'.[19] Then, he would work on areas barely touched on in the book. These included: (a) how we should decide what is in a person's best interests; (b) the claims of distributive justice and what they imply about the increasing inequality between the world's richest and poorest people; (c) what limits can be placed on the demands of morality; (d) how we should assess the consequences of our acts; and (e) what he described as less familiar issues, such as the implications of the growing interdependence between nations, as well as the implications of our newly acquired ability to extinguish the human race.

The goal, Parfit wrote, was 'a general theory' under which all this could be subsumed. As if this were not enough, he also explained how he would work on areas which were only tangentially related to ethics. 'Some examples' included 'the nature of any person's continuing identity, what is involved in the passage of time, the sense in which we have free will, the extent to which we are like mere machines, the limits to our knowledge both about each other and about other kinds of sentient being, and the kinds of objectivity which we can achieve'.[20]

Given that many philosophers have devoted their entire research careers to just one of these fundamental areas (for example, in what sense humans could claim to have free will) this was risibly unrealistic. But perhaps the impracticality of his plan would not have been so apparent to the non-philosophers at All Souls.

. . .

Along with his research outline, Parfit had to include a list of referees and ensure that their references reached the Warden by 1 May 1984.

Isaiah Berlin approached on his behalf the renowned legal philosopher
Herbert Hart, who had a high regard for Parfit but declined to help
because it would demand too much reading. Parfit was permitted five
referees, and R. M. Hare, David Pears, John Rawls, and Bernard Williams all agreed to be among them; the dilemma was who should take
the final slot. Parfit was undecided between A. J. Ayer and Tim Scanlon,
and asked Berlin for advice, telling him that both Scanlon and Ayer had
pros and cons. Most All Souls Fellows would probably not realize just
how good a philosopher Scanlon was and might dismiss what he had to
say, believing 'correctly that he is a friend of mine'.[21] As for Ayer, he was
a public intellectual, and everyone would be aware that he was a substantial figure in the discipline, but the 'one third of the College who are
most likely to vote against my promotion [. . .] may think of Ayer as a
social libertine, whose opinion should be ignored'.[22] Parfit had decided
against asking Peter Strawson for a reference because his flattering verdict on *Reasons and Persons* had already been delivered in *The New York
Review of Books*.

Berlin's response to this letter has been lost, but in the end Parfit
opted for Scanlon over Ayer, so perhaps this is what Berlin advised.
Parfit was anxious. Williams's support would not be much use, he
feared, because the people who objected to Parfit were also those who
had opposed Williams for Warden. Williams had not forgotten the All
Souls snub. Writing to Parfit to ask him to read a draft of his new book,
Ethics and the Limits of Philosophy,[23] he described All Souls as a 'mad
College'.[24] As for Hare, Parfit felt obliged to request a reference from
him, since he was the most recent occupant of the White's Chair, and
had been a referee in 1981, so, 'his omission now might arouse suspi-
cion'.[25] The problem was that 'in a recent discussion group I expressed
in his presence, with injudicious force, my belief that his appeal to moral
language is fundamentally misguided'.[26]

Since details of references for Parfit's previous applications, in 1974
and 1981, have already been given, there is little point in rehearsing at
length here the similar references sent to All Souls in 1984. Of course,
one difference now was that his long-anticipated book had appeared,
which, according to his referees was 'astonishing'[27] and a 'truly great

achievement'.[28] Williams wrote, 'The College has in Parfit a moral philosopher of outstanding gifts and, now, manifest achievement'.[29] Parfit, it turned out, had needlessly worried about Hare's support. 'I see that when I wrote to you on 30 March, 1981, I said that he was probably the best moral philosopher of his generation [. . .]. If anything, I would now remove the "probably"'.[30] Parfit was his natural successor to fulfil the vacant White's Chair, Hare explained. David Pears stressed Parfit's specialness and the need for him to have a job free from humdrum academic responsibilities; the typical teaching role for a don at Oxford was 'not compatible with research on the scale of his'.[31] Rawls, meanwhile, described at some considerable length how Parfit had affected his own thinking, making the point that he was no longer confident that one could do moral philosophy without grappling with the issue of personal identity. Williams launched a preemptive strike against the standard carping of non-philosophers at a work of moral philosophy, including the charges that it was trivial, a criticism which 'cannot in any conceivable sense be applied to Parfit's work', or that it was impractical.[32] Parfit's output would come to shape policy, Williams predicted, but, as with the works of Plato, Rousseau, Kant, and Mill, the impact might take time.

In addition to Parfit's chosen referees, All Souls sought two independent views about Parfit's book, his intellectual ability, and his future plans. The first was from Stuart Hampshire, whom Parfit had known since his Harkness years in the United States, and who reported that Reasons and Persons was remarkable and 'can certainly be instanced when the usual journalistic hacks produce their biennial articles on the triviality of analytic philosophy'.[33] The second was Geoffrey Warnock, a philosopher, husband to Mary, and Principal of Oxford's Hertford College.

The Warnocks must have spluttered about Reasons and Persons over their breakfast cereal. Geoffrey Warnock's criticisms were similar to but even more scathing than his wife's; no doubt he was emboldened by the thought that Parfit would not be privy to his remarks. Parfit, wrote Warnock, had spent so long fiddling with the text and responding to comments from dozens of correspondents that he had forgotten the reader. The book's 'extreme oddity' resulted from 'a rather rigid simplicity of purpose, remorselessly pursued'.[34]

The purpose is to consider certain questions about the nature of persons and about the reasons persons have for acting, and to decide by argument, counter-argument, rebuttal of counter-argument etc., what answers to those questions are and are not rationally sustainable. This is what the reader is offered—and nothing else at all. He is not to be entertained by wit or felicity of style; he is not to be allowed to relax from time to time, or encouraged to keep going by variation of pace or density of ratiocination; he is not to be helped by signposts along the way, or by explicit indications of what is more or less important, more or less novel, more or less interesting. Embarked upon this stream of flat, short sentences, of argument, objection, reply, and further argument, he is to sink or swim; and since completeness is aimed for as well as cogency, the stream is a very long one, and greatly taxes the stamina.[35]

Having given *Reasons and Persons* a sound thrashing, Warnock seemed about to deliver a damning judgement on Parfit's intellectual faculties. But at the end of the demolition, he plucked out a surprise. What you really want to know, he wrote, is how good Parfit is as a philosopher: 'I think the conclusion must be that he is very good.'[36]

On 14 May 1984, a month before the general college vote to determine Parfit's future, there was a meeting of the Academic Purposes Committee, to assess Parfit's academic credentials and his research plan. The Warnocks' influence is clear, but overall the committee adopted the consensus of Parfit's referees. 'While criticisms can be made of the style of his writing there can be no question but that Parfit's work probes issues in moral philosophy at a depth and with an intensity that few living philosophers can rival. He raises profound questions which others have ignored [. . .]. In the unanimous opinion of the Committee, Parfit is well up to the standard which the College expects and his election is unanimously recommended.'[37]

The Parfit camp was now quietly confident. The following day, Isaiah Berlin told his friend Bob Silvers of *The New York Review of Books* that they had crunched the numbers and believed they had a '53.5 % chance of victory'. The Mary Warnock review was 'idiotic', but the Strawson review in the *NYRB* was helpful and would 'considerably add to the ammunition of the party of truth and virtue'.[38] According to one Fellow, the hostile Letwin article was 'so foolishly extreme' that for non-philosophers 'it may well have actually strengthened the case for Derek's election'.[39]

. . .

The college meeting took place in mid-June. Berlin spoke up on Parfit's behalf. To his biographer, he claimed to have made 'a very tear-jerking speech [. . .] and more or less said that there was absolutely no possible reason not to elect him'.[40] It was the last speech Berlin made in All Souls, and for that reason might have been memorable, but others present have no recollection of tears.

In fact, this time a Parfit victory proved a formality. Following the triumph of *Reasons and Persons*, the college would have collectively blushed had he been rejected; even opposition from the crustiest of Fellows melted away. According to Berlin, the final tally was fifty to four.

Parfit would, of course, have survived outside the All Souls cocoon. But, for a man so thoroughly institutionalized, departure would have required considerable upheaval. News travelled fast around the international philosophical community. Rawls sent Parfit a congratulatory note on 17 June: 'It's splendid and heartening that it has finally, after this hard and trying time for you, come to pass.' He advised Parfit to take a well-earned rest and 'lie fallow'.[41] He followed this up with a letter to Berlin about the 'very good news indeed [. . . Parfit's] enormous effort in completing his book so splendidly must have compelled the outcome in the end.'[42] The following month, Berlin wrote to Parfit to thank him for the gift of a Glenn Gould recording, and referred back to the Letwin review: 'Nobody in the College to whom I spoke thought you ought to have replied to that silly woman.'[43]

Parfit would no longer be in need of full-time employment elsewhere, but he could firm up his part-time teaching engagements in America. He decided to opt for NYU over Harvard. He had no fresh ideas, and so the plan for the 1984 Fall semester was a course rehashing parts of *Reasons and Persons.* This would be embarrassing at Harvard, he told Nozick, but not at NYU. How so? Because Harvard students were brighter—though Parfit put it more tactfully. 'Given the kinds of students I'll be teaching' at NYU, he wrote, it would be worthwhile explaining the material at greater length. However, with Harvard students, teaching old material 'would waste their time'.[44]

He hoped to come to Harvard when he felt more inspired. 'I'm still feeling pretty stale and infertile [. . . and] I don't expect to learn much from teaching at NYU [. . .]. But I'm sure I would learn a great deal by trying out ideas at Harvard.'[45]

15

The Blues and the Bluebell Woods

Parfit was exhausted. The exhilaration of seeing *Reasons and Persons* in print soon passed. He felt that he was an intellectually spent force, that he had gone stale. His hair had gone white. He told people that the stress had damaged his brain and that he couldn't think as well as he used to do. He feared he might have nothing more of significance to contribute.

Reasons and Persons had been produced in a rush. A new version, with corrections, was printed later in 1984; a paperback, with further corrections, appeared in 1986, and then there was another paperback edition, containing many more corrections, in 1987. The paperback version usually provides the opportunity for an author to remove any glaring errors that have been identified in the hardback by the author or readers. Parfit had hundreds, perhaps thousands, of edits. Some, such as those on personal identity, were substantial, but almost all the rest were insignificant. Once again, he drove his copyeditor and other OUP staff involved in the book to the edge of sanity. 'He was solipsistic. The book's called *Reasons and Persons* but he had no idea about other persons.'[1] When OUP staff, such as Angela Blackburn, baulked at the extent to which he wished to modify the text, he resorted to his usual tactic of offering to pay. 'I said it's not a question of money. The production team is working very hard and it's discouraging. This came as a great shock to him.'[2]

Close textual analysis is required to spot some of the trivial alterations. The book opens with acknowledgements, dated September
1983. The first line of pre-1987 editions declares, 'Seventeen years ago,
I drove to Andalusia with Gareth Evans.'[3] Parfit wanted to start with his
debt to Evans because of Evans's untimely death (see chapter 10). But at
some stage during 1986, he must have realized that he had made, not one
blunder, but two. The 1987 volume begins, 'Sixteen years ago I travelled
to Madrid with Gareth Evans.[4] As we have seen, that edges closer to the
truth, but doesn't quite reach it: he must have travelled with Evans in
the summer of 1968 (*fifteen* years earlier, that is, than the acknowledgements in the book, dated 12 September 1983).

. . .

As well as his intellectual fatigue, the period following publication of
Reasons and Persons was one of personal trauma and upheaval. Parfit had
just completed the revisions for what would prove to be the final version
of the book when he received devastating news. His younger sister had
been in a car accident.

When they were young, the relationship between Derek and Joanna
was sweet and loving, as is evident from their correspondence. But, with
age, they grew apart. They had painfully little in common. Joanna had
trained to become a nursery nurse, but Parfit had little interest in
children. And she couldn't talk to him about philosophy. She had struggled throughout her life, psychologically and financially. She sometimes
called her brother in despair. Although he dreaded these calls, he would
write cheques to bail her out.

The accident occurred in Dorset. Joanna was in Monckton Wyld at a
country house retreat for single parents, where she had stayed a couple
of times before. On 30 October 1986, she and her Ethiopian-born foster
daughter, Naomi, were driving to Lyme Regis, where they were planning to buy ice cream. Her biological son, Tom, then six years old, was
back at the retreat with others in the household, first sleeping, and then
playing a game called Speak-and-Spell on a handheld console. The car
stalled as it was turning out of the top of a steep, narrow road and was

hit in the middle of a dual carriageway by a car that was trailing a boat. Naomi was only slightly bruised, but Joanna suffered severe abdominal and chest injuries and a massive internal brain haemorrhage.

The eldest sibling, Theodora, who lived in the US but happened to be in the UK on holiday, drove immediately from Oxford to the hospital with their mother, Jessie. Derek rushed down soon after. Joanna died on 3 November, aged forty-two. They took Tom and Naomi to see the body.

Joanna having made no will, the immediate problem was what to do with the children. Tom's biological father had had little part in his son's life and was unable to provide financial support. Theodora moved into Joanna's flat for a short period and considered adopting them both, but that would mean uprooting them and moving them to the US. Moreover, she was forty-six, and with a family of her own. It never occurred to anybody that Derek would be a suitable person to take them in. Despite having a partner, he was perceived as a bachelor, and far too unworldly and unfamiliar with children in general to cope with kids. He never knew what to say to children, though he had learned that he could amuse the younger ones by standing on his head.

The consequence was that, after a few weeks, the London borough of Haringey, where Joanna had lived, placed Tom and Naomi in care. This was only meant to be a temporary solution. Parfit sought out Oxford friends who might take the children in, including the philosopher Galen Strawson (son of Peter). Had it been his decision alone, Strawson might have apprehensively agreed, but his then wife vetoed the idea. However, Jessie, the children's grandmother, was professionally acquainted with Adrian Grant—an epidemiologist and pioneer of randomized control trials, who was part of the Oxford public health community to which both Norman and Jessie also belonged. Adrian and his wife Frinny were in their thirties, already had a daughter of their own, and had been approved as potential adopters of another child. The Grants were informed of the tragedy through a colleague and phoned Jessie immediately. Jessie judged the Grants to be a solid, loving family.

But Haringey Council believed it knew better—and so began a bitter sixteen-month legal wrangle, with the council stalling and prevaricating, and its social workers behaving with what from the outside comes across as bureaucratic indifference bordering on negligence. The council, using a primitive algorithm ('two parents', 'motivation', 'ability to manage Tom's contact with his natural family in Tom's interests'), identified an alternative couple for Tom, whom the Parfits considered unsuitable, in part because they were older and had no children of their own for Tom to play with. Theodora requested that she be allowed to adopt Tom rather than his being sent to this couple.

Jessie, now in her mid-seventies, spearheaded the campaign on behalf of the Grants; Haringey Council regarded her as interfering and possessive and a thorn in their flesh; they tried to limit her contact with her grandson and they cut off all contact between the Parfits and Naomi. On a few occasions, Derek and Janet took the children out, but did not really know what to do with them. Derek became heavily involved in the legal case, meeting with the Haringey social workers, helping to draft affidavits, and appearing in court. In fact, the dispute ended up in the High Court. Derek showed up regularly, and on one occasion became so irate that, according to Theodora, he yelled at the judge. If so, it may have been his only adult yelling episode. His own affidavit stated that the Haringey decision 'rests on grave misjudgements and factual errors, and [. . .] was reached in a careless and unprofessional way'.[5]

Eventually, the battle was won, and Tom joined his new family in 1988. Jessie passed away soon afterwards—Frinny Grant and the Parfits blamed the legal case for hastening her death. The novelist Margaret Forster, a close friend of Theodora's, wrote *The Battle for Christabel*, loosely based on this Parfit tragedy. Once the matter was officially settled, Derek saw little of his nephew, who moved with the Grants to Scotland in 1994. But he kept loosely in touch and, just as he had supported his mother, he would sometimes send Tom generous cheques. The Parfits had no influence over Naomi's fate—because she was not officially family—and she languished miserably in a foster home.

Parfit's emotions about his family ran deep. Not many people knew that he had a younger sister who had died in an accident, but if ever the subject was raised, he was quickly moved to tears.

. . .

In the midst of the legal drama, and to general astonishment, Janet and Derek began an experiment in cohabitation and, to even greater astonishment, in rural living. After Norman's death, a pot of money had been earmarked for Derek, but had been used by Jessie to buy a flat in Oxford where Joanna and her children could come to stay. That flat was now to be sold and the money returned to Derek. Janet suggested they pool their resources to buy a bigger house. She was thinking of an Oxford house, without any dramatic change to their normal life, until one day at All Souls, Derek idly picked up a copy of the glossy magazine *Country Life* and, turning a page, fell instantly and passionately in love.

The object of his infatuation was West Kennett House, decribed by the estate agent as a four-storey, six-bedroom, four–reception room, three-bathroom, eighteenth-century Georgian house, set within three acres. It was not actually as splendid as the estate agent made it sound or as the architect had obviously designed it to look, but it was the look of it that enchanted Parfit, in particular the neo-classical facade and pillared porch. After he had seen the picture of the facade, nothing else mattered. He later said it was like falling for a pretty face. He decided he must have it.

Janet was much less sure. She loved the house, but she was worried about the practicalities of being so far from their normal life: West Kennett was a tiny cluster of cottages near Avebury in Wiltshire, an hour's drive from Oxford and two from the Open University site at Milton Keynes. But she allowed herself to be convinced. There was already an offer on the house, so Parfit made a huge counter-offer. It guaranteed their bid would prevail, though they may have overpaid by a massive £50,000. His friend Bill Ewald was aghast: 'I said to Derek, "You're insane!" But he told me he'd worked it all out. If he reduced his purchase of compact discs he could afford to pay for it. It was delusional.'[6] They sold Janet's Oxford house and bought a smaller one nearby to rent to tenants and to use for themselves as a pied-à-terre. And off they went to West Kennett. They would be there for eight years in all, and at the beginning were very content.

There was still no talk of marriage, but Janet thought it would be a good idea to wear rings, as they were living together in a new place, and on one of their weekly shopping trips to Marlborough in 1988 they bought a matching pair. The following year, Parfit's ring was spotted by his American friend Larry Temkin when they were on a flight to a conference. 'You got married!' he said. 'He didn't say "No"'.[7] Temkin managed to swallow his annoyance that he hadn't been invited to the wedding. He barely knew Janet, but from that moment, whenever he and Parfit met, he would dutifully enquire about Parfit's 'wife'. Parfit never corrected him. Then, one day, about fifteen years later, Parfit said, 'You know, we're not married.'

Temkin had mentioned Parfit's 'wife' to several people, but many others in the philosophical world assumed he was unattached. Some thought he was gay. Once, excusing himself from a conversation at one of the rare social gatherings he attended (after a seminar which both he and Janet had sat in on, given by two renowned evolutionary biologists, John Maynard Smith and Richard Dawkins), he announced, referring to Janet, 'I'm just going to talk to that woman,' with no mention of who 'that woman' was.[8] There are almost no photographs of the pair of them together. Parfit seemed puzzled, moreover, when people talked about Janet. 'How is Janet?', Temkin asked on the phone. There was a baffled silence before Parfit responded, 'Why do you ask?' Temkin explained that it was polite and normal to enquire about a friend's nearest and dearest. Parfit squirrelled this useful information away for the future occasions when others posed the same question. Although he never fully internalized this conversational norm, from this moment, whenever he rang Temkin, the conversation would begin as follows:

PARFIT: This is Derek. I hope I'm not disturbing you. Is this a good time to talk?
TEMKIN: It's always a good time to talk with you, Derek.
PARFIT: How's Meg?[9]

. . .

At West Kennett, Janet was developing an Open University course on equality, and in the early stages of thinking about a book on Darwinism and its implications for human nature. She and Derek had separate studies. He would frequently wander into hers, after becoming frustrated with a philosophical argument or, more prosaically, because his computer was playing up.

He had moved to West Kennett full of enthusiasm for the house, the surrounding landscape, and their proximity to the outstanding architecture of Bath, Wells, and Winchester. And he did love being there. Janet would travel to Milton Keynes and would frequently drive to Oxford with Derek. 'This life suits me!' he pronounced.[10] The commute didn't bother either of them, though Janet was once so tired that she drove off the road.

But, over the course of years, his writing began to consume him. Since they hardly knew any local people, Janet invited a few around for drinks, including the local MP. It was not long after they moved in. 'Derek was as close to angry as I have ever seen him. Having to spend an hour trying to make conversation with people he had no reason to think he would be interested in was simply a total waste of time.'[11] In late April and May, the woods nearby to West Kennett are carpeted in deep violet bluebells. Visitors travel miles to see them. In an essay that Parfit wrote about why the universe existed (of which more later), he imagined nothing existing, wondered what the explanation for that might be, and offered examples of things that would not exist in nonexistence. 'Why would there have been no stars or atoms, no philosophers or bluebell woods?'[12] But it turned out that he was more interested in bluebell woods of the abstract than the real kind. In the years that he and Janet owned the West Kennett house, he took a total of two walks, the first time willingly, the second time under sufferance. The top-floor study had breathtaking views, but the curtains were kept closed. He would not even go round to the back of the house when, one evening, Janet asked him to come and admire a stunning sky.

In the evenings, Janet would sometimes go for a cycle ride around the country lanes, but Parfit could not be persuaded to accompany her. Upon returning home, she would glance up, and often he could be seen through the window, completely naked, pumping his legs on his exercise bike. He began to take only short breaks during the day to eat. He may as well have been in Oxford. He had also stepped up his teaching load in the United States and was going off on his annual trips to Venice and St Petersburg. Janet found herself alone for much of the time. Once, he returned from teaching in the US and immediately began packing for a photographic trip abroad, about which Janet knew nothing. He left the following day. The situation was clearly not ideal. Neither of them was a quarreller, but tensions between them grew.

Parfit must have forgotten the good times. Many years later, he told his friend Ruth Chang that the purchase of West Kennett was the biggest mistake he had made.[13]

. . .

The White's Chair of Moral Philosophy was vacant for seven years from 1983, when Hare retired, until 1990. It was the country's most prestigious position in moral philosophy, and Hare told Parfit it was his duty to apply for it. But the role came with administrative responsibilities, and Parfit showed no interest.

For several years in Trinity term (1986–88), he gave seminars on Sidgwick's *Methods of Ethics*. His Oxford annual seminars with Dworkin and Sen also continued, also in Trinity term. Naturally, there was much discussion in these seminars about Rawls; issues raised by Rawls continued to dominate debate in ethics and political theory—and in the US even more so than in the UK. Parfit found this intensely annoying. He thought Rawls's insight about the need for special concern for the least well-off was important, but that *A Theory of Justice* was spectacularly overrated. Rawls was one of very few philosophers whom Parfit would denigrate—not in print and not about anything personal, but because he was baffled by his prominence.

From 1984, the Sen-Dworkin-Parfit band acquired a new member, a quick-witted, fast-talking, wisecracking, twinkly-eyed, Canadian-born political theorist, G. A. (Jerry) Cohen, who had made his reputation as an 'analytic Marxist', examining Karl Marx's arguments with the tools and logic of analytical philosophy. This was referred to as 'no-bullshit Marxism'. All Souls was not the obvious fit for a Marxist, but Cohen was a gregarious and popular figure, and the Fellows were reassured that if the revolution were to come, it was unlikely to be sparked by the peer-reviewed journal publications of the new Chichele Professor of Social and Political Theory.

Cohen's sympathy for Marxist theory waned over time, and, in any case, he was always a strong critic of human-rights abuses within the USSR's sphere of influence. Of the three other panellists, it was Cohen with whom Parfit would become the closest—yet they had wildly contrasting backgrounds. Cohen was raised in a working-class immigrant family in Montreal—his parents both laboured in the garment industry and met whilst trying to organize trade unions in the face of police brutality. It was simultaneously a very Jewish, anti-Zionist, pro-Soviet, and militantly atheistic household, a combination that induced ambivalent attitudes in Cohen about his ethnic origins. Isaiah Berlin had been the first Jewish Fellow at All Souls, and Cohen held the same chair. When I was a postgraduate student, he once invited me to lunch and showed me a booklet containing the names and photos of All Souls Fellows; sifting through the pages, he proudly pointed out, 'He's a bloody Jew . . . he's a bloody Jew . . . he's a bloody Jew'.[14]

Parfit and Cohen, the old Etonian and the working-class Jew, both loved All Souls and remained there for the rest of their careers. In a reference Parfit once wrote for Cohen, he described him as the best political philosopher in the UK, and praised his intellectual integrity.[15] The phone rang in Cohen's room one day, and Parfit was on the other end. 'Would it be all right', Parfit wanted to check, 'if I call you my friend?'[16] Parfit put the question because he was unsure how to use the word 'friend', but Cohen was profoundly touched.

The seminars went under various titles—'Rationality and Justice', 'Agency, Well-Being and Equality', 'Equality of Reason'—but soon acquired the catch-all nickname 'Star Wars'. Cohen, Dworkin, Parfit, and Sen would be seated behind a long table at one end of the room. The Gladstone Professor of Government and Public Administration, Viennese-born Peter Pulzer, hovered near the edge of the table, in a grey zone between the panellists and the audience. Pulzer had a wide range of expertise, from German politics to the rise of anti-Semitism, but he was no philosopher, and had not been invited to participate as a panellist. He must have felt that his Oxford chair justified a privileged role in the proceedings, and it was clearly too awkward for the philosophers to ask him to move.

Cohen's arrival did not alter the format—one of the four would open a discussion with some informal remarks. A recurring theme was 'equality'. What does treating people equally mean? Why should we value equality or worry about inequality? How could equality be attained? What is the link between equality and rights? Is equality incompatible with liberty?

Most people, of all political persuasions, glibly claim that they favour some form of 'equality'—but, if questioned, would struggle to explain why, or what precisely they mean. Examined under the analytic microscope, the concept 'equality' appears charged with tensions. The US Declaration of Independence proclaims, 'All men are created equal', and the phrase is held to capture a moral truth, that humans are of equal worth and are owed equal respect. But what does this entail for the distribution of goods? Does equal worth mean equal resources—or should we aim at something like equal happiness which resources generate? Different conceptions of equality will support different policies.

Linked to these issues was another, raised by Dworkin; it became known as the 'expensive taste' problem. Suppose there are two people—let's call them Derek and Ronnie. The former is indifferent as to what he eats. He is happy surviving on a diet of cornflakes and broccoli. The latter, on the other hand, relishes white truffles and foie gras, especially when accompanied by a glass of vintage Château Mouton-Rothschild. To allocate equal resources to Derek and Ronnie seems to punish poor Ronnie, whose refined desires may not be satisfied. This line of thought then provoked questions to do with equality, luck, and choice. Some people may end up less well off than others because of a choice they have made; with others, it may be the result of bad luck. Should the state compensate for luck but not choice? Cohen argued that the goal of egalitarianism was to eliminate disadvantage, for which the sufferer was not responsible.

These and similar debates helped Amartya Sen develop what would become the 'capability' approach to equality—focusing on the capabilities of individuals to achieve the kinds of lives they value. In other words, Sen argued, we should look at what people can *actually* be and do, rather than, say, attempt to measure and compare subjective levels of wellbeing or happiness. This approach has become hugely influential within the contexts of international aid and development.

But the Star Wars discussions ranged far beyond questions of equality. For example, there was a session about whether it was rational to vote (given that the likelihood of one vote making a difference was negligible). There were also debates about 'freedom'. The no-bullshit Marxist, Jerry Cohen, was intrigued by what seems like a contradiction within Marxism. Marx insists that historical forces ensured that the revolution was inevitable. At the same time, Marx and Marxists also exhort people to engage in the political activism that will ultimately bring about the revolution. But if the revolution was inevitable, wasn't it rational for a Marxist to remain seated on the sofa, munching capitalist-produced popcorn and watching daytime TV, until it occurred?

Not according to Cohen. Marx did not think the revolution was inevitable *whatever* people might do, but rather *because of* what, acting rationally, they were *bound* eventually to do. In the same way, a huge and well-equipped army will inevitably defeat a tiny, poorly equipped one, but only if, and because, the soldiers in the powerful force participate in the fighting.

The thrill for postgraduate students in the room—and I was one—was in part because many of the issues being discussed had serious implications for how society should be run and restructured. The seminars were taking place at the height of Thatcherism; there was, for a period, mass unemployment, and Britain was riven ideologically. On 29 January 1985, in protest at funding cuts in education, Oxford dons voted to deny Margaret Thatcher an honorary degree: an astounding snub. Thatcherism had its intellectual underpinnings in the monetarism of Milton Friedman, the classical liberalism of the Viennese-born Friedrich

Hayek, and the open society anti-totalitarianism of a fellow Viennese, Karl Popper. More immediate intellectual ballast came from one of Thatcher's key allies in the Conservative Party, the ex-All Souls Fellow Sir Keith Joseph. Although widely loathed in the university sector, Thatcherism was an ideological phenomenon propelled by ideas that had floated down from the ivory towers.

But beyond the socio-political context, there was the spectacle of the seminars. Here were heavyweight intellectual wrestlers, going at each other; the room was saturated with ego. Cohen, Sen, and Dworkin were all garrulous extroverts. Among themselves, the postgraduates gossiped about who amongst the four possessed the most inflated self-image. Nobody said Parfit.

The philosopher Tom Hurka recalls a conversation along these lines with Jerry Cohen. Hurka was on sabbatical in Oxford in the mid-1980s and, one evening, he invited Cohen back for supper after the seminar. Cohen asked him to rank the participants according to (a) how much they cared about 'winning' and (b) how much they cared about the truth. It was obvious, Cohen thought, that Parfit was the one who cared most about the truth and the least about victory.

· · ·

For a few years, Parfit could savour the success of *Reasons and Persons* whilst enjoying a steady flow of academic laurels. An entire edition of the prestigious journal *Ethics* was devoted to the book in 1986, and, in the same year, he received the imprimatur of his peers, with his election to the British Academy.

But, outside the animated and fertile Star Wars seminars, these were relatively fallow years for him, intellectually. A few articles and chapters in edited books appeared, but all of it was essentially reheated material. He began working on an insanely ambitious book, provisionally entitled *Metaphysics and Ethics*, which would cover personal identity, free will, time, death, mind and matter, the universe, and God![17] In the free will debate, Parfit was interested in what sort of freedom was required for moral responsibility and desert. He had deterministic instincts; that is to say, he thought that either our decisions must be caused, or, if not caused, they must be the product of a random process—and in either case we had to rethink radically our reactive attitudes, such as guilt, resentment, indignation, anger, and pride. If people were *caused* to act badly, it made no sense to feel hostility towards them. It might make sense to lock some people up as a deterrent, or because they were a danger to others, but not because they *deserved* punishment.

'Death' raised many issues that intrigued Parfit: what was bad about death, and how would we react to the prospect of immortality? As for 'time', touched upon in *Reasons and Persons,* Parfit believed that there might be a parallel between 'now' and 'here'. 'Here' was relative to a speaker's point of view. If there was no life on the planet, 'here' would have no meaning. Might that also be true of 'now'? Or would time roll out in its forward direction in a lifeless universe, so that some things would happen 'now', followed by other things happening 'now'?

For Parfit, there were no major intellectual breakthroughs in the years immediately following the publication of *Reasons and Persons,* but the time was not squandered. He read voraciously. Socializing had almost disappeared from his schedule, although he would occasionally permit himself a few hours off. He took the historian Adrian Wooldridge to a Leicester Square showing of a film he had already seen, the silent 1927 French movie *Napoléon,* directed by Abel Gance. They went to London by car; Parfit surprised Wooldridge by exhibiting basic competence at both driving and parking. His driving style was to pick a lane and a speed, and to stick with it robotically all the way down the motorway. He paid little attention to other cars on the road; they were merely obstacles to be avoided. According to Janet Radcliffe Richards, 'he seemed to have no real idea of the need to make his intentions clear to other road users, or to try to read theirs'.[18]

To Wooldridge, the five-and-a-half-hour film seemed interminable, but Parfit watched with rapt attention, awaiting one particular shot, in one particular scene, that he regarded as a sublime moment of genius. He had excitedly hyped this scene, but it made no impression on his companion. They drove back to Oxford on one lane, in the same manner in which they had arrived. Janet always advised passengers that if they wanted to stay alive when Derek was driving, they were not to talk philosophy.

Although the chance of being ejected from All Souls was slim, Parfit was still required to submit a study plan every seven years, and the Academic Purposes Committee existed to keep a watchful eye on progress. In 1988, the committee reported that, once again, Parfit's rate of publication was 'disappointing'.[19] In response, he decided to turn his attention to writing another book, about equality, that he thought he could produce quickly. It was provisionally entitled *On Giving Priority to the Worse Off*. By late 1990, he had written eight draft chapters.

On Giving Priority to the Worse Off was never completed—eventually (see next chapter), it would be boiled down to one short but magnificent lecture. Parfit's excuse for not finishing it was that he now had to fulfil another pressing commitment. In 1987, Jonathan Dancy, a philosopher based at the University of Keele, approached him with the idea of editing a book, *Reading Parfit*. This would contain mostly specially commissioned essays, responding to Parfit's arguments in *Reasons and Persons*. Rawls and Nozick had already been honoured with *Reading Rawls* and *Reading Nozick* volumes, respectively. The idea was that the chapters in *Reading Parfit* would be sent to Parfit, and his responses would be published in the same book. Parfit responded to the idea enthusiastically, suggesting a list of contributors. Here was a major project that could engage him until inspiration for original work returned.

By 1991, almost all the chapters were in, and Dancy was waiting for Parfit's replies. He waited. And waited.

16

The Priority View

Those who had written chapters for the *Reading Parfit* volume included Larry Temkin, Simon Blackburn, and Judith Jarvis Thomson; Parfit's response to each of them kept ballooning. He repeatedly promised the volume's editor, Jonathan Dancy, that his final manuscript would arrive soon. Dancy was having to fend off the contributors, some of whom were becoming irate that their papers were taking years to appear.

Parfit had many distractions. These included giving lectures and participating in discussion groups. The longest-running of all the groups he was involved in began in 1990, lasted for nearly three decades, and for all but the first meeting did not include his student Ruth Chang. The Chang-less nature of the group is worthy of mention because, as a DPhil student, she had first suggested it to two young fellow Oxford-based philosophers, Roger Crisp and Brad Hooker. The idea was to meet in her rooms at Balliol; among the appeals of the proposal was that Chang had a stash of imported fine-quality coffee (this was before the British coffee revolution).

Chang already held an embryonic form of the view for which she would become best known. Her instincts told her that values and reasons were wholly unlike physical properties such as height and weight. Physical qualities like height and weight must be greater, lesser, or equal to one another. Brad is taller than Roger, or vice versa, or maybe they are equally tall. But that is not true, Chang believed, of values and reasons. While we can agree that Monet is a better artist than my nine-year-old child, it makes little sense to say Monet is better than Cezanne. Nor are they equally good. When two things are equally good, if you improve one of them, it becomes better than the other. If Monet had used more cobalt blue rather than the much cheaper French ultramarine blue in his *Water Lilies* paintings, those paintings might have been a bit more beautiful, showing even greater artistry. But he would not thereby become a better artist than Cezanne.

Something similar can be said of the tough decisions we all have to make in life. Should you become a lawyer or a philosopher, move to the suburbs or stay in town, stay single or get married? Each option has pros and cons. Overall, neither path might be better or worse than the other, and they also might not be equally good. But it would be madness to flip a coin between them, and the matter would not be settled by someone offering you fifty dollars to take one path rather than the other. Often in life, Chang thought, our options are on a par—really different without one being the correct choice. You have to make one of them correct *for you*, through your commitment to it.

Chang herself had faced such a dilemma, choosing to become a philosopher after qualifying as a lawyer. The solid and well-paid legal profession was the career her immigrant parents had wanted for her. Born on the Chinese mainland, they'd met in Taiwan, before the 1949 revolution. Later, they moved to Minnesota, and before her father qualified as a biochemist he would make ends meet by washing dishes. Moral philosophy appealed to Chang. She had faced constant racist abuse as a child in an almost wholly white neighbourhood (her third-grade teacher told all the other kids in the class to go and inspect her eyes). She was taught by her family to keep her head down, not to stick out. Overnight, when she was about five, her parents had stopped talking to her in Mandarin, and moved to (broken) English, though Mandarin was retained as the language in which they quarrelled.

While the reasons to become a philosopher were no more compelling than the reasons to become a lawyer, in choosing to become a philosopher, Chang was choosing to be the sort of person she could commit herself to being, and to have the sort of life she could commit herself to having. In any case, she was sitting in Parfit's lecture one day, when he touched on the idea of value fuzziness. And the bond between them was forged when they began to discuss it, and the implications for ethics.

Crisp and Hooker, close friends and both likeable and popular, shared Chang's interests in moral philosophy. At the first meeting of their group, Chang put forward the far-fetched proposal that they invite Parfit to the next meeting. It was assumed that he would, politely, refuse, but, to their surprise, he agreed—on condition that it move to his rooms at All Souls. He also discouraged Chang from showing up—because he felt she needed to focus on completing her doctorate. So the Chang discussion group continued, in a new venue, and minus its founder.

Over the next twenty years, the group met on average three or four times a year. It expanded to include other philosophers, some of whom attended for many years, while others only participated for a term. As well as Crisp and Hooker, attendees included Robert Adams, John Broome, Krister Bykvist, Jonathan Dancy, Tom Hurka, Wlodek Rabinowicz, Julian Savulescu, John Skorupski, Philip Stratton-Lake, Larry Temkin, and Ralph Wedgwood. Usually, meetings began at around 2 p.m. and would last until at least 5 p.m. No refreshments were on offer.

It would be misleading to describe Derek as being first among equals within the group; he was first among unequals. Although occasionally a paper presented by one of the others would be discussed, for around 75 per cent of the time the group debated something Parfit was working on. And, about 50 per cent of the time, Parfit would be talking. Since there were not enough chairs to accommodate everyone, there would often be people on the floor. Parfit would sit with his back to the fireplace, in which, alarmingly, there were stacks of books piled high—one participant became mesmerized by Parfit's elbows, because one false move might send the book towers tumbling.

. . .

Seminars, lectures, and discussion groups were far from being Parfit's only barriers to completing his portion of the *Reading Parfit* book. He also became distracted by two issues which were orthogonal to his other philosophical concerns.

The first was equality and distributive justice—how resources in society should be fairly shared. This matter not only dominated the Star Wars seminars, but fascinated his two closest American friends, Thomas Nagel and Tim Scanlon. When the University of Kansas approached Parfit to deliver the 1991 Lindley Lecture, he chose 'Equality or Priority?' as his topic. He must have been honoured to have been invited. The list of Lindley lecturers over the years reads like a *Who's Who* of philosophy, including many thinkers with whom Parfit was well acquainted, such as Hare, Williams, and Dworkin.

On the face of it, equality appears to be one important value which might be weighed on the scales against others. Even fervent egalitarians do not maintain it is the only value. For example, an equal society where everybody is well off must be better than an equal society where everybody is badly off. Usually, the value that is thought to be most in tension with equality is freedom—to redistribute from the rich to the poor, governments have to impose coercive taxes. But, in a Harvard seminar in 1991, Parfit surprised those present by postulating that a more equal society will have worse art, leading to the following exchange with a postgraduate student.

> PARFIT: Consider. Why has there been no great music composed in the twentieth century?
> STUDENT: You're kidding.
> PARFIT: Give us an example then.
> STUDENT: Punk rock.
> PARFIT (THROWING UP HIS ARMS): Pleeeeeease. . . .[1]

Even if we are sceptical of Parfit's dubious correlation between inequality and art, it is obvious that pursuing equality may have other costs. Acknowledging that does nothing to undermine what most of us take for granted, however: that equality may not be the only value, but it is surely a value of intrinsic significance. It was this assumption—one that had received little attention from philosophers, because they, like non-philosophers, took it to be self-evident—that Parfit targeted in his lecture.

Parfit was struck by an example from his friend Thomas Nagel, who towards the end of 'Equality', a chapter in his book *Mortal Questions*, imagined a parental dilemma:

> Suppose I have two children, one of which is normal and quite happy, and the other of which suffers from a painful handicap. Call them respectively the first child and the second child. I am about to change jobs. Suppose I must decide between moving to an expensive city where the second child can receive medical treatment and schooling, but where the family's standard of living will be lower and the neighbourhood will be unpleasant and dangerous for the first child—or else moving to a pleasant semi-rural suburb where the first child, who has a special interest in sports and nature, can have a free and agreeable life. This is a difficult choice on any view. To make it a test for the value of equality, I want to suppose that the case has the following feature: the gain to the first child of moving to the suburb is substantially greater than the gain to the second child of moving to the city.[2]

Nagel's intuition was that there is nonetheless a reason to choose the city, the choice that will be of most benefit to the second child. And the reason, he wrote, was 'equality'. The second child is worse off than the first child, and prioritizing the interests of the second child would make the lives of the two children more equal. He does not insist that this consideration outweighs all other factors. There may be other factors that are more important and which on balance lead one to choose the suburb. But we can all agree that in this dilemma, the value of equality tugs us in the other direction.

Or can we? Parfit's originality lay, in part, in his refusal to embrace intuitively plausible claims until they had been expressed with precision and then tested in a range of, usually hypothetical, cases. His starting point in the equality debate was to compare various hypothetical worlds, in which different groups are more or less badly off—this may be in terms of wealth, health, happiness, or in other ways. For example, imagine there's a divided world in which neither side knows about the other—perhaps there are people on either side of the Atlantic Ocean, there are no modern communications, and the ocean has not yet been crossed. Population is equal on both sides. Now suppose that on one side each person in the population has a wellbeing level of 100, and on the other they are better off, with each having a wellbeing level of 200. Compare that to a divided world in which the level is 140 on either side. The first world is in one sense better, because people are on average better off (the average is 150). But many of us will be tempted to say that, all things considered, the second world is to be preferred, because it is more equal.

So far, so comforting for the egalitarian. However, Parfit pointed out a simple but devastating objection to the claim that equality is intrinsically valuable. He labelled it the 'Levelling Down Objection'. Some people are blind. Would the world be a better place, *at least in one way*, if we slipped some chemical in the water that made everyone blind? Of course, there would be multiple reasons why this would be a monstrous act; surely every decent person must agree that it would be a horrific thing to do. But Parfit is not asking whether we *should* make everyone blind. The chemical would make many people worse off and nobody better off; Parfit's question is whether, nonetheless, its use would be *in one way* welcome, in that it would at least produce greater equality. A similar example is a natural disaster that only affects the better-off, reducing them to the level of the worst-off. Is there really something to be said in favour of this eventuality? This seems an absurd claim.[3]

If Parfit is right about the force of the Levelling Down Objection, then nobody should endorse equality as a value with *intrinsic* significance—though it may have an instrumental rationale. That is, it may help to produce other outcomes that do have intrinsic value. A more equal society may be a more cohesive and therefore a happier society. In such a case, equality is valuable not in and of itself, but because it contributes to more of something else of value (happiness).

Parfit suggests that there is a value close to equality but more fundamental. What matters, he writes, is not that some people in an unequal world are worse off per se. What matters is that they are worse off than the worst-off might have been. Return to the scenarios contrasting

(a) a world in which the population's wellbeing level is split, with half on 100 and half on 200, and (b) a world in which everyone has a wellbeing level of 140. The reason why (b) is at least in one way better is not because it is more equal, but because the worst-off are now better off. Parfit called this the 'priority' view.

Equality was the specialist area of one of his former students, Larry Temkin, who reached slightly different conclusions. In fact, Temkin can claim priority over the priority view. In his 1983 dissertation, he drew attention to the incompatibility of egalitarianism and prioritarianism.[4] Several times, Parfit confessed to Temkin that he felt he owed the younger man an intellectual debt that he had never sufficiently acknowledged. Still, the teasing apart of the distinction between equality and priority was expressed by Parfit with his trademark economy and clarity. It was he who made it famous. It took another four years before the 1991 Lindley Lecture appeared in published form.[5] It remains a seminal contribution to the equality literature.

. . .

Another intellectual detour at this time took Parfit around what he called the most sublime question that there is. Why does the universe exist? Or, to put it another way, why is there something rather than nothing? There was also a supplementary question: why is our universe as it is?

Some people regard these as meaningless questions. The young Freddie Ayer and the logical empiricists would have adopted this stance—for they are not questions open to empirical testing. Parfit, however, believed that not only were they meaningful, but we could even provide some partial answers.

His earliest thoughts on the topic appeared in a short piece in *The Harvard Review of Philosophy* in 1991.[6] But he also addressed it in the only articles he ever wrote for a non-philosophical readership: first in 'The Puzzle of Reality',[7] published in July 1992 in *The Times Literary Supplement*, and then in a long article in two parts for the *London Review of Books* in 1998.[8] Many scientists had pondered the mystery of existence, as had philosophers such as Gottfried Leibniz in the seventeenth century and Arthur Schopenhauer in the nineteenth. In the early twentieth century, Ludwig Wittgenstein wrote, 'It is not *how* things are in the world that is mystical, but *that* it exists'[9]

The world could have been other than it is. So why this world? Each of the ways the world could exist Parfit calls a 'local' possibility. He calls the entire collection of these local possibilities 'cosmic'. Now, among the cosmic possibilities are that none of the local possibilities exist (which he calls the 'Null Hypothesis'), or that all of them exist (the 'All Worlds Hypothesis'). And there could be everything in between. Fifty-seven possibilities might exist. Or fifty-seven trillion.

If all the possibilities exist—if, somewhere there is every world that could have existed—then it ceases to become much of a mystery that we live in *this* world. The question, 'Why is our universe the one it is?' would be, Parfit says, analogous to asking, 'Why is now the time that it is?'

The Null Hypothesis would also be quite a plausible scenario—though we have to ask what it would be for nothing to exist. If nothing existed, this book would not exist. Nothing on planet Earth would exist. Planet Earth itself would not exist. But, according to Parfit, 'there would still have been various truths, such as the truth that there were no stars or atoms, or that nine is divisible by three'.[10]

Since our world does in fact exist, we know that the Null Hypothesis is false. Between the Null Hypothesis and the All Worlds Hypothesis, there exist some possible worlds. Perhaps our world is the only one that exists. Many scientists believe that the conditions that make life possible are highly specific. For example, had the initial conditions in the Big Bang been just slightly different, complex life would have been impossible. In which case, Parfit says, there is a question to answer. He draws an analogy with a lottery. Suppose a thousand people are facing death, and only one can be rescued, determined by a lottery.

[If] I win, I would be very lucky. But there might be nothing here that needed to be explained. Someone had to win, and why not me? Consider next another lottery. Unless my gaoler picks the longest of a thousand straws, I shall be shot. If my gaoler picks that straw, there would be something to be explained. It would not be enough to say, 'This result was as likely as any other.'[11]

The second result was special, the first was not. The first was bound to happen to someone, somewhere. The second may very well not have happened—in most cases, would not have happened. It could, of course, just be a coincidence. But that seems unlikely. The Big Bang seems akin to this second lottery. So, an explanation is in order.

This gives a flavour of some dense and knotty arguments which I presume very few readers of either *The Times Literary Supplement* or the *London Review of Books* managed to wade through. The subject is fiendishly complex, and Parfit was necessarily at his most rarefied and abstruse. It is ironic that this alone among his writings was given a popular airing. The writer Jim Holt reported that the *LRB* articles caused him to 'weep tears of intellectual joy',[12] but not all readers shared his ecstatic reaction. One reader was moved to question, 'Why does a literary magazine exist at all?', before adding, 'The world we live in is unfair enough already, with the *LRB* only appearing fortnightly, and that terrible gap after Christmas, the deepest abyss in the year. To surrender two and a half pages in each of two issues to this meticulous but rather pontifical philosophical analysis is enough to make us cry out "why?" to the heavens.'[13]

Heaven, or its absence, probably had something to do with Parfit's interest in these matters. He had a short but fervently religious period as a boy and, of course, had come from a missionary family. The main reason he couldn't believe in God—at least the Christian God—was the Problem of Evil. An all-powerful, all-benevolent God would surely have arranged the world so that it contained no suffering.[14] He was also scornful of the notion that an all-powerful, all-good God would divide and apportion up spots in heaven and hell, condemning some humans to eternal damnation.

But if God did not exist, where did that leave morality? If the universe was inexplicable, how should this affect how we live our lives? Without God, would anything matter? Here were the seeds of thoughts that would soon become Parfit's overriding obsession.

. . .

In the early 1990s, Parfit also returned to past topics. A year after the Lindley Lecture, he published his only co-authored article.[15] His co-author was not a philosopher, but an economist. Reading *Reasons and Persons*, Tyler Cowen said, 'changed my life'.[16] So taken with it was he that he read all the appendices, including Appendix F. Here, Parfit argued that there was no rationale for the 'social discount rate', whereby the moral significance of future events is discounted at a certain rate— so that, for example, a thousand people having wretched lives now mattered more than a thousand people having wretched lives in ten years' time, which in turn mattered more than a thousand people having wretched lives in a hundred years' time.

Parfit rejected this kind of claim, for reasons Cowen found compelling. From 20 to 22 October 1988, both Parfit and Cowen had attended a Liberty Fund conference in Austin, Texas, on the theme 'Intergenerational Relationships'. Cowen had been eager to meet 'my favourite thinker in the world'.[17] The Liberty Fund format consists of roundtable discussions among a small interdisciplinary group. There were law professors present, as well as philosophers and economists. Parfit was impressed by Cowen, and proposed they co-write a paper.

This turned into an expanded form of the *Reasons and Persons* appendix, and analysed various arguments used to justify an intergenerational discount rate, finding them all wanting. For example, there is the argument from democracy: many people care less about the future, so we should respect their wishes. But Parfit and Cowen drew a distinction between the question of whether we are morally justified in being less concerned about the future and the separate issue of whether a government should enforce the majority view. The argument from democracy was relevant only to this latter issue and had nothing to contribute to the central concern of the paper—whether the majority was right.

They conceded that there are some reasonable grounds to be less concerned about the future. One of these is that the future is uncertain. If Policy A could save a life for certain now, while Policy B would have only a 50 per cent chance of saving a life in a year's time, and we can afford either Policy A or Policy B but not both, we obviously have a powerful reason to adopt Policy A. It makes sense to discount for predictions that are more likely to be false. But that is not because a life in one year's or a hundred years' time is any less valuable than a life today. To repeat a *Reasons and Persons* claim, it makes no moral difference whether discarded broken glass cuts a child today or in a century. There should be no *ethical* discounting of distant lives—lives do not become less valuable the more remote they are in time. Time was relevantly similar to distance, Parfit and Cowen argued, and '[n]o one thinks that we would be morally justified if we cared less about the long-range effects of our acts at some rate of n % per yard.'[18]

The collaboration between the two men turned out to be remarkably hassle-free. Cowen wrote the initial draft, of around fifty pages; Parfit made many points of clarification, but they were more or less in complete agreement. Cowen's distinct contribution was his conversion of Parfit's philosophical insights into economic language—the language, for example, of marginal and opportunity cost. He could do the maths that, though relatively straightforward, made Parfit's head hurt. If there is a discount rate of 1 per cent, Cowen pointed out, a single life today is worth more than a million lives in 1,400 years. If the discount rate is 10 per cent, a single life today is worth more than a million lives in a mere 145 years.

. . .

Throughout this period, Parfit was still delivering annual classes in Oxford. These usually had headings such as 'Ethics' or 'Practical Reason'. He led two joint classes on personal identity, the first, in Michaelmas term 1992, with Quassim Cassam, and the second, in 1995, with Paul Snowdon. The Kenyan-born Cassam was an up-and-coming philosopher based at Oxford's Wadham College. He sent Parfit a paper he had written on personal identity in the late 1980s. Parfit had been very complimentary about it, but since the publication of *Reasons and Persons* he had put the subject of personal identity aside. It was only when he returned to it that he got back in touch with Cassam and suggested they run a joint class. 'And I thought, "Great—a joint class with Derek Parfit!"'[19]

Cassam's enthusiasm soon waned. 'It was my most gruelling experience ever. It was an absolute killer.' The deal was that they would alternate in leading the sessions, and they would send a draft of their lectures to each other. 'So I would send a draft and Derek would call back within an hour or two. He never said hello. He'd say, "Am I disturbing you?"' And then he would give extensive, detailed comments. Cassam felt he had to address these before the seminar began, 'so by the time I got to the session, I was knackered.'[20]

The weekly seminars were held in the philosophy department at 10 Merton Street, and were packed, with several big-name philosophers in attendance. There was a sense of occasion, because it was the first time Parfit had spoken about personal identity since the publication of *Reasons and Persons*.

Much of the class was devoted to animalism. The term 'animalism' had been coined by Paul Snowdon, and it was the view that each of us is a human animal, a biological organism. I begin to exist when this organism begins to exist and I cease to exist when it dies. Animalism had been gaining ground since *Reasons and Persons*, and Parfit was open to it, because of the so-called Too-Many-Thinkers Problem. According to Parfit's psychological-continuity account, people were not identical to their bodies. But bodies think. My body has a brain, so it is a thinking thing. That seems to suggest that at the desk writing these words are two thinkers, the animal David Edmonds and the person David Edmonds. That, in turn, seems like one thinker too many.

To put the puzzle another way: suppose it was possible for just your brain to be transplanted into a different body. According to the psychological-continuity account, the person with the different body but *your* brain would be you—it would have all your memories and so on. This kind of example is more persuasive if we bear in mind that the parts of the brain that sustain biological life-processes—breathing, heartbeat, digestion—are different from those that are the seat of mental faculties. So, an organism that loses the latter to another organism could remain biologically alive. If the original body survived without the brain, would we not want to say that that body was you, albeit without your brain (admittedly a rather crucial organ!)? If so, it looks like you then exist in two places.

There are very few examples of Parfit changing his mind about anything fundamental in philosophy. By the time he reached a firm conclusion, he had usually foreseen and overcome all objections to it. But the Too-Many-Thinkers Problem forced a temporary shift in his position on personal identity and, for a brief period, he was enticed by animalism. Later, he reverted to a more sophisticated view of his original position. A person is distinct from, but still has to exist within, a particular body, rather as a car horn is distinct from, but exists within, a car. So, when the horn is blown, both the horn and the car make a noise, but there is really only one noise and only one noise-maker; it is just that the noise-maker—the horn—is a part of the car. Regardless, what makes a person the same person over time is psychological connectedness. Even during his animalist phase, Parfit insisted on the view that whatever identity consisted in, identity was not what *mattered*. What mattered was psychological continuity. Indeed, he thought that animalism provided him with a fresh argument for his view: sameness of person is sameness of animal, and sameness of animal isn't what matters; it followed that personal identity is not what matters.

Parfit had approached Cassam and Snowdon precisely because they were animalists. 'He was terrifying because he had thought so deep and hard about the issues,' Snowdon says. In one seminar, Parfit imagined visiting Bernard Williams in hospital and chatting to him. If, mid-conversation, Williams's sheet then fell off, to reveal that Williams's head was not attached to a body, 'I would still think I'd been talking to Bernard.'[21] An exasperated Snowdon interjected, 'If I went to pick up a pet at a pet shop and they only gave me the cat's head, I would be extremely annoyed.'[22] The class found this hilarious.

Snowdon stuck to his strong animalist position, but Cassam came round to the view that Parfit was right on the central point—that animalism posed no challenge to Parfit's position about what was important. For Cassam, the most unnerving aspect of the joint teaching experience was how Parfit 'got into my head.'[23] Cassam gave a paper to the Aristotelian

Society in 1993, in which he laid out Parfit's views. He sent this to Parfit, who 'suggested' changes. The paper went through multiple drafts and ended up with Parfit's distinctive voice, unlike any other paper Cassam has written. 'I felt completely out of my depth in a way that I've never felt with anyone else. I felt I ceased to think independently. I felt he'd taken over my brain.'[24]

. . .

As Jonathan Dancy continued to wait for Parfit's contribution to the *Reading Parfit* book, there was yet another distraction. Parfit was now also serving as the editor for an 'Oxford Ethics' series. He had come up with the series idea himself shortly after the publication of *Reasons and Persons*, and had mentioned it in his application for promotion at All Souls. It took another seven years for the first volume in the series, Shelly Kagan's *The Limits of Morality* (1991), to emerge.

In the following two decades, another dozen books appeared, including two by Larry Temkin and no fewer than five by Frances Kamm; the best seller was Jeff McMahan's *The Ethics of Killing*. All the books were on moral philosophy and were personally selected by Parfit (OUP acquiesced in all his suggestions), but other than that had little in common. The series helped launch several careers. A young Kagan had just emerged from an awkward meeting with his department head at the University of Pittsburgh, having faced an uncomfortable interrogation about his non-existent publishing record, when Parfit rang to say, 'I've read your thesis and I want to publish it.' Kagan's reaction was, 'I didn't really believe it. It was the best thing that ever happened to me.'[25] Parfit had been eager to kick the series off with the Kagan book, telling OUP, 'Of all the theses I have read [this] seems to me the very best [. . .]. When revised [. . .] I expect it to be one of the most important books in ethics for many years.'[26]

Oddly, Parfit took very little interest in the design or aesthetic of the series, but for every author who published in it there was, inevitably, a rather gruelling editing process to navigate. Some found this rewarding. It took seven years from Parfit's reading Jamie Mayerfield's thesis and proposing it for publication, to the appearance of the book itself, as *Suffering and Moral Responsibility*. It was about our duty to relieve suffering, and Parfit's first set of comments amounted to around ninety single-spaced pages, 'which I read and savoured, learning a vast amount from them. I felt overwhelmed by and grateful for the generosity he showed me [. . .]. It was remarkable—made more remarkable by the fact that he dedicated similar help to many other scholars. His comments were constructive, brilliant, wise, encouraging, and contained many original and compelling arguments. I felt that I was reading significant philosophical work prepared just for me.'[27]

But Parfit's relentless quest for perfection was exhausting. After dealing with round after round of editing, Kagan told Parfit, 'If you find a passage where I literally contradict myself, I'll deal with it, but I do not have the heart to make any further changes.'[28] Larry Temkin published *Inequality* in 1993, and his magnum opus, *Rethinking the Good*, appeared towards the end of the series. He slaved away at it for years, responding to Parfit's comments on multiple drafts. Just as he thought the thousand-page manuscript was complete, Parfit emailed him with additional comments on every page. 'I said, "Derek, I don't want your comments! Enough's enough!" He said, "But Larry, don't you want your book to be as good as it could be?" I said, "No, I want my book to be done!"'[29] Tom Hurka contributed one book to the series, *Perfectionism*, but declined to include another, *Virtue, Vice, and Value*, because he couldn't face a blitz-krieg of remarks—perfectionism had its limits. The acknowledgements in the various volumes, meanwhile, reflect Parfit's exceptional input. '[My book] got longer [. . .] thanks to the extraordinary and painstaking attention showered on it by Derek Parfit,' wrote Kagan.[30] And Liam Murphy: 'My greatest debt is to Derek Parfit [. . . whose] generosity to me has been literally astonishing.'[31]

Although Parfit had a special obligation to these books, they were far from the only ones to receive this treatment. He kept up correspondence, first by post, then fax, then email, with philosophers all around the world. The speed and extent of his response were remarkable. There was a period in the 1980s and 90s when it seemed that any newly published, highly rated moral philosophy book would contain a boilerplate acknowledgement along the following lines: 'I have been encouraged by Professor Z. I am grateful to Professor X. I would like to thank Professor Y. But by far my greatest debt is to Derek Parfit, whose astute and penetrating comments [. . .].' Sam Scheffler's book *The Rejection of Consequentialism* contains an archetype of the genre: 'My debt to Derek Parfit is, quite simply, extraordinary [. . . . His] written comments on the penultimate draft were almost as long as the draft itself, and I blush to think of the errors the book would have contained but for his detailed and sensitive criticisms [. . .]. I suspect that only those who have received comparable assistance from him, and they are by no means few in number, will be able to fully appreciate the real extent of my debt.'[32]

. . .

Whether he was at West Kennett or staying overnight in Oxford, Parfit's routine remained unchanged. He would read and write from midday until late into the night. A talented young legal philosopher, John Gardner, was elected a Prize Fellow in 1986; he read and was profoundly influenced by *Reasons and Persons*. Gardner died of cancer in his fifties, and an obituary recorded how he and Parfit had become friends and meal companions. 'The famously eccentric Derek Parfit [. . .] would disconcertingly tend to pick up on some chance fragment of John's contribution to the conversation and begin to dissect it in microscopic philosophical detail. Parfit suggested that the two should meet to discuss some matter further. John readily assented. Then Parfit enquired, "Are you free at 3 a.m. on Tuesday?" To which John, of course, answered, "Yes, I am." John turned up at the agreed time. The two had a wonderful discussion, neither remarking at all on the unusual hour.'[33]

There were two years in which Parfit had a rationale for spending more time in college. The period 1992–94 was unique in his life for being burdened with the sort of administrative responsibilities that routinely blight the lives of other academics. The Warden at All Souls is supported by a sub-Warden, who is chosen from among the Fellows on a Buggins's turn system from the most senior Fellow down. In 1992, Derek was Buggins. In theory, he could have declined the role, though this would have been frowned upon. The position involved deputizing for the Warden, sitting on committees, attending funerals if a Fellow died, presiding at dinner when the Warden was absent, and attending various chapel services, where the Warden and sub-Warden had reserved seats on either side of the entrance screen. Parfit's predecessor in the job, Robin Briggs, wrote him a long handover note, setting out his duties. Parfit more or less performed what was expected of him, though he caused consternation whenever he replaced the Warden at dinner. The convention is that nobody leaves Hall until the Warden has left, but Parfit would become so involved in conversation that he would forget to depart, effectively incarcerating his fellow diners.

On 11 December 1992, Parfit turned fifty. The day was no different from his previous or future adult birthdays. It went uncelebrated. It seemed pointless to him to mark one day in the calendar rather than another. He held no party and received no presents. 'He agreed with Humpty Dumpty that unbirthdays were better because there were more of them,' according to Janet, though 'he didn't do unbirthdays either.'[34] He did not buy cards or presents for other people's birthdays—not even for Janet. He did not know when Janet's birthday was. Birthdays *did not matter*.

So what did matter? Did anything matter? Until now, this was not the sort of question Parfit would have thought to pose. That was about to change.

17

Derekarnia

A few philosophers—only a few—gather disciples. Ludwig Wittgenstein was an interesting case in point. His disciples ended up talking like him, dressing like him, developing his mannerisms, even adopting his distinctive customs, such as carrying vegetables in string bags so that they could more easily breathe. The Austrian-born philosopher could have a brutal impact on his disciples, too. He would encourage some talented students to abandon philosophy and do something more worthwhile, as he saw it, such as working with their hands, even when they were entirely unsuited to a manual life.

Parfit was another philosopher to whom students felt a deep attachment. Unlike Wittgenstein, Parfit's influence did not spill over into how students lived their lives beyond academia. The philosophical community did not become populated by lecturers clad in white shirts and red ties. And besides, his influence was far more benign. In the 1970s and early 1980s, when there were few jobs available, he was worried about his students' prospects. But in general, rather than discourage them from pursuing philosophy, he wanted them to dedicate their lives to it, as he had done. When one of his students, Sophia Moreau, told Parfit that she was thinking of transitioning from philosophy to law, he said, 'We need to talk about this. I am very worried. If you go into law, then we won't be able to talk to each other again!'[1]

Parfit believed Wittgenstein had had a pernicious effect on philosophy. 'I am strongly against his influence partly for the common reason that he was so against philosophy.'[2] He also had a low opinion of

Wittgenstein's character. The Austrian, scion of one of the richest families in Europe, had given all his money away, but to his wealthy siblings, which showed, thought Parfit, that he was concerned only with his own purity, not with doing good.

But there are some intriguing parallels between Wittgenstein and Parfit, nevertheless. Both had an otherworldly quality, and both have been described as saintly. One ex-student cites the gravity of Parfit's presence and reports that being taught by him was 'very much like a religious experience. There was a majestic mystique to both the philosopher and his ideas. I wasn't alone in feeling that way.'[3] Both Wittgenstein and Parfit eschewed public recognition. Both were single-minded obsessives and capable of being impossibly inflexible. Parfit's obsessiveness with his photography paralleled Wittgenstein's obsession with the details of the Viennese house he designed for his sister in the 1920s. One memoir of Wittgenstein recalls, 'I can still hear the locksmith, who asked him with regard to a keyhole, "Tell me Herr Ingenieur, is a millimetre here really that important?" and even before he had finished his sentence, the loud energetic "Ja" that almost startled him.'[4] Students of Wittgenstein describe falling under his spell; Parfit had a similar power. Both Wittgenstein and Parfit were odd creatures of habit: Parfit would cite approvingly Wittgenstein's statement that he did not care what food he was served so long as it was the same every day.

. . .

Parfit's relationship with his students merits its own chapter. All Souls was the dream college for Parfit because it freed him from teaching commitments. But it turned out that what he wanted was not to avoid all teaching per se, but merely teaching that was not on his own terms and on subjects in which he had no interest. The deal with US universities was that he would teach classes and take on PhD students. In Oxford, he had no such obligations. Yet, he gave regular classes, and when the topic intrigued him, he would agree to serve as supervisor.

His PhD students (or DPhil students, in the Oxford vernacular) recollect Parfit in much the same way. He was not a man to provide you with pastoral support. You would not turn to Parfit if you were experiencing a bereavement, having problems with a partner, behind with your rent, or feeling depressed. He would not offer worldly advice, comfort you, or feed you cake. But when it came to the philosophy, there was no other advisor who would dedicate as much time and intellectual energy to your work.

'Kind' is the term former students most frequently use to describe him. He was unfailingly kind. He never put students down or took satisfaction in showing them up. (The same, of course, cannot be said of all academics.) He would almost always have something complimentary to say about a piece of work, even when he would then point out serious objections. The positive reaction was usually at the top of the paper, and he would tell students that they should pay more attention to this than the criticisms. His own insecurities gave him an insight into those of others. He once thanked Jeff McMahan for some comments on his own work, but mildly rebuked him for not having said anything complimentary.

His own feedback to students was astonishing, and astonishingly swift. Ex-students talk about this with awe. When a piece of work was handed in in the evening, it would be returned the next day, with pages and pages of notes. Parfit prided himself on his lightning response, and it was a mystery how he managed it. Was there a cave full of Parfitian elves, beavering away, scrawling comments on submitted papers? It could sometimes be frustrating for a student who, having handed in a substantial essay, was hoping that there might be a gap before they would have to think about it again. One student sent Parfit fifty pages in the early afternoon and went shopping. Three hours later he returned to his college room where an email was awaiting him, with detailed comments on the paper and a suggestion that he come around immediately to discuss it.[5]

Some supervisors tend to focus on big-picture points; others are more useful for pointing out many smaller ones. Parfit did both. He corrected punctuation, spelling, and grammar; he cleaned up inelegant or ambiguous sentences. And unlike many philosophers—who see it as their role to attack the weakest links of an argument—he was more

interested in identifying the seeds of a strong argument and then helping to water it so that it could bloom and flourish. Often, what would
emerge was not what the student originally envisaged—many felt that
their thesis should have had Parfit credited as co-author.

Far from it being a chore, Parfit seemed to seek out work. At Harvard,
he would stay in the department in Emerson Hall until late at night—
with curtains semi-drawn and his desk light on. If he spotted one of his
PhD students, he would confront them like a mugger—except with the
demand for a philosophy paper rather than a wallet: 'What have you got
for me? Do you have a new draft?'

In this regard, he was the ultimate egalitarian. It mattered not a jot to
him whether the text was written by a philosopher with an international
reputation or by a twenty-three-year-old with no publications to their
name. 'As time has gone by,' wrote one student, 'I have become more
and more amazed at how much time he was willing to let me spend in
his office hours and how interested he seemed in what I had to say.'[6]
Being taken seriously by Derek Parfit was empowering for students.
Theron Pummer was a visiting student at Oxford, and wrote to Parfit
about his equality paper. 'He was insanely generous with his time.
I would send him a thirty- to forty-page thesis chapter: he would write
back with as many pages of comments. I wasn't a proper Oxford student.
I had no publications. I was a nobody.'[7]

Pummer and Parfit also had several marathon discussions. Conversations with Parfit could start any time from midday to midnight. When
she was a BPhil student, Sophia Moreau would regularly be called to
Parfit's rooms at All Souls for tutorials beginning at 11.30 p.m., and she
and Parfit would talk until 3 or 4 a.m. Another student recalls that he
would become so animated by an argument that he would literally
bounce up and down on the sofa with puppyish enthusiasm. It was
typically the student who had to draw proceedings to an end, not Parfit.
Four- or five-hour sessions were routine, but longer ones were not
unknown. Former student Jeff McMahan had a supervision with Parfit
that, with a short meal break, lasted twelve hours.

Sometimes Parfit would sit on an armchair on one side of the fireplace, whilst the student sat in an armchair on the other side. Other

times Parfit would ask the student—male or female—to sit by him on the sofa; it was evident that there was nothing predatory or untoward about him. Although he had a vodka bottle from which he drank water, it never occurred to him to offer students refreshments. He himself had a bladder that rarely needed emptying, but inevitably, after a few hours, the call of nature would require his students to excuse themselves for a few minutes. So intense and unremitting were discussions that at least one student would disappear for toilet breaks just so that she could gather her thoughts before returning to the fray.[8]

Because of Parfit's idiosyncratic relationship to the clock, students frequently received telephone calls at less than ideal times. One afternoon, Sophia Moreau and Parfit got stuck trying to crack a particular problem. The following morning, her phone rang at 3 a.m., waking her up. 'My friends didn't call me at that hour. But I had family overseas, so I initially thought that something terrible must have happened back home. I picked up the phone with a shaking hand. It was Derek's voice. He didn't say, "Sorry to bother you at this hour" or even "Hello, it's Derek!" He just said, "About the problem on page 5 . . . ." Once he explained his proposed resolution, he paused, and then hung up.'[9]

BPhil students at Oxford are required to write a dissertation and, over the years, Parfit led many BPhil seminars in which students would present their work in progress. He ran these occasions efficiently and assiduously. He was never ill. There were a few occasions when Janet Radcliffe Richards was called on to take the seminars on his behalf, after the students received a note: 'Mr Parfit has been detained in St Petersburg due to bad weather.' The 1950s ordinary-language philosophers at Oxford would have relished this sentence for its ingenious ambiguity. The wording was designed to imply that the delay was involuntary. But Parfit welcomed bad weather in Russia because it was ideal for his photography, so another interpretation was that he had *chosen* to stay away in order to photograph the snow. In fact, his photography was the only cause of any unreliability. 'I may not be here next week,' he might forewarn a student during winter, meaning that if it snowed in St Petersburg he would hop on a flight as soon as he could.

BPhil students would routinely go on to study for a PhD. If Parfit was keen to continue to work with them—as he often was—he would try to persuade them to stay at Oxford or go to one of the US universities with which he had an institutional link. He swayed Sophia Moreau to choose Harvard over Princeton. 'You don't want to go to Princeton!' he said, with great verve. 'All they have there are rows and rows of shops with fluffy tigers in the windows!'[10]

In theory, the drawback of having Parfit as a supervisor was that he would be absent much of the time abroad. In practice, he was always available to respond to work. Some students preferred the long-distance relationship, because in-person tutorials were too exhausting. He had various gears of intimacy, so that early notes and letters ended with 'Yours truly', and then they slowly progressed through the social cogs, from 'Yours with best wishes' and 'Yours with all best wishes', to 'Yours affectionately'. For Sophia Moreau, 'it was as though he was following social rules which he didn't fully understand'.[11]

Replying to email questions, he would interrupt the text with 'zzz' to show where his comments began. If emails went back and forth, new insertions would be marked by 'xxx', and then in a third round, 'DAP'.[12] He was an early convert to the desktop computer and would tell All Souls colleagues how sitting at the screen with the keyboard in front of him made him feel 'like the pilot of a jet plane'.[13] But later he was often defeated by technology and didn't upgrade an old Windows programme, so that he sometimes had difficulties reading certain files. He became comically evangelical about the autocorrect function in Word. He had discovered that he could write faster if he used shortcuts and sent dozens of people a version of the following note:

> What you do is this. You first define some keyboard combination which summons up Autocorrect (so that you don't have to use the Tools menu to summon it up). You can then select some word or phrase in your text, summon up Autocorrect, enter an abbreviation in the long box on the left, and hit 'enter' twice. You never need type this word or phrase again. I have about 5,000 abbreviations. It's best to use a few of the consonants in a word or phrase. If you can't

remember some abbreviation, you can define one or more others. Two examples might be 'Uism' for 'Utilitarianism' and 'cnrr' for 'could not reasonably reject'.[14]

His abbreviations included most common words. 'Would', 'should', 'person', and 'reason', were 'wd', 'shd', 'pn', and 'rn'. 'Using these abbreviations makes typing much faster,' he affirmed.[15] He would adapt his examples to the philosopher concerned: Wittgensteinians, for example, should use 'witt' for Wittgenstein. So enamoured was he of autocorrect that 'he had one of the administrators in the Philosophy Faculty circulate a note to all members of the faculty, recommending that everyone adopt this approach—and noting that his own typing speed had doubled since he had done so himself'.[16] It never occurred to him that typing speed might not be a factor limiting the productivity of others.

There was something else that didn't occur to Parfit. "The perfect is the enemy of the good' is an aphorism often attributed to the French philosopher Voltaire. For the student or early-stage academic, the usual priority is to complete the doctorate and to publish a few papers or a book—which need not be discipline-shattering in its impact. But this was a notion that was hard for Parfit to grasp: for him, there was always time and room for improvement. When one despondent student told Parfit that he really needed to complete his PhD because his financing was coming to an end, Parfit shocked him by saying, 'You could have defended it a year ago. I thought you just wanted to make it better'.[17] He told an All Souls student finishing her PhD (not supervised by him) that she should send it to two hundred people for feedback. 'This was the worst advice possible'.[18]

The one chore he loathed was writing references. He would try and deflect appeals for letters of support. This was no doubt because if he agreed to write a reference, he took the process far more seriously than was either required or expected. He believed that to be in a position to give a reliable reference he had to read everything the student had written. He requested that a Rutgers student, Jake Ross, send him not just his four hundred-page dissertation, but all his postgraduate ethics papers. He then read over twenty of them. But an endorsement from Parfit could be of tremendous benefit to a student, as Ross learned.

However, although his references were invariably favourable, he never fully grasped that, especially in the United States, comments had become so inflated that candidates had to be preposterously hyped if they were not to be disadvantaged. More than once, references were returned to him with a request that he do more to build up an applicant. He was tormented by the process.

. . .

As well as supervising individual students, Parfit continued to give lectures and run seminars, even in Oxford, where this was voluntary. At the lecture podium there was usually a vodka bottle, from which he would occasionally take swigs. Students were not sure what was in it— but it was water.

Here too, Parfit was a model of civility. Traditionally, philosophy has had a macho image within the academy. In Oxford during the second half of the twentieth century, there were philosophers whose modus operandi was to belittle students. It came naturally to Parfit to take the opposite approach. Jeff McMahan witnessed this multiple times. 'There was always a stupid question from the audience. And Derek would say, "Well, as I understand you, you're saying. . . ." And he would produce a fascinating question and then an incredibly interesting answer, involving extraordinary intellectual gymnastics. All prompted by a totally useless question.'[19] The macho norm in philosophy is wrapped in a culture of robust (and sometimes hostile) debate. Parfit enjoyed the spectacle of ferocious argument, but, when he was involved, he took no pleasure in conflict.

Although he was meticulously—indeed doggedly—logical, students and other interlocutors learned that there was one area of philosophy he refused to enter. He would sometimes illustrate arguments and thought experiments with simple bar graphs, used to represent numbers (as with worlds A, A−, B, and so on, in the Repugnant Conclusion), but he *never* used mathematical or logical symbols. Philosophy is, or can be, a highly technical subject. One of the founders of analytic philosophy, Bertrand Russell, argued that our language often leads us astray. It can contain ambiguities: 'I'll give you a ring tomorrow' is an example of such a statement. A telephone call or a piece of jewellery? And it is full of vague statements: 'I'll see you in the morning.' If we can convert language into logic, we can remove some ambiguities and some of the vagueness, and this can help us to resolve philosophical problems. Logic can also clarify and make precise the connections between statements.

But Parfit had a phobia of logical notation. If he was ever sent an article about a topic that included such notation, he would respond with a note like this one:

> I would be particularly interested in reading a full statement of the argument for one of your impossibility theorems—perhaps the final theorem—stated in English without formal symbols. I can't follow such arguments when they are presented in formal symbols.[20]

This irritated a few students and academics who could not see the form of a tricky argument unless it was expressed in notation. But Parfit had a rare ability to follow long lines of thought in his head, keeping in mind the various ways that the argument could branch off; so formal logic was of less use to him than to others. True, sometimes he employed visual aids. There was one Oxford postgraduate class, observed by John Tomasi, in which Parfit took a student through their paper's argument:

> 'At the start of your talk you said X, but I wondered: by X, did you mean A or B?' Student replies 'A'. Parfit continues: 'Good. Later on you said Y, did you mean P or Q?'. Student replies, 'Umm, I think P'. Parfit continues, 'Oh well that can't work because ...' (pointing out a logical error here). 'Let's go back to the start. At the start of your talk did you perhaps mean B instead of A?' Student: 'Yes, I guess I must have meant B.' Derek, 'Ah good. Then, later on, did you mean M or Z?' And so on.[21]

Amazed that he could do this, Tomasi sat next to him the following week. He saw Parfit doodle a sort of maze. So, when his own paper came, 'I prepped extra hard, and the centre of my prep was to war-game the maze that he was most likely to draw when hearing my paper. I even wrote the paper with the idea that it (and I) were going to be dropped into a little maze of Derek's creation, and tried to work out ways to last longer in the maze than some of the others had. I wrote a *much* better paper because of the fear/awe the prospect of facing Derek and his maze inspired in me.'[22]

. . .

Although the experience of being taught by Parfit was life-changing for many students, the benefit was two-way. Parfit gained much from these tutor–student interactions. First, there was the pure satisfaction. Established philosophers have often made their reputation by staking out distinct philosophical positions and their minds are less malleable than younger ones. Parfit found it gratifying to influence students. He was pleased that several of his cleverest students abandoned their belief in God after being confronted with the Problem of Evil.

There was the satisfaction, too, in setting postgraduates off on their career paths. He encouraged them to publish and, when necessary, backed this up with supportive notes to publishers. He was delighted when his protégés landed teaching positions. On hearing that Sophia Moreau had been offered a job at a prestigious university, Parfit sent her an email, the subject line of which was 'Yippee!' and the entire text, 'Yippee, Yippee. Yippee!'[23] (She became a professor of law *and* philosophy.)

Parfit would send drafts of his work to his best students, who treated the request to supply feedback as a flattering but serious responsibility. Ruth Chang had a fresh set of comments with her in the early 1990s when, in a terrifying experience, she was held up at gunpoint. She was walking along Massachusetts Avenue in Cambridge, Massachusetts with two men, following a Thanksgiving dinner. The two men, with guns pressed into their ribs, were ordered to hand over their wallets, and Chang to hand over her bag. Together, the three of them managed to persuade the muggers to keep the money but return what really mattered: Parfit's marked papers.

For Parfit, the real bonus from students was that they (usually) possessed two related qualities that many professional philosophers lacked. First, they were less likely to be entangled with family obligations, and second, they were more likely to have the intellectual stamina and enthusiasm to keep up with his pace. If you were seeking partners in philosophical dialogue willing to go at it for five hours at a stretch from 10 p.m., you were better off trying to find them within the student demographic than among middle-aged professors who had to be up at 6.30 a.m. to ferry their kids to school.

Quite a few students came to think of themselves as Parfitian disciples. It seems unlikely that Parfit ever saw them in these terms himself; nonetheless, some philosophers believed that Parfit set out to enlist certain people into his philosophical orbit—that he was a conscious 'recruiter into Derekarnia'.[24]

18

Alpha Gamma Kant

Reading Parfit eventually appeared in print in 1997—ten years after the initiation of the project. But it did so *without* Parfit's promised replies to the thirteen essays. The patience of the editor had finally been exhausted. In his acknowledgements, Dancy could only thinly disguise his frustration. The reason for the delay was 'my desire to include responses that Derek Parfit had agreed to write to the suggestions and criticisms of the contributors. These responses rapidly grew to such a size that the whole could no longer be contained in a single volume.' Parfit had now produced so much, explained Dancy, that the material would appear in three books, to be called *Practical Realism*, *The Metaphysics of the Self*, and *On What Matters*. 'I end by apologizing to all my contributors, and to a frustrated readership, for my failure to get this collection published in proper time.'[1]

· · ·

Parfit was now dealing with a new contact at OUP. Peter Momtchiloff had become the philosophy editor there in 1993. In the evenings and at weekends, Momtchiloff moonlighted as the guitarist for the indie band *Heavenly*. Though critically acclaimed, *Heavenly*'s album sales were far from stratospheric. Momtchiloff had more commercial success in his day job, becoming a powerful figure in philosophy by transforming OUP into the dominant force in philosophy publishing.

Parfit discussed plans for his three books with Momtchiloff and there were contracts signed. *The Metaphysics of the Self* would contain material on personal identity; *On What Matters* would revisit other aspects of *Reasons and Persons*, but also cover issues to do with equality and justice; *Practical Realism* was to be mostly about metaethics.

Metaethics is a subcategory of metaphysics. The term 'metaphysics' has ancient origins. Aristotle's works were categorized in the first century CE under 'physics' and 'metaphysics'. Metaphysics—or 'after physics'—has come to refer to the branch of philosophy that deals with the fundamental nature of reality: matters such as time and space. Sometimes it is put this way: metaphysics deals with things as they are in themselves, rather than things as they seem to us. The Vienna Circle and the logical empiricists treated the term as a dirty word, precisely because the questions that it addressed were out of reach of scientific scrutiny. Metaphysics, for them, was a type of nonsense.

Parfit was not a complete stranger to metaphysics. His reflections on time, for example, and on why the universe exists, could be classified as metaphysical. Metaethics is a sub-branch of metaphysics—but the metaethical issue that he spent the next fifteen years of his life addressing was very specific. The chapters in *Reading Parfit* cover different aspects of *Reasons and Persons*. But several of them got Parfit to reflect more deeply about what it is to have a 'reason' to do something, and that drew him into metaethics.

Take a statement such as 'Torturing innocent children is wrong.' What is its status? How can such a statement claim to be morally objective? What would such a claim to objectivity mean? How should we respond to a sceptic who insisted that it was merely an opinion, and no more valid than the diabolical judgement that torturing innocent children was just fine, thanks very much. How should we respond to the sceptic's cousin, the relativist, who claims that morality is relative to culture, so that what is morally 'true' in London might not be morally true in Lagos or Lahore?

Of course, believers in God have a ready answer as to why something might be objectively wrong. Things are wrong by God's moral code. But this is a problematic way out. It would seem to follow that if God dictated, 'Torturing innocent children is acceptable,' then torturing innocent children would, in fact, be acceptable.[2] In any case, it's not a response available to the secular world.

For years, Parfit felt he could ignore metaethics. It was just too complicated, he believed, and in any case other philosophers were better equipped than he was to tackle the subject. Larry Temkin was walking with him in Princeton in the 1970s when 'I asked him *his* views on metaethics. Derek looked at me, and very earnestly replied, "I don't do metaethics. I find it *much* too hard."'[3] So he decided that he would stick to his domain, the metaethicists could stick to their domain, and they could happily coexist and need not interact.

But, at around the time that he was responding to the articles for the *Reading Parfit* volume, he changed his mind. And a thought began to grip him.

. . .

The thought was this. Everything he had written to date, every philosophical argument he had ever made, every conclusion he had ever reached, was pointless, worthless, and illusory, unless moral reasoning could be moored to solid ground. The solid ground had to be moral objectivity. If morality was not objective, then it was a waste of time debating it. If morality was not objective, there was no *reason* to act in one way rather than another. He went further. If morality was not objective, life was meaningless. His own life was meaningless, and every human and animal life was meaningless.

Indeed, he came to realize that most philosophers, including many philosophers that he admired, believed that morality was *not* objective, at least in the strong sense that he believed it to be. 'I got increasingly disturbed and alarmed', he later explained, 'by the number of good philosophers who just assumed that there couldn't be any normative truths.'[4]

One of the most important philosophers of the twentieth century, the Harvard-based W.V.O. Quine, had promoted an influential line on ontology. 'Ontology' is the philosophers' term for the philosophical study of what exists. The book *Reasons and Persons* exists, and '*Reasons and Persons* is more than four hundred pages long' is a fact about the world. Values were excluded in Quine's ontology, and statements such as 'Torturing innocent children is wrong' did not capture anything that existed in the world. Philosophers should stick to the empirical world. 'Philosophy of science', Quine once wrote, 'is philosophy enough.'[5]

In 1977, John Mackie, one of Parfit's referees, published *Ethics: Inventing Right and Wrong*.[6] There were no objective moral values, Mackie concluded, putting forward an 'argument from queerness'. If there were objective moral values, they would be of a very peculiar sort, totally different from anything else in the universe. Atoms, and philosophy books, and bluebell woods have an indubitable objectivity. After all, they can be measured, or perceived, experimented on or photographed. But the idea that moral truths exist—well, that is just too odd. He also cited what philosophers label an epistemological problem—a problem about knowledge. We have ways of telling whether a particular bluebell wood exists—for example, by taking a walk to see it. But how are we to know whether a moral truth exists?

. . .

Parfit came to believe that Quine's conception of 'facts' was dangerous idiocy; he would endlessly repeat the charge of the American philosopher Hilary Putnam, that Quinean ontology 'has had disastrous consequences for just about every part of analytic philosophy'.[7] After all, as Parfit pointed out, even Quine was not a Quinean purist. Quine thought that a central role for philosophy was to support the empirical sciences through the application of logic. So he reluctantly had to concede that there were such things as numbers: he had to squeeze the number '2' and all other numbers into his ontology.

But, argued Parfit, if numbers could exist—and if we could acknowledge the truth of '2 + 2 = 4', even if it is not a truth 'in the world' in the same way as books are in the world—then, surely, we could also concede the possibility that moral truths exist? A statement such as 'Torturing innocent children is wrong' is not testable in the way that a scientific claim (for example, 'This paperback of *Reasons and Persons* weighs over 300 grammes') is testable. But not everything that exists in the world, Parfit argued, was physical. Not everything can be seen or touched, prodded or measured. Numbers are not physical. Morality is not physical. There are objective empirical or scientific truths ('The paperback of *Reasons and Persons* weighs over 300 grammes'), there are objective mathematical truths ('$2 + 2 = 4$'), and there are objective moral truths ('Torturing innocent children is wrong'). Only the first is open to empirical investigation; but the latter two are equally objective.

You might protest that while no mathematician doubts that two plus two equals four, in ethics there is much more room for debate. You might expect that if ethics were a part of the world, not quite like books, but nonetheless real, there would be more consensus about its contents. But on the face of it, there appear to be fundamental disagreements. Should there be more redistribution from the wealthy to the poor? Is abortion wrong? Is corporal punishment wrong? Is it permissible to eat meat? Should there be spaces—such as separate toilets—reserved for people of the same biological sex? Is it acceptable to blaspheme? There is fierce debate about these and numerous other ethical matters, sometimes within countries, sometimes between people from different countries. Issues which appear to have become settled in some places—such as the right of same-sex couples to marry—remain contentious, or taboo, in others.

Parfit was unfazed by such examples. One would expect *some* disagreements, he argued. It is precisely because some issues are controversial that they dominate ethical discussion. But we overlook how much *agreement* there is. On most basic areas, in fact, there is agreement. Nobody seriously doubts that it is wrong to torture innocent children just for the fun of it.

To introduce more philosophical jargon: Parfit's position was that of a 'cognitive non-naturalist'. A cognitive non-naturalist holds that there really are normative facts, such as that torturing innocent children is wrong. These are facts, but not like natural facts such as that *Reasons and Persons* weighs over 300 grammes.

. . .

Suppose we concede the point that 'Torturing innocent children is wrong' is an objective fact. Presumably that gives us a reason not to do it? Parfit certainly believed so. But once again, many philosophers adopt a position that seems to defy common sense, and which Parfit thought was crazy. They take their lead from David Hume, who, in *A Treatise of Human Nature*, concluded that reason alone could not motivate us, since '[i]t is not contrary to reason to prefer the destruction of the whole world to the scratching of my finger'.[8]

Within this intellectual tradition, the contemporary article that most disturbed Parfit was Bernard Williams's 'Internal and External Reasons'.[9] Williams analysed a claim such as 'Parfit has a reason to cut his hair'. There are two possible interpretations of this statement. We might be saying something like, 'If Parfit would prefer to have shorter hair (perhaps because it would then be easier to wash), then he has a reason to cut his hair.' This is what Williams calls the *internal* interpretation. Alternatively, the claim could be read as follows: 'Parfit has a reason to cut his hair, whether or not he wants to cut his hair.' This is what Williams calls the *external* interpretation.

Williams's widely cited contention was that external reasons do not exist. If Parfit does not want to cut his hair, he has no reason to cut it, even if he is presented with good arguments for doing so. Reasons, insisted Williams, had to be grounded in motivation. To take a more consequential example: do I have a reason to give money to an efficient charity that helps people in desperate poverty? All sorts of arguments could be made to persuade me: I have more money than I need and I could certainly spare at least a small amount; the money could be used to help transform lives—it would benefit somebody else far more than it would benefit me; giving to charity might make me feel good about myself. But suppose I simply dismiss these points. I don't want to give to charity. I don't care about the poor. I want to spend all my money on myself. In that case, Williams would say, it makes no sense to *insist* that I nonetheless have a reason to donate.

One of Williams's own examples was of a man who treats his wife terribly. We can try to change his attitude. We can tell him that he is ungrateful, sexist, nasty, and brutish. We can offer arguments. We can berate and cajole. But if he remains indifferent to any of this, if he shrugs his shoulders at attempts to improve his behaviour, then, says Williams, it is hard to know what would be meant by our assertion that he nonetheless has *reasons* to be nicer.[10]

. . .

Williams had left the country in 1987 in a disgruntled state of mind, and in protest at the Thatcher government's cuts to higher education. The Oxford-educated Margaret Thatcher was, he thought, a philistine. But he missed Britain, nevertheless, and after three years at the University of California, Berkeley, he returned, somewhat shamefacedly, to take up the White's Professorship of Moral Philosophy. When he retired in 1996, he rejoined All Souls, where he had begun as a Prize Fellow, and so he and Parfit bumped into each other more frequently.

Although Williams was fond of Parfit, clearly respected him, provided him with references, and in 1984 penned a long and appreciative review of *Reasons and Persons*, there was something in Parfit's intensity that now irked the elder man. He would gently tease Parfit to his face and make barbed comments about his social gaucheness and obsessiveness behind his back. He would frequently repeat the story of the time he was living in Cambridge and gave a talk on personal identity in Oxford. Parfit raised objections in the Q&A session. After the talk, there were drinks, and Parfit took the chance to buttonhole Williams and raise more objections. Williams needed to return to Cambridge and eventually fled to his car; Parfit pursued him, talking all the while. It was pouring with rain, and Parfit was still talking and pounding an arm on the bonnet, when Williams wound up the window and drove off, leaving his harasser standing there, drenched and bedraggled.

Parfit was naive about human interactions and largely unaware of how he was perceived, and in his relationship with Williams there was a sharp asymmetry. He had a copy of a magazine that featured an interview and a photograph of the handsome Williams when he was Provost (equivalent to Master) of King's College and, admiring it with his friend Larry Temkin, Parfit commented, 'Isn't he wonderful?'[11] He would tell people that he 'loved' Williams. But the latter stage of Parfit's academic career was essentially a prolonged assault on Williams and a defence of the claim that the man who treats his wife badly, in Williams's example, *does* have a moral reason to improve his behaviour, whether he wants to or not. The fact that he could not convince Williams on this point literally made Parfit cry.

Only academic philosophers could doubt that we had objective reasons to do things, Parfit moaned. One of Janet's close friends was a woman who helped around the house. She had not been to university. Parfit was fond of her and hoped that she would never ask what he was working on, because he would be embarrassed to tell her. If he came clean—that he was defending the view that we can have reasons to care about things for their own sake, 'she would have said, "They *pay* you for doing that?"'[12]

James Griffin succeeded Bernard Williams as White's Professor in 1996, and when Griffin retired in 2000, an obvious inheritor of the crown was Simon Blackburn, with whom Parfit had once travelled to Leningrad. Blackburn was one of five philosophers considered seriously by the Appointments Committee—all five were from the UK. There are conflicting accounts of Parfit's role in this process. He was on the Appointments Committee, and his opinion appears to have carried significant weight. Given his deep disagreement with Blackburn's non-objectivist ethics, he was delighted with the selection of his favoured candidate, John Broome, then in Scotland, at the University of St Andrews.

. . .

Besides metaethics, Parfit developed one other all-consuming preoccupation—Immanuel Kant.

The shift in his attitude to Kant is impossible to date accurately. In *Reasons and Persons*, Kant is notable for his absence. Shelly Kagan recalls commenting to Parfit during a seminar in the early 1990s that he was interested in Kant's *Groundwork of the Metaphysics of Morals.* 'And he [Parfit] turned to Thomas Nagel and said, "Is this really our Shelly?" '[13] Parfit himself later dated his conversion to, approximately, the mid-1990s, when he became 'unexpectedly obsessed with Kant's ethics. For the next two or three years, I thought about little else.'[14] In fact, his Kant period came later, around the millennium. In any case, his book copies of Kant became splattered with 'exclamation marks, question marks, and arrows.'[15] Sometimes he would want to refer to the original German, and, since his language skills were not up to the task, he would consult others, including the All Souls philosopher Edward Hussey.

There was a deep-rooted connection between Parfit's new interests in metaethics and Kant. One of the world's leading Kant experts, Christine Korsgaard, was at Harvard, where Parfit taught regularly from 1989. Korsgaard had attacked the idea that there were moral facts which should move us to act in certain ways. While Kant had credited Hume with 'waking him from his dogmatic slumbers',[16] Parfit, who had previously neglected metaethics, credited books by Korsgaard for motivating him to reread Kant and for waking him from his 'undogmatic slumbers'.[17]

By the time his second book, *On What Matters,* was published, Parfit had become polytheistic: Immanuel Kant had joined Henry Sidgwick as one of his twin gods. Kant was a true genius, even more brilliant than Sidgwick, Parfit came to believe, though he found him exasperating. One reason for annoyance was that Kant 'made really bad writing philosophically acceptable',[18] and another was that he was often contradictory. Most deplorable of all, some of his arguments were sloppy. Nevertheless, he had insights that were original and profound. Parfit concluded that if he were an examiner marking Kant's work, he would award him an 'Alpha Gamma', a grade that once existed for Oxford candidates whose papers were part inspired (Alpha), part dross (Gamma), and never mediocre (Beta). 'Our disagreement should be only about how much of what Kant wrote is Alpha, and how much is Gamma. And if we have found what is Alpha, we can ignore what is Gamma.'[19]

In several works, most especially in the *Groundwork of the Metaphysics of Morals,*[20] Kant sought to identify the fundamental moral principle that applies to all of us. He called it 'the Categorical Imperative'—it is

absolute and unconditional and contrasts with hypothetical impera-
tives, that are linked to specific desires. 'If you wish to sleep but can't, you
should take a sleeping pill', is a hypothetical imperative; 'if you want to
save time, always wear the same-coloured tie', is another. But the Categorical Imperative applies whatever our desires.

Kant formulated the Categorical Imperative in several ways. The first
version is the best known: 'Act only according to that maxim whereby
you can, at the same time, will that it should become a universal law.'
You should not break a promise, because if everyone broke their promises trust would disintegrate and the practice of 'promise-making' would
implode. There is an obvious similarity here to the Golden Rule, a
principle in several religions: 'Do unto others as you would have them
do unto you.'

Another version of the Categorical Imperative runs as follows: 'Act
so as always to treat people as ends in themselves, never as mere means.'
If you lie to somebody, the person lied to cannot reach a free and
informed decision about what to do or what to believe. If you lie to
somebody, you are not treating that person as a rational end—but as a
means for your own purposes. Notoriously, Kant was an absolutist in
his prohibition of lying, and believed that if a murderer was at your door
and demanded to know whether you were sheltering a person he intended to kill, you should tell the truth.

Parfit had reached broadly consequentialist conclusions in *Reasons
and Persons*. Kantianism is usually held to be the main contrasting ethical
approach, and states that there are duties other than that of producing
the best consequences. A utilitarian consequentialist might countenance the killing of an innocent person to save, for example, a hundred
lives. A Kantian would insist that intentional killing is wrong under all
circumstances. Kant is central to the human-rights movement. The idea
that all humans are deserving of equal rights and dignity, and that there
are constraints on what majorities can impose on minorities, are core
Kantian notions. And, on the face of it, these Kantian constraints
are easy to grasp and intuitively plausible.

Parfit was unusual in that consequentialism came entirely naturally
to him; taking Kant seriously meant interrogating his consequentialist

instincts. But when he drilled into the details of Kant's abstract formulations, he found them wanting. He made it his mission to refine and improve Kant's multiple formulations of the Categorical Imperative. It was a project that would take many years.

. . .

In 1995, Parfit conceded that his rural experiment in West Kennett had been a failure. He and Janet put the house on the market, and even though they'd purchased it for an inflated price, they made a tidy profit. With the proceeds, they bought 28 St John Street, in the centre of Oxford. Janet had assumed they would live there together, but Parfit's idea was that he would continue to sleep at All Souls—fifteen minutes' walk away— during the week, returning at weekends. That provoked further friction. The following year, they sold the house, and this time used the money to buy two homes—one just a stone's throw away in Beaumont Buildings, and the other, into which Janet moved, in Huddleston Road, Tufnell Park, in north London.

That is when I came to know Janet. I had returned to philosophy and begun a PhD at the Open University; Janet became my PhD supervisor. Every couple of months, I would visit her to discuss my thesis (on the philosophy of discrimination). We were invariably interrupted by a call from Parfit. He seemed oblivious to the fact that Janet was sixty miles away. 'It matters to him that I exist,' Janet told me. 'It matters much less that I'm around.'[21]

In 1999, Janet became the director of the Centre for Bioethics and Philosophy of Medicine at University College, London—cementing London as her base. A year later, she published *Human Nature after Darwin*, on the implications of evolution for psychology. And not long after that, she began a two-year stint as a panellist on 'The Moral Maze', a BBC radio progamme which debates a moral issue raised by a news story. She was an island of calm reason in the sea of shouting and indignation. The Parfit–Radcliffe Richards relationship remained a source of some gossip back at All Souls. Some of the male Fellows who had seen or met Janet were baffled that Parfit would choose to spend his nights in college. He didn't know how to love, they concluded.

The Beaumont Buildings house lay empty during the week, so it made sense to rent it out. The result was a variant of the hit TV comedy *The Big Bang Theory*, except that, instead of being a household of physicists, it was chock-full of philosophers. At varying times, the lodgers were Nick Bostrom, Guy Kahane, Julian Savulescu, Ingmar Persson, and Anders Sandberg; the philosophers were joined by a token historian (who happened to be the grandson of the Duke of Marlborough, and so a relative of Winston Churchill). Nick Bostrom, later author of the bestseller *Superintelligence*, took responsibility for collecting the below-market-rate rent and depositing it into Parfit's bank account.

A tiny closet room at the top was left empty for Parfit and, about once a week, he would show up late at night. All Souls offered an annual housing allowance of several thousand pounds, but it was intended for Fellows who were fully resident outside college. Parfit may have misunderstood the rules, or deliberately applied an elastic interpretation to them. He carried on claiming the allowance. There was no mechanism for checking how many nights Fellows lived outside college, especially when they never appeared for breakfast.

In his boxroom there was a reclining exercise bike, so that he could read and cycle simultaneously. His habit, as at West Kennett, was to do this naked. Besides the bike, the room was mostly filled with toothbrushes, dental floss, CDs, and empty vodka bottles. The CDs, once played, were never returned to their cases, and if Parfit couldn't find one he was looking for among the haphazard piles, he simply went out and bought another copy. DVDs had been invented by this time, and he would buy them in bulk at Tower Records and watch them after midnight on his laptop. He loved documentaries about musicians, and also about wildlife. He would watch movies too: anything with Fred Astaire, but he was also a fan of 1940s noir, such as *The Big Sleep*, starring Humphrey Bogart and Lauren Bacall, and the Billy Wilder-directed *Double Indemnity*. He repeatedly watched Ingmar Bergman's *Wild Strawberries*, about an ageing professor forced to reassess his life.

The house slowly became dirtier and more decrepit. There was a long-running war of attrition with a kitchen-headquartered mouse, who constantly outwitted the phalanx of philosophers, launching multiple guerrilla attacks on the muesli, whilst skilfully avoiding the (humane) traps they had set. The creature's life came to a tragic end when Dr Sandberg, who among other topics researches the potential for life on Earth to end, threw out some rubbish without looking, and inadvertently crushed it.[22]

Parfit's withdrawal from social life was now almost complete. Brad Hooker, one of the founding members of the All Souls discussion group, invited his former supervisor to his wedding in 2001. 'He wrote a nice note to say he couldn't come because, firstly, at these occasions there was no time to have meaningful conversations and, secondly, that he had to maximize his work time. And I remember thinking, "This is very sad. He's missing out on a happy occasion for somebody he cares about."'[23] It didn't tarnish their relationship, but Parfit told Jonathan Dancy that he was aware that working on his book risked costing him friends, and 'he was sad about this'.[24]

Sitting with Parfit at dinner became a daunting experience, because, at least with people he was not close to, he was awkward and uninterested in small talk. At a formal college dinner in 1995 a non-philosopher, Catherine Paxton, was placed next to him. Knowing his reputation, and somewhat trepidatious, she wondered what they could talk about. She struck lucky when she discovered that they shared a fascination for wildlife documentaries. He had recently seen one about meerkats, and became quite animated; mongooses sustained them through three courses.

Parfit taught at Harvard for parts of 1995–98, 2000, and 2002, and at NYU for various semesters over the same period. He was in Oxford on 11 September 2001 when the planes flew into the twin towers of the New York World Trade Center. That day, he was writing about Kant and had an email exchange that was only about philosophy: I have found no evidence that he discussed the epochal news with anybody.

There was, understandably, an immediate, dramatic collapse in demand for air travel, and some of the invited guests to his nephew's wedding in Aspen, Colorado, on 29 September 2001, decided not to come. Fear of flying was not, however, Parfit's excuse for politely declining his invitation. He had a rule, he told Theodora Parfit. 'I only attend funerals, I do not attend weddings.'[25] But his big sister pulled rank. 'I don't care whether or not you come to my funeral,' she said, 'but I do care that you turn up at Alexander's wedding.' Although browbeaten into going, once there he was his usual benign self. Each relative received one of his photographic prints.

He was already committed to returning to the US the following year, in order to give the lectures that would eventually—after the usual Parfitian delays—transmute into his mammoth second book.

19

Climbing the Mountain

4 July 2002: 'I would be very glad to have this book in the Berkeley Tanner Lecture Series, published by the OUP.'[1] With that seemingly innocuous email, the next eight torturous years began.

Parfit's correspondent was Sam Scheffler, then a philosophy professor at Berkeley. He had known Parfit a little since he had begun to correspond with him as a postgraduate student. They finally came face to face at an American Philosophy Association (APA) gathering in New York. For Scheffler, this meeting was keenly anticipated. Parfit had sent him an absurdly helpful, outlandishly long (sixty-page) response to his book *The Rejection of Consequentialism*, which had been based on his dissertation, and to meet Parfit 'meant an enormous amount' to him. At the APA, he went to introduce himself. 'He [Parfit] turned to me and said, "Oh yes, hello," and then turned away! I couldn't compare the effort he'd put into my work with this lack of interest in me.'[2] But despite this wounding start, interactions between Parfit and Scheffler continued. 'I realized that getting to know Derek as a person was not like getting to know other people.'[3] Scheffler included an article by Parfit in his edited OUP book *Consequentialism and Its Critics*. Later, in 1990, Scheffler was a visiting Fellow at All Souls and so they spent more time together.

In 2001, when Scheffler was on the committee for the Berkeley Tanner Lectures on Human Values, he proposed that they invite Parfit. For the Tanner Lectures, an eminent visiting lecturer is expected to deliver a series of three lectures. Parfit readily agreed and proposed the title 'What We Could Rationally Will'. It could comprise, he suggested, much of the content of the second part of the book he was working on. Once called *Practical Realism*, this had mutated into *Rediscovering Reasons*. He was still planning the two other books, *The Metaphysics of the Self* and *On What Matters*.

There was a hitch. The expectation was that the lectures would be turned into a short book—which would consist not just of the lectures but of comments from three respondents—to be published by the University of California Press. Meanwhile, it had been seventeen years since the appearance of *Reasons and Persons*. OUP was awaiting a follow up, and philosophy editor Peter Momtchiloff had discovered that his job required Job-like patience. He had been meeting Parfit annually at All Souls, and each year the philosopher would explain why no manuscript was completed, and that he now had a clear plan to proceed. When the usually mild-mannered Momtchiloff heard about the proposed defection to the University of California Press, he expressed his displeasure. Parfit was chastened. He told Scheffler that, upon reflection, his long-standing obligation to OUP meant he could not publish with another press.

By pure coincidence, a solution emerged. The University of California Press was in the midst of a torrid period, slashing jobs and philosophy titles. It had nothing to do with Parfit's quandary, but a decision was taken to move the publication of the Tanner Lectures to OUP, thereby resolving the dilemma. On hearing the news, Parfit sent an email to Scheffler at 2.08 a.m. on 4 July 2002: 'Yippee!'[4]

The lectures were delivered, uneventfully, from 4 to 6 November 2002, in Alumni House in Berkeley. Each had a different title— 'Kant's Formula of Ends-in-Themselves', 'Kant's Formula of Universal Law', and 'Contractualism'—and each had a different respondent: Allen Wood from Stanford on Monday, Susan Wolf from the University of North Carolina on Tuesday, and Harvard's Tim Scanlon on Wednesday. There was a culminating seminar on Thursday, involving Parfit, Wood, Wolf, and Scanlon. Samuel Scheffler made the opening introduction to the lecture series, describing Parfit as someone with 'inexhaustible dialectical energy'.[5]

Much of the material in the lectures would later reappear in *On What Matters*. In the opening lecture, Parfit analysed Kant's claim that we should always treat people as ends in themselves, never merely as means. Did this cover all cases of wrongdoing? He gave the example of his mother and the Chinese robbers. 'When my mother was travelling on a Chinese river in the 1930s her boat was held up by bandits whose moral principles permitted them to take only half of anyone's property. These bandits let my mother choose whether they would take her engagement ring or her wedding ring. Even if these people acted wrongly, they did not treat my mother merely as a means.'[6] So, the wrongness of the bandit behaviour could not be captured by Kant's maxim. If they had treated Jessie as 'a *mere* means' they might have taken everything; they would certainly have given her no say about what she was permitted to keep.

One problem with Parfit's bandit example was that it was untrue. How the story came to be handed down from mother to son in this form is unclear. But, as explained in chapter 1, a contemporaneous account of the boat assault shows the bandits took what they wanted—Jessie Parfit *was* treated as a mere means.

Factual quibbles aside, this was a vivid illustration of some of the broader points Parfit was making—that we accept some Kantian formulations too readily, without sufficient reflection. As he would write in *On What Matters*, the doctor who prods my chest and asks, 'Where does it hurt?' is treating me as a means, but presumably not a 'mere' means.[7] What is required is a more detailed account of the work being done by the word 'mere'. And, however we understand it, it is obvious that we can act badly without treating people as mere means. The multibillionaire who does not give even a cent to the poor could be said to be acting wrongly—but he isn't treating those who are harmed by his meanness as 'mere means'.

That was Lecture One. Lecture Two was on Kant's Universal Law. It took place on US election day in the middle of President George W. Bush's first term. Susan Wolf announced that, if anybody had to leave early to vote, that was acceptable because it passed the formula of Kant's Universal Law—act only according to that maxim by which you can at the same time will that it should become a universal law. The drumbeat towards the Iraq War was already audible, and, despite the political leanings of academic philosophers, the Republicans would hold the House and regain the Senate.

Kant's Universal Law has always been taken as an argument against coercion, or lying, or promise-breaking. If we all broke promises, the practice of promise-making would collapse. But what exactly did Kant mean by the Universal Law? Once again, Parfit took a Kantian maxim which has a surface plausibility and set to work on it, going back and forth with example and counterexample, addressing the Law with that inexhaustible dialectical energy Scheffler had referred to. Pinning Kant down: perhaps, for example, Kant meant that it was wrong to act on a maxim unless we could all successfully act upon it? But that formula cannot be accepted, because it would condemn a maxim such as 'Give more to charity than other people do.'

Lecture Three was devoted to contractualism. Crudely put, a contractualist believes that the principles of morality are those that would be agreed upon if they were discussed under certain ideal conditions. Some of the most important political theorists in history—Thomas Hobbes, John Locke, Jean-Jacques Rousseau—can be labelled contractualists. But Parfit took Rawls as his representative contractualist.

As we have seen, according to Rawls, the ideal conditions require 'a veil of ignorance'. We are to imagine that we don't know who we are—how well off we are, whether we are male or female, what our values and interests are. The principles we choose to be governed by under these conditions are, by definition, just and fair ones. And it is rational to act upon these principles. So what general judgements would we make from behind the veil of ignorance? Well, according to Rawls, if we did not know what position we occupied, we would choose to make the worst-off people as well off as possible.

Parfit had trenchant criticisms both of the way Rawls framed the veil of ignorance and of the judgements that he claimed would be made under its conditions. For example, Rawls wanted us kept in the dark about probabilities, and whether we were more likely to be rich than poor; a stipulation, Parfit argued, that was difficult to justify. Even if we accepted Rawls's somewhat arbitrary set-up, it did not follow that we should adopt a principle of always benefiting the least well off.

Suppose we had to choose how to use some scarce medical resources. In one possibility, Mrs Green lives to the age of twenty-five and a thousand people live to eighty. In another, Mrs Green lives to twenty-six, and a thousand people live to thirty. According to Rawls, we should opt for the second policy. Parfit thought it obvious that we should select the first.

. . .

Once the lectures were over, it would surely be a simple matter to transform them into a book. The lectures themselves constituted over thirty thousand words. All the book required was an editor. 'I would love it if you felt you had time yourself,'[8] Parfit wrote to Sam Scheffler. Scheffler was not enthusiastic, but having already had some experience of dealing with his dialectically turbo-powered friend, 'I felt that I couldn't ask anyone else to do it.'[9]

The format for the book series was for it to contain an adapted version of the three lectures. Parfit wanted to add a fourth (undelivered) 'lecture' to the text and argued that there was a precedent for this.[10] In part, this fourth chapter would be used to discuss Tim Scanlon's contractualism, which he had barely referred to in the lectures. As for the actual lectures, they 'might also be lengthened a bit',[11] and perhaps one extra commentary might be added.

'Lengthened a bit' would prove to be perhaps the greatest underestimation since the assurance when war broke out in August 1914 that it would all be over by Christmas. But, in 2002, Parfit was maintaining that, even with a fourth chapter, it would be a slim volume—by his reckoning only a third of the length of *Rediscovering Reasons*. He saw the virtue in publishing a short book, though he was worried about the implications it might have for his planned major one. 'I think that people will tell their undergraduates to buy the Tanner Volume rather than *Rediscovering Reasons*. In some ways I regret that prospect. It's been a long time since my last book, and I was hoping to produce another large book that might have the fairly good continuing sales that *Reasons and Persons* has had. The Tanner Volume will make that less likely.'[12]

Already, by 2002, Parfit had amassed a huge body of unpublished writing. A month after the Tanner Lectures, he turned sixty. He would not himself have noticed the passing of this milestone, but Larry Temkin spotted it and suggested that it be marked by a conference at Rutgers on Parfit's published oeuvre. The author was lukewarm, so Temkin put a counter-proposal. How about a conference on his unpublished manuscripts? Here was a far more appealing prospect. Parfit relished the idea of receiving comments from serious philosophers on his work in progress.

The conference took place over the weekend from 10 to 12 April 2003, and was a memorable event. Leading moral philosophers—including John Broome, Steven Darwall, Allan Gibbard, Thomas Hurka, Shelly Kagan, Frances Kamm, Christine Korsgaard, Jeff McMahan, Thomas Pogge, Peter Railton, and Tim Scanlon—delivered papers, to which Parfit responded. 'Each is regarded as a leader in his or her field, many are regarded as the world's foremost experts in their subspecialties. But for two days straight it was clear that Parfit was the star of the conference.'[13] There was a pattern in several presentations, whereby the speaker raised some objection or other, with Parfit courteously making the point that they had misunderstood his position.

On the Friday night, six speakers gave mini-speeches about Parfit's impact on their lives. According to Temkin, 'when they were done, there was literally not a dry eye in the room. Never have I seen such an outpouring of gratitude, affection, love, and respect in an academic setting.'[14] Philosophers' memories are as fallible as those of ordinary mortals, and this may be an exaggeration. Others present report that the general mood was festive rather than lachrymose. Parfit, however, was certainly moved. When he stood up to give a response, he found himself overcome with emotion and unable to speak. Tears flowed and, after a few seconds of silence, all he could manage was, 'You've made me very happy.'[15] He then sat back down and tried to control his weeping. Not everyone at the conference was so touched; one attendee complained that it had the atmosphere of a cult.

. . .

Over the next few years, there would be many hundreds of emails between Parfit and Scheffler. Scheffler would ask about the progress of the promised book, and Parfit would respond that there was one more section he had to write, one more argument he had to counter. Many birthdays and Christmases would come and go. Scheffler would remind him that it was supposed to be a short book and try to discourage him from adding fresh material. He could develop lengthier arguments in the big book, Scheffler pointed out. Sometimes these exchanges became testy. Scheffler would despair that the book would ever appear but, if he pressed Parfit, Parfit would respond, 'You don't want my book to be the best it could be.' 'He was impossible to deal with, stubborn and inconsiderate. He had a will of iron. He was not going to yield on any point.'[16] In the spring of 2006, Scheffler took the decision to wave the white flag. 'I decided there was no point in trying to dissuade him from the path he was taking, which involved greatly expanding the manuscript in ways that departed from the original plan.'[17]

. . .

The years from 2003 to 2010 had little to distinguish them, one from another, in terms of Parfit's life and output. Just as *Reasons and Persons* was the product of various strands of his thinking, so the book that eventually emerged in 2011 was a combination of diverse thoughts recycled and packaged up under one title. The idea of producing three books was abandoned. Instead, these three books became one manuscript in two volumes. The title was altered several times. Initially it was to be called *What We Could Rationally Will*, then there were several changes before it became *Climbing the Mountain*. Finally, it emerged from its extended chrysalis phase as *On What Matters*.

Most academics are fiercely protective of their ideas, and so anxious that their intellectual authorship be acknowledged that they show prepublished work only to a few trusted friends and colleagues. Parfit took the opposite approach. Versions of his manuscripts travelled around the globe like migratory birds. His insouciance about intellectual theft showed a touching faith in human nature. In fact, his unconventional approach was vindicated; not a single philosopher, as far as I can tell, took advantage of his apparent naivety to pass his ideas off as their own.

Many people were asked to comment on, not just one version of the book, but two, three, or four. There was widespread scepticism as to whether it would ever appear. Brad Hooker's feeling was typical: 'The degree of tinkering had got so obsessive that I thought it would never make it.'[18] Once a philosopher had commented on one draft, Parfit would then send them the updated version. After a time, when they had been through the second, third, fourth, fifth, and sixth drafts, many of these correspondents gave up. This was not only because they had their own lives to lead, their own papers and books to write, but also because, like Shelly Kagan, they thought that they were no longer helping Parfit. 'I stopped commenting because I thought I'm not doing him, or the profession, a favour by delaying it.'[19] Bob Adams took the same approach, 'because I thought if I didn't stop I would be collaborating in the procrastination. I didn't tell him, I just stopped.'[20]

For Parfit, other philosophers had become a means to his most valued end: he had an insatiable appetite for feedback on his writings. John Skorupski was a visiting Fellow in All Souls in the 2002–3 academic year and, conducted many conversations with Parfit about some of the issues in *Climbing the Mountain*—not always quite willingly. 'We'd start talking in the All Souls Common Room after lunch. On one occasion he followed me out and we ended up in my room with me in an armchair and Derek kneeling in front of me, emphatically making a philosophical point.'[21]

At Harvard, he would teach *Climbing the Mountain* in his class with Tim Scanlon. In the spring of 2006, students were asked to fork out $30 for the course packet, which included *Climbing the Mountain*, only to be told in the first class that parts of it were already redundant because the text had been updated. Moreover, the replacement text that Parfit had prepared, and handed out to them, was also out of date. Would it not be easier just to send a file containing the entire manuscript, a student asked in an email. Parfit sent it immediately, but with a request to 'email me again at the end of the weekend, because I will have updated versions of chapters 9 and 10 by then.'[22]

By this time, scores if not hundreds of philosophers had read at least a portion of the draft. In November of that year, a conference on the draft entitled 'Parfit Meets Critics' was held at the University of Reading. The conference convener declared, optimistically, that *Climbing the Mountain* was shortly to be published. By the following year, the manuscript had acquired its new (and, as it turned out, final) title—so a book on the conference papers was published as *Essays on Parfit's 'On What Matters'*.[23]

This was in 2009; it was still another two years before *On What Matters* actually appeared. This curious chronology—a book being published about a book that had yet to be published—was not entirely unprecedented. James Joyce's *Finnegans Wake*, known before publication as *Work in Progress*, was the subject of a collection of essays that appeared a decade before the novel itself.[24]

. . .

Even before the new millennium, Parfit's obsession with philosophy had been running in fifth gear. He now eased into a sixth gear, all of his own. Work was his only priority. He developed a motivational system for getting things done. The tasks that he considered most important—and they were all work-related—would be tagged in his head with a gold star. He never failed to complete a gold-star task. He explained the method to one of his students, who recalled, 'It was almost childish, but it worked for him. He said, once you've got the system up and running you can make more and more things gold stars.'[25]

The ruthless relegation of non-work aspects of his life caused collateral damage. He felt no nostalgia for any period of his life, nor the emotional ties most people feel about those to whom they were once close. Mary Clemmey, his first girlfriend, bumped into him at a memorial event at All Souls and suggested they get together. 'He replied in a cold, off-hand way, "Why, what would we talk about?"'[26] In March 2007, Bill Ewald, who had been helpful in the final stages of *Reasons and Persons*, was in Oxford on a trip from the US. Their mutual friend Susan Hurley had been diagnosed with cancer, and it was not clear how long she had to live. She invited Ewald to supper at All Souls on 6 March, and asked Parfit to join them—so that the three of them could be together like the good old days. But Parfit demurred; he could not spare the time because he was working on his book. After supper, Bill and Susan went to his rooms to say hello, but he told them that he was very busy and ushered them out. Hurley was hurt, but shrugged it off: 'Oh well, that's Derek.' But Ewald wanted to say, 'Derek, you're writing a book of moral philosophy called *On What Matters*. Well, *this* matters.'[27]

At approximately this time, another very old friend, Edward Mortimer, bumped into Parfit in Oxford and invited him for lunch at his home in the Cotswolds. 'I'd love to come,' Parfit replied, 'but I'm preparing for a seminar.' 'And I said, "No, I didn't mean today, I mean next week or in a few weeks' time". But he said, "No, no, no—the seminar's in six months."'[28] There are numerous similar stories. Parfit's Eton buddy Anthony Cheetham, with whom he had co-edited a book as a student, tried to re-establish a connection and rang him at All Souls. 'I said we must meet up in London. And there was a rather chilly silence at his end. Then he said, "I'll put you on my agenda." I felt a little bit left out from my once closest friend.'[29]

'No' became the default response to requests. Could he come and address a university philosophy society? 'Unfortunately, I am too busy.' Would he be willing to be interviewed for the podcast 'Philosophy Bites'? 'Unfortunately, I am too busy.' Would he address an Oxford seminar on personhood in ancient philosophy? 'I'm afraid I never do ancient philosophy.' Would he come to the Dragon School reunion (in 2006)? 'No, because I have no memory of faces.' Would he like to come for dinner at (another) college? 'No, although I would love to talk to you, I would also have to spend time talking to other people, and I don't want to do that.'

His social awkwardness grew more debilitating. If there was a dinner after an event, he would fret about seating arrangements and whom he would have to converse with. A friend from his undergraduate days, Deirdre Wilson, who knew him sufficiently well to have spent a few weeks living at 5 Northmoor Road after her Finals, found herself sitting next to him at an All Souls dinner. She had been looking forward to reminiscing about the past and reminded him of their old friendship. 'He said, "I don't talk about the past," and he turned away and didn't address another word to me for the rest of the evening.'[30]

On the other hand, in June 2006 he was pressured to attend an extended family reunion at the summer house of his sister Theodora and brother-in-law Van, in Deer Isle, Maine, along with two nephews, two first cousins, and various partners and offspring, and was pleasantly surprised to find that he liked his cousins; and they, in turn, enjoyed his presence. When he surfaced from his books, and was in relaxed mood, he could be a fluent conversationalist on a broad range of topics. 'Derek was wonderful company,' recalled his cousin Gavin, 'holding us rapt as he held forth.'[31] This was an exceptional occasion, but it is worth noting that, when it did not interfere with his work, his generosity was limitless. He might not have had time to see Hurley, but she had the pick of his photographs for a special present for two wealthy friends of hers who had helped with her cancer treatment. She wrote to thank Parfit four months before she died: 'It's a strange kind of thank you, for a gift that enabled me to give a gift to people who have given so much to me. By doing so I impose on your incredible generosity in a strange sort of way [. . . and] it means a very great deal to me.'[32]

He hardly ever travelled to London, except for the occasional philosophy lecture or to renew his US visa. After Janet had moved to London, their relationship became principally telephonic. He would call several times a day, though these calls were often brief. It was only in 2007, when Janet became a Distinguished Research Fellow at Oxford's Uehiro Centre for Practical Ethics, that there was a resumption of part-time cohabitation. Janet began to spend a few nights a week in Oxford, and would stay at the house in Beaumont Buildings, along with the philosopher tenants. Initially, she slept in the tiny top room reserved for Parfit, with its single bed. But on the day that she installed a sofa-bed in the previously unused common room, Parfit rang to say that he would 'toggle along' that evening.[33] So he did, and his toggling along at night, and returning to All Souls during the day, became the pattern.

Parfit was prepared to devote time away from work to only one person other than Janet, and that was Patricia Zander, the British-born,

Boston-based pianist he had first met in 1965. Contact had been severed in the early 1990s, but it was re-established when Parfit was informed that Patricia had developed cancer. Initially, most of their email correspondence centred on Parfit's photographic prints: he sent many of these to her, and she became almost as fixated as he was on the ways in which they could be improved, advising him on everything from colours and dimensions to whether clouds or raindrops should be added or removed. As her illness progressed, Parfit would call her regularly: Patricia's daughter says these conversations would often last an hour. Parfit was teaching at Harvard in the spring and early summer of 2008 and then returned to the UK. But in July, when it was clear that she was dying, he flew back to the US especially to see her, with Janet's knowledge and encouragement. Sitting by her hospital bed, he read *Alice's Adventures in Wonderland* aloud and worked quietly on his laptop when she slept.

. . .

Parfit ceased attending the Tuesday Group, because most of the papers had little to do with his own work. He far preferred the All Souls discussion group which, by the millennium, had become dominated by his mushrooming manuscript. Each meeting would last at least two hours, and usually longer. 'It was challenging stuff,' recalls Krister Bykvist. 'By the end, we were all exhausted. All except Derek, who wanted to continue. Sometimes he would go down on all fours on the carpet, and would be drawing invisibly on the floor, grouping things, clarifying ideas.'[34] At the end of the meeting they would decide what to focus on at the next meeting, and Parfit would be quick to say, 'I've got a new version of chapter X'—often a slightly modified version of one they had already debated. One participant, Julian Savulescu, stopped attending, 'as it was just Derek talking to himself about his own book.'[35]

It happened gradually, but, as a philosophical interlocutor, Parfit slowly ceased to be a receptive listener who would give a sympathetic hearing to an opposing position. The gymnastic imagination, with its shape-shifting flexibility, receded. Its place was taken by a more rigid mind. This was manifest in the narrowing of his interests. There had been a time when he would become engaged with a myriad of philosophical questions that his colleagues were grappling with. Now he was only interested in the few issues that mattered to him. Almost everything he did became an extension of his own project.

This growing rigidity was also revealed in a new dogmatism. He had spent so many years working on the same topics that he came to believe he had seen every counter-move that could be made. Many philosophers felt he had ceased to listen attentively and that positions had congealed inside him. They became frustrated when he assumed that they were making a particular point, a point to which he had a pre-prepared response, when they thought they were making a different point. He would interrupt before they had finished a question, believing he could anticipate what they were going to say. Sometimes, when responding to a question, whole passages from drafts of *Climbing the Mountain/On What Matters* would tumble from his mouth, word for word, like a document spewing from a printer. At other times, two people would raise a similar objection, and rather than attempt to vary his answer, with a different way of clarifying his response, he would simply repeat it.

There is a yarn involving prisoners serving life sentences who have heard each other's jokes so many times that they give each joke a number. One of them says, '42', and they all burst out laughing. Another says, '73', and they all guffaw. Then somebody shouts out, '219', and one prisoner laughs louder and longer than the others. 'What's so funny?' he's asked. 'I hadn't heard that one before', he replies. The story reminded Roger Crisp of the last few years of the All Souls gatherings. By the early 2000s, whenever somebody put an objection to Parfit's position, he would speed through the rolodex in his brain, until he identified the relevant counter-objection.

Because Parfit no longer seemed to be intellectually flexible, some meetings became tense. Bob Adams and Ralph Wedgwood took issue with his arguments about metaethics, believing them too weak to publish. John Broome was irritated that Parfit would not countenance the use of logical notation, which Broome thought could remove several ambiguities. The most fraught meeting took place on 18 December 2008.

The participants cannot recall the substance of the debate with confidence, but it was probably about moral naturalism.[36] Parfit objected to the analogy made by some naturalists that, just as we have discovered that water is H_2O, we might discover that moral rightness is the same as some natural property. This dispute centred around what counted as a fact. Parfit insisted that the claim, 'Water is H_2O' is of a completely different type from the claim that, for example, 'what is good is what makes people happy'. In any case, the meeting ended unresolved, with some participants upset that disagreement had become so sharp. Parfit was left feeling 'devastated'. At 8 p.m. that evening he wrote to Broome to apologize 'for my rudeness'. He'd worked so hard on this subject that 'I get too easily upset by criticisms from any of the few people whose judgement I admire and trust the most'.[37]

The gatherings stuttered on for another year, becoming more and more intellectually barren. The final meeting took place on 15 February 2010.

. . .

Reasons and Persons had been proudly revisionist. Some of our ordinary, commonsense positions were wrong, Parfit believed, and he aimed to put us right and to use reasoned argument 'to challenge what we assume'.[38] He was happy to stake a position outside the mainstream—indeed, he regarded it as the philosopher's duty to attack and shift false beliefs.

But now he became desperate to reconcile conflicting views. Disagreement began to worry him more and more. And in later years, his response to audience members who sought to make critical points would often be of the form, 'I actually don't think we disagree.' The Israeli philosopher Saul Smilansky preferred early to late Parfit. Parfit was one of his Oxford DPhil examiners in 1990; early Parfit, he says, 'wanted to open rather than close, he wanted people to be excited rather than agree, he sought breakthrough rather than consensus'.[39]

A psychoanalyst might trace this aversion to disagreement to Parfit's parents' fractious marriage, or to his relationship with his father. It

certainly became a core mental trait. He himself explained it in philosophical terms—citing a section with which he was much taken in his
favourite book, *Methods of Ethics*. In this section, Sidgwick remarked
that 'if I find any of my judgements, intuitive or inferential, in direct
conflict with a judgement of some other mind, there must be error
somewhere: and if I have no more reason to suspect error in the other
mind than in my own, reflective comparison between the two judgements necessarily reduces me [. . .] to a state of neutrality.'[40]

Many have reflected on this passage. Parfit internalized it. 'I am
deeply worried by disagreements with people who seem as likely as I
am to be getting things right.'[41] If another philosopher, particularly one
he respected, had an important objection, he now felt compelled to
counter it and persuade them that it failed. If he was unsuccessful in
convincing them, he would be forced to conclude that his argument was
not superior to theirs.

This cannot fully explain why he found disagreement so profoundly
disturbing. After all, disagreement and debate are the norms within philosophy. One of the founders of Western philosophy, Socrates, used to
irritate his fellow Athenians by confronting them in the public square
and marketplace with teasing questions about the nature of beauty and
justice. But Parfit came to believe that dissent about ethics—especially
dissent between leading philosophers—was evidence for its relativism.
And he thought that relativism essentially collapsed into nihilism. If
your moral truth conflicted with, but was no less valid than, my moral
truth, this would show that, ultimately, nothing mattered.

Most moral philosophers can engage in metaethical debates without
this bleeding into the rest of their life—they still have hobbies and projects, they support certain political parties, they believe in and promote
certain values, they care about the flourishing of their friends and family.
But for Parfit, the thought that moral values might be merely something
we project onto the world caused almost existential anguish. If moral
values were relative, then we must conclude, he believed, that almost
everything in his life was pointless.

No disagreements distressed Parfit more than those with Bernard
Williams, whom he so revered. Williams, as we have seen, had argued

that if a person has no desire to do something, then they have no reason
to do it. This had things topsy-turvy, Parfit thought. What gives me a
reason to want friendship is not that I desire friends. Rather, it is because
friendship is valuable that I have a reason to want it.

Parfit needed his morality to be anchored in bedrock. There had to be
an objective reason to relieve from suffering someone who is needlessly
in pain. This had nothing to do with semantics, with how we use language. It is not mere opinion. It is to do with our relationship to the world.
And it is independent of our desires. If I see a child drowning in a pond,
I have a reason to save her, whether or not I want to. If I am not motivated
to save the child, that is evidence that I am irrational—or wicked.

But can we really make sense of our having a reason to do something
that we have no desire to do—or, conversely, having a reason not to do
something that we do desire? Yes, argued Parfit. And he conjured up a
gloriously ludicrous individual with 'Future Tuesday Indifference'. This
person is indifferent to what happens to him on any future Tuesday. He
would prefer agony on a future Tuesday to the mildest of pains on a Monday. We can all agree, said Parfit, that Future Tuesday Indifference man
is irrational. Despite his desires, he has a reason to choose the mild
Monday pain rather than the agonizing Tuesday one. This simple contention had a powerful effect on some leading philosophers. 'For much of my
life as a philosopher', writes Peter Singer, 'I was a Humean about practical
reason. This example helped to persuade me that Hume was wrong.'[42]

Nor was it merely in the domain of prudence, or self-interest, that
reasons could be objective and independent of our desires. In terms of
epistemology (questions about knowledge), for example, we can have
reasons to believe something. Thus, I have a reason to believe that Paris
is the capital of France; and, presented with the evidence, I ought to
believe this fact. If I have reason to believe it is very sunny outside, and
I also have reason to believe that I am susceptible to sunburn, then that
gives me an objective reason to wear sun cream. We have reason to believe some things that we don't desire. Parfit liked an example from the
philosopher Tom Kelly: if you haven't seen a film, and a friend spoils it
by revealing the denouement, you have a reason to believe this is how
the film ends, even if you don't want to believe it. Belief in God is

another example. There are strong reasons to believe that God does not exist and that there is no afterlife; but you may want to believe that God does exist and that there is an afterlife.

This all seemed so obvious to Parfit that he simply could not understand that some people would deny that there were external reasons for action. The fact that these people included the brilliant Bernard Williams made it even more baffling. Over the years, scores of people would be on the receiving end of a tormented conversation with Parfit—'How could Bernard not see that there were external reasons? Bernard. Bernard!' He would insist—implausibly—that Williams had somehow misunderstood and did not have the concept of a normative reason.

He went to see the philosopher Adrian Moore, a protégé of Williams, to see if Moore could give an explanation. 'For Parfit it was as though someone he totally revered had said the moon was made of custard.'[43] In Harvard, he would occasionally meet up with Selim Berker. 'He was so obsessed with Williams, that he had to get it out. When we'd meet up to talk, I knew within five minutes we'd be talking about why Williams didn't have the concept of a normative reason.'[44]

. . .

Meanwhile, the manuscript of *On What Matters* was ballooning. One of Scheffler's jobs, as editor, was to write an introduction for the book. He was determined to put off this task until Parfit's text was complete—otherwise he might have to rewrite his contribution to take account of additions or, less likely, deletions. Parfit kept telling him the book was finished but would then have a change of mind. The book was in a state of constant evolution. It had to be perfect: he was writing it for posterity. Finally, in the autumn of 2007, Parfit's insistence that he was close to dotting the final i in the final appendix convinced Scheffler that he should not put off writing the introduction any longer.

Mistake. Parfit was still dispatching copies of the manuscript far and wide, and his compulsive fiddling went on and on. Amia Srinivasan arrived at All Souls in 2009 and had lunch with Parfit, who was appointed her college advisor. He asked whether she would be interested in reading his work, and '[t]he next day I received two hefty boxes'. He became upset during the lunch when she said that she thought morality was not objective in his strong sense; that it was, in her view, dependent on the human mind. 'He said it implied that there was nothing wrong with torture.'[45]

Even after *On What Matters* went into production in 2010, Parfit was still pushing to include new material. A new appendix was added early that year, after typesetting had begun. And Scheffler had to revisit his introduction, after all. Throughout the final years leading up to publication, about the only person who believed that a book would eventually appear was its OUP editor, Peter Momtchiloff. He noticed a change in Parfit's motivation. 'The key factor was the shadow of the reaper. He became increasingly worried that he didn't have enough time left to do all the things that he wanted to do. He started to think more pragmatically about what he could get done.'[46]

With the manuscript at last complete, the baton of pain was passed to OUP.

20

Lifeboats, Tunnels, and Bridges

In what typeface is this book printed? You may well not know. There are many decisions made in the course of a book's production to which readers pay little attention. *On What Matters* looks much like any other book, with a cover and pages, words, sentences and paragraphs, headings, and footnotes. But of course, it has a certain look, it has a typeface and a font, it has margins and gaps between the paragraphs.

On every decision about the aesthetics of the book, Parfit wanted a say, and scores of emails on these matters went back and forth. How many previous authors have gone to the trouble of identifying and recommending a specific printer for their books (Biddles, please, based in Kings Lynn)? A note to Momtchiloff discussed whether indented paragraphs should have justified right margins and how much space there should be above and below indented material. As for the font, initially Parfit had requested Palatino, but OUP considered it 'dated'. Parfit, unusually, backed down, though he was unconvinced by the 'dated' objection. 'The main building of the OUP, for example, looks dated compared with the modern addition to the North on Walton Street, but the dated building looks much better.'[1] They settled on Minion Pro. He wanted the font to be big. Just as an Englishman abroad supposedly believes that, if he raises his voice sufficiently, the natives are bound to understand, so Parfit seemed to believe that if his philosophy was presented in large enough letters, it would inevitably persuade.

In his approach to OUP, Parfit deployed three familiar tactics. First, he always found a previous OUP book which contained an example of the style he was after. Second, he wrote to members of the OUP production team individually, rather than taking on the team as a whole. And third, if they objected to the cost, he would offer to pay. He'd adopted a similar strategy for *Reasons and Persons*.

As the book edged closer to production, the negotiations between Parfit and OUP became more intense. 'I am sorry if this letter seems hostile,' reads one email on 4 October 2009, in possibly the most hostile letter he ever wrote.[2] Volume 1 of *On What Matters* had already been prepared for the printing press. Parfit had seen how it would look and was upset. At this late stage, he decided that the typeface was not right. One member of the OUP team, Louise Sprake, attempted to hold the line. It was too far down the process to change, she claimed.

Her resistance greatly disconcerted Parfit. He composed numerous responses, which laid out what he regarded as the pertinent facts. OUP had agreed that he would be involved in decisions about the book's appearance. He had been browsing through past OUP books and discovered a book whose appearance he approved of—*Metaethics after Moore*.[3] *On What Matters*, he proposed, should be printed in a similar way. When that proved impossible (because *Metaethics after Moore* had been digitally as opposed to litho printed), Parfit found a litho-printed OUP book, *The Oxford Book of Modern Science Writing*, which seemed to him ideal. Louise Sprake demurred, since the typesetting had already been completed for Volume 1, and Parfit replied that this was hardly his fault, but that he was nonetheless prepared to pay any extra costs incurred.

OUP declined this offer, and Parfit implored Sprake to reconsider. 'Of course I realize that I couldn't reasonably expect that the OUP would print my book in whatever way I happened to prefer. Many requests would be quite unreasonable. But my request is only that my book be printed, at no extra cost to the OUP, in the same way as another recent similar OUP book.' He then mooted the nuclear option: that he move to another publisher if what he regarded as his perfectly reasonable demands were ignored. This might, technically, put him in breach of contract, but, he pointed out, it was unlikely OUP would sue him. And in a veiled threat, he warned that to do so would risk their reputation. An apology for what might appear his aggressive tone came in a postscript: 'That is not intended at all, and if it seems so, that is only because I am so upset. Perhaps I care too much about the appearance of my book. But I've spent most of my time for nearly 20 years writing this book, and it seems now the most important part of my life.'[4]

Sprake soon left the philosophy list, and her replacement was Jen Lunsford, who wasn't fully briefed about, and didn't fully appreciate, the sensitive nature of the task she had inherited. Thanks to Parfit, there had already been many delays. Her immediate priority was to push the book through the final stages of the production process. She had to commission a proofreader for the first volume, reorganize the typesetting, and find a copyeditor and indexer for the second volume. 'I'm the kind of person who has to stick to a schedule,' she says. That is an admirable virtue in a production editor; but there was no schedule so immovable that it could withstand Parfit's unstoppable force. 'I've worked with well over two hundred authors. I've never dealt with anybody like him. It took everything I had to get that book published.' Parfit responded directly to copyeditor points, but Lunsford had to confront his typesetting demands. The spacing resurfaced as an issue. 'The space between the lines and words are set by a program. But he would demand changes in individual spacing between words—more space here, less space there—and on the whole document. I wanted to pull my hair out.' She tried to explain that tinkering with individual spaces was impractical, but Parfit was insistent. And the corrections never ceased. 'I'd say, "I need the final, final, final set of corrections on Friday." And on Friday he'd say, "Here's a set, but there's more coming."'[5]

Meanwhile, both Lunsford and Momtchiloff were facing multiple demands about the cover—which disturbed Parfit even more than the gaps between words. The photograph for the cover of Volume 1 was of St Petersburg's Winter Canal, taken through an arch. Volume 2 is graced with a stunning image of the University Embankment, also in St Petersburg. 'The tower [on the Volume 1 cover] needed more gold, the snow [on the Volume 2 cover] needed to be whiter.'[6] He moved the buildings around on the photograph to make more room for the spine. 'We don't have time to do this for most books. We made an exception for Derek.'[7]

Various image adjustments were made, but Parfit remained unhappy. More than unhappy; Janet rang Momtchiloff because 'Derek was in total despair.'[8] Eventually, when OUP believed that they had finally secured consent for the covers, they sent him the sample proofs. That wasn't good enough. He wanted to see the wet proofs—in other words how it would turn out from the actual print plates. It was an unprecedented proposal, and OUP had to approach the printer to check the cost. The quote came back at £3,000—far too much for a university press. 'I'll pay,' said Parfit. And so he did.

Momtchiloff witnessed the toll these troubles took on the author: 'We're not used to authors weeping in our presence.'[9] It was just as bad, if not worse, for those at the receiving end of his anxieties, such as Jen Lunsford. 'I didn't want to kill Derek. But more than once I did think to myself that if he sends one more email, I'll jump off a bridge!'[10] OUP never had the heart to tell him that printing is an inexact science. The quality of a print will vary according to when the ink is put on, the temperature and how the chemicals interact, the type of paper, and so forth. But by the time the book appeared, Parfit had reached some sort of psychological accommodation with it. And, after it was published, OUP never again heard from him about the book's aesthetics.

. . .

In Volumes 1 and 2 of *On What Matters*, which were finally published in 2011, Parfit aimed to demonstrate that three important moral theories converge, and that morality is objective.

That is the substance of 1,400 pages, condensed into the length of a tweet. The claim about the objectivity of ethics was described in chapter 19 above. In theory, convergence and objectivity were distinct issues. It is possible to believe that morality is objective without believing that disputes between the main moral systems can be reconciled. But for Parfit they were connected: he felt that disputes undermined the case for objectivity.

In the Preface, he writes that '[m]y two masters are Sidgwick and Kant. Kant is the greatest moral philosopher since the ancient Greeks.

Sidgwick's *Methods* is, I believe, the best book on ethics ever written.'[11] As well as comparing their many virtues, Parfit points out that they were not without their faults. 'Sidgwick is sometimes boring, for example, and Kant is sometimes maddening.'[12] Nevertheless, they were the book's twin guiding spirits. Its bare bones were already present in the Tanner Lectures. The title of the book changed, but for many years *Climbing the Mountain* did seem apt, because of a metaphor Parfit used repeatedly. He argued that the disciples of three core ethical traditions, Kantians, consequentialists, and contractualists, were climbing the same mountain from different sides. It was only when they reached the summit that they would become aware of their common goal.

Over the years, many people commented on the vividness of the mountain metaphor, but in fact it was not entirely novel. It was adapted from a line used by John Stuart Mill and previously cited in *Reasons and Persons*. There, Parfit made the point that commonsense morality and consequentialism are not as far apart as had been assumed, and that it might be possible to reduce disagreement between them significantly. If so, '[w]e might find that in Mill's words we are "climbing the hill from the other side"'.[13] Parfit was obviously struck by Mill's powerful image; he had mentioned it as early as January 1976 in a letter to Rawls.[14]

In Parfit's Tanner Lectures, John Rawls had been the contractualist mountaineer. But by the time of *On What Matters*, this line of thought was represented by Tim Scanlon, as it was expounded in his book *What We Owe to Each Other*. This paid Scanlon an enormous compliment. Parfit chose his version not because it was easy to critique but, on the contrary, because he felt it was the most plausible account of contractualism.

On the face of it, the project to show that Kant, consequentialism, and contractualism are compatible appears hopeless. There seem to be irreconcilable differences: for example, on the question of whether it can ever be right to torture somebody (Kant: 'No'; consequentialist: 'Yes'). But, by probing various hypothetical cases, Parfit sought to show that to preserve what is best in each tradition, they each need to be reformulated. And, after his 'improvement' process, it would become clear that they no longer conflict—they simply become different ways of expressing the same thing. They are bedfellows in a queen-size bed.

The hypothetical cases are variations of the trolley problem (see chapter 9), and to each of them Parfit gave a name. They usually involve individuals endangered in unfortunate circumstances, where there is the option to help, but at the cost of harming others. They include 'Lifeboat', 'Tunnel', and 'Bridge'. In 'Lifeboat', I am on one rock and five people are on another. Before a rising tide drowns all six people, you could use a lifeboat to save either me, or the five. In 'Tunnel', a driverless runaway train is about to kill five people. You are a bystander and you could flick a switch and so divert the train onto another track and through another tunnel. Unfortunately, I am in this other tunnel. And in 'Bridge', the train is again speeding towards five people, but this time there is no other track or tunnel and only one way to save the five. I am on a bridge and by remote control you could open the trap door on which I am standing, so that I would fall in front of the train, triggering its automatic brake function. I, of course, would die.

As Parfit explains, in 'Lifeboat', 'Tunnel', and 'Bridge', the outcome of your saving the five is the same—my death. But in each case,

> my death would be differently causally related to your saving of the five. In *Lifeboat*, you would let me die because, in the time available, you would not save both me and the five. In *Tunnel*, you would save the five by redirecting the train with the foreseen side-effect of thereby killing me. In *Bridge*, you would kill me as a means of saving the five.[15]

There are also several thought experiments involving earthquakes. Take 'Third Earthquake', in which

> [y]ou and your child are trapped in slowly collapsing wreckage, which threatens both of your lives. You cannot save your child's life except by using *Black's* body as a shield, without her consent, in a way that would crush one of her toes. If you also caused Black to lose another toe, you would save your own life.[16]

All these thought experiments are used to test the plausibility of the implications of certain moral principles. In 'Third Earthquake', we might want to say that treating Black in this way is using her as a 'mere means', and so is prohibited by Kant. But this cannot be right. For suppose you choose to save your child but not yourself, such that Black loses only one toe, rather than two—well, clearly in this case Black is not being treated as *a mere means*.

Conversely, there are cases where Person A does treat Person B as a mere means, and yet does not act wrongly. For example, suppose an egoist 'saves some child from drowning, at a great risk to himself, but his only aim is to be rewarded. Since this man treats these other people merely as a means, Kant's principle implies that, in [. . .] saving this child's life, this man acts wrongly. That is clearly false.'[17]

Traditionally conceived, each of the three traditions, Kantianism, consequentialism, and contractualism, is inadequate to explain our intuitions, Parfit claimed. But, once reformulated so that their implications are plausible, they converge on the same truth. To gain an idea of how the Parfitian process operates, think about how Kantians might reason in 'Lifeboat'. Each of the six might rationally will that they be saved. But I, alone on my rock, might also rationally sacrifice myself to save five lives. Reason does not compel me to do this, but it surely allows me to do so. So choosing to save the five rather than the one is the only option that could be rationally willed by all six of us, and is therefore the option that should be chosen. Obviously, the consequentialist will reach the same conclusion, for saving five lives is clearly better, on consequentialist grounds, than saving one.

The upshot was to demonstrate, at least to Parfit's satisfaction, that there was no disparity between the best version of each theory. It was a strenuous climb up the slope, but exponents of the three moral traditions could now embrace each other on the mountain summit. According to Parfit, the ultimate principle of morality can be expressed in three ways, reflecting the three traditions: an act is wrong when it is disallowed by some principle that is either:

(1) one of the principles whose being universal laws would make things go best; or
(2) one of the only principles whose being universal laws everyone could rationally will; or
(3) a principle that no one could reasonably reject.

. . .

At last, he had done it. He had come up with the supreme principle of morality—a task that others before him, such as Kant and Sidgwick, had tried and failed adequately to accomplish.

Except that he had not satisfied all his critics. They came at him with multiple objections. Some were scathing about his entire methodology, and, in particular, the use of artificial thought experiments. It is not easy to identify what so irks some philosophers about these cases, 'why it turns the grey matter of [some] philosophers red';[18] but a common complaint is that since they are often ludicrously unrealistic, our intuitions about them are unreliable and can tell us nothing about how we should make judgements in the messy, complex, real world. This was a point forcefully made by Allen Wood in his response to the Tanner Lectures, published in Volume 2 of *On What Matters*. Parfit ignored this objection in his reply to Wood, but when he was asked about it in lectures, he advanced the defence that the value of such cases lay precisely in their artificiality. Just as a scientist tries to work out the impact of one variable by changing it whilst holding all other variables constant, so the moral philosopher seeks to understand the significance of one factor by holding all other factors constant.

For Wood, however, trolley-like dilemmas were more than just unrealistic. They were repugnant. They asked us to define the conditions in which we could justifiably kill innocent people for the greater good. Merely raising the question was, Wood believed, morally corrosive, an objection that Parfit simply could not comprehend. After all, since there were rare occasions when such dilemmas actually occurred, how could it be wrong to consider them hypothetically?

Wood's criticisms were of Parfit's methodology. Putting these aside, Parfit had to deal with even more fundamental attacks. Some philosophers thought that the entire venture—with its aim to derive a single account of morality—was misconceived. Tensions and conflict between values was inevitable, and it was futile to try to clean morality up. This was the thrust of Susan Wolf's critique, made in the spirit of Isaiah Berlin, who held that there was a plurality of ideals, and that it was reasonable for people to disagree about whether, for example, freedom should, in a particular case, be granted more weight than equality. Producing a single formula covering all cases was almost as silly as the supercomputer, in Douglas Adams's *The Hitchhikers Guide to the Galaxy*, offering '42' as the answer to the question, 'What is the meaning of life, the universe, and everything?'

There was and is another frequent criticism of Parfit's position that is worth highlighting. This is that when he 'improved' the moral theories he was examining, he shed all that was distinctive about them. In particular, by 'cleaning up' Kant, by scrubbing off the defects and inconsistencies and making Kantian maxims coherent and watertight, he lost what was central to Kant's appeal.

This critique was at the heart of Roger Scruton's review of *On What Matters*. In a variation of 'Lifeboat', called 'Second Lifeboat', we have the option to save our own child, or else five strangers. Consequentialism might imply that we should save the five, and to some people this is an outrageous demand. Parfit, however, explains why there is no such consequentialist imperative. True, if we were not powerfully disposed to help our own children more than the children of others, things might occasionally go better (as in 'Second Lifeboat'). But, far more often, they would go much worse. And for that reason, Parfit argued, consequentialism permits us to give strong priority to our own children. This, wrote Scruton, was a bizarre way to reach the right conclusion.

> What is remarkable about this line of reasoning is that, even if it upholds common sense, it does so on grounds that entirely undermine the obligations on which common sense is founded. It ignores the fact that our children have a claim on us that others do not have, and that this claim is *already* a reason to rescue them in their hour of need, and needs no further argument. It ignores, one might say, the human reality of the situation that Parfit claims to be imagining, in favour of the spectral mathematics that provides the measure for all his comparative judgements.[19]

Nevertheless, Scruton described the book as endlessly engaging and 'a landmark in moral philosophy'.[20] On this, at least, there was consensus.

Academic philosophy is a minority sport—mostly of negligible interest to the world beyond. But *On What Matters* had been anticipated for so many years that within philosophy it constituted an Event with a capital E. And all serious newspapers, in the Anglo-American world at least, acknowledged the birth. *The New Yorker* honoured it with a lengthy article, and it was the lead review in *The New York Review of Books*.

There were some effusive reviews. In *The Times Literary Supplement*, Peter Singer rated it even higher than *Reasons and Persons*, describing it as 'the most significant work in ethics since Sidgwick's masterpiece was published in 1874'.[21] Another praised it for being 'one of the richest, most exciting contributions to moral philosophy in decades'.[22] A largely critical article conceded that the book was nevertheless 'the work of a philosophical genius'.[23]

But the general tenor of the reviews was that Parfit's project resembled a vast baroque cathedral that evoked a sense of awe less for its beauty than for its sheer construction. 'It stands as a grand and dedicated attempt to elaborate a fundamentally misguided perspective,' declared *The New Republic*.[24] Several of the reviews mentioned the daunting length of the volumes; one reviewer went to the trouble of putting Volumes 1 and 2 on the scales: they weighed in at '4.8 pounds' (2.18 kilos).

The most brutal judgement was by Simon Blackburn. So scathing was it that the *Financial Times* eventually published it only in a modified form. Even in the version that appeared, Parfit's argument was described as so 'idiosyncratic' that 'Vice-Chancellors bent on finding excuses to close philosophy departments must be rubbing their hands'.[25] The undiluted article is quite something. Blackburn is a delightfully elegant writer, and his hatchet was clothed in velvet. Is this book really as significant as some have claimed, the author asked, or is it 'a long voyage down a stagnant backwater?'[26] There was no doubt about Blackburn's verdict. He accused Parfit of a crass misunderstanding of Hume. And here's the final paragraph, representative of the tone of the whole:

'It would be a tragedy', he [Parfit] tells us on page two, 'if there is no single true morality.' Well, outside the charmed walls of All Souls College, there actually are tragedies. Often the messy pluralities of conflicting moral demands—one might have said, the conflicting demands on human life itself—are part of the cause. Inside the charmed walls I fear that the tragedy is more like that of Ajax slaying sheep, or perhaps it is the comedy of Don Quixote tilting at windmills.[27]

. . .

The highest hurdle for *On What Matters* to overcome, however, was an almost inevitable sense of anticlimax. It was as if a movie trailer had generated feverish anticipation, only for the audience to discover later that it contained all the film's best bits. The text of *On What Matters* had been circulating in some form or other for so many years that many of its potential readers had read at least portions of it before. And truly, there was not enough novelty in the published book for them to bother to read it again. There was also a sense that, as with *Reasons and Persons*, Parfit had artificially bundled together an assortment of thoughts and topics that would have been better served by being kept apart. He threw in material that did not need to be there. There are ten appendices in Volumes 1 and 2 combined, including Appendix D, 'Why Anything, Why This?' which reprises Parfit's work on why there is something rather than nothing and why our universe is as it is. Riveting though this material may be, it is not evident why it warrants space alongside everything else.

That the book appeared at all, however, was some sort of miracle. OUP's Jen Lunsford was pleased to see the back of it and did not want to be reminded of the experience: 'So much so that while I kept copies of his volumes on my shelf at work after publication, I couldn't bring myself to take them home.'[28]

21

Marriage and Pizza

Nothing mattered to Parfit more than *On What Matters*. But with the book approaching the finishing-line, he could reflect on less weighty affairs. These included marriage.

By 2010, Parfit and Janet Radcliffe Richards had been together for nearly three decades. There had been ups and downs, as in all relationships, and Janet had to accustom herself to her partner's unusual and uncompromising lifestyle. He spent large chunks of time in the US, he had travelled many times on holiday alone to take photographs, and even when he was in the UK, his work always took priority. Parfit showed sufficient self-awareness to describe his decision to continue his annual pilgrimages to Venice and St Petersburg long after he had met Janet as 'shamefully ruthless'.[1] Few partners would have tolerated it.

It was Janet's proposal that they marry, and for entirely pragmatic reasons. She wanted to formalize the relationship so that they were each other's next of kin. This would give them the right to make decisions for each other if either of them became incapacitated and incapable of exercising autonomy. Derek was happy to be married, for tax and inheritance purposes. Both he and Janet had made wills leaving everything to each other.

The date was set for 31 August 2010. On Monday, 29 August, Parfit rang his closest living relative, Theodora. 'I just want you to know that Janet and I are getting married on Wednesday.' 'That's wonderful,' Theodora spluttered, 'but I won't be able to get there in time.' 'That's OK,' said her brother. 'I am not *inviting* you. I just wanted you to know.'[2]

No invitations were issued to friends, either. The two official wit-
nesses to the ceremony were Janet's sister and brother-in-law, Judith and
Richard. In an article about Parfit and Radcliffe Richards, I recounted
the following story about Parfit literal-mindedness:

> The night before they were due to get married [. . .] Derek and Janet
> were walking down Little Clarendon Street in Oxford on the way to
> a low-key celebration at an Indian restaurant. As they approached the
> restaurant, they passed a wedding shop. In the window was one of those
> meringue bridal dresses, all petticoats, hoops, and trains. 'That', said
> Janet, jokingly, 'is what I shall be wearing tomorrow.' 'Do you mean
> that exact one,' replied Derek, in all seriousness, 'or one just like it?'[3]

The wedding was on a glorious day. They walked the few minutes
from Beaumont Buildings to the registry office. Janet was wearing a red
dress, not the meringue dress or even one just like it. Parfit had a red tie.
Janet's niece and her boyfriend were waiting outside with confetti. Then
the six of them went punting under a cloudless sky. They drank bubbly
and ate a picnic Judith had prepared. No best men or bridesmaids, no
banquet or marquee, no speeches or toasts. It was an occasion devoid
of stress, 'the best wedding I've ever been to', according to Judith.[4]

For a few hours there was no philosophy, and Parfit was abnormally
relaxed. The biggest upset of the day was that he enjoyed it. He even
started to make sentimental remarks. 'We should look at the marriage
certificate and gloat,'[5] he said to Janet. But, when the punting was over,
it was straight back to All Souls. A honeymoon had never been contemplated and, given the timing, was out of the question. Parfit was in the
final throes of *On What Matters*. What is more, he had to vacate the All
Souls rooms that he had occupied for over four decades, since he had
now reached the statutory age for retirement. And, in a couple of days,
he was due to be on a flight to New York, where he would be teaching
in the Fall semester.

The next forty-eight hours were manic and mostly spent in All Souls.
Parfit was printing out reams and reams of documents in the college
office, frantically running up and down the stone stairs. Book, marriage,
moving, travel—all were playing on his mind, and together they

triggered some kind of neurological chain reaction. Suddenly his mind went blank. He could not remember how he came to be in All Souls or what he was doing there. Naturally, he became agitated. Janet diagnosed (correctly) that he might be suffering from transient global amnesia—a condition involving the rapid and temporary loss of memory, which she had once experienced herself. She rang the emergency healthline, and they took a taxi to the all-night doctor, a mile or so away on the Cowley Road.

Sufferers from transient global amnesia typically repeat questions, because they cannot remember the answers they have just been given. So it was with Parfit. In the car he kept asking, 'Have I had a stroke?' and several times he told his wife, 'I'm so lucky to have you.' The doctor put him through a series of questions. Parfit informed the doctor that he was writing a book, called *Reasons and Persons* (*sic*). He could not re- member getting married, but when the doctor pointed at Janet and asked, 'Who's that?' Parfit responded, 'She's the love of my life.'

The following day, Parfit's memory had returned, but he was still feel- ing groggy and so had to postpone his US trip by twenty-four hours. Janet finished emptying his All Souls rooms (it took three days). Parfit arrived in the United States over the Labor Day weekend and, because it was a national holiday, he did not have immediate access to his office. Sam Scheffler was in his New York apartment when his home intercom buzzed. It was Parfit; he said, 'I need to call my wife.' Janet was worried about him, he explained, and he had to reassure her that all was fine. 'Did you notice I called her "my wife"?', he asked Scheffler. He then related the global amnesia episode and reached the point when the doc- tor asked who Janet was: 'Fortunately I replied, "the love of my life".' He was pleased with this response, Scheffler detected. 'He had trained him- self to know what sorts of things one was supposed to say. He recog- nized that this was an emergency, and he was glad that he had been able to make an appropriate comment.'[6]

Parfit's official retirement day in the UK was 30 September 2010, and the following day, 1 October, he was elected Emeritus Fellow at All Souls. There was no Oxford philosophy faculty event to mark his retire- ment, but on 2 March 2011, after he had returned to the UK from the

United States, All Souls put on a low-key farewell dinner. It was hosted by the Warden, John Vickers. Parfit had been told he could invite some close friends, and it was suggested he also invite one or two of the younger Fellows. 'But I don't really have any friends,'[7] he told Janet, matter-of-factly. Nevertheless, invitations were dispatched. In addition to the Warden and Lady Vickers, in attendance were John Broome and Ann Broome, Julian Savulescu and Miriam Wood, Hanna Pickard and her partner, Ian Phillips, Jeremy Waldron, then Chichele Professor of Social and Political Theory, legal scholar Carol Sanger, Amia Srinivasan, and Ingmar Persson. Janet wore her red wedding dress; Parfit was dressed in his traditional combo: white shirt and red tie. There were no speeches and no presentations of carriage clocks or fountain pens. It was all over in about two hours.

The tenants in his Beaumont Buildings house had been asked to leave. After a decade of occupation by (male) philosophers, the house was badly in need of renovation. Half-way through the redecorating, Parfit was interviewed in Beaumont Buildings by Larissa MacFarquhar of *The New Yorker*. As one would expect from *The New Yorker*, the result was an elegantly drawn (and sympathetic) portrait (although it would seem that the renowned *New Yorker* fact checker must have been on vacation that week).[8] Parfit was a philosopher's philosopher and, until then, had been virtually unknown outside the ivory tower. The profile had no major impact on his life. He went unrecognized even in Oxford streets. But a profile in *The New Yorker*, the magazine he'd worked for half a century earlier, was the ultimate endorsement by intellectual US society and Parfit was pleased—with a few reservations—to have it.

Although he was retired in Oxford, his teaching in the United States continued. He taught at Harvard in the Spring semesters and at NYU in the Fall of 2010, 2012, and 2015, and spent three semesters at Rutgers, teaching joint seminars with Larry Temkin, Jeff McMahan, and Ruth Chang—mostly material from *On What Matters*. At Harvard in 2010, when he gave a class on the metaethics of the soon-to-be-published volume, he became visibly anguished when not all the students were convinced by his arguments about the objectivity of ethics. At one point, he fell to his knees, virtually pleading with the class: 'Don't you see, if morality isn't objective, our lives are meaningless.' He seemed genuinely to fear that if the idea that morality was not objective took root, it would sway behaviour, and people would cease to care about being 'moral'. If only his fellow philosophers could be persuaded about the objectivity of morality, then together they could make real progress in the still nascent area of secular ethics. . . .

. . .

Six months later, during the 2011 Spring semester at Rutgers, Volumes 1 and 2 of *On What Matters* were rolling off the presses. There was nothing more Parfit could do to change it. And a miracle occurred. 'He agreed to go for a pizza!'[9]

Parfit did not do pizza, certainly not 'recreational pizza'. He did muesli. And salad. And the odd meal out if food was washed down with philosophical discussion. He avoided, as far as possible, all large social gatherings, small dinner parties, book launches, receptions, and drinks. When Temkin rang up his friend Jeff McMahan to enquire whether McMahan and his wife Sally would like to come for the hour's drive to the coast with him and his wife, Meg, to go to a pizza restaurant, the inclusion of Parfit in the invitation was a mere courtesy. It was inconceivable that Parfit would agree to join them.

Except he did. And when they expressed surprise, he looked at them and said, 'Do you think I'm some kind of monster?'[10] It dawned on Temkin that perhaps he had not shut himself away, socially, because he was wholly anti-social, but rather because he felt that he had a higher calling.

Julian Savulescu and Miriam Wood had a similar social success in persuading him and Janet to come for supper in Oxford in 2012. Parfit brought along a bottle of Chateau Pichon Comtesse de Lalande, worth perhaps £200, which he had either been given by a grateful student or had acquired cheaply from the All Souls cellar: he poured a small amount into his wine glass, and topped it up with water. 'My jaw dropped,' recalled Savulescu, 'and then I thought, "Well, it's his wine, he can drink it how he wants to."'[11] That same year, they invited him to their June wedding outside Oxford, and on Janet's insistence he turned up. Roger Crisp gave them and Ingmar Persson a lift.

> Derek was in fantastic form. As we drove through various villages, he would talk about what happened there during the civil war and who was buried there. Our children fell in love with him. He continued talking about history until we got to the wedding. But at the wedding he and Ingmar began a philosophy conversation, and after that it was just philosophy.[12]

He also entered into an animated conversation about cryonics with Peter Singer and Anders Sandberg, near the barbecue. Cryonics involves the frozen storage of the human head and/or body shortly after death, in the hope that one day they can be resurrected. Sandberg paid an annual fee (about $1,000) for a 'neuro-suspension'—to have just his head frozen (it's more costly to pay for the body too) and openly wore a cryonics tag. He found himself in the middle of a pincer attack. Singer objected to cryonics on the grounds that the money could be far better spent on helping others. Parfit pressed personal identity points—to what extent was this future person identical to oneself, and to what extent did it make sense to want to have this psychologically connected person appear in the future? He appeared to relish the debate. For him, such conversations constituted a form of relaxation—allowable now that the book was out and he had established, he believed, that there was an objective morality.

In spring 2013 he was back at Rutgers, teaching a course on advanced ethics with Ruth Chang. The semester passed more or less without incident, apart from one strange episode in May. Parfit was preparing to lead a seminar in the philosophy department at Seminary Place, and students were entering the room. There was hubbub and pre-seminar banter. The air-conditioning system had malfunctioned, and the atmosphere was stifling. A PhD student, Tim Campbell, was chatting to him: 'We were sitting at one end of a long table and Derek was at the head of it. And at one point he said, "It's quite hot," and he unfastened his trousers and pulled them down to his ankles, and he just sat there in his underpants. He sat there for at least two minutes continuing to talk, as though nothing weird had happened. As though, if you were hot and you needed to cool down, what would be more sensible?'[13]

. . .

If popular recognition meant very little to Parfit, the judgement of his peers meant a great deal. So he was delighted when the news arrived on 12 February 2014 that he had won the Rolf Schock Prize. There is no Nobel Prize for philosophy; the Schock Prize is the closest that exists. Established in 1993, it is administered, like the Nobels, by the Royal Swedish Academy of Sciences. Schock was a philosopher and artist, but there tends to be less money made from art than arms, and his endowment is a fraction of Alfred Nobel's. Still, recipients receive a significant sum, 400,000 Swedish krona (at the time of writing, the equivalent of around £32,000 or $40,000). Among the first winners were W.V.O. Quine, Michael Dummett, John Rawls, Saul Kripke, Thomas Nagel, and Hilary Putnam.

Within the small world of Swedish philosophy, there were some dedicated Parfitians. They included the philosopher who, in 2010, became chair of the Schock committee, Wlodek Rabinowicz, a Swedish philosopher of Polish-Jewish origin. He was a previous visiting fellow at All Souls, and had met Parfit at various talks in Oxford and elsewhere; he had once joined him for a meal at an Indian restaurant, when the discussion had become so animated that they forgot to eat.

From the beginning, the Schock Prize had a bias towards those who made seminal contributions in logic—the prize was officially for 'Logic and Philosophy'. But it did not exclude philosophers working in other fields, and behind the scenes Rabinowicz lobbied enthusiastically for Parfit. 'It didn't take much convincing because everyone recognized his brilliance,' he says.[14] He wrote a synopsis of Parfit's philosophy and explained why he was worthy of the prize. Once the philosophy committee had endorsed Parfit, it had to be voted on by the social science class within the Academy, and then approved in a vote by the Academy as a whole. Except in extraordinary circumstances, these final stages were a formality. The citation emphasized Parfit's groundbreaking contributions to personal identity, population ethics, and analysis of moral theories. The ceremony and symposium, to which various philosophers and dignitaries would be invited, was fixed for 21–23 October.

It was the Schock Prize that helped earn Parfit a place in a March 2014 poll, run by *Prospect* magazine, on the most important world thinkers. There was a somewhat random long-list of fifty, and I contacted *Prospect* to point out that another person on their list, Janet Radcliffe Richards, knew Parfit rather well. (As it turned out, too, Nobel Prize winner Amartya Sen, the man who had introduced Parfit to his future wife, topped the poll.) The result of this initiative was the long article about their idiosyncratic relationship mentioned in the Preface to this book.[15] I spoke to Derek and Janet at Janet's home in Tufnell Park, and tried to capture something of their conversational interactions:

> JANET: Derek has no idea what it is for a building to exist without a manciple and domestic bursar.
> DEREK: Are you implying that I require looking after?
> JANET: Not at all. That's what's so interesting. You don't demand looking after at all.[16]

Parfit soon tired of my personal questions and retreated upstairs to work. But, at a subsequent appointment, he allowed the magazine's photographer to take some photos of himself and Janet—of which there had been very few. The photographer sent me an email afterwards: 'They were so friendly and helpful—the loveliest couple one could wish to meet!'[17] Later, there was an almost inexplicable misunderstanding between Parfit and myself (recounted in the Preface above), but eventually he expressed his satisfaction with the piece. I mentioned in it that Janet had been a regular panellist on the BBC's 'Moral Maze', 'although she wasn't rude enough really to excel in that format and she had what must have been the exasperating habit of telling the presenter and her fellow panellists that they were posing the wrong question.'[18] Parfit was pleased with this reference. He rarely denigrated anybody, but in an email to me earlier had made an exception for the right-wing polemicist Melanie Phillips. '[Janet] should be on this programme as a regular panellist instead of Melanie Philips (or some such name),' he wrote.[19]

A further mini-measure of fame came later in the setting of the hit television series *The Good Place*. This was about a heaven-like world of the afterlife, populated by people who had led blameless lives (and a few who have been sent there in error). One character is a moral philosopher, and there's a scene in the second episode of Season 1 in which he chalks the blackboard with the names of Aristotle, Kant—and Parfit. The Harvard-educated writer of the series, Michael Schur, explained in one interview that Parfit's books had 'totally dominated the college years of philosophy students of my generation'.[20]

. . .

Meanwhile, with the Schock ceremony still a few months away, Parfit was back to work. A University of Warwick philosopher, Victor Tadros, visited him at his Oxford home in February 2014. They discussed whether the intention with which an act is done could make that act wrong. Might an act done with a good intention be acceptable, while the same act carried out with a bad intention be wrong? Tadros thought so—Parfit disagreed. Four hours after they began talking, at about 6 p.m., Tadros needed food, and so they headed to a Lebanese restaurant in the Jericho district, talking philosophy all the while. Debate continued throughout the meal, when the subject of World War I came up.

> Suddenly, in the middle of that discussion, Derek started to cry, really quite a bit. He was crying at the sadness of all of those lives ended prematurely in the war. I wasn't quite sure what to make of this. Did Derek have an admirable connection with human beings whose lives were distant from our own in time that most of us, including me, lack? I found that kind of reaction really odd, and, yes, in a way admirable. Thinking about it later, I wasn't sure whether it was compatible with the kind of deep interaction that most people hope to have with some particular people—their families and close friends. His reaction to those who lost their lives in World War I was a bit like the reaction that a person would have during a discussion of a close friend or family member who had recently passed. And so perhaps

there was something admirable about it, but [. . .] this might come at a price—the price of the distinct personal relations that we have with those who are special to us.[21]

Indeed, Parfit's consequentialism, and the view that we should not draw a sharp distinction between strangers on the one hand, and our nearest and dearest on the other, may have been the product of his rational philosophical reasoning, but it was relatively easy for him to embrace, because it chimed with his atypical emotional reactions. His sensibility with regard to suffering was constrained by neither time nor place. One particular instance would reliably evoke tears: he was touched by the infamous case of the young Missouri woman Nancy Cruzan, who, after a car accident, was kept in a vegetative state for years. He would become upset whenever he mentioned her tombstone inscription, 'Departed Jan. 11, 1983, At Peace 26 Dec. 1990'.

Despite discouragement from OUP, Parfit was still thinking about a revised edition of *Reasons and Persons*, with the title *Reasons, Persons, and Reality*. He had not given up on his efforts to crack Theory X, the theory that would rescue us from the Repugnant Conclusion whilst facing up to the Non-Identity Problem. He always regretted that the Non-Identity Problem had what he regarded as a perverse impact on some readers, who concluded that if no individual was harmed by, for example, a policy that damaged the environment (since this policy led to a different set of people being born), there was less reason to care about it. Parfit hoped to reinforce his earlier view that this was erroneous and that, all else being equal, we should adopt policies that would produce lives with the highest level of wellbeing, irrespective of whether these were the same lives that would have been lived with an alternative approach.

In May, his friend Sam Scheffler delivered the H.L.A. Hart lecture, and Parfit went along to the reception afterwards.[22] Scheffler noticed his own wife, Katy, in a long and animated conversation with Parfit. What could they be discussing, he wondered, for Parfit was not renowned for his small talk and Katy was not a philosopher: 'Afterwards I asked my wife about the topic of conversation. She said, "Apparently Bernard Williams doesn't have a concept of a normative reason."'[23]

Parfit was at Rutgers in the autumn of 2014, and then flew to Sweden in October with Janet for the presentation of the Schock Prize. He was required by custom to deliver a talk, and he chose as his topic population ethics. There were four other contributors to the day-long symposium: two Swedes, Gustaf Arrhenius and Ingmar Persson, and two Americans, Ruth Chang and Larry Temkin.

Parfit's talk in Stockholm came last, and everyone remembers it in much the same way. He was pacing up and down, and because the stage was so brightly lit, and the audience was in near-darkness, it was nigh impossible to make out the edge of the platform. Several times, he came perilously close to tumbling off. Then, towards the end of his talk, he mentioned Johann Sebastian Bach's last and unfinished work, *The Art of Fugue*—he did so just as an aside, in raising the possibility that there might be some higher or superior values, such that some amount of these values is to be preferred to any amount of an inferior value: one composition by Bach, for example, might be considered of greater value than ten thousand songs by Barry Manilow. But there was also the problem known as 'lexical imprecision': it might be impossible to say whether Bach was superior to Wagner.

Mid-paper, and quite suddenly, Parfit stopped talking and began to cry. Not just moistening of the eyes, but full-on weeping. And not for just a few seconds- -it went on for around a minute and a half. There were approximately a hundred people in the audience, and there was some uncomfortable shuffling in seats, with people not knowing where to look or how to react. Eventually, Parfit managed to pull himself together, apologize, and carry on.

Wlodek Rabinowicz and Parfit were staying in the same hotel, and the following day, Rabinowicz questioned him about it: 'Why did you cry?' 'It's such a beautiful piece of music', Parfit replied, 'and it is so tragic that Bach died before he could complete it.' And then he began to cry all over again.[24]

. . .

By the time Parfit retired, he had become something of an All Souls treasure. He had almost wholly retreated inside philosophy, but remained a benign college presence, friendly, modest, respectful. There had been a demographic revolution in college: since Susan Hurley's arrival, the percentage of female Fellows had continued to rise. Many traditions had survived, but the college had become a more tolerant, progressive place. There was nobody left who publicly doubted that Parfit merited his fellowship—indeed, he had come to represent precisely the sort of scholar who justified the existence of this privileged institution. Parfit had needed All Souls as much as any other scholar had ever needed it. And if All Souls was not for people like Parfit, then who was it for? His transgression of social norms at mealtimes was now just part of the furniture of college life, as traditional as the pre-meal grace.

He now worked mostly at home, in Beaumont Buildings, sometimes kept company by Janet, but often alone, apart from a giant stuffed giraffe which had been abandoned in the house by one of the previous philosopher-tenants and which was propped next to the upstairs window—it was eventually given to a five-year-old girl from the same street who used to chat to it when she passed.[25] Once his All Souls rooms had been emptied, Parfit rarely returned to the college. His decades-long association with it produced no sentimental yearning. When he did pay a visit, he preferred not to go to the common room, which might have embroiled him in unnecessary chitchat. If he had an appointment with an All Souls Fellow, such as Amia Srinivasan, he preferred to meet in their rooms. Srinivasan later described their last meeting in her study: 'While jostling his papers he knocked over a glass. He was unfazed. We sat and talked for a few hours, his feet in a pool of water and shattered glass.'[26]

He was not entirely disengaged from Oxford or All Souls affairs. Although he was not a member of the appointing committee to the White's Chair of Moral Philosophy, he had many conversations with some of its members on what he saw as the merits and demerits of the various candidates to succeed John Broome. In the end, two candidates having turned down the offer, Parfit was delighted that the third, Jeff McMahan, accepted it. He also helped to set the exam for the All Souls Prize Fellowship, which he himself had been awarded in 1967. Oxford exam-setters relish devising questions that are ambiguous and open to interpretation and where half the challenge is figuring out what the problem is supposed to be. Parfit's inclinations were quite opposite. He pushed to make the questions as straightforward as possible—such as 'Utilitarianism: true or false?'. He thought the best philosophers were not necessarily always the fastest and most agile under pressure. What was needed was to give them the chance to demonstrate deep prior knowledge.

No longer having his own space in All Souls, Parfit had to debate philosophy elsewhere. Theron Pummer met him for lunch at the Quod restaurant on the high street. They had an extended discussion about what dishes they would order, for reasons Parfit didn't explain. 'Then, after a few bites, he said, "I think it would be better if we swapped dishes." So we did. And then, after another five minutes he said, "I think we should swap thrice." And so we switched dishes two more times.'[27]

Now that he was no longer catered for in college, his diet at home became narrow and fixed, as it always was when he taught in the US. For his (very late) breakfast he wanted muesli, yogurt, juice, and instant coffee. In the evening, he ate raw carrots, cheese, romaine lettuce, and celery dipped in peanut butter. At some unannounced stage, he had become vegetarian. He had, some years earlier, taken to drinking camomile tea before going to bed, because Ruth Chang had told him it might help him sleep, and he had promised to try it.

. . .

Parfit's new edition of *Reasons and Persons* would never appear. But he had two additional projects. Peter Singer had conceived the idea of a book of essays on Parfit's metaethics, with replies from Parfit. Parfit was enthusiastic and, in all, thirteen chapters were produced, by leading philosophers. On 16 March 2012, Parfit was sent every chapter bar one, and told Singer that it would take him less than a year to send back his responses. As any student of Parfit's life would predict, this was overoptimistic. In fact, as with *Reading Parfit* twenty years earlier, his replies became so lengthy that it was no longer feasible to include them in one volume—and OUP, Parfit, and Singer together agreed that it made more sense for the essays and replies to appear in separate volumes,

Does Anything Really Matter? and *On What Matters, Volume 3*, with matching covers of a photograph Parfit had taken of the Winter Palace in St Petersburg. *Does Anything Really Matter?* was three hundred pages long and, for each page, Parfit replied with, on average, a page and a half. He delivered his manuscript a mere two and a half years late.

Even producing the preface for Parfit's volume was a tortuous process. To his delight, two of the heavyweight contributors to the Singer volume, Allan Gibbard and Peter Railton, reached some sort of accommodation with his views on the objectivity of ethics, and contributed additional essays for Volume 3 of *On What Matters*. Railton, unlike Parfit, was a naturalist, believing that objective reality was discoverable only by means of observation and experimentation. Gibbard, also unlike Parfit, was an expressivist, believing the main function of sentences such as 'It is wrong to torture innocent children' is not to assert a fact, but to express an attitude (for example, as here, of disapproval).

Parfit sent one letter to Railton, in which he wrote, 'I'm enormously heartened by the way in which our main disagreements seem to have been resolved, like fog or cloud drifting away from the mountain';[28] and to Gibbard he wrote that both he and Railton were 'eager to have you join us on the sunlit upper slopes'.[29] But devising a formula to describe their degree of agreement necessitated the sort of skills normally required of a diplomat shuttling between warring sides to draw up a peace treaty. Various versions of the text, expressing their accord, bounced back and forth, until Parfit received the green light for the following in his preface: 'Railton agrees that our disagreements have been wholly resolved, and Gibbard agrees that our disagreements have been partly resolved. I am deeply worried by disagreements with people who seem as likely as I am to be getting things right. That is why, like Railton, I find it "immensely heartening" that Railton, Gibbard and I now have similar beliefs.'[30]

Parfit was also responding to papers assembled for a new book from Routledge. This was edited by Simon Kirchin, from the University of Kent, and, like Jonathan Dancy's book on Parfit, was to be entitled *Reading Parfit*. It included articles by different philosophers on various aspects of *On What Matters*, not just the metaethics. Kirchin had approached Parfit with the idea in 2012, and sent him a full set of papers in June 2014. Parfit promised to restrict his response to one chapter and not to repeat the mistake of writing replies as long as the original articles. His forty-eight-page chapter was submitted in November 2015, a month before he completed Volume 3 of *On What Matters*.

. . .

In the year he left All Souls, Parfit had accepted an affiliation with Oxford University's Uehiro Centre for Practical Ethics, where Janet was already a Distinguished Research Fellow. The Uehiro Centre was established in 2003 to investigate applied moral questions—actual dilemmas in the real world. The driving force behind the Centre was the Australian-born Julian Savulescu; Parfit himself had nothing to do with its founding, but it was the natural institutional culmination of his pioneering seminar, three decades earlier, with Jonathan Glover and Jim Griffin.

Practical ethics was becoming mainstream at Oxford, though not without a struggle. In 2016, there was a vote in the Oxford philosophy faculty about the introduction of an optional practical ethics paper in the PPE degree. The paper would cover, amongst other topics, war, the treatment of animals, punishment, bioethics, charity, racial and gender equality, and future generations. Some within the faculty opposed the new paper, haughtily dismissing it as lacking rigour. Parfit no longer had a right to vote, but promoters of the new paper asked him to show up in silent support, which he did. His mere presence was designed to make a mockery of the notion that practical ethics was not proper philosophy; the vote passed.

Parfit had devoted his life to the realm of ideas, and had remained aloof from politics and policy. But he had always held that philosophy should matter, that it should not merely be of academic interest. In his retirement, an organization with which he felt a natural affinity approached him for support.

The Oxford-based charity Giving What We Can (GWWC) was set up by Toby Ord, an Australian-born philosopher, and another young philosopher, Will MacAskill. The charity's direct inspiration came from

Peter Singer. Singer had devised a thought experiment that was simple but devastatingly effective in making people reflect on their behaviour and their attitude to those in need. Imagine that you are walking past a shallow pond and see a toddler thrashing about in the water, clearly struggling. There is no one else to rescue her. You could easily wade in and save the toddler, at no risk to yourself, but you're wearing a fancy suit and your best brogues, and it would cost, say, £150, to have them cleaned or replaced. Plus, it would make you a few minutes late for work. What should you do? Ruin your suit and save a life, or let the toddler die?

Of course, it's not supposed to be a genuine dilemma. That is precisely the point. Nobody is expected to answer that it is acceptable to allow the child to drown. But, argued Singer, the hypothetical scenario was analogous to our position vis-à-vis desperately poor people on the other side of the world. If we contributed a relatively small amount of money to an effective charity, we could easily save a life. The only difference from the pond case is that this person is far away and we don't know their identity. But that, says Singer, is morally irrelevant.[31]

This thought experiment has generated a significant secondary literature. Certainly, the GWWC initiators found it compelling. Their mission was to persuade people to give more of their income away and to donate to effective organizations that could make a real difference. Not all charities are equally effective. Some are better managed than others. Some focus on more pressing issues than others. Some sufferings are easier and cheaper to fix than others. So the impact of donating £100 will vary dramatically, depending on where the money is directed. GWWC was created to help donors select charities that do the maximum amount of good.

There were spin-off organizations from GWWC, such as 80,000 Hours. The number refers to the rough number of hours we might have in our career, and 80,000 Hours was set up to research how people could most effectively devote their time (rather than their money) to tackling the world's most pressing problems. In 2012, the Centre for Effective Altruism was established to incorporate both GWWC and 80,000 Hours.

Since it launched, the Effective Altruism movement has grown slowly but steadily. Most of the early backers were idealistic young postgraduates, many of them philosophers. If Singer was the intellectual father of the movement, Parfit was its grandfather. It became an in-joke among some members that anybody who came to work for GWWC had to possess a copy of *Reasons and Persons*—some owned two copies, one for home, one for the office.

But it took Parfit until 2014 to sign the GWWC pledge—and he agreed to do so only after wrangling over the wording. Initially, those who joined the GWWC campaign were required to make a public pledge to donate at least 10 per cent of their income to charities that work to relieve poverty. Parfit had several issues with this. For reasons the organizers never fully understood, he said that participants should make a 'promise' rather than a 'pledge': he may have believed that a promise entailed a deeper level of commitment. Nor was he keen on the name—'Giving What We Can'. Ten per cent of a person's income is certainly a generous sum (and in line with what adherents to some world religions are expected to give away). Nevertheless, Parfit pointed out, it was obvious that people *could* donate more. The GWWC organization had settled on the figure because it was enough to make a significant difference, but not so much that it would deter potential supporters. So this became a skirmish between philosophical honesty and marketing. Parfit also cavilled at the word 'giving'. He believed this implied that we were morally entitled to what we hand over, and morally entitled to our wealth and high incomes. This he rejected. Well-off people in the developed world were merely lucky that they were born into rich societies. They did not *deserve* their fortune.

Linguistic quibbles aside, the issue that Parfit felt most strongly about was the movement's sole focus (initially) on poverty and development. While it was indeed pressing to relieve the suffering of people living today, Parfit argued, there should be an option that at least some of the money donated be earmarked for the problems of tomorrow. The human population has risen to eight billion, but faces existential risks, such as meteors, nuclear war, bioterrorism, pandemics, and climate change. Parfit claimed that between (a) peace, (b) a war which killed 7.5 billion people, and (c) a war which killed everyone, the difference between (b) and (c) was much greater than between (a) and (b).

Why would human extinction be such a tragedy? Parfit had little to say about this, but he once told a friend that 'what really distressed him about the thought that mankind might cease was that there would be nobody anymore to listen to Mozart'.[32] Given how grim human existence had been for much of its history, Parfit believed that it was not at all obvious that, on balance, human life up to this point had been a good thing. But, as long as we did not mess things up, he said, there was every prospect that lives would be much better in the future. This was the prize to fight for. There were all sorts of exciting possibilities for intelligent life—who knows: perhaps lasting billions of years and populating other galaxies.

In any case, Parfit wanted the Effective Altruism movement to swivel its orientation to the long term, and not dedicate itself merely to the here and now. Others came to agree. The pledge was rewritten; it currently runs as follows:

> I recognise that I can use part of my income to do a significant amount of good. Since I can live well enough on a smaller income, I pledge that from now until ___ I shall give ___ to whichever organisations can most effectively use it to improve the lives of others, now and in the years to come. I make this pledge freely, openly, and sincerely.

In 2016, the movement sought Parfit's explicit endorsement. He responded to the first email immediately, and with enthusiasm. 'Would be happy to be involved as an adviser. With best wishes, and gladness for your activities, Derek.'[33]

Now, it would be natural to assume that a movement that campaigned for more charitable donations would be beyond criticism and would receive universal support. Who could possibly object? In fact, it has been at the receiving end of a surprising degree of hostility and contempt. This is partly because its instinctive consequentialism produces some counterintuitive recommendations. If one wants to help the poor in the developing world, then rather than work in the charity sector, a job that perhaps someone else might be able to do just as well, it could be more effective to become a bond trader on Wall Street and earn enough to donate millions to good causes. The problem here is that identified by Bernard Williams in *Utilitarianism: For and Against*,[34] and mentioned in chapter 10: consequentialism, the critique runs, treats people as mere inputs into a giant do-gooding algorithm, and cannot carve out adequate space for the role of integrity and personal projects.

But the more fundamental criticism is that the Effective Altruism movement is too individualistic, too ahistorical and is, in some ways, too apolitical. That is, it does not interrogate how structural inequalities and injustices have contributed to suffering. It does not ask whether we should focus on systematic and radical transformation in how society functions, rather than on the short-term impact of charitable giving.

Proponents of Effective Altruism have pushed back against these attacks. They acknowledge that sometimes the most effective way of doing good is not in direct charitable work, but in advocacy or political activism. But they also defend the legitimacy of an individual reflecting on the current state of affairs, and then asking, 'What difference can I personally make, in the world as it exists today, to improve the lives of others?' Privately, some supporters of the movement make a more cynical point; they speculate that the motivation of some of their critics is to be released from any sense of obligation to engage in the tough personal sacrifices that the movement demands.

As for Parfit, once he had helped shift the movement towards longtermism, he expressed no fundamental doubts about its raison d'être. Between 7 and 9 July 2014, he took part in a conference on effective altruism at All Souls, called 'Good Done Right'. The following year, in April 2015, he spoke on effective altruism at Harvard, and in June 2015 he delivered a well-attended talk at the student-run Oxford Union. By now a white-haired, slightly stooped figure, slightly out of breath, he leant on the podium, swigging water from a bottle, occasionally fiddling with his shirt sleeves or scratching his head, while offering some practical measures that could be taken to improve the state of the world. We should go vegetarian, and possibly vegan, we shouldn't have more than two children, we should invest more and consume less. It was inevitable that those who initially pledged to give away 10 per cent of their money when they were young and idealistic would lapse, and Parfit had a suggestion for how to keep them from erring. Why not use the fear of shame, and have an annual newsletter that included all the names of those who ceased to make contributions?

What is striking about the talk is how his priorities in his seventies mirror those of his twenties. Recall the editorial line he took as a student at *Isis* magazine: 'The aim of all actions should be to reduce suffering. Two kinds of suffering stand out above all others: the hypothetical suffering of a nuclear furnace (fuel: one third of the world, 1000 million bodies), and the actual suffering, now, of the other two thirds.'[35] Half a century on, he was making the same case.

2 2

Incompatible with Life

Parfit was back at Rutgers in the autumn of 2014, when a meal out nearly killed him. It was the evening of 2 September, and Larry Temkin had taken him to the Pad Thai Restaurant in Highland Park, New Jersey. They typically ate together after their joint class, and this was their first class of the term. They had different tastes. Temkin always chose mild dishes. Every time Parfit would query whether Temkin's meal wasn't a bit boring, and suggest that he try some of his own spicier dish. Every time, Temkin would explain that he did not care for spicy food.

That evening, Temkin deposited Parfit back at Jeff McMahan's house at around 10 p.m., returned to his own home, and retired to bed. At around 1 a.m., he was woken by a call from a very shaken McMahan: 'Jeff clearly thought that Derek was about to die.'[1] Parfit, it transpired, was now in hospital, hooked up to a ventilator because his body was incapable of breathing without support. McMahan had been in the bath when he heard Parfit violently coughing and wheezing, and went to check on his welfare. He found Parfit sitting in a chair, struggling for air. McMahan looked up 'collapsed lung' on the internet, and when Parfit's shortness of breath worsened, he bundled him into his car and drove him the short distance to the Robert Wood Johnson University Hospital in New Brunswick.

That quick decision probably saved Parfit's life. At the hospital, one of the nurses requested Parfit's permission to intubate him. He was unresponsive; his breathing was extremely shallow and rapid. McMahan told him to nod to indicate permission, but there was still no reaction. The medical staff hastily ushered McMahan out. When Parfit's clothes were eventually returned to him, it became clear that after McMahan had left the room, they had ripped his shirt off, not bothering to unbutton it.

He was put under a general anaesthetic and was still unconscious the following day, when McMahan returned. Emerging finally from unconsciousness with a tube in his throat, he couldn't speak, but he gestured for a pad and a pen. 'He didn't ask, "Where am I, what's happening to me, what's my condition?" He didn't ask, "Am I going to live?" He wrote that he was supposed to be on Johann Frick's thesis committee—and he needed to go to Harvard for his viva.'[2] Frick was one of Parfit's doctoral students. It had to be explained to Parfit that he would not be able to fulfil this obligation.

Temkin went to see Parfit that day. 'It was frightening. He was haggard. He had whiskers. He looked like hell.'[3] He still wanted to philosophize, but had to communicate in writing. When he was eventually taken off the ventilator, it was painful for him to talk, and his voice was raspy. That did not deter him. Frick's viva would have to go ahead without Parfit, though Parfit had written to the examiners suggesting a postponement: 'I'm sorry for these typos, but I'm having to type only one bandaged ffinger. Affextionately Derek.'[4] After Parfit had been in hospital for a few days, Frick was given the green light to visit him: 'He was still in intensive care, with tubes coming out of him, and I stuck my head through the door. Derek saw me and literally his first words were, "Johann, so good of you to come. I've only read your dissertation twice so far, but I have some questions." He gave me a two- or three-hour viva, which was much tougher than anything I had a few days later.'[5]

Even more pleased to see Frick were McMahan and Ruth Chang, who had by now spent hours by Parfit's bedside. 'They had been a captive audience and were grateful when I showed up because they could have a break from philosophy,' Frick recalls. Other visitors followed. One of the nurses joked to Parfit that Jesus had had only twelve disciples and he seemed to have many more. 'What do you work on?' she enquired. 'I work', he replied, 'on what matters.'[6]

Parfit had no qualms about being seen in bed. Chang once or twice covered him up when he was unaware that he was exposing more of his body than was appropriate. Doctors would be prodding and poking him whilst he asked her about her latest philosophical paper. In general, he showed little interest in his medical condition but became curious about the US medical system and began to read up on the Patient Protection and Affordable Care Act (ACA), known as Obamacare. He was astonished to discover that one of his nurses thought that the doctors deserved their huge income and that it would be unfair if their salaries were cut.

What had caused Parfit's health scare? The chief cardiac surgeon speculated that the spicy food had sparked a coughing fit, leading to barotrauma—the left lung had over-filled with air, which was forced to circulate in his upper body. The right lung, it turned out, was totally ineffective, because of a paralysed muscle that Parfit had probably lived with since childhood. It was about 2.5 inches (6.5 cm) in size and completely squashed. The medics had to inflate the one, previously functioning, lung, and wait until it healed. With Jeff McMahan present and taking notes, the surgeon showed Parfit a CAT-Scan of his lungs and told him that what it showed was almost incompatible with life. McMahan later reminded Parfit of that phrase and it made Parfit inordinately proud. 'My body was almost incompatible with life,' he bragged to many people. He was proud of the ripped shirt too—and kept it.

There was a discussion about whether there should be a further operation to fix Parfit's atypical organ arrangements, but eventually it was agreed that this was too risky. Also, Parfit was told, an operation would give him an 'American pot-belly'. He was as thin as he was in part because intestines that would in normal circumstances be in his abdomen were in his right chest cavity. 'I'm not climbing the mountain any more,' he concluded, 'so perhaps it's not worth it.'[7]

. . .

The illness did not slow him down. Indeed, some of his American students detected a renewed urgency; here was a man with an eye on the tick-tock of his life-clock. During the Spring 2015 seminars at Harvard, he ran a joint seminar with Selim Berker (Tim Scanlon had retired).

Selim pressed him on a technical point; Parfit shook his head and inter-rupted. 'Selim,' he said, in a calm but stern voice, 'if we were immortal, it would perhaps be worth trying to settle these issues. However, our time here is limited, and we must move on to more pressing matters.'[8]

In the summer, Parfit went with Janet to stay with his sister Theodora and her husband Van at their holiday home in Deer Isle, Maine. There he mainly worked, sitting in a wicker chair, and kept cool by means of a ru-dimentary electric fan, but there is photographic evidence that on at least one occasion he went on a motorboat trip, and, on another donned a life-jacket, over-sized sunglasses, and a beige fishing hat to go kayaking. According to Janet, he would have preferred to remain in the wicker chair, but felt duty bound to engage in a couple of holiday-type activities.

There were to be only two more teaching semesters in Parfit's life. They almost didn't happen at all, after a large knife he was carrying was caught by a metal detector at the US embassy in London, where he was renewing his visa. He was always impatient with practical matters and, leaving home to catch the bus, he had grabbed the knife as the first object he saw that could serve to sharpen his pencil. It was unreasonable to expect him to know that knives were banned, the philosopher argued. Fortunately, the security staff accepted his explanation.

In the autumn of 2015, he taught an NYU course on metaethics, with Sharon Street. He was still brooding incessantly over Bernard Williams having no concept of a normative reason, but Street took the Williams view that mind-independent reasons made no sense. 'He thought my position was nihilistic. He was worried about it being true and felt it needed beating back with arguments.' They talked past and sometimes over one another. Parfit would become so agitated that, after each seminar, he felt the need to apologize for interrupting. 'On the very last day of class, one of the students asked whether either of us felt that we had learned anything during the seminars. My memory is that both of us said "No!"', says Street.[9] Nevertheless, she approved of his passion: his attitude to his philosophical positions brought to her mind a religious fervour.

Another member of the NYU faculty, Dale Jamieson, was surprised when Parfit approached him, complimented him on his work (on envi-ronmental ethics) and declared that he was devoting the rest of his life to thinking about climate change and similar humanity-threatening issues. 'I was flabbergasted. Then, without missing a beat, he started talking about the metaphysics of reasons, and how mystifying it was that Williams had no concept of normative reasons.'[10]

In spring 2016, Parfit taught a course at Rutgers with Larry Temkin. It would be his final American teaching semester.

. . .

There was more than just Parfit's own health worries to contend with. When he was back in the UK, Janet too fell seriously ill. Two years earlier, in late summer 2014, she had begun to feel a pain in her foot. It worsened and spread to her hands. A doctor diagnosed rheumatoid arthritis, a debilitating, chronic inflammatory disease that affects the joints.

Janet was supposed to be making progress on a book for the Oxford Uehiro Centre. In November 2012, she had delivered the annual Uehiro Lectures. The Uehiro lecturer was expected to adapt their three lectures into a short volume, to be published by OUP. Radcliffe Richards's lectures were entitled *Sex in a Shifting Landscape*. They re-trod some of the ground from *The Sceptical Feminist*, but also drew on the new and burgeoning field of evolutionary psychology and her book *Human Nature after Darwin*. She pointed to the double standard whereby promiscuous men were lauded as studs, and promiscuous women shamed as sluts. One explanation, she argued, was that until the advent of DNA testing, men, unlike women, could never be 100 per cent certain that they were the father of their partner's children. Sexual shaming was a means of controlling female sexual behaviour such that men who invested time and resources in their children's upbringing could do so with greater confidence that they were supporting their biological offspring. That was the evolutionary explanation, but it had a discriminatory impact—with monogamy norms arbitrarily punishing women more than men.

As in *The Sceptical Feminist*, Radcliffe Richards argued that it was wrong to infer that if women were paid on average less than men, or were outnumbered in a particular profession, this logically entails that they have been treated unjustly. Once again drawing on research in evolutionary psychology, she maintained that selection pressures may have shaped the minds of men and women in different ways. At the very least, this possibility could not be dismissed a priori—it was an empirical matter. But even if there were average differences between the sexes, that still left open the normative issue of how to respond.

This, then, was her contentious subject matter. On 25 June 2016 Parfit wrote a letter to Julian Savulescu, the director of the Uehiro Centre. Janet was now out of hospital, but Parfit asked Savulescu not to pressure her about the book, as she was still ill, in chronic pain, and depressed; and her depression was 'partly caused by her failure to fulfil her obligation to you to write a book based on her lectures'. She was 'racked with guilt'. It might be natural for the Uehiro Foundation to be disappointed by the book's non-appearance, he wrote, but they should not interpret that as suggesting that their generosity had been disregarded. 'They wouldn't respond in that way if some Uehiro Lecturer failed to produce a book because this person died, and Janet's illness and depression are having effects like those of being dead.'[11]

Parfit was not in good health himself. He had been becoming more forgetful in the previous few years—several people noticed and commented on this. When the young Cambridge philosopher Simon Beard went to visit him in Oxford on 20 July 2016, they had a discussion about personal identity. Parfit interrupted his own soliloquy to report that 'my doctor tells me I have early-stage Alzheimer's, and so I know for sure that in twenty years' time there will be nobody alive who is psychologically continuous with me now. But it really doesn't matter to me if there is someone then who is still *called* Derek Parfit or not.' Then, recalled Beard, 'he just carried on with what he was saying as if this news was totally inconsequential'.[12]

It is quite possible that Beard misheard or misinterpreted this in some way; for Parfit had not mentioned it to anybody else, not even Janet. But the story is consistent with his behaviour, and he might not have told Janet because of her health. If it was true that Parfit was facing a future increasingly impacted by dementia, he was at the start of a journey that, according to his own view of identity, would slowly strip away 'what matters'.

A few weeks later, on 9 September, when Parfit was with Janet at her Huddleston Road home in Tufnell Park, there was another health crisis. Suddenly, Janet could not move her limbs. Parfit managed to get her into a taxi, with the help of the driver, and they drove to University College Hospital. She was there for a week before being transferred to a neurology hospital in Queen Square, where she remained for two months, until 10 November. For a time, the doctors were baffled, but she was eventually diagnosed with vasculitis of the brain, another inflammation illness (which may or may not have been connected with her rheumatoid arthritis).

Parfit spent the entire two months in Huddleston Road. Judith, Janet's sister, moved down to London to help out. She taught Parfit how to use a washing machine; he was pleased to have mastered it, but did not risk meddling with the settings. He visited Janet regularly—though not every day—carrying his laptop so that, when they were not talking, he could work. He was worried and emotional. He wept as he told Judith that he felt he had let Janet down. He was not 100 per cent himself. He was becoming increasingly out of breath. He would walk the short distance from Euston station to the hospital but would need to stop for a rest mid-way. On one occasion, he inadvertently left two bags by a bench, including Janet's laptop; it was handed in to the police.

Janet finally emerged from hospital on 10 November. Two days later, on a drizzly Saturday, Parfit travelled to Oxford to examine the latest proofs of the cover of Volume 3 of *On What Matters*. He had lost some of his fight. He didn't like the cover much, but told Ingmar Persson and Jeff McMahan that 'it didn't matter much because hardbacks didn't have jackets in libraries'.[13] Had he applied this logic to previous volumes, he would have saved himself endless trouble with OUP. The following weekend, on 20 November 2016, he gave a talk at an Effective Altruism conference in Oxford. He bemoaned the damage that had been done by his writing about the Non-Identity Problem, with some people wrongly assuming that we had less reason to care about policies that destroyed the environment if these policies did not harm particular people.

. . .

As people age, it is no doubt natural for them to reflect more on death. The body weakens and wilts, more friends and contemporaries die. Isaiah Berlin passed away in November 1997. Bernard Williams died in 2003, Susan Hurley in 2007, Patricia Zander in 2008, Jerry Cohen in 2009, and Ronnie Dworkin in 2013. Parfit was, to varying degrees, affected by each loss. About a month after Williams's death, his widow Patricia was invited to dinner at All Souls. She was placed next to Parfit, and when talk turned to Bernard, Parfit immediately burst into tears. 'I ended up comforting him. Only afterwards did I realize how strange this was.'[14] At Jerry Cohen's funeral, Jerry's daughter Miriam reminded Parfit that he had once rung Cohen to check whether it was acceptable to describe Jerry as a friend. Parfit began to weep.

Aided by his philosophy, Parfit had gone some way to accommodate himself to mortality. Sally Ruddick, the wife of his old friend Bill, passed away in 2011, and Derek sent a note to Bill on 27 June, as soon as he heard the news.

When I think of someone dead whom I loved, it helps me to remember that this person isn't less real because she isn't real now, just as people far away aren't less real because they aren't real here. But it's awful to know that Sally isn't real now.[15]

Ruddick reflected on this note, and, rather than let it pass, responded in an email the following day. He wasn't clear how reflections about the past and present bore on the sense of daily absence that was his prime source of grief. His wife's death felt to him not like a wound that would heal, but rather like a partial amputation of the heart. A lengthy correspondence ensued. Parfit cited Timeless, his character from *Reasons and Persons*. Although we cannot look forward to an ongoing future relationship with a loved person who has died, we can look back to what was good about the relationship in the past. Ruddick was not consoled. His memories of his wife were not discrete, and almost any pleasant memory 'becomes bittersweet when tainted by awareness of her absence now. Timeless, apparently, has no such reflux of the present.'[16]

As it happens, Parfit had sent an almost identical message of condolence to the writer Joyce Carol Oates when her first husband, Raymond Smith, died. 'I am very sorry to learn that Ray died a couple of weeks ago. When someone I loved died I found it helpful to remind myself that this person was not less real because she was not real now, just as people in New Zealand aren't less real because they aren't real here.'[17] Parfit had become acquainted with the Princeton-based author through his friend Jeff McMahan, and she had attended several of his lectures. Oates was grateful for his good wishes, and sufficiently moved to reproduce the note in a book she published about her grief; but privately, she too was unconvinced that Parfit's suggestion provided much solace. She compared it to trying to console an amputee that his leg was still real and existed in New Zealand.

As for Parfit's own mortality, he had argued in *Reasons and Persons* that bodily survival was not what really mattered. He would say to students, 'I find it very comforting to think that all [death] means is that there will be no future person who is related to me in a certain way.'[18] And this thought genuinely seemed to lift his spirits.

And yet the latter half of his life is only comprehensible when understood as his response to mortality. There were things he wanted to achieve before he died, questions he wanted to answer, people he needed to convince. Parfit was in a hurry. Even in his seventies he remained 'the Alexei Stakhanov of the philosophy world'[19]—working all day, seven days a week, as he had done for decades. Sam Scheffler recalls Parfit admitting that everything he had ever written was motivated by fear of death. Peter Singer thinks there was not one, but two motivational fears: 'death and eviction from All Souls'.[20]

The corollary to anticipating death was reflecting on his past. What had he achieved? His old friend Jonathan Glover approached him before a talk on personal identity at University College London, and asked how close his life had come to his hopes. 'He said, "My life is my work. I believe I have found some good reasons for believing that values aren't just subjective and that some things really do matter. If my arguments don't succeed, my life has been wasted."[21]

This struck Glover as absurd. Not all Parfit's philosophical arguments are universally accepted; that is normal. But, 'he wrote some of the deepest and most brilliant philosophy of our time, likely to be thought about long after the rest of us are gone. In discussions that made us all think, he was a great stimulus to huge numbers of colleagues, students and friends. If *his* life was wasted, what hope for the rest of us philosophy teachers?'[22]

23

Parfit's Gamble

Sometime during the hours separating 1 and 2 January 2017, Derek Parfit stopped breathing. He was in bed at 21 Huddleston Road with Janet. Although he had been suffering from a severe cold, New Year's Day had been much like any other day, with the only difference being that he did not feel up to exercising on his bike. Nevertheless, he had put in a full day's work, sending in a draft of an article on future people to the journal *Philosophy and Public Affairs*,[1] and not finishing until 10 p.m., after taking a short break for supper.

Later that night, he began to cough violently: a worried Janet suggested they go to hospital, but he insisted he was all right, and left the room briefly so as not to disturb her. When he returned, he asked for a fan. At around 1 a.m., Janet looked at him, thinking that he had finally fallen asleep. When she realized her mistake, she rang the emergency services, who told her to get him onto the floor and pump his heart. It was too late.

The autopsy found that there were two main causes of death. The first had to do with the lungs, and involved pulmonary sarcoidosis (an abnormal collection of inflammatory cells in the lungs), and diaphragmatic paralysis (causing tiredness and weakness of breath). The second was heart-related: Parfit had ischaemic heart disease (his heart was receiving insufficient blood and oxygen). The cause of death was unhelpfully given as 'natural causes'. But it seems highly probable that it was linked to the illness that had nearly taken his life in New Jersey.

When the philosopher Isaiah Berlin died, two decades earlier, the BBC cleared the schedule and immediately broadcast two hour-long programmes about him. But Parfit was not a name familiar to TV producers or obituary editors. There was neither a television nor a radio special. Word eventually reached the newspapers that he was a substantial philosophical figure, and tributes appeared in some—not all—of the broadsheets.

Parfit's body was cremated in Golders Green in north London. The funeral service took place on 9 February in All Souls chapel. The Queen's College choir sang Purcell's *Funeral Mass for Queen Mary*, and there was *St John's Passion* from his beloved Bach. On 3 June there was a memorial event in the All Souls Codrington Library. Janet had scooped up all the red ties she could find and those who went to the memorial were invited to help themselves. They were not exactly fragments from the Turin shroud, but they were seized upon enthusiastically. Each red tie came 'ornamented with spots of Derek's dinner.'[2]

. . .

How to sum up Derek Parfit's legacy? There are thinkers who achieve prominence but who after they die are quickly forgotten, and others, less renowned in their lifetime, who develop a posthumous reputation. Parfit's legacy remains contested; no doubt a more settled judgement will be reached in the decades to come. Certainly, there are many respected philosophers who argue for his inclusion in a moral philosophy pantheon that would house the likes of Hobbes, Kant, Mill, Nietzsche, and Sidgwick. Few philosophers exhibit Parfit's imagination and depth and rigour; few philosophers are capable, as he was, of bringing fresh perspectives to age-old puzzles. There are not many important new discoveries to be made in philosophy, and Parfit made several, including the Non-Identity Problem and conundrums around population size. In the words of the eminent moral philosopher Peter Railton, 'He blew the windows wide open.'[3]

Some of his students likened *Reasons and Persons* and *On What Matters* to the Old and New Testaments. Parfit believed *On What Matters*—the product of a quarter of a century of hard graft—was his enduring masterpiece. That is a minority view. There is a broad consensus that the Parfitian Old Testament was the more significant work; many contend it is the greatest work of moral philosophy of the twentieth century, and a book that will be read for decades to come.

Parfit would be distraught to discover that *On What Matters* has so far acquired only a tepid reputation. He could not hate, but he could be hurt, especially by people dismissive of his work. And his harshest critics claim he spent two decades plodding down a cul-de-sac. Certainly, judged by how much literature a book generates in response, and how many additional ideas it seeds (what Peter Railton calls 'export value'), *Reasons and Persons* is more influential. There have probably been more than a thousand papers published just on Parfit's work on future people. It is hard to think of another work in moral philosophy that has had such reach, though in political theory John Rawls's *Theory of Justice* can boast greater impact still. *On What Matters* has had only a fraction of this export value. The truth is that even some of Parfit's closest philosophical colleagues have not read it—often because they effectively read it years earlier, in an earlier draft.

Because of Parfit's psychological need to cover every point and every objection, both *Reasons and Persons* and *On What Matters* were longer than they needed to be; they could have been cleaner and more streamlined. Parfit believed that the aesthetic value of a building could suffer if an ugly extension was added to it. Regrettably, he did not apply the same attitude to his books. Bernard Williams once praised a book because the author 'did his best thinking off the page.'[4] Parfit left too much on it.

· · ·

Less than a fortnight after Parfit's death, the Peter Singer-edited volume *Does Anything Really Matter?* came out, followed, a week later, by Parfit's responses, published as the third volume of *On What Matters*. The other volume to which Parfit gave responses, *Reading Parfit*, edited by Simon Kirchin, also appeared in 2017.

At the time of his death, Parfit still had multiple philosophical plans. One ambition was to work on 'the sublime', that sense we have when we see a spectacular waterfall, or when we listen to a Mozart opera. In aesthetics, the sublime is normally contrasted with the beautiful. The beautiful can be explained and categorized. We can deconstruct the beauty of a piece of music, or a building, or a novel, in terms of narrative, pace, tension, balance, structures, and symmetries. But the sublime is somehow beyond categorization. It is like pain: you know it when you experience it. The sublime is not wholly good. It might be awful, as well as awesome. Indeed, on some accounts, for something to be sublime, a sense of gloom or fear or foreboding is a prerequisite.

Parfit had a deep aesthetic sensibility, but had never undertaken a serious study of aesthetics. Personally, he was more likely to sense the sublime in music than in architecture. 'The best buildings in Venice and St Petersburg, though very beautiful, are not sublime,'[5] he said. Janet once asked him if he would sacrifice his own life in exchange for giving Mozart another thirty-five years to compose, and he said he would willingly do so. But what interested him most was whether the sublime had a normative component. He thought it did. That is, just as everybody who has experienced pain must believe that pain is something that we should try to minimize, so nobody who experiences the sublime will say that it doesn't matter, that it isn't valuable.

Besides his interest in the sublime, Parfit was considering a volume on effective altruism and the best ways we could help those in greater need than ourselves. He thought, too, about writing more about time. And he was still holding out hope that he could crack Theory X, a theory that would embrace the Non-Identity Problem whilst avoiding the Repugnant Conclusion.

Throughout his life, Parfit wrote, wrote, and wrote. No doubt some works will arise from beyond the grave—for he left behind a vast stack of unpublished material. Going through it is like swimming in murky water. Although he printed out his early papers, he rarely used paper-clips or staplers, and the pages are jumbled up and often unnumbered. Later papers exist on computer file, but there are challenges even here, because most exist in multiple forms. Parfit, helpfully, had a folder on his computer in which he dropped all the files that could be useful for posthumous publications.

Less helpfully, it is empty.

. . .

Parfit's portrait now hangs in the blue corridor—painted in 'Eton blue'—
that runs from Eton College's school library. The corridor is lined with
portraits and photographs of notable old Etonians. Parfit has been
placed to the left of John Maynard Keynes, and below Freddie Ayer.

He leaves some concrete legacies beyond the books. His enormous
library has been donated to Oxford's Uehiro Centre, and there is now a
Parfit Scholarship,[6] and an annual Parfit Lecture, as well as a fellowship in
his and Janet's names. There is a touching story to this. In 2012, a young
student, Jonny Pugh, who was applying ideas from *On What Matters* to
debates in bioethics, contacted Parfit, who, in his typically generous
fashion, sent back multiple comments on some draft work. Pugh was at
that stage in a precarious financial position, after some funding had
fallen through, and Parfit sent him an encouraging note: 'If you are
forced financially to give up the hope of becoming a paid philosopher,
as so many excellent philosophers had to do in the previous period
when funds and jobs were scarce, you should remember that you can
still be an unpaid philosopher who also does something else.'[7] After
Parfit's death, Pugh became the Parfit-Radcliffe Richards Fellow—and
thus a paid philosopher.

Parfit's impact outside academia is hard to assess. He is certainly not
as influential as Rawls; at least, not yet. Rawlsian ideas have percolated
into policy in the democratic world. But it is possible that aspects of
Parfit's theoretical work will be similarly absorbed, most especially the
consideration of people still unborn. Larry Temkin has attended many
conferences and meetings with organizations such as the World Health
Organization and the World Bank where 'I have been overwhelmed at
how the discussion of many of the world's most pressing practical problems concerning health, poverty, inequality, ageing, and global warming
has been fundamentally shaped by Parfit's ingenious insights and arguments'.[8] The Effective Altruism movement and the relatively new study
of existential risk are indirectly Parfit's progeny.

. . .

So much for Parfit's intellectual bequest. What of the verdict on Parfit the man, not the philosopher? Since his life became his work, he might resist any such partition. To non-philosophical eyes, Parfit appears, in the words of the writer Joyce Carol Oates, to be 'the very quintessence of the otherworldly philosophy don who prevailed in a sort of exquisite bubble of intellectual inquiry'.[9] Because he dedicated almost every hour to philosophy, he believed his life was uninteresting to others. But it is precisely that monomaniac dedication that makes him a figure of fascination.

The famous ethicist Peter Singer says that 'talking to Parfit was the closest I've ever come to talking to a genius'.[10] And many other substantial figures in philosophy have similar reports. There is a double edge to this. Philosophy has a problem with genius. Historians don't tend to believe that being a historian requires an innate ability that cannot be taught. But most philosophers do believe this with regard to philosophy.[11] Behaviour that might be frowned on elsewhere can receive a sympathetic reading in philosophy, shrugged off as 'genius'. This often involves a gendered element, moreover: men's eccentricities are more likely than women's to be marked down to genius. There appears to be an inverse correlation between the belief that a subject requires innate brilliance and the low number of women in a discipline; and although the situation has much improved, women have historically been hugely underrepresented in philosophy, more so than in other disciplines. None of this is to say that Parfit's life was in any way phony, or that he consciously cultivated the image of a genius. If anything, he was exceptionally authentic: his inner life and his outer behaviour were unusually aligned. But his image within the philosophical world is, and was, shaped by the cult of genius.

The philosopher Tom Kelly remembers Parfit as 'unique';[12] in her talk at the Schock award ceremony, Ruth Chang said he was 'probably the strangest person I know'.[13] He was in multiple ways a wonderfully generous and kind man. Numerous students and colleagues attest to that. He was also loved by many—several people interviewed for this book broke down when they spoke about him. But in the pursuit of what he considered a higher calling, he was also capable of monstrous selfishness.

His friend Bill Ewald's verdict is that although 'he never did anything cruel, he also never did anything that was deeply self-sacrificing'.[14] A colleague at All Souls, Richard Jenkyns, reached a related conclusion: 'He was, I think, both entirely selfish and entirely benevolent—an unusual combination.'[15] Former All Souls Fellow Hanna Pickard described him as 'very warm and cold at the same time'.[16]

Parfit told one friend that his biggest regret was 'not being able to be more for Janet'.[17] It is hard not to judge his treatment of his nearest and dearest harshly. Note this odd fact: Parfit wrote only two philosophy books, the second one in three parts. It is normal for an author to dedicate a book to a partner. But *Reasons and Persons* is dedicated to his parents and sisters; the first two volumes of *On What Matters* are dedicated to two American philosophers, Thomas Nagel and Thomas Scanlon; while Volume 3 is dedicated to three other American philosophers, Larry Temkin, Jeff McMahan, and Ruth Chang. Within these books there are hundreds—literally hundreds—of acknowledgements of yet more philosophers. Janet Radcliffe Richards's name is absent.

At least from the time of writing *Reasons and Persons*, philosophy had become walled off and more significant to Parfit than his private life. Derek and Janet were together for over three decades, but Janet is clear-eyed about her position in the hierarchy: 'I was a side show in his life. The real show was philosophy.'[18] She also wrote, 'I can't think of anything we did together that wasn't what he wanted to do.'[19] All the concessions in the relationship were made by her. On the other hand, she has few regrets, and knew early on what kind of a life she was letting herself in for. 'You shouldn't take up with Derek if you want a normal domestic relationship,' she once said.[20]

. . .

It was only when reading Oliver Sacks's book *An Anthropologist on Mars*,[21] published in 1997, that Janet began to feel she understood Parfit. The book had been his own recommendation. It contains case studies of individuals with neurological conditions, and Parfit was particularly interested in an animal behaviourist, Temple Grandin. Janet already knew about her, but Parfit proceeded to describe how she had great powers of concentration and single-mindedness, a passionate sense of right and wrong; how virtually her entire waking life was devoted to work, and how she had difficulty reading social codes. But, 'He didn't realize the similarity between himself and this woman.'[22]

Grandin had been diagnosed with an autism spectrum disorder.[23] In the recent past, the condition might have been labelled Asperger's Syndrome,[24] named after the 1940s Viennese paediatrician Hans Asperger, who observed a basket of symptoms possessed by some troubled children he was examining. These symptoms included literal-mindedness, narrow and obsessional preoccupations, and the failure to read social signs. Parfit ticked these particular boxes. Ruth Chang described him as 'intensely uncomfortable in the normal social world'. She served as a 'gate-keeper' in the United States, when people attempted to invite him to social events. 'I would tell people that they shouldn't take it personally, but he didn't want to go.'[25] Even philosophy-related events were of little interest to him if he did not think they would advance his work.

Hans Asperger did not believe that the condition he described was wholly negative, of course. It was often accompanied by 'a particular originality of thought and experience, which may well lead to exceptional achievements in later life.'[26]

I myself have gone through three stages in reflecting about Parfit. When I began writing this book, I assumed that he did, indeed, have an autism spectrum disorder. I once put it to him, directly, that he had Asperger's, and took as weak evidence that he did the fact that he found the subject uninteresting, conceding only that there 'may be something in this suggestion'.[27] But he had himself considered the matter during a period of introspection, several years earlier. He sent an email to his friend Patricia Zander that touched on his ignorance 'about matters of the heart', which he tried to explain in a bracketed clause: '(perhaps I have Asperger's Syndrome)'.[28] In 2004, he asked Ruth Chang to read a draft of something he had composed to another philosopher, 'since you may notice something that I shouldn't have written (having a touch of Asperger's Syndrome in me)'.[29] And, to Tim Scanlon he wrote, 'I do hope I haven't been unfriendly. I know that I'm a borderline case of Asperger's Syndrome.'[30]

So Parfit himself thought it a possibility. But then I became less confident of this diagnosis. Of course, autistic people can be quite different from each other, but the differences between Parfit and Temple Grandin are quite as notable as the similarities. Temple Grandin had no idea what it was to fall in love. She was relatively unmoved by art, and had no sense of the sublime. 'I felt there were modules missing,'[31] said one of Parfit's former students, and many people I spoke to about him spontaneously mentioned autism. But these were all people who knew him later in life. Not a single person from his early life raised the subject of autism of their own accord, and many were scathingly dismissive of applying it to Parfit. It is not a condition that one develops in mid-life: one either has it from childhood or not at all.

And the contrast between the young and old Parfit is glaring. In his early sixties, he said to his friend Ingmar Persson, 'People never change';[32] a curious remark for someone who had himself changed so dramatically. The first part of Parfit's life was full of—precisely—life; the second part was full of philosophy; and, as it turned out, life and philosophy were not wholly compatible. The young Parfit was relaxed, curious in multiple domains, relished friendship and life in general. The older Parfit was intense, shunned social interactions, and was dedicated to his work to a fanatical degree. Recall how the ten-year-old Derek evoked a delectable meal on his French exchange trip, with its starter of watery melon and black olives, and contrast that with his functional, monotonous, bleak, and joyless meals as a mature adult. How could this be one and the same person!

There are certainly character traits that were present throughout Parfit's life—a benign gentleness; a lack of negative reactive attitudes, such as blame, envy, or hostility. But in other ways there appears to have been a rupture—and behaviour patterns that might indicate autism are far more prominent later than earlier.

. . .

So, in my second stage, I concluded that there must be some other explanation—not to do with autism—for the disjuncture between Parfit I and Parfit II. Perhaps his daily concoction of pills and vodka was having an effect?

Then I made contact with some autism experts—and the autism hypothesis took on renewed plausibility. Scientific investigation into autism is ongoing. In the past, it was thought that autism predominantly affected men. But researchers have recently come round to the view that more women are on the autistic spectrum than previously believed, and that many have been able to hide their condition through 'masking'— mimicking the social behaviour of others in order to fit in.

So, here is one possibility. Perhaps, in the first part of his life, Parfit was a male masker? Masking might well not have been very difficult in the kinds of environments in which he was raised: private schools, Oxford University; insular, cloistered worlds. But wearing a mask for many years takes a heavy toll. Presenting an image to the world that is not authentically one's own is exhausting. And there is evidence that, in periods of stress, the mask will slip. It can also be dispensed with if, for whatever reason, camouflage becomes superfluous.

The major change in Parfit's behaviour can be traced to the early 1980s. From this period, there was a notable intensification of his more atypical traits. There were two pivotal episodes at the time. The most stressful period for him was when he was rebuffed for promotion in 1981—a promotion he had complacently taken for granted. That forced him to devote two manic years to *Reasons and Persons*. Then, in 1984, with his appointment to the position of Senior Research Fellow, he was effectively handed job security for life. He was no longer required to be who he was not.

Perhaps for that very reason, a *diagnosis* of autism is misplaced, in so far as this is normally applied when a person is having trouble functioning, or settling in, and suffering or being harmed as a result. To that extent, it involves a social component. Parfit did not suffer in the academic institution in which he spent almost all his adult life, however; on the contrary, he thrived. As a leading authority on autism spectrum disorder puts it, 'he wouldn't have needed a diagnosis of autism.'[33]

. . .

Because Parfit did not believe in free will, he did not believe that people deserved blame for bad actions or praise for good ones. But for most of us, our views on causation calibrate our attitudes to moral responsibility; for example, if a person has an autism spectrum disorder, we might hold them less responsible for at least some of their actions.

Let us grant that Parfit may have had an atypical neurological structure. Nevertheless, the world is not monocausal. There can be more than one reason for a phenomenon. Could we not permit a second reason for Parfit's unusual choices, one that admits more agency, more freedom, as it is traditionally understood, and therefore enlarges the space for responsibility?

Perhaps Parfit made a clear-headed choice. He decided that there were certain fundamental questions and that he was in the small category of people with the intellectual capacity to make progress on the answers. This was a privilege, but also a burden. The need to make progress weighed upon him. The urge to convince others weighed upon him. The fear of time running out weighed upon him.

Ingmar Persson likens him to those who undergo a religious conversion, such as Saint Francis of Assisi, who abandoned a life of leisure and pleasure for veneration of poverty and complete religious immersion: 'There was something of a religious fervour about the older Derek's attitude to "what matters".'[34] An echo of the Parfit family missionary zeal . . .

Parfit sacrificed the ingredients that for most people make up a good life—the simple pleasures to be derived from family, friends, play, food, love. Because he had to climb the mountain from all sides, he missed out on so much—on walks in bluebell woods, on lounging on a beach and feeling sand between his toes, on nursing a glass of wine in companionship with people he liked, on joyful occasions such as birthday parties and weddings. 'Ordinary' people believe that *these are among* the things that matter.

Parfit presented one of his early girlfriends, Judith De Witt, with a book about Keats and told her that 'Keats would have chosen to die young and be the best as opposed to living longer and being second best.'[35] Accomplishment was Parfit's most valued virtue. The accomplishment he cared most about was demonstrating that morality was objective—for if it was not, he believed, his life was useless, as were all our lives. The ambition of his last two decades was to rescue ethics.

We do not need to adopt Parfit's narrow view about what matters in order to realize that forfeiting the things that other people find fulfilling is a risky strategy. If the work produced is of seminal value, then the life devoted to it might reasonably be judged as worthwhile, in spite of its self-sacrifice. But if it is not, then it will seem wasted and impoverished.

Readers can turn to Parfit's work, and reach their own verdict. My own view, and the reason I wrote this book, is that his gamble paid off.

Derek Antony Parfit

1939: Theodora (Theo), Derek's sister, born in Chengdu, Sichuan

11 December 1942: Derek born in Chengdu

March 1944: the Parfits—Norman, Jessie, Theo, and Derek—leave China, eventually arriving in the US.

May 1944–June 1945: the Parfits live in Manhattan, near George Washington Bridge.

13 October 1944: Joanna Parfit born

June 1945: the family takes the *Queen Mary* to Britain. Jessie lands a job in Surrey.

Spring 1946: the Parfits move to 116 Croxted Road, Dulwich, south-east London.

1947–49: attends Dulwich College Preparatory School

Summer 1949: the Parfits buy and move to 5 Northmoor Road in North Oxford and Derek attends Greycotes Junior School. Theodora is sent to Dartington Hall School in Devon.

1950: starts at the Dragon School, North Oxford

1956: wins a scholarship to Eton and starts there, aged thirteen

December 1958: O-Level exams, after which Derek specializes in history

March 1960: wins a scholarship to Balliol College, Oxford

May–August 1961: works in New York as an intern at *The New Yorker* magazine, sharing Theo's Upper West Side apartment

1961–64: studies for history degree at Oxford

3 June 1962: Parfit's poem 'Photograph of a Comtesse' published in *The New Yorker*

Trinity (summer) term 1963: edits the Oxford student magazine *Isis*

18 May 1963: ends up in hospital after attempting a midnight entry into Balliol

November 1963: wins the Gibbs Prize

June 1964: awarded a First-Class degree in history

Autumn 1964: publication of *Eton Microcosm*, co-written with Anthony Cheetham

October 1964: unsuccessful application for an All Souls Prize Fellowship

1965–66: Harkness Fellow, studying at New York University, Columbia University, and Harvard University. At Harvard Parfit has extensive conversations with John Rawls.

Summer 1965: US road trip with Mary Clemmey

January 1967: begins a BPhil degree back in Oxford

November 1967: elected a Prize Fellow at All Souls

1967–74: Prize Fellow/Examination Fellow at All Souls

27 January 1970: unsuccessful interview to become the Balliol philosophy tutorial Fellow

Trinity 1970: leads a class with James Griffin and Jonathan Glover. It then runs for several years, attended by both postgraduates and established philosophers.

January 1971: publication in *The Philosophical Review* of Parfit's breakthrough paper on personal identity

Fall semester 1971: visiting lecturer at Harvard

Fall semester 1972: visiting lecturer at New York University

1973: becomes the convener of an Oxford Civic Society working group on the city's street lights. He continues in this role into the 1990s.

9 March 1974: elected a Research Fellow at All Souls, a seven-year fellowship

June 1977: wins the T. H. Green Prize with a long essay, 'Against Prudence'

October 1978: signs contract with OUP to write a short book entitled *Against Prudence* (never published)

16 November 1978: delivers a lecture at the British Academy, 'Prudence, Morality, and the Prisoner's Dilemma'

Autumn 1979: teaches at Princeton

13 June 1981: has his All Souls Research Fellowship extended for three years

5–12 February 1982: leads All Souls delegation to Leningrad

1983: meets Janet Radcliffe Richards

10 September 1983: final deadline to complete *Reasons and Persons*

12 April 1984: publication of *Reasons and Persons*

23 May 1984: death of father, Norman Parfit

June 1984: elected a Senior Research Fellow at All Souls (effectively giving job security for life)

3 June 1986: becomes a Fellow of the British Academy

3 November 1986: sister Joanna dies from injuries following a car accident

15 January 1988: buys West Kennett House, Wiltshire, with Janet

1 April 1988: death of mother, Jessie Parfit

20–22 October 1988: attends Liberty Fund conference on 'Intergenerational Relationships', in Austin, Texas

Autumn 1990: first meeting of the Ruth Chang discussion group (though Parfit dissuades Chang herself from attending subsequent sessions)

1991: publication of Shelly Kagan's *The Limits of Morality*, the first book in the Parfit-edited 'Oxford Ethics' series

Spring 1991: 'Why Does the Universe Exist?' published in *The Harvard Review of Philosophy*

21 November 1991: delivers the Lindley Lecture at the University of Kansas, from which comes his influential paper on equality, 'Equality or Priority'

1992–94: sub-Warden at All Souls. During this period Janet teaches an Open University course on equality.

3 July 1992: publishes 'The Puzzle of Reality' in *The Times Literary Supplement*

September 1995: West Kennett House is sold. Parfit and Janet move to 28 St John Street in Oxford.

1996: St John Street house sold. Janet moves to Huddleston Road in Tufnell Park, north London, and Parfit buys a house in Beaumont Buildings, Oxford.

1997: publication of *Reading Parfit*, edited by Jonathan Dancy (but without Parfit's contribution)

December 1997: publication of 'Equality and Priority' (based on Parfit's 1992 Lindley Lecture) in *Ratio*

January and February 1998: two-part essay, 'Why Anything? Why This?', published in the *London Review of Books*

Fall semester 1998: first teaching at Harvard

1999: Janet takes a job as director of the Centre for Bioethics and Philosophy of Medicine at University College London, where she remains until 2007

4–6 November 2002: delivers his three Tanner Lectures at the University of California, Berkeley

10–12 April 2003: Rutgers conference in Parfit's honour

2–3 November 2006: Reading University conference, 'Parfit Meets Critics', on the manuscript *Climbing the Mountain*

Spring 2007: teaches at Rutgers

Autumn 2007: Janet returns to Oxford, to the Uehiro Centre for Practical Ethics

23 July 2008: death of Patricia Zander

2009: publication of *Essays on Parfit's 'On What Matters'*, based on the 2006 Reading University conference papers

October 2009: Parfit and several philosophers in 9 Beaumont Buildings fail to kill a mouse.

15 February 2010: last meeting of the All Souls philosophy group

31 August 2010: Parfit and Janet Radcliffe Richards marry at the Oxford Registry Office

30 September 2010: retires

1 October 2010: elected Emeritus Fellow at All Souls

2011: publication of first two volumes of *On What Matters*

Spring 2011: last teaching at Harvard

12 February 2014: learns he has won the Rolf Schock Prize ('the philosopher's Nobel'), 'for his groundbreaking contributions concerning personal identity, regard for future generations and analysis of the structure of moral theories'

7–9 July 2014: participates in a conference on effective altruism, 'Good Done Right', held at All Souls

August 2014: Janet suddenly develops rheumatoid arthritis

September 2014: falls ill during a Rutgers semester and is rushed to hospital in New Brunswick

21–23 October 2014: symposium and ceremony in Stockholm for the Schock Prize

23 August–5 September 2015: a rare holiday with Janet, at Theodora and Van's summer home in Deer Isle, Maine

Autumn 2015: last semester teaching at NYU

2016: publication of Frances Kamm's *The Moral Target*, last book in the Parfit-edited 'Oxford Ethics' series

Spring 2016: last semester teaching at Rutgers

9 September 2016: Janet falls ill, and is in hospital in London until 10 November. Parfit remains at her Tufnell Park home.

20 November 2016: gives talk at Effective Altruism conference in Oxford

2 January 2017: death of Derek Parfit in the early hours

12 January 2017: publication of *Does Anything Really Matter?*, edited by Peter Singer

19 January 2017: publication of third volume of *On What Matters*

9 February 2017: Parfit's funeral service in All Souls college chapel

21 March 2017: publication of *Reading Parfit*, edited by Simon Kirchin

3 June 2017: memorial event for Parfit in All Souls library

15–16 December 2017: joint NYU/Rutgers conference on Parfit

11 May–30 June 2018: central London exhibition of Parfit's photography at Narrative Projects gallery

18–20 May 2018: conference in Oxford to honour Parfit's work

NOTES

Preface: What Matters

1. *The Times*, 4 January 2017.

Chapter 1. Made in China

1. Obituary of A. H. Browne, Church Mission Society archive.
2. Ellen Browne (née Roughton), Church Mission Society archive.
3. Jessie Parfit's unpublished memoir.
4. Church Mission Society archive.
5. Jessie Parfit's unpublished memoir written for Joanna Parfit.
6. Ibid.
7. *Daily Mirror*, 12 July 1934.
8. Ibid.
9. Published in *Chengdu News Letter*, Church Mission Society archive.
10. https://www.youtube.com/watch?v=pQUc1ZZfSA8, accessed 18 May 2022.
11. Jessie and Norman Parfit's unpublished memoir, 'China—There and Back 1935–1945'.
12. Ibid.
13. Jessie Parfit's unpublished memoir.
14. Ibid.
15. Jessie and Norman Parfit's unpublished memoir.
16. Ibid.
17. Ibid.
18. Ibid.

Chapter 2. Prepping for Life

1. Joanna van Heyningen, interview with author.
2. Parfit (2011) (c).
3. Annie Altschul at Jessie Parfit's memorial event, 25 June 1988, the transcript of which is in Parfit's private papers.
4. Michael Prestwich, email to author.
5. My thanks to Stephen Jessel for supplying these nicknames (and many more!)
6. Bill Nimmo Smith, Parfit's memorial event, Oxford, 3 June 2017.

7. Ibid.

8. *The Draconian*, Easter 1951.

9. *The Draconian*, Summer 1954.

10. *The Draconian*, Christmas 1954.

11. *The Draconian*, Summer 1955.

12. *The Draconian*, Summer 1956.

13. Joseph T. Parfit, Norman's father, who died on 21 July 1953.

14. Parfit's diary, 23 July 1953.

15. The bus station terminal is called Gloucester Green.

16. Parfit's diary, 23 July 1953.

17. Ibid., 28 July 1953.

18. Ibid., 21 August 1953.

19. Ibid.

20. Parfit's diary, 23 August 1953.

21. Ibid., 25 July 1954.

22. Ibid., 23 July 1954.

23. Ibid., 2 August 1954.

24. Ibid., 7 August 1954.

25. Ibid., 17 August 1954.

26. Tim Hunt, interview with author.

27. *The Draconian*, Easter 1956.

28. Parfit (2011) (c).

29. *The Draconian*, Summer 1956.

30. As recalled by Bill Nimmo Smith, interview with author.

Chapter 3. Eton Titan

1. Edward Mortimer, Parfit's memorial event, Oxford, 3 June 2017.

2. Sam Leith, 'The Social Politics of Eton', *The Spectator*, 6 July 2019.

3. James Wood, 'These Etonians', *London Review of Books*, 4 July 2019.

4. Adam Ridley, interview with author.

5. Ibid.

6. Edward Mortimer, unpublished memoir.

7. Adam Ridley, interview with author.

8. Anthony Cheetham, interview with author.

9. The final two-year period at school during which pupils in the UK (except for Scotland) prepare for their A-Level (advanced level) exams.

10. As recalled by David Jessel, email to author.

11. *Eton Chronicle*, issue no. 3234 (1960).

12. Ibid.

13. *Eton Chronicle*, issue no. 3201 (1959).

14. *Eton Chronicle*, issue no. 3205 (1959).

15. *Eton Chronicle*, issue no. 3224 (1960).

16. *Eton Chronicle*, issue no. 3234 (1960).

17. *Eton Chronicle*, issue no. 3241 (1960).

18. *Eton Chronicle*, issue no. 3246 (1960).

19. Ibid.

20. The Public Schools, in the English educational system, being a select group of private, fee-paying ones.

21. *Eton Chronicle*, issue no. 3252 (1961).

22. O-levels were replaced in 1986 by the GSCE (General Certificate of Secondary Education) exams.

23. Parfit (2011) (c).

24. Parfit's handwritten note on his Trevelyan Prize essay, in his private papers.

25. Ibid., pp. 1–2.

26. Ibid., p. 4.

27. A 'Blue' is awarded to those who play in the Oxford vs. Cambridge match.

28. As recalled by Edward Mortimer, interview with author.

29. Balliol College Historic Collections, Derek Parfit dossier.

30. Parfit to Joanna, 11 October 1959, Parfit's private papers.

31. Ibid.

32. Parfit to Joanna, 14 February 1960, Parfit's private papers.

33. Khrushchev branded Lorenzo Sumulong 'a jerk, a stooge, and a lackey'. The Soviet leader may or may not have banged the rostrum with his shoe—accounts differ.

34. Parfit to Joanna, 12 October (probably 1960), Parfit's private papers.

35. An anecdote from Edward Mortimer, from the Parfit memorial event, Oxford, 3 June 2017.

36. Parfit to Joanna, 9 February 1961, Parfit's private papers.

37. Parfit (2011) (c).

38. Georgina Robinson, email to author.

Chapter 4. History Boy

1. Parfit (2011) (c).

2. MacFarquhar (2011).

3. Patten (2017), p. 55.

4. Forsyth (1989), p. 59.

5. Patten (2017), p. 53.

6. Cobb (1985), p. 18.

7. Stonier and Hague (1964).

8. Parfit (2011) (c).

9. Ibid.

10. Gareth Stedman Jones, email to author.

11. The information comes from Jonathan Glover, in McMahan (forthcoming).

12. The meeting was held on 27 February 1963.

13. 27 February 1963, in Bodleian Libraries, University of Oxford, Dep. e. 335, ff. 61–62.

14. Ibid.

15. It has proved impossible to date this episode accurately, but it probably took place in 1964. This story was recalled by Aitken in an interview with the author.

16. Jonathan Aitken, email to author.

Chapter 5. Oxford Words

1. Rowbotham (2000), pp. 45–46.

2. *Isis*, 29 November 1961. Skidelsky was to become an economic historian, the biographer of John Maynard Keynes, and a member of the House of Lords.

3. *Isis*, 9 May 1962.

4. *Isis*, 23 May 1962.

5. *Isis*, 30 May 1962.

6. Parfit (2011) (c).

7. Parfit, Trevelyan Prize essay, 1960.

8. *Isis*, 13 March 1963.

9. *Isis*, 17 October 1962.

10. Wally Kaufman, *Isis*, 18 November 1962.

11. *Isis*, 28 November 1962.

12. *Isis*, 6 March 1963.

13. Not to be confused with his Cambridge-educated namesake, born 1957.

14. *Isis*, 1 May 1963.

15. *Isis*, 19 June 1963.

16. Parfit to Joanna Parfit, undated letter, Parfit's private papers.

17. Ibid.

18. Mary Clemmey, interview with author.

19. Ibid.

20. Parfit to Mary Clemmey, December 1962, Parfit's private papers.

21. Parfit to Mary Clemmey, undated, Parfit's private papers.

22. Ibid.

23. Mary Clemmey to Parfit, undated, Parfit's private papers.

24. Mary Clemmey to Parfit, undated, Parfit's private papers.

25. Mary Clemmey to Parfit, undated, Parfit's private papers.

26. Parfit to Mary Clemmey, 1964, Parfit's private papers.

27. Stephen Fry, *Isis*, 28 May 1963.

28. Parfit to Caroline Cracraft, recalled in email to author.

29. Stephen Fry, *Isis*, 28 May 1963.

30. Ibid.

31. Robin Briggs, interview with author.

32. Anthony Cheetham, email to author.

33. Cheetham and Parfit (1964), p. 11.

34. 'The Fish', in ibid., pp. 182–83.

35. Cheetham and Parfit (1964), p. 100.

36. Ibid.

37. Cheetham and Parfit (1964), p. 101.

38. Ibid.

39. Anthony Cheetham, interview with author.

40. Balliol College Historic Collections, Derek Parfit dossier, letter to the Master, 14 October 1963.

41. Ibid.

42. Commonwealth Fund Archive, held at the Rockefeller Archive Center.

43. Ibid.

44. Ibid.

45. Ibid.

46. Ibid.

47. Ibid.

48. Ibid.

49. John B. Fox Jnr, 8 May 1964, Commonwealth Fund Archive.

50. Parfit, 11 May 1964, Commonwealth Fund Archive.

51. Commonwealth Fund Archive.

52. Ibid.

53. As recalled by Deirdre Wilson, interview with author.

54. Robin Briggs, email to author.

55. Edward Mortimer at Parfit's memorial event, Oxford, 3 June 2017. Almost two decades after Parfit's exams, Hugh Trevor-Roper 'authenticated' the forged Hitler diaries; evidence, perhaps, that he was not quite as exceptional a historian as he believed himself to be.

56. Hugh Trevor-Roper, *The Sunday Times*, 2 August 1964.

57. Robin Briggs, interview with author.

58. Heald (2011), p. 101.

59. Commonwealth Fund Archive.

60. Parfit to Mary Clemmey, undated [1964]

61. I'm grateful to Robin Briggs for explaining the exam process to me.

62. Sarah Lyall, *New York Times*, 27 May 2010.

63. A claim made by Lyall, ibid.

64. Armand d'Angour, https://www.armand-dangour.com/2013/07/failing-souls/, accessed 9 June 2022.

Chapter 6. An American Dream

1. David Lodge wrote his breakthrough novel *The British Museum is Falling Down* whilst on his Harkness Fellowship.

2. Miller (1987), p. 513.

3. Miller (2002).

4. Parfit (2011) (c).

5. Ibid.

6. As recalled by David Wiggins, interview with author.

7. Lovibond and Williams (1996), p. 222.

8. Mary Clemmey, email to author.

9. Ibid.

10. Edward Mortimer, email to author.

11. Ben Zander, interview with author.

12. Ibid.

13. Bob Wolff, email to author.

14. Ibid.

15. Ibid.

16. Balliol College Historic Collections, Derek Parfit dossier.

17. Ibid., 20 February 1966.

18. Ibid., 3 February 1966.

19. Ibid., 28 February 1966.

20. Ibid., 2 March 1966.

21. Balliol College Historic Collections, Derek Parfit dossier.

22. Bob Wolff, Commonwealth Fund Archive.

23. John Rawls, reflecting on his first memories of Parfit, in a reference to All Souls, 27 April 1981, Parfit's private papers.

24. Parfit, Commonwealth Fund Archive, 31 October 1966.

25. Parfit, Commonwealth Fund Archive, 24 November 1966.

26. Ibid. Hilary Putnam was a leading US philosopher in the second half of the twentieth century.

27. Ibid.

28. Edward Mortimer, Parfit's memorial event, Oxford, 3 June 2017.

Chapter 7. Soul Man

1. For a lengthier discussion of Vienna Circle ideas, see Edmonds (2020).

2. John Passmore in Edwards (1967), pp. 52–57.

3. See Parfit (2011) (c).

4. See MacFarquhar (2011).

5. See Parfit (2011) (a), p. xl.

6. Ibid., p. xxxiii.

7. Crisp (2015), p. x.

8. Parfit, as recalled by Roger Crisp, interview with author.

9. Parfit to Joanna Parfit, 27 June 1967, Parfit's private papers.

10. Ibid.

11. Ibid.

12. Ibid.

13. Ibid.

14. Parfit to Joanna Parfit, undated, Parfit's private papers.

15. Ibid.

16. Briggs, *ODNB* online.

17. Isaiah Berlin to John Lowe, 27 February 1989, in Raina (2017), p. xvi.

18. To keep non-Oxonians on their toes, heads of colleges have different titles—'Warden' at All Souls, 'Master' at Balliol, 'Principal' at Somerville.

19. Balliol College Historic Collections, Derek Parfit dossier, 1 November 1967.

20. Ibid.

21. Balliol College Historic Collections, Derek Parfit dossier.

22. Ibid.

23. Dancy (2020), p. 40.

24. Norma Aubertin-Potter, interview with author.

25. These quotes are from Budiansky (2021), p. 148.

26. Cohen (2010), p. 144. Cohen joined All Souls when he became the Chichele Professor of Social and Political Theory in 1985.

27. Willie Abraham was the first and (as of 2023) the only African elected to an All Souls fellowship.

28. A. L. Rowse, quoted in a *Financial Times* article, 3 August 2018, available at https://www.ft.com/content/c57bc460-94c5-11e8-b67b-b8205561c3fe, accessed 18 May 2022.

29. Balliol College Historic Collections, Derek Parfit dossier, 4 March 1968.

30. Parfit (c) 2011.

31. I was given this information by Álvaro Rodríguez.

32. Parfit (1986), p. vii. In the 1987 paperback, the words 'fledgling' and 'merciless' have been removed.

33. Mike Rosen would become better known as the children's writer Michael Rosen.

34. Mike Rosen, *Cherwell*, 6 November 1968, quoted in Raina (2017), p. 544.

35. Quoted in Raina (2017), p. 542.

36. Jonathan Glover, in McMahan (forthcoming).

37. Anthony Quinton, quoted by Jonathan Glover in McMahan (forthcoming).

38. Singer (2017) (b).

39. David Heyd, email to author.

40. Jonathan Glover, in McMahan (forthcoming).

41. This thought experiment reappears in J. Glover and M. Scott-Taggart, 'It Makes No Difference Whether or Not I Do It', *Proceedings of the Aristotelian Society,* Supplementary Volume 49/1 (1975), pp. 171–209.

42. Parfit, 7 January 1969, OUP archive.

43. Anthony Kenny, email to author.

Chapter 8. The Teletransporter

1. Parfit (2011) (c).

2. Ibid.

3. We are never told definitively how the *Star Trek* transporter worked. Were the molecules of Captain Kirk disassembled, sent to another location, and reassembled? Or were they copied and 're-created'? In *Star Trek: The Next Generation* (a series that began to air a few years after *Reasons and Persons* was published), talk of the 'pattern buffer' may indicate transportees are

reassembled. But the *Star Trek* writers adopted a woefully inconsistent approach to this important issue. I put out a question on Twitter about this and received scores of responses. I'm grateful for replies from, among many others, Stefan Forrester, Stephen Tweedale, and Dominic Wilkinson.

4. See Shoemaker (1963) and Wiggins (1967).

5. *Reasons and Persons*, as we shall see, was delivered to OUP at the last moment. This explains why, in the early editions, there are some copyediting lapses. For example, 'Teletransported' here is with a capital T, but in the previous paragraph is with a small t.

6. Parfit (1986), p. 199.

7. Ibid., pp. 254–55.

8. You can hear the neuroscientist V. S. Ramachandran talking about this at https://youtu .be/PFJPtVRlI64, accessed 18 May 2022.

9. This is, necessarily, a highly truncated account of a deeply worked-through theory. Parfit argues, plausibly, that if only one brother survived, we might say that identity *was* preserved. We could not say the same if both brothers survived, for the reasons given. Yet this would clearly be a double success and only goes to reinforce Parfit's central claim, that identity is not what matters. My thanks to Paul Snowdon for help with this section.

10. See Mill (1991), pp. 13–14.

11. Parfit (1986), p. 281.

12. Ibid., Appendix J, p. 502.

13. Ruth Chang, in a talk at the Schock Prize symposium, 21–23 October 2014.

14. Alan Montefiore, interview with author.

15. Janet Radcliffe Richards, interview with author.

16. Parfit to Mary Clemmey, Parfit's private papers.

17. Mary Clemmey to Parfit, October 1968. Richard Nixon was elected US president on 5 November 1968.

18. 1969 US visa application form, Parfit's private papers.

19. Mary Clemmey has no recollection of receiving it.

20. Parfit to Mary Clemmey (undated letter), Parfit's private papers.

21. Ibid.

22. Patricia Zander to Parfit, undated letter, Parfit's private papers.

23. Patricia Zander to Parfit, undated letter, Parfit's private papers.

24. Patricia Zander to Parfit, 11 September (undated year), Parfit's private papers.

25. Patricia Zander to Parfit, undated letter, Parfit's private papers.

26. Patricia Zander to Parfit, undated letter, Parfit's private papers.

27. Patricia Zander to Parfit, undated letter, Parfit's private papers.

28. Parfit to Joanna Parfit, 3 July 1970, Parfit's private papers.

29. Ibid.

30. Patricia Zander to Parfit, undated letter, Parfit's private papers.

31. Judith De Witt, interview with author.

32. Richard Jenkyns, email to author.

33. Judith De Witt, interview with author.

34. Balliol College Historic Collections, Hare Papers, 5.35, 26 February 1973.

35. Peter Strawson review, in Parfit's private papers.

36. David Pears, in Parfit's private papers.

37. R. H. Hare, in Parfit's private papers.

38. John Rawls, in Parfit's private papers.

39. Isaiah Berlin, in Hardy, https://berlin.wolf.ox.ac.uk (Michael Ignatieff tape 27/31), accessed 3 December 2021.

40. Charles Wenden, as recalled by Edward Hussey in email to author.

41. Larry Temkin, email to author.

Chapter 9. A Transatlantic Affair

1. Parfit (2011) (c).

2. Tim Scanlon, interview with author.

3. Voorhoeve (2009), p. 179.

4. Scanlon (1998), p. 235.

5. Thomas Nagel, *London Review of Books*, 4 February 1999.

6. The following account of Nagel's work has been lifted from Edmonds (2018).

7. Nozick (1974), p. 183.

8. Kamm (1996).

9. They are called 'trolley' dilemmas because the first time they were introduced into the literature, in a 1967 article by Philippa Foot, the runaway train was actually a tram, or trolley. For an introduction to 'trolleyology', widely acknowledged (at least within the author's household) as an enduring literary masterpiece, see Edmonds (2014) (a).

10. From the BBC World Service documentary *Would You Kill the Big Guy* (2010; available at https://www.bbc.co.uk/programmes/p00c1sw2, accessed 18 May 2022), and quoted in Edmonds (2014) (a), p. 53.

11. Kamm (1999), p. 186.

12. Parfit, in Edmonds (2014) (b).

13. Thomas Kelly, unpublished remarks for Parfit's Princeton remembrance day, 7 February 2017.

14. Ibid.

15. Simon Rippon, interview with author.

16. Larry Temkin, in McMahan (forthcoming)

Chapter 10. The Parfit Scandal

1. Richard Jenkyns, email to author.

2. OUP archive BLB 251/BACKB1355.

3. Nigel Warburton, told to author in conversation.

4. Quoted in several of his obituaries, e.g., *The Times*, 14 June 2003.

5. Williams's example concerns a creative artist—'let us call him Gauguin'; Williams (1981), pp. 22–26.

6. Williams, in Smart and Williams (1973), p. 116.

7. Isaiah Berlin, in Hardy, https://berlin.wolf.ox.ac.uk (Michael Ignatieff tape 27/34), accessed 3 December 2021.

8. Ibid.

9. Ibid.

10. Patricia Williams, email to author.

11. Isaiah Berlin, in Hardy, https://berlin.wolf.ox.ac.uk (Michael Ignatieff tape 27/34), accessed 3 December 2021.

12. Parfit to Marshall Cohen, 24 June 1981, Parfit's private papers.

13. Although it is difficult to be sure, this argument was most probably put by Rodney Needham.

14. Description of All Souls attributed by Isaiah Berlin to John Sparrow, and cited by Paul Seabright at Susan Hurley's funeral, 24 August 2007.

15. Paul Seabright, interview with author.

16. Ibid.

17. Patricia Morison, interview with author.

18. Bill Ewald, interview with author.

19. Ehrlich (1971) (the co-author Anne Ehrlich is not credited).

20. Parfit, in Papers of John Rawls, 1942–2003, HUM 48, Box 19, Folder 3, Harvard University Archives.

21. The lecture was on 16 November 1978.

22. Adam Hodgkin, 9 August 1978, OUP Archive.

23. R. M. Hare, 28 October 1978, OUP Archive.

24. Taurek (1977), p. 309.

25. Parfit (1978).

26. Parfit to Ronald Dworkin, 15 August 1980, Parfit's private papers.

27. Balliol College Historic Collections, Hare Papers, 5.45, 9 October 1980.

28. Ibid., 5.45, 20 October 1981.

29. Parfit to Patrick Neill, 26 March 1981, Parfit's private papers.

30. Ibid.

31. Ibid.

32. Ibid.

33. *The Independent*, 13 December 2006.

34. Richard Jenkyns, email to author.

35. Ibid.

36. Adrian Wooldridge, interview with author.

37. Bill Ewald, interview with author.

38. Thomas Nagel to Parfit, Parfit's private papers.

39. R. M. Hare, 30 March 1981, Parfit's private papers.

40. John Rawls, 27 April 1981, Parfit's private papers.

41. Ronald Dworkin, undated, Parfit's private papers.

42. Jonathan Glover, undated, Parfit's private papers.

43. Ronald Dworkin, undated, Parfit's private papers.

44. Thomas Nagel, 20 April 1981.

45. Jonathan Glover, undated, Parfit's private papers.

46. Ibid.

47. Thomas Nagel, 20 April 1981, Parfit's private papers.

48. Parfit to Adam Hodgkin, 11 May 1981, OUP archive.

49. Adam Hodgkin to Parfit, 15 May 1981, OUP archive.

50. Amartya Sen, interview with author.

51. Amartya Sen, https://news.harvard.edu/gazette/story/2021/06/tracing-amartya-sens -path-from-childhood-during-the-raj-to-nobel-prize-and-beyond/, accessed 18 May 2022.

52. Amartya Sen, interview with author.

53. William Waldegrave, interview with author.

54. Parfit to 'Michael' (possibly Dummett), 23 June 1981, Parfit's private papers.

55. Parfit to Marshall Cohen, 24 June 1981, Parfit's private papers.

56. Quoted back at Marshall Cohen by Parfit, 24 June 1981.

57. Ibid.

58. Parfit to 'Michael', 23 June 1981, Parfit's private papers.

59. Isaiah Berlin to Bernard Williams, 22 November 1981, in 'Supplementary Letters 1975–1997', ed. Henry Hardy and Mark Pottle, in Hardy, https://berlin.wolf.ox.ac.uk, accessed 3 February 2021.

60. Isaiah Berlin, in Hardy, https://berlin.wolf.ox.ac.uk (Michael Ignatieff tape 27/35), accessed 3 December 2021.

61. Nick Bostrom, interview with author.

62. Jeff McMahan, email to author. The discussion took place on 11 September 2005. Besides McMahan, the others present were Shelly Kagan, Larry Temkin, Thomas Hurka, and Thomas Nagel.

63. Parfit, as recalled by Roger Crisp, interview with author.

64. Douglas Kremm, email to author.

65. Richard Jenkyns, email to author.

66. Tim Scanlon, 4 July 1981, Parfit's private papers.

67. Parfit to Marshall Cohen, 24 June 1981.

Chapter 11. Work, Work, Work, and Janet

1. Richard Jenkyns, email to author.

2. Balliol College Historic Collections, Hare Papers, 1a, 3 October 1981.

3. Ibid., 7 October 1981.

4. Dale Jamieson, interview with author.

5. Bernard Williams, as recalled by Galen Strawson in interview with author.

6. Simon Blackburn, email to author.

7. Hanna Pickard, email to author.

8. A. J. Ayer, in his 1973 reference for Parfit, Parfit's private papers.

9. Humaira Erfan-Ahmed, interview with author.

10. The Vietnam War ended in 1975. This witticism is credited to musicologist Alan Tyson.

11. Parfit (1986), p. viii.

12. Shelly Kagan, interview with author.

13. John Broome, interview with author.

14. Adam Hodgkin, letter to Parfit, 16 August 1983, Parfit's private papers.

15. Jeff McMahan, email to author.

16. Parfit, as recalled by Bill Ewald, interview with author.

17. Parfit (1986), p. 443.

18. Nietzsche (2001), p. 199, §343.

19. Susan Hurley, as recalled by Bill Ewald in interview with author.

20. Parfit (1986), p. 454.

21. OUP employee Angela Blackburn (wife of philosopher Simon Blackburn).

22. Parfit to Angela Blackburn and Adam Hodgkin, 29 October 1983, OUP archives.

23. Paul Seabright in an address delivered at Susan Hurley's funeral, 24 August 2007.

24. Paul Seabright, in a memorial for Susan Hurley, 26 April 2008.

25. Amartya Sen, interview with author.

26. Mill (1977), p. 27.

27. Janet Radcliffe Richards in Edmonds (2014) (b).

28. Janet Radcliffe Richards, interview with author.

29. Janet Radcliffe Richards in Edmonds (2014) (b).

30. Truer in the 1980s than today.

31. Janet Radcliffe Richards, email to author.

Chapter 12. Moral Mathematics

1. Parfit (1986), p. ix.

2. See Hannah Sparks, 'If cats were people, they'd probably be psychopaths, scientists say', *New York Post*, 6 December 2021, available at https://nypost.com/2021/12/06/if-cats-were-people-theyd-be-psychopaths-scientists-say/, accessed 18 May 2022.

3. Theodora Ooms, relayed to author by email.

4. Parfit's private papers.

5. Ibid.

6. Hobbes (2012), p. 192.

7. Parfit (1986), p. 68.

8. Ibid., p. 70.

9. Ibid., p. 80.

10. Ibid.

11. Parfit (1986), pp. 165–66.

12. Adapted from Parfit (1986), p. 358.

13. Kant (1996), p. 33.

14. Ibid., preface.

15. Jeff McMahan, email to author.

16. More catastrophic still, this other person might not have bought this book.

17. Parfit (1986), pp. 361–62.

18. Ibid., p. 367.

19. Ibid., p. 338.

20. McTaggart (1927), pp. 452–53.

21. Ibid., p. 453.

Chapter 13. The Mind's Eye in Mist and Snow

1. Larry Temkin, in a talk at Rutgers Philosophy Club.
2. Ibid.
3. Ingmar Persson, interview with author.
4. Now called the MetLife Building.
5. Edward Mortimer, interview with author.
6. Parfit, quoted in MacFarquhar (2011).
7. Edward Hussey, email to author.
8. Parfit to Jan Narveson, relayed in email to author.
9. Frances Kamm, email to author.
10. Parfit to Angelica and Neil Rudenstine, 3 May 2003, Parfit's private papers.
11. Simon Blackburn, interview with author.
12. Ibid.
13. John Vickers, at Parfit's funeral service, 9 February 2017.
14. Adrian Wooldridge, interview with author.
15. The famous Oxford bookshop is in fact called Blackwells.
16. Frances Kamm, email to author.
17. The Winsor lamp is named after Frederick Winsor, a lighting pioneer. Winsor lamps are now usually called Windsor lamps. But anyone who tells you that they are connected to the town of Windsor is gaslighting you.
18. Curl (1977), p. 95.
19. Parfit to John Ashdown, 13 March 1993.
20. Norma Aubertin-Potter, interview with author.
21. This section owes much to an interview with Adam Zeman.
22. As explained by Jake Nebel, in interview with author.
23. Srinivasan (2017).

Chapter 14. Glory! Promotion!

1. Alan Ryan, *The Sunday Times*, 3 June 1984.
2. John Gray, *The Times Higher Educational Supplement*, 18 May 1984.
3. Samuel Scheffler, *The Times Literary Supplement*, 4 May 1984.
4. Roger Scruton, *New Society*, 19 April 1984.
5. Peter Strawson, *The New York Review of Books*, 14 June 1984.
6. John Banville, *The Guardian*, 23 March 2017.
7. Bernard Williams, *London Review of Books*, 7 June 1984.
8. David Wiggins, interview with author.
9. Mary Warnock was appointed a Dame in the 1984 New Year Honours list.
10. Mary Warnock, *The Listener*, 26 April 1984.
11. Shirley Letwin, *The Spectator*, 19 May 1984.
12. Shelly Kagan, interview with author.
13. https://www.amazon.com/Reasons-and-Persons.
14. Parfit (1986), p. 153.

15. See Nozick (1974), pp. 160–64.

16. Parfit to Robert Nozick, 12 May 1983, Parfit's private papers.

17. Ibid.

18. Parfit to John Rawls, 26 March 1984, Papers of John Rawls, 1942–2003, HUM 48, Box 40, Folder 30, Harvard University Archives.

19. Ibid.

20. Ibid.

21. Parfit to Isaiah Berlin, 3 March 1984, Parfit's private papers.

22. Ibid.

23. Williams (1985).

24. Bernard Williams to Parfit, 30 November 1983, Parfit's private papers.

25. Parfit to Isaiah Berlin, 3 March 1984, Parfit's private papers.

26. Ibid.

27. R. M. Hare, 24 April 1984, Parfit's private papers.

28. David Pears, 27 April 1984, Parfit's private papers.

29. Bernard Williams, 1 May 1984, Parfit's private papers.

30. R. M. Hare, 24 April 1984, Parfit's private papers.

31. David Pears, 27 April 1984, Parfit's private papers.

32. Bernard Williams, 1 May 1984, Parfit's private papers.

33. Stuart Hampshire, 14 March 1984, Parfit's private papers.

34. Geoffrey Warnock, 27 March 1984, Parfit's private papers.

35. Ibid.

36. Ibid.

37. Academic Purposes Committee, 14 May 1985, Parfit's private papers.

38. Isaiah Berlin to Bob Silvers, 15 May 1984, in 'Supplementary Letters, 1975–1997', ed. Henry Hardy and Mark Pottle, in Hardy, https://berlin.wolf.ox.ac.uk, accessed 3 December 2021.

39. Edward Hussey, email to author.

40. Isaiah Berlin, in Hardy, https://berlin.wolf.ox.ac.uk (Michael Ignatieff tape, 27/35), accessed 3 December 2021.

41. John Rawls, Papers of John Rawls, 1942–2003, HUM 48, Box 40, Folder 30, Harvard University Archives.

42. John Rawls to Isaiah Berlin, 20 June 1984.

43. Isaiah Berlin, 13 July 1984, Parfit's private papers.

44. Parfit to Robert Nozick, 16 July 1984.

45. Ibid.

Chapter 15. The Blues and the Bluebell Woods

1. Angela Blackburn, interview with author.

2. Ibid.

3. Parfit (1986), p. vii.

4. 1987 reprint of Parfit (1986), p. vii.

5. A copy of this affidavit is in Parfit's private papers.

6. Bill Ewald, interview with author.

7. Larry Temkin, in McMahan (forthcoming).

8. This story was relayed to the author by Ingmar Persson.

9. Larry Temkin, in McMahan (forthcoming).

10. Parfit, recalled by Janet Radcliffe Richards in email to author.

11. Janet Radcliffe Richards, in McMahan (forthcoming).

12. Parfit (1998 [22 January]).

13. Ruth Chang, interview with author.

14. Jerry Cohen to David Edmonds, 1986 or 1987.

15. Parfit, in Jerry Cohen's private papers.

16. Parfit to Jerry Cohen; as told to the author by Jerry's daughter, Miriam.

17. Later he gave his work in progress on these issues a new title, *Truth, Evil, and the Sublime*. He often changed the title of his various book projects, sometimes shifting material between one planned book and another.

18. Janet Radcliffe Richards, in McMahan (forthcoming).

19. Quoted by Parfit in his renewed fellowship application, 5 October 1990, Parfit's private papers.

Chapter 16. The Priority View

1. The student was Timothy Sommers, who relayed this story in an email.

2. Nagel (1979), p. 124.

3. There might be reasons why the poor would be made better off, in some ways, from the impoverishment of the rich. But the assumption here is that they are not.

4. See Temkin (1983), pp. 231–52.

5. Parfit (1995).

6. Parfit (1991).

7. Parfit (1992).

8. Parfit (1998).

9. Wittgenstein (1974), §6.44.

10. Parfit (1998 [22 January]).

11. Parfit (1998).

12. See Jim Holt, https://artsbeat.blogs.nytimes.com/2012/07/18/no-small-talk-jim-holt -on-why-the-world-exists/, accessed 9 June 2022.

13. Leonard Pepper, *London Review of Books*, 19 February 1998.

14. Or, at the very least, less suffering. Various arguments have been put forward to explain the compatibility of an all-powerful, all-good God with some suffering. For example, it has been argued that some suffering is necessary for a greater good. Perhaps the virtue of endurance would be impossible without pain.

15. Parfit and Cowen (1992).

16. Tyler Cowen, interview with author.

17. Ibid.

18. Parfit and Cowen (1992), pp. 166–67.

19. Quassim Cassam, interview with and email from author.

20. Ibid.

21. Parfit, as recalled by Karin Boxer in interview with author.

22. Paul Snowdon, as recalled by Karin Boxer in interview with author.

23. Quassim Cassam, interview with author.

24. Ibid. The paper, 'Parfit on Persons', was published in *Proceedings of the Aristotelian Society* 93/1 (1993), pp. 17–37.

25. Shelly Kagan, interview with author.

26. Parfit, OUP archive OP2708/1914.9

27. Jamie Mayerfield, email to author.

28. Shelly Kagan, interview with author.

29. Larry Temkin, in McMahan (forthcoming).

30. Kagan (1991).

31. Murphy (2000).

32. Scheffler (1982), pp. v–vi.

33. https://www.law.ox.ac.uk/content/john-gardner-1965-2019, accessed 18 May 2022.

34. Janet Radcliffe Richards, in McMahan (forthcoming).

Chapter 17. Derekarnia

1. Parfit to Sophia Moreau, email to author.

2. Parfit to Anthony Gottlieb, in an email of 28 May 2014.

3. Matt Rohal, email to author.

4. Hermine Wittgenstein, in Rhees (1984), pp. 6–7.

5. The student was Johann Frick.

6. Ben Vilhauer, email to author.

7. Theron Pummer, interview with author.

8. Ruth Chang, interview with author.

9. Sophia Moreau, email to author.

10. Parfit to Sophia Moreau, recalled in interview with author. The tiger is the Princeton mascot.

11. Sophia Moreau, interview with author

12. I.e., 'Derek Antony Parfit'.

13. Parfit, recalled by Bill Child in interview with author.

14. Parfit, email to Jake Nebel, 2 January 2014.

15. Ibid.

16. Bill Child, email to author.

17. Parfit, recalled by Rahul Kumar in interview with author.

18. Hanna Pickard, interview with author.

19. Jeff McMahan, interview with author.

20. Note from Parfit to Gustaf Arrhenius, 29 January 2013.

21. Parfit, as recalled by John Tomasi in email to author.

22. John Tomasi, email to author.

23. Parfit, as recalled by Sophia Moreau in interview with author.

24. Dale Jamieson, interview with author

Chapter 18. Alpha Gamma Kant

1. Dancy (1997), p. viii.

2. A version of this objection, the Euthyphro dilemma, was put two and a half millennia ago by Plato.

3. Larry Temkin, quoted in Singer (2017) (a), p. 2.

4. Parfit, speaking at the Oxford Union in June 2015, https://www.youtube.com/watch?v =xTUrwO9-B_I, accessed 18 May 2022.

5. Quine (1976), p. 151 (ch. 14, reprinted from *Mind* 62/248 [1953], pp. 433–51).

6. Mackie (1977).

7. Putnam (2004), p. 2.

8. Hume (1978), p. 416.

9. Reproduced in Williams (1981), pp. 101–13.

10. This example is from 'Internal Reasons and the Obscurity of Blame', reproduced in Williams (1995), p. 39.

11. Parfit, as recalled by Larry Temkin in MacFarquhar (2011).

12. Parfit at his Harvard 'Effective Altruism' talk, 21 April 2015.

13. Parfit, as recalled by Shelly Kagan in interview with author.

14. Parfit (2011) (a), p. xli.

15. Krister Bykvist, interview with author.

16. See ch. 12 n. 13 above.

17. Parfit (2011) (a), p. xlv.

18. Ibid., p. xli.

19. Ibid. p. xliv.

20. Kant (1948). The book was first published in 1785.

21. Edmonds (2014) (b).

22. The mouse was given a solemn burial behind the Ashmolean Museum.

23. Brad Hooker, interview with author.

24. Jonathan Dancy, interview with author.

25. Parfit, recalled by his sister Theodora in interview with author.

Chapter 19. Climbing the Mountain

1. Parfit, email to Sam Scheffler.

2. Sam Scheffler, interview with author.

3. Ibid.

4. Parfit, email to Sam Scheffler.

5. Tanner Lectures: https://tannerlectures.berkeley.edu/2002-2003/, accessed 9 June 2022.

6. Ibid.

7. See Parfit (2011) (a), p. 213.

8. Parfit, in email to Sam Scheffler

9. Sam Scheffler, interview with author.

10. Christine Korsgaard's *The Sources of Normativity*.

11. Parfit, email to Sam Scheffler.

12. Parfit, email to Sam Scheffler.

13. Larry Temkin, in McMahan (forthcoming).

14. Larry Temkin, nomination of Parfit for the 2014 Rolf Schock Prize, 3 January 2013 (unpublished).

15. Parfit, as recalled, with slightly different wording, by Jake Ross in interview with author, and Jeff McMahan, email to author.

16. Sam Scheffler, interview with author.

17. Sam Scheffler, email to author.

18. Brad Hooker, interview with author.

19. Shelly Kagan, interview with author.

20. Bob Adams, interview with author.

21. John Skorupski, interview with author.

22. As recalled by Paul Schofield, tweet to author.

23. Suikkanan and Cottingham (2009).

24. I am grateful to Andy Wimbush for bringing this example to my attention.

25. Johann Frick, interview with author.

26. Mary Clemmey, interview with author. This was in 2001. The memorial was for the musicologist Alan Tyson, who had died in November 2000.

27. Bill Ewald, interview with author.

28. Edward Mortimer, interview with author.

29. Anthony Cheetham, interview with author.

30. Deirdre Wilson, interview with author.

31. Gavin Parfit, email to author.

32. Susan Hurley, email to Parfit, 4 April 2007.

33. As described by Janet Radcliffe Richards, in McMahan (forthcoming).

34. Krister Bykvist, interview with author.

35. Julian Savulescu, interview with author.

36. This is the recollection of Philip Stratton-Lake.

37. Parfit to John Broome, 18 December 2008.

38. Parfit (1986), p. x.

39. Saul Smilansky, email to author.

40. Sidgwick (1981), p. 342.

41. Parfit (2017), p. xiii.

42. Peter Singer, email to author.

43. Adrian Moore, interview with author.

44. Selim Berker, interview with author.

45. Srinivasan (2017).

46. Peter Momtchiloff, email to author.

Chapter 20. Lifeboats, Tunnels, and Bridges

1. Parfit to Peter Momtchiloff, 27 January 2009.

2. Parfit to Louise Sprake, 4 October 2009.

3. Edited by Terry Horgan and Mark Timmons (Oxford University Press, 2006).

4. Parfit to Louise Sprake, 4 October 2009.

5. Jen Rogers (née Lunsford), interview with author.

6. Ibid.

7. Peter Momtchiloff, interview with author.

8. Janet Radcliffe Richards to Peter Momtchiloff, recalled by Momtchiloff in interview with author.

9. Peter Momtchiloff, interview with author.

10. Jen Rogers, interview with author.

11. Parfit (2011) (a), p. xxxiii.

12. Ibid.

13. Parfit (1986), p. 114.

14. Parfit to John Rawls, 19 January 1976, Papers of John Rawls, 1942–2003, HUM 48, Box 40, Folder 30, Harvard University Archives. Parfit correctly gives the reference as 1, 373 in Russell and Russell (1937).

15. Parfit (2011) (a), p. 219.

16. Ibid., p. 222.

17. Ibid., p. 216.

18. Edmonds (2014), p. 169.

19. Scruton (2014), pp. 622–23.

20. Ibid., p. 621.

21. Peter Singer, *The Times Literary Supplement*, 20 May 2011, pp. 3–4.

22. Setiya (2011), p. 1288.

23. John Cottingham, *The Tablet*, 21 April 2012.

24. Philip Kitcher, *The New Republic*, 11 January 2012.

25. Simon Blackburn, *Financial Times*, 6 August 2011.

26. Simon Blackburn; the full version is available at Simon Blackburn's website www2.phil.cam.ac.uk/~swb24/, accessed 9 June 2022.

27. Ibid.

28. Jen Rogers, email to author.

Chapter 21. Marriage and Pizza

1. Parfit email, as recalled by Theodora Ooms.

2. Theodora Ooms, email to author.

3. Edmonds (2014) (b).

4. Judith Richards, interview with author.

5. Janet Radcliffe Richards, interview with author.

6. Sam Scheffler, interview with author.

7. Parfit, recalled by Janet Radcliffe Richards in interview with author.

8. There are many, mostly trivial, errors. For example, it is not true that Parfit could not play a musical instrument; nor was Joanna in her thirties when she died in a car accident; etc.

9. Larry Temkin, interview with author.

10. Parfit (2011) (c).

11. Julian Savulescu, interview with author.

12. Roger Crisp, interview with author.

13. Tim Campbell, interview with author.

14. Wlodek Rabinowicz, interview with author.

15. Edmonds (2014) (b).

16. Ibid.

17. David Killen, 4 July 2014.

18. Edmonds (2014) (b).

19. Parfit to David Edmonds, 22 February 2012.

20. https://www.vox.com/future-perfect/2019/9/26/20874217/the-good-place-series-finale-season-4-moral-philosophy, accessed 18 May 2022.

21. Victor Tadros, email to author.

22. The date was 27 May 2014.

23. Katy Scheffler, as recounted by Sam Scheffler in interview with author.

24. Wlodek Rabinowicz, interview with author.

25. It has been named 'Imogen, the philosophical giraffe'.

26. Srinivasan (2017). Amia Srinivasan later became the Chichele Professor of Social and Political Theory at All Souls.

27. Theron Pummer, interview with author.

28. Quoted in an email from Parfit to Allan Gibbard, 30 May 2013.

29. Ibid.

30. Parfit (2017), p. xii.

31. Singer's thought experiment is presented in various forms, but first makes an appearance in Singer (1972). It was this puzzle that Frances Kamm was responding to with her 'long arms' thought experiment, mentioned in chapter 9.

32. Richard Jenkyns, note to author.

33. Parfit, email to Michelle Hutchinson, executive director of GWWC, 14 July 2011.

34. Smart and Williams (1973).

35. *Isis*, 1 May 1963.

Chapter 22. Incompatible with Life

1. Larry Temkin, interview with author.

2. Jeff McMahan, interview with author.

3. Larry Temkin, interview with author.

4. Parfit, email to Tim Scanlon, Frances Kamm, and Johann Frick, 3 September 2014.

5. Johann Frick, interview with author.

6. As witnessed and recalled by Johann Frick, in interview with author.

7. Ditto.

8. Parfit, as recalled by Douglas Kremm in email to author.

9. Sharon Street, interview with author.

10. Dale Jamieson, interview with author.

11. Parfit to Julian Savulescu, 25 June 2016.
12. As recalled by Simon Beard in email to author.
13. Recalled by Ingmar Persson in email to author.
14. Patricia Williams, interview with author.
15. Parfit, email to Bill Ruddick.
16. Bill Ruddick, email to Parfit, 27 July 2011.
17. Oates (2011), p. ix.
18. Parfit, as reported, among others, by Paul Linton, in interview with author.
19. Edmonds (2014) (b).
20. Peter Singer, email to author.
21. Parfit, quoted by Jonathan Glover in McMahan (forthcoming).
22. Jonathan Glover, in McMahan (forthcoming).

Chapter 23. Parfit's Gamble

1. The article, 'Future People, the Non-Identity Problem, and Person-Affecting Principles', was published later that year in *Philosophy and Public Affairs* 45/2.
2. Janet Radcliffe Richards, email to author.
3. Peter Railton, at a conference held at Rutgers, 15–16 December 2017, in memory of Derek Parfit, at which philosophical papers were presented.
4. Quoted by G. A. Cohen: Cohen (2011), p. 226.
5. Parfit (2011) (c).
6. https://globalprioritiesinstitute.org/parfit-scholarship/, accessed 18 May 2022.
7. Parfit, email to Jonathan Pugh, 5 May 2012.
8. Larry Temkin, unpublished submission in support of Parfit's Schock Prize, 3 January 2013.
9. Joyce Carol Oates, email to author.
10. Peter Singer, interview with author.
11. See Leslie et al. (2015).
12. Tom Kelly, interview with author.
13. Ruth Chang, at Schock symposium, Stockholm, 21–23 October 2014.
14. Bill Ewald, interview with author.
15. Richard Jenkyns, note to author.
16. Hanna Pickard, interview with author.
17. Ruth Chang, interview with author.
18. Janet Radcliffe Richards, interview with author.
19. Janet Radcliffe Richards, in McMahan (forthcoming).
20. Janet Radcliffe Richards, quoted in Edmonds (2014) (b).
21. Sacks (1997).
22. Janet Radcliffe Richards, interview with author.
23. I am grateful to Simon Baron-Cohen and Jessica Eccles for help with this section.
24. Asperger's was removed from the latest Diagnostic and Statistical Manual of Mental Disorders (DSM-5) as a separate disorder, though it is still recognized by the World Health Organization.

25. Ruth Chang, interview with author.

26. Quoted in Sacks (1997), p. 234.

27. Quoted in Edmonds (2014) (b).

28. Parfit to Patricia Zander, undated note, probably early 2003.

29. Parfit to Ruth Chang, 2 June 2004.

30. Parfit to Tim Scanlon, 9 June 2007.

31. Galen Strawson, interview with author.

32. Parfit to Ingmar Persson, in McMahan (forthcoming).

33. Simon Baron-Cohen, email to author.

34. Ingmar Persson, email to author.

35. Judith De Witt, interview with author.

BIBLIOGRAPHY

Briggs, R., 'Sparrow, John Hanbury Angus', in *Oxford Dictionary of National Biography* online (oxforddnb.com), https://doi.org/10.1093/ref:odnb/51324

Budiansky, S., *Journey to the Edge of Reason* (W. W. Norton, 2021)

Cheetham, A. and D. Parfit (eds), *Eton Microcosm* (Sidgwick & Jackson, 1964)

Cobb, R., *People and Places* (Oxford University Press, 1985)

Cohen, G. A., *Finding Oneself in the Other* (Princeton University Press, 2010)

——, 'Rescuing Conservatism: A Defense of Existing Value', in *Reasons and Recognition: Essays on the Philosophy of T. M. Scanlon*, ed. R. J. Wallace, R. Kumar, and S. Freeman (Oxford University Press, 2011), pp. 203–30

Crisp, R., *The Cosmos of Duty* (Oxford University Press, 2015)

Curl, J. S., *The Erosion of Oxford* (Oxford Illustrated Press, 1977)

Dancy, J. (ed.), *Reading Parfit* (Blackwell, 1997)

Edmonds, D., (a) *Would You Kill the Fat Man?* (Princeton University Press, 2014)

——, (b) 'The World's Most Cerebral Marriage', *Prospect Magazine*, August 2014

——, 'What Makes Life Worthwhile?', *Jewish Chronicle*, 12 March 2018

——, *The Murder of Professor Schlick* (Princeton University Press, 2020)

Edwards, P. (ed.), *The Encyclopedia of Philosophy*, Volume 5 (Macmillan, 1967)

Ehrlich, P., *The Population Bomb* (Ballantine, 1971)

Forsyth, F., *The Negotiator* (Bantam Press, 1989)

Hardy, H. (ed.), *The Isaiah Berlin Virtual Library*, https://berlin.wolf.ox.ac.uk/

Heald, T. (ed.), *'My Dear Hugh,': Letters from Richard Cobb to Hugh Trevor-Roper and Others* (Frances Lincoln, 2011)

Hobbes, T., *Leviathan*, ed. N. Malcolm (Oxford University Press, 2012)

Hume, D., *A Treatise of Human Nature*, ed. L. Selby-Bigge (Clarendon Press, 1978)

Kagan, S., *The Limits of Morality* (Oxford University Press, 1991)

Kamm, F. M., *Morality, Mortality*, Volume 2: *Rights, Duties, and Status* (Oxford University Press, 1996)

——, 'Famine Ethics: The Problem of Distance in Morality and Singer's Ethical Theory', in *Singer and His Critics*, ed. D. Jamieson (Blackwell, 1999), pp. 162–208

Kant, I., *The Groundwork of the Metaphysics of Morals*, trans. H. Paton (Routledge, 1948)

——, *Prolegomena to Any Future Metaphysics*, ed. B. Logan (Routledge, 1996)

Leslie, S.-J., A. Cimpian, M. Meyer, and E. Freeland, 'Expectations of Brilliance Underlie Gender Distributions across Academic Disciplines', *Science*, 16 January 2015, pp. 262–65

Lovibond, S. and S. Williams, *Essays for David Wiggins* (Blackwell, 1996)

MacFarquhar, L., 'How to Be Good', *The New Yorker*, 5 September 2011

Mackie, J., *Ethics: Inventing Right and Wrong* (Penguin, 1977)

McMahan, J. (ed.), *Derek Parfit: His Life and Work* (Oxford University Press, forthcoming [2023])

McTaggart, J., *The Nature of Existence* (Cambridge University Press, 1927)

Mill, J. S., *On the Subjection of Women* (MIT Press, 1977)

———, *'On Liberty' and Other Essays*, ed. J. Gray (Oxford University Press, 1991)

Miller, A., *Timebends: A Life* (Methuen, 1987)

———, 'The Chelsea Affect', *Granta* 78 (2002)

Murphy, L., *Moral Demands in Nonideal Theory* (Oxford University Press, 2000)

Nagel, T., 'What Is It Like to Be a Bat?', *The Philosophical Review* 83/4 (1974), pp. 435–50 (reprinted in Nagel [1979], pp. 165–80)

———, *Mortal Questions* (Cambridge University Press, 1979)

———, *The View from Nowhere* (Oxford University Press, 1986)

Nietzsche, F., *The Gay Science*, ed. B. Williams (Cambridge University Press, 2001)

Nozick, R., *Anarchy, State, and Utopia* (Basic Books, 1974)

Oates, J. C., *A Widow's Story* (Fourth Estate, 2011)

Parfit, D., 'Personal Identity', *The Philosophical Review* 80/1 (1971), pp. 3–27

———, 'Innumerate Ethics', *Philosophy and Public Affairs* 7/4 (1978), pp. 285–301

———, 'Prudence, Morality, and the Prisoner's Dilemma', *Proceedings of the British Academy* 65 (1979), pp. 539–64

———, 'Rationality and Time', *Proceedings of the Aristotelian Society* 84/1 (1984), pp. 47–82.

———, *Reasons and Persons* (first paperback edition) (Oxford University Press, 1986)

———, 'Why Does the Universe Exist?', *The Harvard Review of Philosophy* 1/1 (1991), pp. 2–5

———, 'The Puzzle of Reality: Why Does the Universe Exist?', *The Times Literary Supplement*, 3 July 1992, pp. 3–5

———, *Equality or Priority?* (University of Kansas, 1995)

———, 'Why Anything? Why This?' [in two parts], *London Review of Books*, 22 January and 5 February 1998, pp. 24–27; 22–25

———, (a) *On What Matters*, Volume 1 (Oxford University Press, 2011)

———, (b) *On What Matters*, Volume 2 (Oxford University Press, 2011)

———, (c) 'Responses to Questions from L. MacFarquhar' (unpublished, 2011)

———, *On What Matters*, Volume 3 (Oxford University Press, 2017)

Parfit, D. and J. Broome, 'Reasons and Motivation', *Proceedings of the Aristotelian Society*, Supplementary Volumes 71 (1997), pp. 99–146

Parfit, D. and T. Cowen, 'Against the Social Discount Rate', in *Justice between Age Groups and Generations*, ed. P. Laslett and J. Fishkin (Yale University Press, 1992), pp. 144–61

Patten, C., *First Confession* (Allen Lane, 2017)

Putnam, H., *Ethics without Ontology* (Harvard University Press, 2004)

Quine, W.V.O., *The Ways of Paradox*, revised edn (Harvard University Press, 1976)

Raina, P., *John Sparrow: Warden of All Souls College, Oxford* (Peter Lang, 2017)

Rhees, R. (ed.), *Recollections of Wittgenstein* (Oxford University Press, 1984)

Rowbotham, S., *Promise of a Dream* (Allen Lane, 2000)

Russell, B. and P. Russell (eds), *The Amberley Papers* (George Allen & Unwin, 1937)

Sacks, O., *An Anthropologist on Mars* (Picador, 1997)

Scanlon, T., *What We Owe to Each Other* (Harvard University Press, 1998)

Scheffler, S., *The Rejection of Consequentialism* (Oxford University Press, 1982)

Scruton, R., 'Parfit the Perfectionist', *Philosophy* 89/350 (2014), pp. 621–34

Setiya, K., '(Review of) Derek Parfit, *On What Matters*', *Mind* 120/480 (2011), pp. 1281–88

Shoemaker, S., *Self-knowledge and Self-identity* (Oxford University Press, 1963)

Sidgwick, H., *The Methods of Ethics* (Hackett, 1981)

Singer, P., 'Famine, Affluence and Morality', *Philosophy and Public Affairs* 1/3 (1972), pp. 229–43.

——— (ed.), (a) *Does Anything Really Matter?* (Oxford University Press, 2017)

———, (b) 'A Life That Mattered', *Project Syndicate*, 14 March 2017, available at https://www.project-syndicate.org/commentary/life-that-mattered-derek-parfit-by-peter-singer-2017-03

Smart, J. and B. Williams, *Utilitarianism: For and Against* (Cambridge University Press, 1973)

Srinivasan, A., 'Remembering Derek Parfit', *London Review of Books*, 6 January 2017

Stonier, A. and D. Hague, *A Textbook of Economic Theory* (Longman, 1964)

Suikkanan, J. and J. Cottingham (eds), *Essays on Parfit's 'On What Matters'* (Wiley-Blackwell, 2009)

Taurek, J., 'Should the Numbers Count?', *Philosophy and Public Affairs* 6/4 (1977), pp. 293–316

Temkin, L., 'Inequality', PhD thesis, Princeton University, 1983

Voorhoeve, A., *Conversations on Ethics* (Oxford University Press, 2009)

Wiggins, D., *Identity and Spatio-Temporal Continuity* (Blackwell, 1967)

Williams, B., *Moral Luck* (Cambridge University Press, 1981)

———, *Ethics and the Limits of Philosophy* (Fontana, 1985)

———, *Making Sense of Humanity* (Cambridge University Press, 1995)

Wittgenstein, L., *Tractatus Logico-Philosophicus* (Routledge, 1974)

Archive Sources

Balliol College, Oxford: Balliol College Historic Collections. Quotations by permission of the copyright holders and the Master and Fellows of Balliol College.

Bodleian Libraries, University of Oxford.

Canning Club, Oxford: Papers held at the Bodleian Library, University of Oxford. Quotations by permission of the Oxford Canning Club.

Church Mission Society Archive, University of Birmingham, Cadbury Library. Quotations by permission of the Church Mission Society.

Commonwealth Fund Archive, Rockefeller Archive Center.

The Dragon School, Oxford. Quotations by permission of the Head (Preparatory), Emma Goldsmith.

Eton College Archives. Quotations by permission of the Provost and Fellows of Eton College.

Harvard University: Harvard University Archives. Quotations by permission of Harvard University Archives.

The Isaiah Berlin Literary Trust. Quotations from Isaiah Berlin by courtesy of the Trustees.

Oxford University Press Archives. Quotations by permission of the Secretary to the Delegates of Oxford University Press.

INDEX

Throughout the index, "DP" refers to Derek Parfit.

Hussey, Edward, 188, 260
Huxley, Aldous, 55
H.W.C. Davis Prize, 42

identity, personal: body and, 99, 106–7; commonsense understanding of, 98–99; cryonics and, 300; implications and consequences, 104–5; joint classes on, 234–37; memory and, 99; names and, 92; Non-Identity Problem, 178–84, 304, 321, 328; 'Personal Identity' (DP), 98–99; psychological continuity and, 103–4, 235–36; the Teletransporter, 99–101; Too-Many-Thinkers Problem, 235–36; triplets case, 102–3; Wiggins and, 70–71. See also future people
Institute for Advanced Study (IAS), Princeton, 88–89
'Internal and External Reasons' (Williams), 256–57
Isis magazine, 45–50, 54, 314

Jamieson, Dale, 153, 318–19
Jenkyns, Richard, 128, 141, 152, 191, 331
Jessel, Stephen, 24
Jim Crow, 71–72
Johnson, Lyndon, 71
Joseph, Keith, 221
journalism: Cherwell, 45, 93; The Draconian, 17; The Eton Chronicle, 29, 55; Isis, 45–50, 54, 314; Mesopotamia (Balliol), 45
Joyce, James, 273
justice, distributive, 227–30

Kagan, Shelly, 148, 157, 201, 237–38, 259–60, 271, 273
Kahane, Guy, 263
Kamm, Frances, 123–24, 189, 194, 237, 271, 362n31
Kant, Immanuel, 128, 179, 259–62, 264, 267–69, 287–92, 326
'Kant's Formula of Ends-in-Themselves' (Tanner Lecture), 267–68

'Kant's Formula of Universal Law' (Tanner Lecture), 268–69
Keats, John, 335
Keen, Maurice, 39, 60
Keir, David Lindsay, 39
Kelly, Thomas (Tom), 124–25, 281–82, 330
Kennedy, John F., 60, 68–69, 93
Kenny, Anthony, 96–97
Keynes, John Maynard, 329
Khrushchev, Nikita, 35, 345n33
Kirchin, Simon, 308–9
Korsgaard, Christine, 260, 271
Kripke, Saul, 92, 154, 301

Labour Club, Oxford, 42
language: linguistic philosophy, 67, 70, 79, 81; ordinary language philosophers, 67, 79, 245; phenomenology of, in 'Wanton Beauty,' 33
la Sablière, Jean de, 19–20
Le Carré, John (David Cornwell), 27
legal positivism, 143
Leibniz, Gottfried, 231
Lemmon, John, 97
Leningrad (St Petersburg), 111, 118, 187–93, 245, color insert 2
Letwin, Shirley, 199–200, 208
Levelling Down Objection, 229–30
Lévi-Strauss, Claude, 140
Lewis, Richard, 195
Liberty Fund conference (Austin, Texas, 1988), 233
Lifeboat cases, 289, 290, 292
'Like Pebbles' (DP), 48
Lindley Lecture, University of Kansas, 227–30
linguistic philosophy, 67, 70, 79, 81
local possibilities, 231
Locke, John, 99, 269
Lodge, David, 65, 347n1
logical empiricism (logical positivism), 80–81, 230, 253
logical notation, 248–49

logical symbols, 248–49
lottery case, 231–32
love, random vs. chosen, 53
Lowther, Nicholas, 29
luck, moral, 130
Lukes, Steven, 96
Lunsford, Jen, 286–87, 294

MacAskill, Will, 309–10
Maccoun, Robert, 195
MacFarquhar, Larissa, 37, 298
macho norm in philosophy, 248
Mackie, John, 143, 255
Macmillan, Harold, 25, 43
Malthus, Thomas, 135
Mao Zedong, 59
Marcuse, Herbert, 59
Margáin, Hugo, 92
Marx, Karl, 56, 59, 217–18
mathematics, moral, 174–75
Mayerfield, Jamie, 237–38
McDowell, John, 154
McGilchrist, Iain, 191, 193
McMahan, Jeff, 126, 148, 158, 179, 237, 243–44,
    248, 271, 298–99, 306, 315–17, 321, 323, 331
McMahan, Sally, 158, 299
McTaggart, John, 183–84
McWatters, Stephen, 33
means, ends, and mere means, 268, 290
Mehta, Ved, 38
memory and identity, 99
Mere Addition Paradox, 182–83
mere means, 268, 290
Merleau-Ponty, Maurice, 80
Mesopotamia magazine, 45
metaethics, 79, 92–93, 253–59, 278, 280
Methods of Ethics (Sidgwick), 82–83, 126,
    139, 198, 204, 217, 280
Mill, John Stuart, ix, 73, 97, 104–5, 165,
    288, 326
Miller, Arthur, 66
Mills, C. W., 66
mind, philosophy of, 163
mirror neurons, 163

Momtchiloff, Peter, 252–53, 267, 283, 284,
    286–87
Monet, Claude, 160, 194, 224–25
Montefiore, Alan, 74–75, 80, 86, 91, 96
Moore, Adrian, 155, 282
Moore, G. E., 79
'Moral Maze, The' (BBC radio), 262, 302
moral objectivity, 253–59, 287, 298–99, 308
moral philosophy: DP's summary of history
    of ethics, 160; metaethics, 79, 92–93,
    253–59, 278, 280; ultimate principle of
    morality, 290–91. See also thought
    experiments; specific topics and
    philosophers
moral thinking, intuitive vs. critical, 138
Moray, Oswyn, 96
Moreau, Sophia, 241, 244–46, 250
Morgenbesser, Sidney, 67
Mortimer, Edward, 25–28, 31–32, 49, 72, 78,
    85–86, 187, 274
Mortimer, Elizabeth (Wiz), 85–86
Mozart, Wolfgang Amadeus, 18, 312, 327–28
Murphy, Liam, 238
music: beauty of, 305; in childhood, 15–16,
    18; at Eton, 28; in New York, 38–39, 72–73

Nagel, Thomas, 114, 118, 120–21, 142–44, 154,
    161, 203, 227–28, 260, 301, 331, color insert 1
Naomi (foster daughter of Joanna), 211–13
Napoléon (film; Gance), 222
Narveson, Jan, 135, 181
naturalism, moral, 279, 308. See also
    cognitive non-naturalism
Nebel, Jake, 197
Needham, Rodney, 140
Neill, Patrick, 132–33, 150, 161
New School for Social Research, 59–60, 66
Newton-Smith, Bill, 96–97
New York City: APA meeting in, 266;
    architecture in, 187; Clemmey in, 108;
    in DP's childhood, 9–10; DP's lodgings
    in, 66; Museum of Modern Art, 194;
    New Yorker internship, 37–39; 9/11 attacks,
    264; at Scheffler's apartment in, 297;

Slugs jazz club with Mortimer, 72.
See also specific universities
New Yorker internship, 37–39
New York University (NYU): Harkness
Fellowship at, 59–60, 66; job offer from,
202–3; teaching at, 118, 122–23, 126–27,
208–9, 264, 298, 318–19
Nietzsche, Friedrich, 158–60, 326
Nimmo Smith, Bill, 17–18, 24, 26, 27, *color
insert 1*
Nkrumah, Kwame, 38, 42–43
Non-Identity Problem, 178–84, 304, 321, 328
Nozick, Robert, 121–22, 202–3, 209, 223

Oates, Joyce Carol, 323, 330
objectivity, moral, 253–59, 287, 298–99, 308
O-Levels, 32
ontology, 254–55
On What Matters, Vols. 1 and 2 (DP), as
Climbing the Mountain, 272–74; constant
evolution of, 282–83; convergence of
Kantianism, consequentialism, and
contractualism, 287–92; *Essays on
Parfit's 'On What Matters'* (Suikkanan
and Cottingham), 273; feedback on,
272–73; image used on Vol. 1, *color
insert 2*; legacy of, 326–27; length of, x;
Lifeboat, Tunnel, Bridge, and Third
Earthquake cases, 289–92; morality as
objective, 287; mountain metaphor, 288;
negotiations on aesthetics of, 284–87;
photo of, *color insert 1*; plans for, 252–53;
reception of, 291–94; release of, 299;
Scheffler as editor, 270, 272; Scheffler
introduction, 282–83; Tanner Lectures
and, 267–68; titles, early, 272; 'Why
Anything, Why This?' (Appendix D), 294
On What Matters, Vol. 3 (DP), 321, 327,
color insert 1
Ooms, C. Alexander, 170
Open University (OU), 166, 214, 216, 262
Ord, Toby, 309–10
ordinary language philosophy, 67, 79, 245
Oxford Civil Society, 195

Oxford Ethics series, 237–38
Oxford Group, 4–5
Oxford Philosophical Society, 82
Oxford Union, 42, 46, 313–14
Oxford University: application to, 34;
Appointments Committee, 259; BPhil
application, 74–75; H.W.C. Davis Prize,
42; Glover-Griffin-Parfit seminars,
93–96, 114; Harkness Fellowship
application, 57–60, 62–63; Parfit-
Dworkin-Sen seminars, 156; philosophi-
cal emphases at, 67–68, 79–80, 92–93;
photos of, *color insert sections*; Star Wars
seminars (Sen-Dworkin-Parfit-Cohen),
218–21, 227; Tuesday Group, 153–55, 277;
White's Chair of Moral Philosophy, 81,
205–6, 217, 258, 259, 306. *See also* All Souls
College; Balliol College
Oxford University Press: Berkeley Tanner
Lectures, 266–67; *Does Anything Really
Matter?* (ed. Singer), 307–8; DP's planned
publications, 96, 128, 136, 204, 252–53;
Oxford Ethics series, 237–38; *Reasons and
Persons*, 156, 158, 160–62, 210; *On What
Matters* (vols. 1 and 2), 283, 284–87; *On
What Matters* (vol. 3), 307–8, 321

Parfit, Cyril (uncle of DP), 186
Parfit, Derek: aesthetics, sense of, 193–96,
328; aphantasia of, 196–97; autism
spectrum, question of, 331–35; birth and
early childhood, 6–10, 11–12; character
change in, 116–17, 279, 333–34; childhood
and home life in England, 11–16; chronology, 337–41; death, brushes with, ix, 6,
54–55, 315–17; death and funeral, 325–26;
declining health, 320–21; disagreement,
aversion to, 279–82; driving style, 222–23;
eccentricity, reputation for, 141–42, 239;
emotional reactions, atypical, 304–5;
family background, 1–6; at family reunion,
276; habits, distinctive, 152; kindness of,
243; legacy of, 326–36; love life, 51–54,
68–73, 83, 85, 107–12, 162–68, 214–18,

Parfit, Derek (*continued*)
240, 262–63, 276–77; money, attitude to,
126–27; name of, 6; nationalism of, 153;
nocturnal schedule and insomnia, 116,
123; perfectionism of, ix–x, 128, 143,
167–68, 194, 238, 247; philosophical range
of, 91; photography hobby, 185–94, *color
insert section 2*; photos of, *color insert
section 1*; at prep school, 12, 16–24;
publication record, poor, 96, 128, 136–37,
139–40, 143–44, 146, 223; religious faith
and, 13; retirement, 296–98, 305–6;
retribution, loathing of, 147–49; rigidity
and dogmatism later in life, 277–79;
social awkwardness of, 107, 197, 246, 258,
264, 274–76; students, relationship with,
241–51; summary of history of ethics, 160;
transient global amnesia, 297; wedding,
295–96; writing style of, 101
 —letters: Mary Clemmey, 51–54,
108; Joanna Parfit, 35, 36, 51,
83–85; Patricia Zander, 109–11
 —writings: *Against Prudence*
(planned), 136, 151; 'Against
Prudence,' 136; diaries, 19–21;
'A Dream,' 22–23; *Eton Microcosm*
(with Cheetham), 55–56; 'Innumerate Ethics' (counterargument
to Taurek), 137–38; 'Like Pebbles,'
48; *Metaphysics and Ethics*
(planned), 221–22; *The Metaphysics of the Self* (planned), 252–53,
267; *On Giving Priority to the Worse
Off* (planned), 223; 'Personal
Identity,' 98–99; 'Photograph
of a Comtesse,' 46–48; *Practical
Realism* (later *Rediscovering
Reasons*) (planned), 252–53, 267,
270; 'The Puzzle of Reality,' 230;
Reasons, Persons, and Reality
(planned), 304; 'Wanton Beauty,'
33; 'The Warfare State,' 48–49.
See also *On What Matters*;
Reasons and Persons

Parfit, Eric (uncle of DP), 4, 8
Parfit, Jessie Brown (mother of DP), 2–13,
15–16, 24, 212–14, 268, *color insert section 1*
Parfit, Joanna (sister of DP), 9–10, 14, 51,
83–85, 110, 211–12, *color insert section 2*
Parfit, Joseph (grandfather of DP), 1–2, 19
Parfit, Norah Stephens (grandmother
of DP), 2
Parfit, Norman (father of DP), 2–15, 200,
214, *color insert section 1*
Parfit, Theodora (sister of DP), 6–10, 13–14,
37, 84, 170, 212–13, 265, 276, 295, 318, *color
insert section 1*
Parfit-Radcliffe Richards Fellowship
(Uehiro Centre), 329
Paris, 56–57, 111
Parry, Raymond (R. H.), 33–34, 58
Patten, Chris, 39–40
Paxton, Catherine, 264
Payne, Raef, 33
Pears, David, 80, 91, 113–14, 154, 205–6
personal identity. See identity, personal
'Personal Identity' (DP), 98–99
Persson, Ingmar, 263, 298, 300, 305, 321,
333, 335
Phillips, Ian, 298
Phillips, Melanie, 302
philosophy club, Eton, 30
'Photograph of a Comtesse' (DP), 46–48
photography, 185–94, *color insert section 2*
Pickard, Hanna, 155, 298, 331
poetry: DP on, 33; at Dragon School, 18, 21–22;
'Photograph of a Comtesse' (DP), 46–48
Pogge, Thomas, 271
political philosophy, 76–78
Popper, Karl, 76, 151–52, 221
Pop Society, Eton, 36
Population Bomb, The (Ehrlich and Ehrlich),
135
population ethics, 95, 135, 178. See also future
people
positivism. See legal positivism; logical
empiricism
possibilities, local vs. cosmic, 231

Scanlon, Tim (Thomas), 118–20, 125, 143, 150,
    205, 227, 267, 270–71, 273, 288, 317, 331–32
Scheffler, Samuel, 198, 239, 266, 269–72,
    282–83, 297, 304, 323
Schock Prize, 301–2, 305, 330
Schopenhauer, Arthur, 231
Schrödinger, Erwin, 12
Schur, Michael, 303
Scruton, Roger, 198, 292–93
Seabright, Paul, 134, 163, 172, 191
self-defeating theories, 170–75
self-interest, 136, 170–73
Sen, Amartya, 145–46, 156, 164, 172, 217–21,
    302
separateness of persons, 122
Sex in a Shifting Landscape (Radcliffe
    Richards, Uehiro Lectures), 319–20
Shawn, William, 37, 38–39
Shoemaker, Sydney, 99–100
'Should Numbers Count?' (Taurek), 137–38
Sidgwick, Henry, ix, 73, 82–83, 126, 135,
    139, 158–59, 171, 198, 217, 260, 280, 287–88,
    291, 326
Silvers, Robert, 198
Singer, Peter, 94, 281, 293, 300, 307–11, 323,
    327, 330, 362n31
Skidelsky, Robert, 46, 346n2
Skorupski, John, 226, 273
Smart, J.J.C., 131
Smilansky, Saul, 279
Smith, John Maynard, 215
Smith, Raymond, 323
Snowdon, Paul, 154, 234–37
social choice theory, 145–46
Socrates, 280
Soviet Union, 50
Sparrow, John, 42, 43, 64, 86–87, 91, 93,
    114–15, 129, 134
Sprake, Louise, 285–86
Srinivasan, Amia, 197, 282–83, 298, 306,
    362n26
Star Trek, 99, 349n3
Star Wars seminars (Sen-Dworkin-Parfit-
    Cohen), 218–21, 227

St Petersburg (Leningrad), 111, 118, 187–93,
    245, *color insert section 2*
Stratton-Lake, Philip, 226
Strawson, Galen, 155, 212
Strawson, Peter, 80, 81–82, 92, 144, 154–55,
    198, 205, 207–8
Street, Sharon, 318
streetlamps, 194–96
Stuart, Charles, 60–61
sublime, the, 327–28
suffering: additive, 137–38; DP's sensibility
    on, 304; in Eton debate, 30; God and, 232,
    357n14; moral desert and, 148–49; Problem
    of Evil, 232, 250; two kinds of, 50
Suffering and Moral Responsibility
    (Mayerfeld), 237–38

Tadros, Victor, 303–4
Tanner Lectures (Berkeley), 266–72, 288, 291
Taurek, John, 137–38
Taylor, Charles, 145
Teletransporter, 99–101
Temkin, Larry, 116–17, 125–26, 185–86, 215,
    224, 226, 230, 237–38, 254, 259, 271,
    298–99, 305, 315–16, 319, 329, 331
Temple University, 118
Tennant, Stephen, 72–73
Thatcher, Margaret, 153, 201, 220–21, 258
Theory of Justice, A (Rawls), 76–78, 121–22,
    202, 217, 327
Theory X, 184, 304, 328
Thompson, Dennis, 77
Thomson, Judith Jarvis, 224
thought experiments: additive suffering
    (Taurek), 137–38; bean bandits (Glover),
    95–96; Bridge (DP), 289; Chinese
    bandit example (DP), 268; drunk
    drivers and moral luck (Williams), 130;
    'expensive taste' problem (Dworkin),
    219–20; George and Jim (Williams),
    131–32; harmless torturers (DP), 96,
    174–75; Lifeboat (DP), 289, 290; long
    arms (Kamm), 124; lottery (DP), 231–32;
    parental dilemma on equality (Nagel),

For additional resources for *Parfit,* please see

press.princeton.edu/resources/parfit